Gerald L. Wilson

Groups in Context
Leadership & Participation in Small Groups

Ninth Edition

Pearson Learning Solutions, 501 Boylston Street, Suite 900, Boston, MA 02116
A Pearson Education Company
www.pearsoned.com

Printed in the United States of America

3 4 5 6 7 8 9 10 V092 16 15 14

000200010271842076

CW

ISBN 10: 1-269-61599-8
ISBN 13: 978-1-269-61599-0

This book is lovingly dedicated to my beautiful daughter
Hannah Beth Wilson

About the Author

Gerald L. Wilson is professor of communication at the University of South Alabama, where he teaches courses in small group communication. He received his B.S. degree from Bowling Green State University, his M.A. degree from Miami University of Ohio, and his Ph.D. from the University of Wisconsin–Madison. Wilson has also taught and conducted research at Northern Illinois University and Indiana University–Indianapolis.

contents in brief

contents

part
II

PREPARING FOR GROUP MEETINGS   35

2 Preparing for Group Meetings   37

part
III

PARTICIPATING IN GROUP MEETINGS 133

5 Encouraging Group Development and Evolution 135

part

IV

preface

Our work in various groups is a significant part of what we do. We interact in family groups, social groups, school groups, work groups, civic groups, and many special interest groups. It is important for us that our experiences in these groups are satisfying and successful. It is from these groups that we gain a sense of who we are as social beings and also as productive members of society.

Each person who reads this book comes with a wealth of experience from being in and working in groups. That experience has allowed you to gain a good deal of confidence in your ability to work in groups and a good deal of experiential knowledge regarding groups and group process. It is the aim of this book to carry you further in both your effectiveness in groups and the knowledge base that supports that effort. It is my hope that you will develop a high level of skill in participating and leading in groups.

APPROACH TO THE STUDY OF SMALL GROUPS

Groups in Context takes a balanced approach, blending current theory and research with practical skills and applications. Clearly, there is a relationship between theory and practice. A book that is mostly theoretical does not fully meet the needs of most students. A book that is mostly a listing and discussion of prescribed behaviors does not fully meet the needs of students either. Understanding and skill go hand in hand. To this end, I have carefully presented clear explanations of theory, documented with both classic and current research. I also provide specific suggestions for enhancing individual and group effectiveness. I have worked diligently to illustrate important concepts with real-life examples from a broad range of contexts. I am convinced—on the basis of my teaching, research, and consulting experience, as well as on the extensive use of the seven previous editions of this book—that such an approach is greatly appreciated.

The title *Groups in Context* reflects my belief that the study of small group communication is best understood when the concepts are presented within specific contexts. We all meet with others to make decisions in the workplace, in neighborhoods, in churches, in social groups, and in civic organizations. Thus I have drawn examples and illustrations from these and similar contexts.

My use of context flows out of another concern. I want students to communicate better in groups and to diagnose and act on decisions made about their group. To achieve this goal, I believe the student must be able to make the connection between what he or she is studying and real-world groups. My use of contexts to provide illustrations and examples of important principles shows students how to make the transfer.

Groups in Context focuses on task-oriented and decision-making groups. I selected this focus for three reasons. First, decision making is one of the most difficult tasks a group can undertake. These groups require systematic analysis of the particular group situation, vigilance in the decision-making process, and well-developed communication and leadership skills. Second, decision making is one of the most prevalent group activities. We deliberate to plan and set policies for groups in both our private and professional lives. The ability to carry out the group decision-making activity is vital to the life of an educated person. It is an activity that most adults cannot avoid. Third, the decision-making group provides an excellent framework for understanding the many interpersonal and group processes that operate in other task-oriented groups.

I also carefully reviewed my experience as teacher and consultant to discover what has helped my students function more effectively in groups. The features of this book are designed to respond to student needs on the basis of this careful review.

SPECIAL FEATURES

I believe in a balanced approach that blends theory, research, and practice. I have made every effort to achieve an appropriate blend of *current theory and research with practical explanations, skills, and applications.*

I firmly believe that examples can make the difference between books that are truly useful to students and books that are not. So I have filled this book with *examples from group contexts* to allow the students to see how concepts actually work in the real world.

Each chapter encourages students to analyze their own communication behavior and to place that *behavior in a group context.* For example, this book includes exceptionally *thorough coverage of leadership, cohesiveness, and conflict*—and not merely from the view of a designated leader but from the view of all potential group participants.

I have been especially sensitive to the need to provide comprehensive coverage of new developments in group communication, such as culture, conflict management, gender, group development, and technology.

Finally, I have included a new feature to help the reader stay focused on important points that have been made throughout each chapter. Each chapter contains a series of boxed summaries titled "Looking Back: A Quick Review." It is hoped that these summaries will help fix the important points in the reader's mind.

ADDITIONS AND REVISIONS TO THE NINTH EDITION

Some materials from the eight edition are not included in the ninth. Two pieces that for me no longer serve the purposes they did earlier in my teaching of small group decision making were removed. The pieces not included are:

- System Properties in Groups, Chapter 1
- Figure 9.4, Model of Groupthink Syndrome, Chapter 9

Additions to this edition include:

- New topic: Synergy in Groups, Chapter 1
- More on the effect of size of the group, Chapter 1

- New definition of ethics, Chapter 1

- New topic: Social loafing, Chapter 1

- New topic: Encouraging and supporting diversity as an ethical responsibility, Chapter 1

- New topic: Members with a high preference for procedural order, Chapter 2

- New topic: Application of high/low cultural contexts to groups, Chapter 4

- Edit and additions to the discussion of Poole's Multiple Sequence Model, Chapter 5

- New topic: Self-centered roles as deviant roles, Chapter 6

- New topic: Procedures for dealing with deviant members, Chapter 6

- New topic: Discussion of power use and gender, Chapter 7

- New topic: Adverse effects of transformational leadership, Chapter 7

- Chapter title change, Relational Communication in Groups, Chapter 8

- New topic: Mentoring, Chapter 8

New Figure 9.4, A Review of Janis's Groupthink, Chapter 9

References were updated to include the new material added.

ORGANIZATION OF THE BOOK

Part I: Approaching Communication in Group Contexts

This book is organized in deductive fashion. Part I, "Approaching Communication in Group Contexts," clarifies what small group communication means; this part provides a conceptual foundation for the rest of the book.

Chapter 1: Introduction to Groups and Group Processes   Chapter 1 explains the terms *groups* and *teams* and describes the communication process. The focus is on how groups develop culture and norms as they seek to manage task and relationship concerns. Ethical responsibilities are important, too, so that topic is addressed also.

Part II: Preparing for Group Meetings

Part II helps the reader understand what is involved in and how to prepare for group meetings.

Chapter 2: Preparing for Group Meetings   Chapter 2 examines concerns about the need for structure; selecting participants; and securing, preparing, and critically analyzing information for use. Listening skills are also important in preparing for group discussion, so they are addressed here, too.

Chapter 3: Preparing for Group Meetings   Chapter 3 highlights the importance of making choices about and planning for meetings. How should a business meeting be organized? If a decision is to be made, should an individual or group make it? How should the group organize its effort when its task is to make a decision? What special group techniques might facilitate the group's effort?

Chapter 4: Communication Processes   Chapter 4 examines the nature of verbal and nonverbal messages. Recurring problems with these kinds of messages are explored, along with suggestions for handling them.

Part III: Participating in Group Meetings

The six chapters in Part III form a thorough treatment of the theories, applications, and skills that allow a member to participate more effectively in group meetings.

Chapter 5: Encouraging Group Development and Evolution   Chapter 5 focuses on the evolutionary processes of groups. It begins with a discussion of the motivations for joining a group. This discussion is followed by an explanation of the development phases, social tension, and idea development.

Chapter 6: Roles and Role Emergence   Chapter 6 presents the concepts of roles and how they emerge in a small decision-making group. Group task roles, maintenance roles, and self-centered roles are explained. Conclusions are drawn about critical role functions for groups.

Chapter 7: Leading Group Meetings   Chapter 7 focuses specifically on the leadership function in groups. The connection between power and leadership is explored, along with perspectives on leader behavior, and conclusions are drawn regarding effective leadership. Concrete suggestions are provided for improving leadership to meet specific group goals.

Chapter 8: Relational Communication in Groups   Chapter 8 looks at relational issues that can help a leader or member manage the relationships and climate. Members have needs that must be understood and addressed. Beyond this, a group must foster a relationship-building process. Members will want to understand and be able to facilitate an appropriate relational climate for achieving group goals.

Chapter 9: Promoting Group Cohesiveness and Satisfaction   Chapter 9 addresses cohesiveness as a central concern of group effectiveness. What can be done to enhance the cohesiveness of a group? How can cohesiveness be promoted? These two central issues are addressed in this chapter. Then, too, participants need to be aware of and guard against the effects of too much cohesiveness.

Chapter 10: Managing Conflict in Groups   Chapter 10 takes the perspective that conflict in groups can be managed so that it is functional. Whether the conflict is substantive or affective, understanding the source of the conflict and how to manage it effectively allows for a potential beneficial outcome.

Part IV: Analyzing Small Group Decision Making

Members can make greater contributions to their understanding of groups if they are able to analyze the process carefully. Part IV provides the understanding and tools to carry out analysis.

Chapter 11: Observing and Evaluating Groups   Chapter 11 provides instructions in the process of observing and analyzing groups. Data-collecting instruments are provided to study interaction, roles, leadership, cohesiveness, and the decision-making process.

Appendixes

A: Public Small Group Presentations   This unit describes the various public small group presentation formats and tells when they are useful. Information is also provided for preparing and delivering an oral presentation.

B: Designing Presentation Graphics   This unit provides an overview and step-by-step guide for the process of creating computer-generated graphics.

LEARNING AIDS

Effort has been made to make the key concepts, chapter by chapter, as clear as possible to readers. Each chapter begins with a list of *objectives* that highlight the most important themes in the chapter. Throughout the chapter ideas are reviewed in boxed material labeled "Looking Back: A Quick Review." *Chapter summaries* and *key terms and concepts* at the end of each chapter recast the important ideas into overview statements and a listing of terms that should leave no doubt in the reader's mind as to what are the key ideas.

Over the years I have found that an understanding of the material is facilitated by *exercises*. Some of these can be used in an ongoing *journal assignment*. Others may be selected to emphasize particular concepts.

Recommended readings at the end of each chapter have been carefully selected to reflect the best, and in some cases the most influential, works available. I think students should be encouraged to be familiar with the benchmark work in a discipline. I also think less well-known works, when they are especially relevant, should be brought to the reader's attention, and so I have mentioned some of them, too. I have also included a *glossary* of terms of small group communication at the end of the book.

ACKNOWLEDGMENTS

I extend a very special thanks to those who have provided developmental and editorial help. These people at Pearson have shared their exceptional skills by providing advice, support, problem-solving ability, flexibility, a creative spirit and friendship.

Beth Whitehurse, Karen Hamilton and Bret Holmes provided encouragement when I needed it. Thank all of you so much. I owe a special thanks to Joshua A. Uehlin and Corina Wilshire for sharing their exceptional expertise and knowledge in the production of this book.

Finally, I thank my beautiful bride, Linda, for her patience, understanding and encouragement during the revision of this book

GERALD L. WILSON

part

I

APPROACHING COMMUNICATION IN GROUP CONTEXTS

chapter 1

INTRODUCTION TO GROUPS AND GROUP PROCESSES

OBJECTIVES

After reading this chapter you should be able to

- Recall and explain the components that make up the basic communication model.
- Specify and explain the defining characteristics of decision-making groups.
- Name and describe the different categories of group meetings.
- Explain the concepts of norms and culture.
- Distinguish between the task and relationship dimensions of group communication.
- Describe how a group is a system. Name and explain system properties.
- Describe a personal code of ethics for group discussion.

Your decision to study small group communication is an important one. Learning to be an effective contributor in group meetings is among the critical life skills you will want.

John J. Franco, the president of Learning International, argues that business is increasingly done in the group and that the higher a person rises in an organization, the more work he or she will do in meetings. Franco's argument is borne out by the fact that the average chief executive officer in the United States spends about six hours of every day working on or participating in meetings.

We know, too, a good way to enhance upward mobility in your profession is to become an effective group participant and leader. That stands to reason. Groups, whether they be business meetings or conferences, are the best place to meet and work with (and impress) individuals from other parts of your organization. Groups give you the best setting in which to demonstrate your interactional skill, your analytical ability, and your emotional stability. Groups also give you the opportunity to cultivate important relationships.

Of course, work is only one part of your life. Your study of group communication also will benefit your personal and social life. You will be a member of many groups during your life. You may be a member of a church-related group. You certainly are a member of more than one informal, social group. You are undoubtedly a member of a family group. Both the social groups and the family group make decisions. These groups give you an opportunity to make a contribution, enhance the quality of others' lives, and cement your relationships with other members (Larkin, 1986).[1] Your study of group communication will help you perfect task and social skills useful in these pursuits.

Groups are everywhere. Groups are at school, at church, at work, in the political process, in your social life, in your avocational and recreational life, and in your private life. If you think about it, you will discover that you are a member of many groups. You even have cards to prove your membership in some groups.

Not all the people who participate in groups have the skill and knowledge to make meetings productive. Executives complain about the meetings they have to attend. They wish they knew how to get more out of those meetings and how to make them less a waste of time.

Clearly, you cannot afford not to be a skillful group member. You want the advantages that skill will bring, and every one of your groups will benefit because you have it.

WHY STUDY GROUP COMMUNICATION?

Important advantages come to those who learn to be successful and skillful in a group. You stand to gain enormous benefits at the personal level ranging from monetary and position-enhancement rewards to self-actualization (Maslow, 1970). The better you are in group contexts, the more likely you are to accomplish your goals. The more of your goals you accomplish, the better you feel about yourself.

At a second level, you can make important contributions to the success of any group you join. Not everyone understands group processes, and fewer still understand how to intervene on behalf of better groups and more successful participation. These are two conditions that are important to group success. If, because of your study of small group communication, you can help a group member to participate and if you can intervene to help the group work more effectively, your contribution will be significant.

At a third level, you can make a better contribution to the world you live in if you have better group skills. If that sounds idealistic or altruistic, consider that the decision-making processes that run our society take place in small groups and that those groups do not always include highly placed people.

Consider the ongoing problem that most communities face to maintain high-quality education for children. Often groups of ordinary citizens organize—as they did in one Alabama community—to do something about the situation. To some, the schools seemed too small and in poor repair. Private citizens met in groups to propose solutions, and their efforts had a significant influence.

Groups and group behaviors are fundamental to your world and culture. Groups meet for personal growth, for study and learning, for cooperative activity, for public discussion, for problem solving, for civic action, and for countless other tasks.

Yet most of us take groups and group behaviors for granted. We fail to perceive and understand how our personal effort affects what does or does not happen in a group. Rarely do we consider our performance and how to make it more effective. This neglect is unfortunate. The better you perform in group contexts, the more likely you are to achieve your goals.

COMMUNICATION: THE BASIC IDEA

In every small group meeting, everyone involved is both sending and receiving messages—a variety of messages and through a variety of channels—at the same moment. Communication is not a static thing; it is ongoing and continuous.

To illustrate this idea, consider a meeting of a local service club. A member is speaking to the group about upgrading the facilities of an inner-city youth center. Although she is doing all the talking and although she is primarily in control of the pacing of the talk, she is still receiving messages from her fellow club members.

The responses of members are easily noticed. Group members fidget, they whisper, they take notes, they listen. In doing so, they communicate something to the speaker. Hence the speaker is both a source and a receiver.

So a contemporary communication model is patterned after what happens in dyads where two people are talking. This model is displayed in Figure 1.1. It includes the following key elements: exigency, source/encoder, messages, channels, receiver/decoder, feedback, noise, context, and culture. Each of these is important enough to need a working definition. The basic model in Figure 1.1 applies in nearly all group contexts.

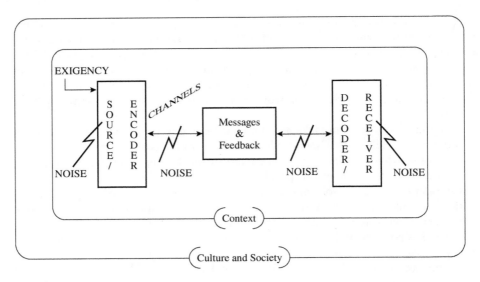

FIGURE 1.1
A Transactional Model of Communication

Exigency

The communication process begins with an **exigency**—a need, demand, or requirement that motivates the desire to communicate. For example, a member of a classroom group might communicate out of a desire to show knowledge, to get an A on the assignment, to exert influence, or to hear himself or herself talk.

Source/Encoder

The **source** is the location of the idea that is to be communicated as a result of the exigency. This idea is **encoded**—that is, translated into words and behavior. This part of the process is identified as the **source/encoder**. A **code** is a set of symbols used to express an idea. Generally our codes are a language and such nonverbal messages as facial expression, body position, vocal characteristics, and clothing. The process of encoding is not simple. A person's personal experience, society, and culture partly affect what codes are available to the group member. The breadth of understanding of both the overall culture and the group culture, coupled with the individual member's communication skill, affects the encoding process.

Messages

Messages are arrangements of symbols that have meaning for the source. That is, the source selects and arranges symbols to create information for the receiver.

An interesting thing is that meaning is not contained in the message we send and receive. Meaning is created and negotiated by the people who send and receive the message. What meaning a person is able to attach to what is said is a function of what he or she is able to bring to the situation from living in the culture and society. *Understanding* is a function of assigning meaning and of the message exchange itself. Thus communication has an inherently transactional nature. Meaning is attached to symbols through a process in which one person initiates a message, the other person or persons take in the message and respond, and the initiator notes the response. Meaning has its basis in your experience of daily living in your culture and society.

The meanings one group member may have for the codes used to transmit an idea may be different from those of other members. For example, when one group began talking about male–female relationships, a female member seemed particularly emotionally involved. Later the group discovered that she was processing the information through the memory of an intensely unpleasant experience with a male. A person's understanding of meaning lies not in the word itself but is based on what he or she takes the word to mean.

Channels

In order for the source/encoder to communicate, the ideas that are encoded must be transmitted as messages through channels. A message is created by the arrangement of symbols that are meaningful to the source/encoder. **Channels** are the mediums through which the message is sent. Thus the channels may be aural (such as speech sounds, music, pausing, and phrasing), or they may be visual (such as gestures and facial expressions).

Notice that, up to this point, the final letter *s* in the words *channels* and *messages* has been consistently *italicized*. This is to emphasize that you rarely communicate through only one channel and that you rarely communicate only one message. Consider a group leader who is trying to motivate sales managers. He might be especially careful to pick the right words. But he would also try to maintain direct eye contact, raise the volume of his voice slightly, use more emphasis, and so forth. He would be using multiple channels to enhance the reception.

Use of multiple channels can complicate the effort to create clear messages. When multiple messages convey the same idea, they reinforce one another. On the other hand, when they contradict one another, they send mixed messages.

Receiver/Decoder

Just as a source has to encode ideas into messages, the **receiver** of the messages must decode and process them. Thus our model includes language that appears to be opposite that of the source/encoder. There is a sense, of course, in which this approach is correct. When you are sending, you want the other person to receive.

In a larger sense, however, the use of opposites—source/encoder and receiver/decoder—creates a false impression that the transactional model is like a linear model. This is not true. Each person in the communication event is at once source and receiver. The arrowheads on both ends of the line between source/encoder and receiver/decoder serve to symbolize a simultaneous, two-way flow of messages.

Feedback

Feedback is information that is provided in the receiver's response or lack of response to the source's message. The arrowheads in the model suggest the notion of feedback. Feedback is the idea that one participant's response helps to correct and control another's message by an ongoing exchange process. For example, consider Susan, a member of a program committee at her church. Imagine that, as she speaks to the group, she notices the other members shifting in their chairs, gazing out the window, and looking glassy eyed. The feedback is telling her that she has lost them. So the feedback could serve the purpose of correcting and controlling her behavior.

Feedback is an important part of a group's communication transactions. Feedback has a role in improving a group's development over time. It needs to be of two kinds in order to accomplish this: task feedback—about the task activities and technical competencies of the group—and teamwork feedback—about the group's interactions and members' relationships, communication, cooperation, and coordination (McIntyre & Salas, 1995).

Noise

A communication event can be pretty noisy. **Noise** is anything in the situation that tends to damage the fidelity of message exchange among group members. Noise inside the participant may be either physiological or psychological. Noise outside the participant may be either physical or systemic. Let's examine these.

Physiological noise results from the physical functioning of the body. A person might experience pain that draws his or her attention. A person might have impaired hearing or vision. Something physiological is hindering the person's communication. **Psychological noise,** on the other hand, comes from the thought process. It may come from a reaction to a word itself. Such **semantic noise** can be created in several ways. One typical way is through the use of emotionally charged words, such as a racial slur. It may come from attaching highly judgmental labels to ideas. The potential for semantic noise is great in groups. This noise can be reduced by avoiding emotionally charged words.

Similarly, group members bring to each communication event their own feelings, wants or expectations, and intentions. They bring with them their attitudes and beliefs. They bring with them a constantly shifting latitude of acceptance for other people and their ideas. They bring with them images of themselves and images of the other communicators. These are always there, and they often generate semantic noise.

Every group communication event includes two dimensions: a **content dimension**—the behavior and ideas related to the task—and a **relationship dimension**—the behavior and ideas related to how people are connected socially. Semantic noise related to content—topics and ideas—generally involves words. Relational noise is often expressed nonverbally. This noise is generated through cues that communicate about the relationship—a relational definition that, perhaps, one or more of the group members believes inappropriate.

To illustrate this relational noise, suppose your boss says to the group, "I have noticed a lot of complaining lately. I want to talk with you about what is going on!"

How she says this may communicate how she is defining her relationship to you. Perhaps it reminds you that she is the boss and that her job is to give orders and yours is to take them. Thus the relationship dimension of the communication event allows you to know how to understand the content dimension. The fit between the content and relational communication can be a source of semantic noise if the way the relationship is defined seems inappropriate to the content.

Physical noise is that which exists in a situation but is outside the participants. The clattering and humming of the air-conditioning system produce noise. The unnecessary chill in the room temperature that distracts you is a form of noise. The glaring light that distracts you is a form of noise. If something outside the group participants gets in the way of the fidelity of message exchange, it is physical noise.

Systemic noise occurs as a product of the communication system in which any particular communication occurs. It is a noise that affects a group but is generated outside the group. For example, many decision-making groups meet as part of the expectations of some larger organization of which they are a part. A sales and marketing department might meet as a group, for example, to hammer out its quota for the next two quarters. Suppose it does that and agrees on a tentative quota system only to discover that the production group cannot accommodate that plan. Such a situation might create frustration and error in the message exchange. An even better example is the loss of a communiqué from the sales department to the production group manager. As you will see, systemic noise can be very perplexing to groups.

Context

Finally, the communication event occurs within some situation. The box around the model in Figure 1.1 is marked "Context." A particular **context** is always embedded in cultures and a society. There will be a group culture, perhaps an organizational culture, and certainly the culture of the society. There may even be a variety of cultures represented within a group if people of different identifiable groups are present. Thus the Context box is surrounded by one marked "Culture and Society."

It is important for you to understand what these words imply. First, of course, all the marked elements of the communication process happen in the context. But the context includes much more. It includes such data as the temperature, lighting conditions, and noise in the environment; the color of the walls; and the acoustics in the room. More important, it also includes what members bring to the event: their motives, their fears and hopes, their self-confidence, their skill with language, their images of one another, and the like.

The specific context, however, also has to have a beginning and an ending. Interaction sequences, like word sequences, must be grouped to make sense. To illustrate this idea, imagine two members of a management team reporting their experience of a fight they witnessed in the Monday morning meeting. Naomi says, "I couldn't believe Linda this morning. She was really riding Josh about those sales figures." John replies, "I didn't see it that way. I thought she was being reasonable. Josh was the person being unreasonable. He ought to have those figures and be able to explain them." Naomi continues, "I agree that he ought to have the figures, but Linda was really being testy! I don't think that kind of behavior is called for." John replies, "I think Linda calls them like she sees them. She is a good team player. Remember last week . . ."

Each event in a group meeting at any given time is related to the events that surround it. In our illustration Naomi observed the event, began to understand it from its place in the sequence of events, and drew conclusions. Her conclusions were that Linda was being testy and that the situation did not warrant this behavior. John, on the other hand, selected a different sequence of events. He came to a different conclusion—that Linda's behavior was necessary, perhaps even justified.

Who was correct, Naomi or John? Correctness depends on perspective. How the incident is understood will depend on *where* you start to understand it. This idea is called **punctuation.** A group member who does not understand the idea of punctuation may assume that his or her view is the only one possible. This can lead to serious consequences.

Culture

Culture is a learned system of behavior, attitude, beliefs, values and norms shared by a group of people. A culture provides the "codes," the language—verbal and nonverbal—and the meaning for the language that make communication possible.

A culture, including a group's culture, develops from the values or ideals of the group, as agreed upon over time by its members, and from the customs or ways of doing things that the members traditionally follow.

Cultural diversity in groups is recognized for the most part as an important advantage. Members of many groups go beyond tolerating differences to celebrating them and using them to create a better outcome. The keys to making this happen appear to be sensitivity and effective communication. Haslett & Ruebush (2000) looked at this productivity issue in the context of diverse groups. They concluded that groups that do not have awareness and sensitivity experience problems, such as poor management of conflict, differential rates of participation, and in-group—out-group divisions.

These values and customs may be artifacts that evolve out of the collective support of the members (Ellis & Fisher, 1994). You can say that they evolve as the result of the functioning of human interaction.

Small groups evolve behavior patterns, beliefs, rituals, and ways of doing things that affect the group's communication. This process begins with the first group meetings, which lay the groundwork for the group's culture. The process "begins" because a group's culture changes to meet members' needs. An observer of a group does not usually see patterns emerging until the third or fourth group meeting. This delay occurs because members react with tentative behavior as they feel their way along in their attempt to understand group members' actions and reactions. Even the established culture of an ongoing group is fluid. Yet, once established, the evolution of a group's traditions and values may be so slow that members adjust without noticing the change. The following description of a group provides a narrative of how one group's culture evolved.

Six engineers who work for a large papermaking company in Oregon were hired for six months to help run an automated plant that makes pasteboard for boxes. The plant was state of the art, meaning that all the equipment and all the processes were technologically sophisticated. The individual engineers identified with one another. They were relatively new. They were relatively young. They were highly trained but relatively inexperienced. They had been hired by the company to meet the same company goals. As these six worked together to make decisions, they began to evolve a group ideal. Their performance became as sophisticated as they perceived their plant to be.

To accomplish this informal group goal, these engineers met regularly after hours to discuss ways of ensuring excellent performance. Their thinking was that they might be able to help one another do their jobs better. They decided that group performance would improve if they planned to cover one another's assignments. Each member learned not only his or her own job but also one of the other group members' jobs. Thus they were able to minimize the effect of an absence. In addition, they became intolerant of "halfway measures." By using this phrase, the group enforced the emerging norm that each member was to do his or her best. "Just good enough" was not enough.

In time the members decided that it would be wise to double-check one another's work. They read, criticized, and sometimes edited technical reports and major capital requests to help one another. The effect was unusually high-quality output. The double-checking was time-consuming, but rewarding. Thus this group evolved a value of quality and a plan to ensure that quality.

This example shows that a group's culture reflects a number of aspects. Social concerns are evident in repeated behaviors that build and reveal the group's identification with its members and task. Task concerns are evident in the group's patterns of behaving and the "rules" these patterns create. The group develops its values and customs for dealing with social and task concerns through its interaction and communication rules it establishes.

Culture on a broader level brings both challenges and benefits. The members of a group may come from differing social and ethnic cultures. **Ethnic diversity** is present in a group when members are from two or more cultures. Culturally diverse groups may have issues to work out in addition to the task. Of course, a stronger group will probably emerge if these are managed well. On the other hand, serious harm can come if they are not managed well. Consequently, culturally diverse groups may need more time to complete their task (Northcraft et al., 1995; Oetzel & Bolton-Oetzel, 1997).

We might speak of culture as if the people of the United States, or any country for that matter, were a single culture. The reality is that we may speak the same language and share some overall social customs, but be very different. Diversity is a term we use to describe the many variations we find among us. It means difference. It is based on a different life experiences that leads to different perspectives on a variety of life issues. It can mean people who speak differently from us and also look different. It might mean people whose first language may be other than English, whose economic situation may be different, and whose access to education may be different.

Diversity may make our life more difficult. We may not share meaning for important words that we have taken for granted that others share. People may not be as predictable as we would like. When we put these people in a group and ask them to work together we may find the situation is more difficult than we had imagined.

Focus on Research

GROUP NORMS AND CULTURE VARIATIONS

Your group may find the process of establishing norms difficult due to cultural variations in members. Recall that individual autonomy and initiative are valued in some cultures, for example the Anglo-American culture, while collective well-being is valued in others, for example the Japanese culture. One implication of this is the time members may want to spend in the task and social dimensions. Members of a collectivist culture may want to discuss a decision until they get 100 percent agreement, no matter how long it takes to get there. Members of an individualistic culture may want to take a vote after a deliberation has gone on "long enough." Of course, most groups have norms about these matters and so it may very well be a point of contention. Beyond this, the cultural orientation may affect the perceptions of each other. People from individualistic cultures may see collectivists as weak and too group dependent, while the people from collectivistic cultures may see individualists who act assertively as too self-centered (Bantz, 1993). A word of caution seems reasonable here. There is significant evidence to suggest that there are wide variations within a single culture. Researchers suggest it is not possible to predict that an particular cultural orientation will match that orientation (Park and Levine, 1999).

C. R. Bantz (1993). Cultural diversity and group cross-cultural team research, *Journal of Applied Communication*, 21, 1–20.

H. S. Park & T. R. Levine (1999). The theory of reasoned action and self-construal: Evidence from three cultures, *Communication Monographs*, 66, 199–218.

COMMUNICATION: A DYNAMIC PROCESS

A model of communication shows a frozen moment in time and space and includes these elements—exigency, source/encoder, messages, channels, receiver/decoder, feedback, noise, context, and culture. Keep in mind that these elements are always in a state of flux. They change to meet the evolving interpretations of the individuals as they negotiate meaning, as well as to accommodate the constantly changing world in which meaning exists. To fully understand this process, we will need to examine what happens inside of the individual communicator. This understanding is very important to group members, for it makes clear that merely because one person defines something in a particular way does not mean the others will understand. We will examine this issue further in Chapter 4.

ADVANTAGES AND DISADVANTAGES OF GROUP WORK

Distinct advantages of working in a group flow from the fact that members provide information and thinking from different perspectives. Each member brings to the group unique experiences relative to the group's goal and issues surrounding it. Of course, that experience includes information that the group has in common, but it also includes unique individual information and experiences. Thus a group brings to bear on its goals a perspective that is distinct and different from that of any individual.

The broad perspective a group is able to achieve is useful in the group's information processing. Members thinking together about an issue create a potential to see the issue in a number of different ways (Stasson & Bradshaw, 1995).

This broad perspective also provides the potential for correcting group thought-process errors (Laughlin, Vander Steop, & Hollingshead, 1994). Members are likely voice the potential problems in the thought process if they are encouraged to be open in their analysis of the issue. Thus the group becomes self-correcting of its errors in thinking.

This broad perspective members bring to an issue can enhance the group's creative thought process. Members' shared ideas can stimulate the thinking of other members. A person may expand on an original idea and/or present it in light of his or her own thinking. This potential for a mix of ideas, and new ways of thinking, provides the potential for exciting creativity.

Synergy comes from a Greek word that means "working together." **Synergy** is the power that comes from people working together, rather than working apart. The group works together, sharing their ideas, operating with an open mind, respecting each other, and managing conflict well. McShane and Von Gllinow (2000, p. 312) describe synergy and its outcome, "Several individuals working together and building on each other's strengths can potentially generate more and better solutions than if these people worked along."

It is the group process that creates an outcome that is different and often superior to what any individual member might generate on his or her own. This is an advantage of group process. Members can "bounce" ideas off one another and the parts of many

Looking Back: A Quick Review

ADVANTAGES AND DISADVANTAGES OF GROUP WORK

Advantages:

Information provided is from differing perspectives.

Members thinking together provide broad perspective.

Members can check thinking for errors.

Working together enhances potential for creativity.

Members working together produce synergy which enhances the group process.

Working together can be satisfying.

Disadvantages:

Increased cost in terms of time.

Enhanced opportunity for conflict if members choose not to cooperate.

ideas can be combined to form new and different ideas. The result is often a product that is new, unexpected and superior.

Finally, the opportunity to work with a group can be more fun and more satisfying than working as an individual. Interaction among members feeds many needs. Among these are the needs for stimulation, belonging, and esteem.

Of course, there also are disadvantages to working in a group. A chief disadvantage is cost in time or revenues. A meeting or meetings must be called, members have to prepare, each may have input to give, and so forth. All this activity takes time. In addition, a group meeting may be costly in terms of actual cost in wages. Productivity lost by pulling people from their work to attend a meeting is expensive.

Group discussion also can be a disadvantage if the climate of the meeting is not cooperative. For example, members may have a high stake in the outcome and may be unwilling to weigh issues without bias. Coalitions may form that completely block the group's progress. Perceived differences may be identified as real and may intensify as the result of a group meeting. We may choose to meet in a group anyway, however, because the circumstance and advantages outweigh the disadvantages. In this case the group leadership will be challenged to manage difficulties like these if they develop.

GROUPS DEFINED

So pervasive is the communication process in groups that we need to focus and limit our consideration if this book is to be of reasonable length. After all, communication takes place in all kinds of groups, and it happens all the time, in an amazingly complex process of variables that can have an effect on accuracy and efficacy. So some terms need to be defined at this point to limit the arena in which you will be.

Group

In our study we will understand the term **group** to mean a collection of three or more individuals who interact about some common problem or interdependent goal and can exert mutual influence over one another. A **small group**—the kind that is of most interest to us—is one in which members communicate with one another face to face, aware of one another's roles. The three key elements in this definition are size, goal orientation, and mutual influence.

Size   By this definition, two people cannot be a group. When three people join together, they create a unique environment because of the ability of two of the members to unite and exert pressure on the other. Size exerts a significant impact on the group (Miller, 1978). If we are in an interaction with one other person and a third person joins us, the dynamic of the group changes. If you were to be making a decision, for example, one possibility is two people with one view and one with another. Often, because the two people share an opinion, they win out. So, size changes the dynamic.

It turns out that a group of five to seven people is ideal for decision making. This is true for a number of reasons. Two reasons are that it is more likely to provide for diversity of ideas and also to provide an opportunity for all to participate. Often, if the group is too large some members will not participate because they do not see the opportunity.

Almost everything that may be said about two persons interacting can apply to groups, but this book focuses upon those variables that influence group processes. Along the way, ideas about interpersonal communication are integrated, of course.

Goal orientation   A group usually shares a problem or wishes to deal with a commonly shared need or meets to achieve some shared goal. Group members will almost always share some degree of interdependence. The group's members depend in some way on each other to achieve the group's goal. By this requirement, a collection of people who do not experience a need to work jointly on a goal does not constitute a group. A good word to describe a gathering of individuals is a **collection.**

Mutual influence   The interactions and behaviors of individual group members influence all the members of the group; that is, they exert mutual influence. They listen to one another. They talk with one another. They attempt to affect one another's attitudes, thinking, and behavior. They influence the collective mentality and the collective behavior of the group. They respond to each other in a variety of ways. The members of a group are **interdependent.** This suggests that each member action affects other members and the group's outcomes (Brewer, 1995). Members are related by talk and intention, and they interact from a shared motive. It is because of this mutual influence that the group itself is a "new experience" each time it meets.

Groups versus Collections

Let's examine some examples of groups and collections to clarify these concepts. By our definition, five students who meet by prior agreement to study for an examination would qualify as a group. Five students who bump into one another outside a classroom building and pause to chat between classes would not be a group of interest to us. In the first example, the students share a common goal or problem and probably have an awareness of each other's roles. The social dynamics of this second group are of interest to scholars and students who are studying the social dynamics of groups. This is not the focus of this book. On the other hand, an ad hoc committee appointed to recommend dates for an upcoming student event also would be a group of interest.

To provide another example of the groups that are and are not of concern to us, suppose five members of a sales department met to plan their biannual sales meeting. They would be a group of concern to us. But if five sales department members gather to celebrate the end of a busy month by holding a picnic in the park, they would not be of concern to us.

With this idea of what we mean by group in mind, let's draw an additional distinction regarding groups and teams.

GROUPS AND TEAMS

Groups are sometimes referred to as teams or as work teams. Not all groups are teams. The word team is also used to designate a particular kind of group.

Dennis Kinlaw, teamwork consultant to corporations and government agencies, clarifies the distinction between groups, teams, and work groups. He suggests that the designation group includes both teams and work groups. The distinction Kinlaw makes is that a **team** is a group that has reached a higher level of quality. It has developed cohesiveness among its members; it creates critical work processes; it provides leadership for its own development and performance (Kinlaw, 1991). Katzenbach and Smith (1993, p. 45) expand on this idea: "A working group relies primarily on the individual contributions of its members for group performance, whereas a team strives for a magnified impact that is incremental to what its members could achieve in their individual roles." Harris and Sherblom (1999) add that teams generally share leadership.

This definition of team actually describes the high-level functioning, decision-making groups this book presents. All the processes we describe apply to decision-making groups and enhance groups' effectiveness, so if a "team" is engaged in decision making, it is precisely the same group we describe in this book.

There are two differences between a team and a decision-making group. One is the expectation that a team will be ongoing or, at least work together for the duration of the task, requiring a number of meetings. A decision-making group may or may not be ongoing. The second difference is that roles team members take in relation to the team's task are often formal roles. For example, a management team will have members who have designated titles and roles within the organization. They are part of the team because they can represent their unit and bring information that is available only from a person connected to that unit. These people have titles such as "manager of" or "vice president for" (Katzenbach & Smith, 1993, p. 88).

A *team*, then, is a group of three or more individuals who interact on an ongoing basis about some common problem or interdependent goal (task), provide their own leadership for development and performance, and exert mutual influence over one another. You will find that everything we say in this text pertains equally to both teams and decision-making groups.

A well-trained team has the advantage of its members being **cross-functional.** This means that team members understand each other's responsibilities and are ready to step in to perform these when a member is absent. This allows the team to achieve its goals even under circumstances that are less than ideal (Devine et al., 1999). In order for this to work, team members must have clearly defined goals that are linked to the group's common goal. Members must also understand how individual efforts fit together to achieve this common outcome. Training can help facilitate members' understanding of each other's roles and duties and thus help ensure team success (Salas et al., 1999). Of course, the essential ingredient in bringing all this about is communication that allows this coordination and collaboration (Hollingshead, 1998).

What does it take to achieve this aim? LaFasto and Larson (2001) identified six characteristics of an effective team member. These are:

- Experience with the issues they will address.

- Problem-solving ability.

- Openness to discussing new ideas and discussing issues.

- Supportiveness in listening to each other and an optimism about the team.

- Action oriented in responding to pitching in to get the job done.

- Positive orientation toward each other and the task.

Cross-Training in Teams

A team may engage in **cross-training.** Cross training is one way teams plan to pick up the slack when members are absent. This gives members a working knowledge of the duties of others. There is more than "picking up the slack" involved here. This kind of training promotes a team mentality. Volpe and colleagues (2002) discovered this training takes on one of three forms. The training may be *positional clarification* in that members are provided with verbal or written information about jobs and responsibilities of each member. The training may go further to *modeling* that provides opportunities for observation and discussion. Instead, the training may be *positional rotation* where members actually step in and perform each other's jobs. How does management decide which level is appropriate? Researchers suggest it depends on the level of interdependence (Blickensderfer and Bowers, 1998; Volpe et al., 1996).

Looking Back: A Quick Review

How Groups and Teams Compare

Groups	Teams
Roles evolve as the group works together.	Roles are assigned and clearly identified. Members may be cross-trained in several roles.
Goals may be discussed and agreed to by members. Goals provide a general direction.	Goals are clearly defined by members.
Members interact and evolve methods of working together. They may also work separately and then come together to work.	Members formally collaborate and coordinate their efforts to work together.
Members are somewhat interdependent.	Members are interdependent.
Rules and procedures generally evolve as the group meets, according to its needs.	Rules and procedures are explicitly discussed and developed in order to coordinate effort.

KINDS OF GROUP MEETINGS

Many groups have a primary focus. The following are some of the typical kinds of meetings and their focuses.

Information-Sharing Meetings

One kind of group meeting—found in families, learning groups, work groups, community groups and groups generally—is the **information-sharing meeting.** This type of meeting occurs on a regular basis, with a predictable agenda and a clear set of traditions, and yet there is no expectation that decisions will be made.

To illustrate the information-sharing meeting, consider the regular Monday morning conference of department heads at a local hospital. In that meeting the group follows a predictable agenda—announcements, ongoing concerns, assignments for the week, and adjournment. Such a meeting allows members to express themselves, to be informed and inform others of the activities of the group, to get and give assistance, to clarify the group's goals, to clarify their own short-term goals, and to establish and maintain their working relationships. Such meetings happen in corporations, churches, schools, service clubs, social fraternities and sororities, town meetings, and other organizations or agencies.

Decision-Making Meetings

A second very important group experience you will almost certainly encounter is the **decision-making meeting.** This experience can occur in ad hoc (one meeting only or a limited number of meetings) and ongoing groups. These task groups meet to focus upon some particular concern. They may follow a loose agenda but are often free to deviate from that agenda. Effective leadership will monitor the progress of a decision-making meeting through the various stages in the evolution of an agenda designed to get the task accomplished. We can expect some amount of information sharing in meeting this goal. This kind of sharing may be brief if members are well informed and already share the basic information necessary for a decision. Otherwise, it may be extensive.

Decision-making group experiences are very common. They occur in families, therapy groups, work groups, and community groups. In fact, routine information-sharing meetings may evolve into decision-making meetings if it becomes clear that decisions must be made. For example, the regular Monday meeting group of hospital department heads may discover that it has to generate a holiday schedule, make a decision about the problem of sudden higher-than-normal power and heat consumption, or generate some creative means to reduce hospital spending by 3 percent.

Special Kinds of Information-Sharing and Decision-Making Meetings

A third, and somewhat less frequent, kind of group experience is the **special-event meeting.** A group's annual conference is a special event. A group of employees being entertained by a sales representative from one of the company's suppliers—typically called a sales meeting—is involved in a special-event meeting. Individuals who gather at a resort hotel to attend

Looking Back: A Quick Review

Types of Small Groups

Type	Task
Information sharing	Share information. Predictable agenda. Clear traditions.
Decision making	Focus is on a particular concern. Flexible agenda. Information and problem solving leads to decision.
Special event	One-of-a-kind meeting. Occasional and often traditional event. Often large group. Includes information sharing and perhaps decision making.

a seminar on fund raising for nonprofit organizations are involved in a special-event meeting. The special-event experience is different in some very particular ways, but it is also sufficiently like the others in that it may involve information sharing and/or decision making.

Groups work within a variety of contexts. These contexts tend to overlap in some ways, but they will often have a primary focus. Groups abound in private and professional life. Groups are so important to a culture that they are fundamental to the culture's pursuits and to our own pursuits and well-being.

UNDERSTANDING SOME BASIC DYNAMICS OF GROUPS

If you want to prepare for a small group discussion, either as a participant or as a group leader, you will want to understand the basic dynamics of groups. How a group evolves norms and rules bears directly on participation in that group. Beyond this, you will want to understand the task and relationship dimensions.

Group Norms

Culture is a concept that designates what can be known about living within a society, a segment of a society, or even a small group. Culture is passed to new members of groups so that the people in them demonstrate behavior and hold values that are important to the group. Some of what people know about living in their society or group can be identified as norms. A **norm** is an informal standard for behavior within a culture; it refers to a specific aspect of the broader culture. When a norm becomes formalized in a culture, it is referred to as a **rule** or *law*. For example, at one point in the history of the United States it was widely believed that working hard at one's job could be expected of people. Since there wasn't a rule governing this behavior, but people adhered to the norm.

Small groups adopt some societal and organizational norms as well as develop their own. A **norm,** then, is a standard model, or pattern, of behavior. Group norms evolve in at least three areas: social, procedural, and task. Groups learn to work together, and they develop a history and tradition as a result of their interactions. Members learn "how it's supposed to be" as a result of rewards and punishment that the group gives individuals.

Many norms govern behavior in a decision-making group, yet behavior governed by these norms seems so natural that members may not notice them. Examples of norms in a decision-making group are understanding how to proceed, how long a member should talk, what kind of evidence is acceptable to support an argument, how a member should argue, how long a meeting should last, how members might be confronted about unacceptable behavior, how personal their relationships can be, how much humor is appropriate, and how to express feelings and emotions. Norms are pervasive.

Conformity to norms is related to attraction to the group. When our attraction is high, we will identify with the group and conform to norms. When we are not, their is little motivation to conform (Abrams et al., 1990).

The term *norm* comes from the word normal. Behavior is normal if it seems to fall within the guidelines that a group accepts—guidelines that the group validates.

The evolution of group norms is important to a group. Norms bear directly upon a group's success. They also make an enormous difference to a member's satisfaction and the group's cohesiveness. But the emergence of norms can also create problems that flow from habit, rigidity, and loss of creativity.

Members adjust and adapt to new members. This process is called *group socialization* (Anderson, Riddle, & Martin, 1999). The new member will need to learn the group's roles, norms, and interaction patterns and follow these so he or she can be a productive member.

The Unproductive Norms

To illustrate the problems, consider those six engineers again. Their habit of double-checking each other's written work may seem like a good idea. But every job includes some things that are not important. For example, engineers often write "for the file." That is, they write to create a paper trail in case something goes wrong.

The custom of waiting until each can check the other's work probably constitutes an unnecessary delay where such a report is written for the file. The group risks its efficiency even further if this habitual way of doing things were to evolve into a norm.

Remember norms evolve not only in the task area but also in procedural and social dimensions. Suppose a group began to adhere rigidly to customary ways of doing things in the procedural area. In that case the group would risk creativity.

If a group evolves a norm that is damaging, what can a member do to provide leadership to change it? You won't be surprised that we advise you to talk about it.

First, identify your concern. Say something like, "I'm worried that we've fallen into a habit of . . ."

Second, ask the group members to discuss their perceptions of the situation so that everyone has a chance to become aware of the dysfunctional norm. "I'd like to know if the rest of you think there's a problem with . . ."

Third, ask the group for an agreement to change the norm. "Well, we all agree this is a problem. Can we also agree to discuss ways to act differently?"

After the group has identified a way to resolve the problem, restate the agreement. "So we're agreed, then, that we'll . . ."

The point here is important. Understanding a group's culture can make a difference, whether you play a participant or a leadership role. It can influence the efficiency and the effectiveness of the group, and it can influence its cohesiveness. The group's notions of how it's supposed to be can also create serious problems.

Norms and Diversity

The importance of understanding norms is underscored when we examine the rapidly changing makeup of society, including dramatic changes in demographics, multicultural backgrounds, and interest (Harris, 1997). The U.S. Department of Labor projected in a 1999 report that "about half of all Americans will belong to what are now considered minority groups" by the year 2050 (Associated Press, 1999, p. 15B).

Tasks and Relationships

If you examine a communication event closely, you will discover that it has two dimensions (Ellis, 1979; Fisher, 1979).[2] In one dimension the participants work on some object, phenomenon, or event dealing with topics or tasks. The **task** is the focus of the work of the group, and that work centers on the achievement of the group's goal. In a civic action group, the task may be promoting better schools. In a marketing department, it may be a new marketing approach for a product. In a city government meeting, it might be allocating funds to various departments. In the group's relationship, sometimes referred to as the **maintenance function,** the participants work on learning their relationships, refining them, nurturing them. This process is a significant benefit of group interaction (Senge, 1990). The **relationship** focuses on who we are with respect to others and the management of the surrounding circumstances. This social dimension refers to the social fabric that promotes relationships among members. It is the affective, expressive dimension. To illustrate these two dimensions of communication, suppose a friend who owns a sailboat invites you to a meeting of the Buccaneer Yacht Club. You attend the meeting and hear this conversation:

SUE: I think that in addition to the race on the thirteenth we should plan a workday to do some repairs to the clubhouse.

DON: I appreciate that idea, Sue. Some of us are a little beyond our racing years. We still want to be included, and the workday is something we can help with.

This exchange illustrates the task dimension of communication. Sue talked about objects, phenomena, and events in her suggestion. The objects were herself, sailing, and

Focus on Research

HOW DIVERSITY ISSUES IMPACT GROUP DISCUSSION

The issue of the impact of diversity on conflict in group process has received significant attention from scholars. Ralph Rodriques (1998) attempted to isolate the variable that has the most impact on group process. He concluded it was not race, gender, or age per se that affects the group performance, but the underlying value structure and approach to the problem. Other scholars disagree. Leonard Karakowsky and Jacob Seigle (1999) attribute diversity-related conflict to the proportion of minority members in the group. Their research revealed that when the number of minority members was small, only one or two, these members were reluctant to press their position. On the other hand, when the number of members of a racial minority was sizable, it was difficult to ignore their opinion so the group dealt with it. So the group gains the advantage of being able to consider diverse opinions and there is evidence that this frequently enhances performance (Farmer & Roth, 1998). Managing this conflict effectively is facilitated by having clear group goals that are understood by every group member and that the conflict be focused on the issue rather than on personalities (Oetzel, 1998).

Farmer, S. M. & J. Roth (1998). Conflict-handling behavior in work groups: Effects of group structure. Decision processes, and time, *Small Group Research*, 29, 669–713.

Karakowsky, L. & J. P. Siegel (1999). The effects of proportional representation on intergroup behavior in mixed-race decision-making groups, *Small Group Research*, 30, 259–279.

Oetze, J. G. (1998). Explaining individual communication processes in homogeneous and heterogeneous groups through individualism-collectivism and self-construal, *Human Communication Research*, 15, 202–224.

Rodriques, R. (1998). Challenging demographic reductionism: A pilot study investigating diversity in group composition, *Small Group Research*, 29, 744–759.

a workday. The phenomena include sailing and working. The events include joining together, racing, and meeting new people and old friends. The task dimension of this talk is the planning of a race and consideration of a workday.

This example also illustrates the relationship dimension, but for this communication you really have to be at the yacht club for this dimension to make much sense. Traditional task groups, as is true for people in our culture, delegate much of their communication about relationships to nonverbal messages. So we must take in the nonverbal behavior to be able to say much about the relationship dimension. Interestingly, there is a gender difference here. Women talk about relationships more than men; compared to men, women may do more than observe and guess.

TASK-DIMENSION CONCERNS IN GROUP COMMUNICATION

In the context of a group meeting, there are task-dimension concerns. Those that are most compelling include such notions as whether or not to have a meeting, decision making, leadership, and participation. The concerns are those that contribute to productivity.

The **productivity** of a group refers to its task-related output. Productivity is what comes from a group's activities. Productivity is always centered in the tasks or goals of a group, measured against either quality or quantity criteria. This statement is true whether the task is making a decision or providing emotional support.

To compare and contrast these criteria we might talk about a city government planning commission. The productivity of this group is measured in terms of the quality of its decisions with respect to variances it passes during its meetings. It could be said: "This commission has exceedingly high standards with very high reliability."

Similarly, it might be said of the commission: "The commission's output, measured in number of decisions per meeting, has increased dramatically over the past few years." That statement would also be about the commission's task productivity. It refers to the quantity produced by the commission over a given period of time. So a working group's task productivity can be judged by the number of units it produces or by the quality of each unit. This distinction can be an important one for groups, since it is directly related to their goals. One group may say of itself, "We want to be a good group," and mean, "We want to turn out many . . . We also want to enjoy each other." Another group may say of itself, "We want to be a good group," and mean, "We want to turn out a few high-quality . . . We want members to like working together." Still another group might wish to be judged by all these criteria.

Productivity, then, is the yield of a group's effort to accomplish its projects. As such, productivity flows from communication in the task and relationship dimensions. In a meeting at a local church, a group met to provide emotional support to people recently divorced. Productivity for this group was measured by the degree to which members feel supported. This result is difficult to measure, but members can report an improvement in the quality of their life.

Relational-dimension concerns in group communication In the **relational dimension,** the one that gives rise to members' attraction to the group, the appropriate concerns are about managing and developing relationships. A list of these considerations includes norms and their evolution; roles and their evolution; power and power use; conflict and conflict management; and, of course, the relationships per se.

THE SMALL GROUP AS AN INFORMATION-PROCESSING SYSTEM

It is useful to view small decision-making groups as **information-processing systems** because the individuals share and process information from their experience and/or study to produce output. The group processes this information for members' purposes. Figure 1.2 presents the various components of a decision-making group that make up this system.

Notice that the system includes *inputs, processes, outputs,* and *feedback* loops operating within an environment. People and things are brought together, processes take place, and products are created. Notice also that the group monitors its processes and outputs and feeds back information as inputs. In other words, the group's feedback is

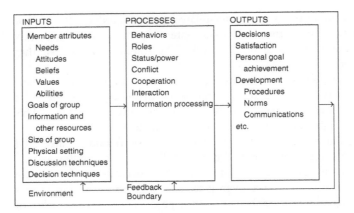

FIGURE 1.2
The Small Group as an Information-Processing System

based on what it learns from its experiences and provides input to improve its process. The environment surrounds the group, providing a basis for both understanding and constraining the group's actions. What happens outside the group may change members' attitudes, and the nature of available resources, change the group's goals, and so forth. Rarely does a group operate in isolation.

Information-processing groups are systems. A **system** is "a set of objects or entities that interrelate with one another to form a whole (Warnemunde, 1986, p. 392)." The *objects* here are the group members. The group may be viewed as a whole and as an interacting set of individual parts. Often the group is part of an organization and, therefore, would be considered a subsystem of the organizational system.

The group as an information-processing system is displayed in Figure 1.2 and serves as the framework for organizing the remainder of this book. It includes and orders the major variables that affect a small group in its decision-making effort. Thus Part II (Chapters 2 through 4), "Preparing for Group Meetings," considers the input variables shown in the model. **Input variables** are such things as member attributes, group goals, resources, size, meeting place, and discussion and decision techniques. Part III (Chapters 5 through 10), "Participating in Group Meetings," addresses the process variables. Examples of **process variables** are behaviors of members, roles, status, power, conflict/cooperation, interaction, and information processing. Part IV (Chapter 11), "Analyzing Small Group Decision Making," focuses on observing **outputs,** measuring outputs, assessing goal achievement, and providing feedback.

In a practical sense how do these variables play out in an effective group? Gloria J. Galanes, Katherine Adams, and John K. Brilhart (2004) speak directly and succinctly to this issue in their list of system characteristics of an *effective* discussion group, displayed in Figure 1.3. You will find this figure useful as you form groups through out the term. This provides a basis for evaluating the effectiveness of your group.

Input Variables
1. Members share values and beliefs toward the purpose of the group and each other.
2. The number of members is small enough for all to be active participants who are aware of each other yet large enough to supply knowledge and competencies.
3. All members understand and accept the group's purpose.
4. Resources needed to achieve group goals are available.
5. The group's relationships to other groups and organizations are clear.
6. The group has sufficient time to do its work.
7. The group has a meeting place that provides for members' needs and is free of distractions.

Process Variables
1. Members can predict each other's behaviors.
2. Roles are stable, mutually understood, and accepted.
3. Members have relatively equal status, so they can exert influence based on knowledge, ideas, and skills.
4. Norms and the values underlying them are understood and adhered to, or discussed openly and changed if counterproductive.
5. Communication flows in an all-channel network.
6. Members are skilled and considerate when expressing themselves.
7. All members understand and share procedures that are efficient and lead to goal achievement.

Output Variables
1. Members perceive that the group purpose has been achieved.
2. Members feel satisfaction with their roles, the group process, and their relationships with other members.
3. Cohesiveness is high.
4. There is consensus on the role and leadership structure.
5. The parent organization (if one exists) is strengthened by the group's work.

Environmental Factors
1. The environment (usually an organization) should publicly recognize and reward the accomplishments of the group.
2. The environment should supply whatever informational resources the group needs.
3. The environment should supply whatever resources and expertise the group needs.
4. The environment should provide a supportive atmosphere for the group.

FIGURE 1.3
System Variables Related to an Effective Discussion Group

Source: Galanes, Adams & Brilhart (2004, p. 35).

ETHICAL RESPONSIBILITIES OF MEMBERS AND GROUPS

Ethical Responsibilities of Members

When people engage in group discussion for the purpose of solving problems, they agree that they will give up some of their individual rights so group process can work. They become, for a time, interdependent. In doing so, they assume an obligation to one another to live by higher ethical conduct. The Random House College Dictionary (2nd edition, page 665) defines **ethics** as the "rules or standards for right conduct or practice." Here are some important ethical small group standards for you and your group members to follow. Here are some important ethical small group standards.

Determine to do your best   As an individual you have a lot to offer. You are knowledgeable, and you have ideas and opinions. Your strengths and your weaknesses *are* you when you commit yourself to group processes. You should determine to give your best.

But sometimes individuals hold back. They avoid taking the leadership role, for example, because others are willing to take it. They learn that if they freely offer their skills, they will be called on to do that again and again. So they hold back.

If something is worth doing, it is worth doing well. If a goal is worth achieving, it is worth the best efforts of everyone involved in achieving it. If group process is worth participating in, it is worth the most skillful participation you can manage. To choose not to give your best violates a profound personal ethical standard.

Determine to behave with the group's good in mind   An individual must sometimes put aside personal goals in favor of group goals. An individual must sometimes put aside private convictions so that group consensus is achievable. An individual must sometimes put private truths in second place to public and group facts and opinions. Determining to work for the group's good means making a commitment to keep an open mind and to listen to evidence and arguments, to evaluate them carefully, even though they may appear to contradict one's own view. Determining to behave in the group's best interests means, in the end, making a commitment to completing tasks on the basis of the evidence and the group's best understanding of that evidence.

Such a commitment means making personal decisions on the basis of facts, and it may mean persuading other group members to open up to those facts. Such a commitment means keeping personalities out of conflicts, examining and accepting or rejecting ideas while valuing the person whose ideas they are. Such a commitment means determining the behavior that is essential if group discussion is to be worthwhile. Group members have a right to expect your commitment to the best interests of the group.

Make a commitment to fair play   Group problem solving must be understood to be a cooperative event. It is not a debate, because, for the most part, it is not a competition. So fair play means determining to seek and present all the ideas and evidence.

In a debate the opposing sides agree to disagree. In making that decision, they agree further that they will present only the strongest and best arguments and evidence on their side of the issue. They agree to minimize or refute altogether the evidence and arguments of the opposing side. But group discussion is not debate. When groups are working together well, the group goals are the individual members' most important goals.

Every member of a discussion group has a right to expect that you will accept a standard of behavior in which you do not grind your private ax at the expense of the group project. Every member has a right to expect that you will play fairly, just as you have a right to expect that every member will play fairly with you.

Determine to listen carefully and to participate fully   When you say something, you have a right to expect that the other members of the group will give you a fair hearing. Sometimes members do not participate fully. The research literature calls these people social loafers. A **social loafer** is a person who does not contribute much to the group effort and is willing to let others carry the load. We believe it is a central responsibility of every member to avoid this label and fulfill the role of participant-analyst. You have a right to expect that they will listen carefully, provide you with feedback, come to understand what you are trying to say, evaluate what you have said, and treat your ideas seriously. None of this means that they will ultimately agree with you, of course.

Listen carefully and fully to other people's ideas. Listen carefully and fully to what others are *not* saying, too. Participate with them when they are talking, for not to do so is to endanger the problem-solving benefits of the group process. To do so, on the other hand, will foster group satisfaction (Hartung, Hagen, & Burch, 1985).

Take on the responsibility to encourage and support diversity.   Diversity in every way, race, ethnicity, religion, sexual orientation and age, generally makes a stronger group. It yields a better decision and an enhanced group performance than when it is not present. So, diversity is a *powerful tool* for enhancing group process. This is true because diversity brings a variety of experiences and information to the problem being discussed.

For example, we recognize that a lone male in a group of females might encounter a situation that makes it difficult for this person to have his opinions and perspectives heard and seriously considered. (This might also happen if the group were male with one female.) This is why this principle is important. The majority, in this case the women, have an ethical responsibility to make sure to include this member and give equal consideration of his ideas to those of other group members. This responsibility extends to encouraging this man to participate fully.

Take on a participant-analyst role   You must be willing to take on a participant-analyst role. The **participant-analyst role** requires you to engage in the group process and also to direct your attention to observing and evaluating what is happening. No two groups are alike. Therefore, you will need to analyze and make decisions about *what is happening now and in the particular group*. You must be an analyst to be a good group member.

You cannot necessarily fall back on what worked before. You must adapt your behavior to what the group needs at the moment. If you cannot personally meet the need, it is in part your responsibility to seek what is needed from others.

Groups that have members who are being participant-analysts will be most productive when they take this activity seriously by observing and inputting data about the groups' performance and, then, feeding these data back into the groups. Groups that have members who are performing these tasks are more likely to be effective in both task performance and positive relationship development (Dominick, Reilly, and McGourty, 1997).

Ethical Responsibilities of Groups

The group as a whole has ethical responsibilities to its members and its larger organization, and a civic responsibility to society. Members collectively share responsibility to be ethical toward each other; that is, they allow members to express their views freely. They should treat each other's ideas with respect. They should not place unreasonable pressure on members to conform. They should provide the opportunity to participate. In other words, the group has an ethical responsibility to ensure all members' free and full participation.

The group has obligations to its organization. It has an obligation to act within the bounds of its authority. If it only has authority to recommend, then it should not make a decision and implement it. If it is given a particular problem to address, it should not assume it can move on to other issues or problems without permission.

A group also has an obligation to represent the organization's view when it speaks in an official capacity to others outside the organization. Generally a group's task will not include sensitive issues, but it may. Sometimes issues that don't seem sensitive to the group may be for the organization. Members should take the time to understand the organization's thinking about the issues they address. Comments made to those who have no need to know and/or to outsiders should represent the organization's position.

Finally, groups must understand that they have a civic obligation to society. This obligation is referred to as **social responsibility.** Groups have a responsibility to operate with the best interests of their society in mind. Thus a group would not advocate actions that would endanger members of the society. A group would not advocate actions that would take unfair advantage of others outside the organization. A group would not deliberately deceive others or misrepresent its position to those outside the organization.

Consider that ethics is an issue not only for individual members; it is clearly also an issue for the group—toward its members, organization, and society.

COLLECTIVE EFFICACY

Collective efficacy is the belief among members that their work on a particular task will lead to success. Of course, this belief in the group's ability is important because if they believe their efforts will result in goal achievement they will probably make the effort; if they do not they may not. Bandura (2000) suggests that high perceived collective efficacy pays big dividends for a group. He concludes that the higher the perceived collective efficacy, the higher the group members' motivation toward their task, the stronger their will to face difficulties and setbacks, and the greater their task performance. There is also evidence that when members believe in themselves they are likely to set higher goals and accomplish them (Little & Madigan, 1997; Prussia & Kiniki, 1996).

Looking Back: A Quick Review

ETHICAL RESPONSIBILITIES

Do your best.

Focus your effort on the group's goals.

Be fair in dealing with other members.

Be a participant-analyst.

A Question of Ethics and Responsibility

A Leader Who Doesn't Lead

Groups experience a variety of situations that challenge members to be ethical and/or responsible. You are encouraged to pause and think about how you would respond to the situation described here.

Mary generally takes her commitments seriously. She is a member of a student professional society that takes on an annual charity event. Mary is a busy person who likes to stay busy. She has a full-time sales job at a local retail computer shop and also manages to go to college part-time. She has not had much opportunity to make a contribution to the Public Relations Student Society (PRSS) since she joined a year ago, but she sees this charity event as her chance to help. She asks to serve as chair of the committee to plan annual philanthropic activity for this group. This committee organizes a holiday party with gifts for disadvantaged children. Others wanted the opportunity to take the leadership of this committee, but Simon, the PRSS president, wanted to give a new person some responsibility. He sensed that Mary really wanted to take on this job.

Mary found that her classes were demanding more time than she had anticipated. She held off calling the first meeting of her committee, thinking that things would get better. When Simon asked her how things were going, she avoided answering him. Mary finally found time to call a meeting. She had not really thought about what the committee should try to achieve, and so the meeting turned into a social event during which little was accomplished. Mary had intended to set a date for a second meeting, but she forgot to do so. The time for reporting plans was closing in on her, and she didn't know what to do. Simon called, and she told him that all was going well. One group member, Hannah, has become particularly concerned. She has called Mary several times but only got her answering machine. She thinks that Mary doesn't answer the phone because she knows who it is and doesn't want to be confronted by the situation.

Assume you are a member of this group. What would you do to solve this problem of ethics and responsibility?

So how do groups come to have confidence in their ability to accomplish tasks? One factor is past performance. Members of a group that has been successful in the past believe in themselves and are likely to set even higher goals for their current endeavor (Mulvey & Klein, 1998; Prussia & Kiniki, 1996). Another factor is adequate resources and skills, belief that other members are committed, and encouragement that they can perform the task. The knowledge that similar groups have been successful at the task is encouraging (Prussia & Kiniki, 1996).

SUMMARY

The study of group communication may be among the most valuable educational investments a student can make. Personally and socially, the ability to work with and in groups has enormous potential for increasing your success and the success of the people around you.

Communication is a process. A model of that process includes an exigency, a source/encoder, messages, channels, a receiver/decoder, feedback, noise, context, and culture. Communication is transactional in that meaning is generated through the process of message exchange.

A number of important terms were defined as a way of making clear the focus and limitations of the book. The focus is on group communication, as opposed to interpersonal communication or mass communication or public communication. Therefore, the scope of this book is limited to the study of communication in contexts where three or more individuals relate to one another out of some common goal. The kind of group that is of most interest in this book is the small decision-making group. Its members are aware of one another's roles, and they communicate face to face.

A team is a group that has reached a high level of productivity. It has developed cohesiveness, creates critical work processes, and provides leadership for its development and performance. A team is similar to a mature decision-making group except that a team may have more formally defined roles and an ongoing mission.

Decision making, in this text, refers to a group task, rather than to an individual task. In this regard group goals are achieved by means of group choices among alternative behaviors or conceptualizations.

Some of the most common group experiences are information-sharing meetings, decision-making groups, and special-event meetings. Each of these group experiences always involves certain task-dimension concerns—such as identifying problems, analyzing data, and testing alternatives—and relationship issues—such as developing cohesiveness, power and its use, and managing personality differences.

Groups evolve ways of doing things that derive from the group's values through a process of trial and error and reward and punishment. From this evolution, a group draws its norms—its behavioral rules. Then, too, behavior within the group develops along both task and relational dimensions.

In large measure, learning to be a good contributor to a group means learning to provide leadership in the task and relationship areas. Leadership is not the prerogative of any one individual; rather, leadership is everyone's business. In this regard productivity is the outcome of talk about tasks, and cohesiveness is the outcome of talk about relationships—the two dimensions of all group communication.

In our study we view small groups as information-processing systems. People and things are brought together, processing takes place, and products are created. Feedback about the processes and products then becomes input. The group as an information-processing model provides the basic structure for this book.

All these concerns lead to the argument that people in groups must have certain ethical responsibilities to their groups: to do their best, to behave in the best interests of the group, to play fair, to listen carefully and take an active part, to encourage and support diversity, and to take on a participant-analyst role. The group shares responsibility to its members, its organization, and its society.

KEY TERMS AND CONCEPTS

channels	information-sharing meeting	receiver
code	input variables	relationship
collection	interdependent	relationship dimension
collective efficacy	maintenance function	rule
content dimension	messages	semantic noise
context	mutual influence	social loafer
cross-functional	noise	social responsibility
cross-training	norm	source
culture	outputs	source/encoder
cultural diversity	participant-analyst role	special-event meeting
decision-making meeting	physical noise	small group
encoded	physiological noise	synergy
ethics	productivity	systemic noise
ethnic diversity	process variable	task
exigency	psychological noise	task dimension
feedback	punctuation	team
group		

EXERCISES

1. Keep a personal journal of your experiences in class groups for this term. Make an entry as soon as possible after each group meeting. A journal entry should tell what happened in the group, describe your contributions, and evaluate them. Set a goal for your next meeting based on the analysis of this meeting. Begin your next entry by evaluating your success with your goal.

2. Consider the best small group experience you have had recently. List reasons that this experience was especially good for you and your group. Bring your ideas to class to share with others.

How are your ideas similar? How are they different? How can you account for the similarities and differences?

3. Gather in small groups and identify the component parts of the communication model presented in Figure 1.1. Define each component without referring to your text. Finally, construct a model of communication that suits your group. Draw your model on the chalkboard and present it to your class.

4. Identify a small group you can observe. Write a two- to three-page report on your observations and evaluations. Focus on the following:
   a. Identify the task of the group. Next tell how you would evaluate the group's productivity. Make an assessment of the group's productivity.
   b. Identify the norms of the group. Provide evidence of each norm's existence. Evaluate the effect each norm has on the group's productivity.
   c. Evaluate the group's cohesiveness by rating it on a five-point scale. What evidence do you have to support your rating? How did the cohesiveness affect the group's productivity?

5. Think about the idea of being a participant-analyst in a small group. Consider these questions:
   a. Of what value is it for members to develop this focus?
   b. Which behaviors would you observe in members who have this focus?
   c. Suppose you wanted to adopt this focus in your group. What could you do to help your group do so?

6. Assess your current levels of skill and knowledge regarding small group communication. Look to the table of contents to identify the fifteen most important group skills. Now assess your current level of skill and knowledge regarding each skill. You might use "excellent," "good," "okay," "needs improvement," and "none at all" to assess the skills. Set some goals for this course based on your assessment.

RECOMMENDED WEBSITES

Public Involvement Techniques for Transportation Decision-Making, at www.fhwa.dot.gov/reports/pittd/smlgroup.htm, is a site provided by the U.S. Department of Transportation Federal Highway Administration. This site gives a basic summary of small group characteristics in an easy-to-read question and answer format.

The website at www.biology.iupui.edu/Biology_HTML_Docs/biocourses/K345/PBL_Web_Pages/SmallGroupPBL.html gives a description of small group problem-based learning, including the advantages and disadvantages of small groups. There are also links to two forms: one providing feedback on roles played by group members and one providing feedback on the problem-solving ability of members.

The Small Group Network at smallgroups.com/ has several informative sections such as small group resources, which has an entertaining section on humor. Along with a free newsletter, there is also a great small group library within the website at smallgroups.com/sgdyn.htm that contains links to various categories of small group behavior.

At www.pitt.edu/~groups/main2.htm there is a well-organized and informative website developed by professors from the University of Pittsburgh that contains six detailed sections with handy intrawebsite links to various elements of small groups.

At ezpinion.epinions.com/educ-review-67CD-165AE8CD-390417F0-prod5, Paramendra Bhagat gives 10 practical tips for communicating well in small groups.

You can set up an e-group account by logging on to the site www.groups.yahoo.comm/local/news.html.

RECOMMENDED READINGS

L. D. Henman, "Groups as systems," in R. Y. Hirokawa, R. S. Cathcart, L. A. Samovar, & L. D. Henman eds., *Small group communication: Theory and practice,* 8th ed. (Los Angeles: Roxbury, 2003), 3–7.

R. Y. Hirokawa & M. S. Poole, eds., *Communication in group decision-making* (Beverly Hills, CA: Sage, 1996).

J. A. Jaksa & M. S. Pritchard, *Communication ethics: Methods of analysis,* 2d ed. (Belmont, CA: Wadsworth, 1994).

F. LaFasto and C. Larson, *When teams work best: 6,000 team members and leaders tell what it takes to succeed* (Thousand Oaks, CA: Sage, 2001), 1–32.

NOTES

1. Group membership is important because it satisfies a need. Groups help by providing a mechanism whereby people can make a contribution to something greater than themselves. Thus groups can fulfill the motivation to give.

2. The task and relationship dimensions are discussed separately here to make them easier to talk about; they are in fact interrelated and complement each other.

PREPARING FOR GROUP MEETINGS

PART

II

PREPARING FOR GROUP MEETINGS

chapter

2

PREPARING FOR GROUP MEETINGS

"When I look back on the time that I started to move up in the company, I recall George, then my boss, commenting on how pleased he was at the active role I took in departmental meetings. It hadn't started out that way. I had to learn how to be productive in conferences," commented a 45-year-old area manager.

"Too many people don't know how to run a meeting. That kind of consultation is important, but I don't want someone to waste my time. That's why anyone in a leadership position around here needs group skills." This comment was made by a 47-year-old senior vice president of a large manufacturing firm.

"Being seen as a team member is a critical factor in my business. If you don't know how to pull your weight in the group, it's noticed," said a 29-year-old sales representative from New Orleans. He was among the top several representatives of his company's southeast district.

"I was never so embarrassed in my life. On my first job the boss asked me if something was wrong as we were coming out of a meeting. He was concerned that I didn't have much to say. I've learned a lot since then. If you want to move up in your career, you have to learn how to help the group along with its goals." That was a 39-year-old middle manager from Dallas who works in the hubbub of advertising.

Each of these individuals is well qualified to make suggestions to people who are studying toward a career objective. Each has suggested that in order to be a successful professional you have to know what to do in groups. The purpose of this chapter is to focus attention upon behaviors that will help you prepare effectively for groups.

This chapter presents information that is helpful in preparing for meetings. It begins by addressing participant selection. Then it examines the problems of posing a discussion issue and selecting appropriate structure for the discussion. Next, it provides guidelines for securing, evaluating, and preparing information. Finally, the topic of preparing to listen is addressed. You will want to keep these ideas in mind as you prepare.

SELECTING THE PARTICIPANTS

The first step in planning for a meeting is participant selection. When you are in control of the meeting, identifying participants is relatively easy. When you are not in charge, there are still important considerations about identifying participants.

But suppose you are in charge of the meeting. New employees are often surprised when they are asked to plan meetings. You should know from the outset how to do this.

If You Select Participants

In general, identifying participants depends upon the context. For instance, in many organizational settings, identifying participants is accomplished by looking for those who are interested in and have the expertise related to the particular problem.

Interest in a particular problem area does *not* imply agreement among the members. One individual may be liberal in her views about the economy, population control, and local politics; another may be on the conservative side; both may be equally motivated to join a discussion about such topics. Disagreement can be healthy because it helps a group weigh evidence and reach better conclusions.

Some groups that meet regularly invite outside participants. Consider, for example, the weekly meeting of a group of department heads in a public relations agency. During one meeting the group discussed ways to make maximum use of space acquired by the company. They invited to this meeting an architect/builder, an accountant, and someone from upper levels of management. Whom to invite depends on the expertise needed and the specific subject. Significant "political" ramifications might determine some of the individuals to be invited. Of course, you will not always be able to control who attends. However, you can try to influence membership in a group when that makes sense. For example, you might want to suggest a couple of members whose views would add to the richness of the discussion. Keep in mind, though, that there is an important balance between enough similarity to work together and enough difference to bring a variety of perspectives.

Diversity in small group appears to enhance performance even if the task is "male-oriented" (Rogelberg and Rumery, 1996). When there is an opportunity to select members, a maximum effort to have ethnic minorities and women represented pays off. There is a 20 percent rule. The **20 percent rule** suggests that 20 percent or more of a group's members be ethnic minorities and/or women. Pettigrew and Martin (1987) observed that discrimination against minorities, and presumably women, drops substantially when no less than 20 percent of the group, and not fewer than two members, are from a minority. So, by applying the 20 percent rule, you may enhance your group's performance by helping the minority voices be heard.

Looking Back: A Quick Review

SELECTING PARTICIPANTS

Is there anyone who should participate in our group because of special qualifications or expertise?

Is there anyone who should participate in our group because of political sensitivity of the subject matter?

Have we duplicated ourselves in any way that may inhibit the group—or inadvertently damage the organization of which the group is a part?

A Question of Ethics and Responsibility

RENEGING ON AN AGREEMENT

Lakita, a faculty member in the communication department, was responsible for forming a task force to investigate installing a campus radio station at her university. She took the job with the understanding that it was to be her committee. She assumed that she would be able to pull together a competent committee of her choosing.

Hannah Allen, her dean, called her in to make it clear to her what choices she would prefer. Lakita did not agree to the names suggested by the dean, but neither did she make it clear that she objected. She merely nodded affirmatively in an attempt to smooth over what she viewed as inappropriate behavior from the dean. Lakita had a different group of people in mind for service on this task force and good reasons for her choices.

There are a couple of obvious ethical questions here. First, Dean Allen knew that Lakita agreed to serve as chair of this group believing that she could pick her own committee. Now the dean seemed to be backing off from their agreement. It seemed downright unethical to Lakita for the dean to be pulling back from their agreement. Second, Lakita's response to the dean seemed to be affirming the suggested choices. Her choice to remain silent seems a bit unfair to the dean. If she were being ethical and responsible, shouldn't she have said something about her concern? Now that she has left the dean's office, Lakita regrets her silence. Lakita is well aware of how her response was interpreted by Dean Allen and now is faced with some choices.

How would you manage this situation of ethics and responsibility?

If Your Participants Are Preselected

In many group situations we do not have the option to select members. Our task as members or leaders is simplified if we know the people who are to be part of our group.

You will want to think about these people and their relationship to the task. Why do you think each member is part of this group? Are they volunteers, or were they appointed? If they are volunteers, why might each person volunteer? What might the volunteers know about the topic or task? What kinds of individual goals might members bring to the group? Are members likely to embrace the goals of the group ornot? Do members possess the talents to achieve the group's goals? What is your role in this group?

CONSIDERING DISCUSSION ISSUES AND QUESTIONS

Kinds of Discussion Issues

Both decision-making groups and teams face a wide range of issues to discuss. Each kind of group will find that its work will profit from understanding what kind of issue it is facing. Some issues are straightforward, as when a group needs to establish a fact. Other issues may prompt multiple questions, nested inside each other so that questions of fact, value, and policy will all surface from a single issue. This situation often occurs when a group is faced with a complex problem that it is charged with solving. Identifying and managing these issues will be easier if your group understands the kinds of discussion issues.

Some discussion issues are primarily questions of fact. **Questions of fact** can be answered by data that prove or support the truth or falsity of a statement. For example, groups in the business community might worry about the question "Are we going to make a profit in this quarter?" Similarly, a business group might discuss the question "What level of output can we expect this quarter for this production line?" Questions of definition and cause are subsets of questions of fact. **Questions of definition** are questions of fact: "What do we mean by poverty?" "What are the limits of a certain acreage?" "How many units of production are optimal?" So are **questions of cause**, although we may not always be able to discover the cause: "What caused this override of our cost estimate?" "Why did this well-planned strategy fail?" "How did this problem occur?" Sometimes we guess at causes when we cannot collect all the data.

Groups typically encounter issues of fact as they try to understand a situation. Some questions of fact that might be asked when a group is trying to understand a situation are "How can we describe the problem?" "What kind of harm is being done?" "How much harm is being done?" "Who is doing the harm?" and "Who is being harmed?"

Questions of value ask about the goodness, worth, or desirability of something. They also may be questions regarding the ethics of taking an action. Issues of value often call for the group to make a judgment or to make a statement about broad philosophical issues. Questions of value cannot be answered by discovery of objective truth. Questions of value often follow from questions of fact. For example, we might ask what harm is taking place because of a situation. This question might be followed by asking what level of harm is acceptable under these circumstances, a question of value.

In a problem-solving discussion, such a question of value might be stated as "How significant is the harm?" Other questions of value might be "What standards can we use to judge the adequacy of the solutions proposed?" and "How should we prioritize our standards?"

Questions of policy invite the group to some action—some course of behavior. They ask what positions or actions should be enacted, adopted, and implemented. Answers to policy questions guide behavior.

Questions of policy differ from the other questions even if those questions address policy. A question about what policies exist is a question of fact. A question about whether an existing policy is appropriate is a question of value. Policy questions are characterized by the terms *should* and *ought*. A question of policy is generally a response to questions of value and fact.

Of course, a number of questions of fact and value precede the answering of a question of policy. These questions are often in terms of exploring a problem, its harm, and standards for judging the quality of the policy to be considered. In problem-solving discussions we address this kind of issue when we ask "What action should be taken?" and "What policies should be put in place to avoid this harm in the future?"

Focusing the Discussion Issue

An issue for discussion can be so broad that a group cannot manage it. When the possibilities for problem identification and solution are nearly limitless, you know the issue needs focus. Most discussion groups discover that they must focus and narrow their concerns to manageable limits. You will see at a glance that the following policy issues are too broad for concrete proposals to emerge:

> What should be done to strengthen the world economy?
>
> What should be done to prevent teenage pregnancy?
>
> What should be done to raise the educational level in the various states?

How might members go about narrowing the issue if a group wanted to focus upon poverty and ignorance? A first step is to identify the time available for the discussion. An hour-long meeting could treat only a small fraction of the problem area.

Perhaps the first inclination might be to address the question "What should be done to interrupt the poverty–ignorance cycle in urban centers?" Such a question focuses the issue somewhat. Nevertheless, a group could work for years to answer it. But notice that the range of the issue may be cut to manageable proportions merely by focusing it upon a single problem: "What should be done to reduce poverty in urban centers?"

Better yet, the issue could be focused still more by considering one agency or one geographical area: "What actions, if any, could our organization take to reduce poverty in our city?" Even with this narrow focus, the issue remains complex, but a group could manage the discussion. The larger issue might be divided into several questions to be taken up in several meetings.

Wording Discussion Questions

The following simple guidelines will allow you to create clear, answerable questions:

1. Ask about one idea per question.
2. Phrase it in terms of the type of question being asked—fact, value, or policy.
   a. Ask *questions of fact* in terms that can be measured or proved, which usually means being answered in terms of numbers, historical record, research, or expert testimony.
   b. Ask *questions of value* in terms of worth, priorities, or consistency with moral or ethical values.
   c. Ask *questions of policy* in terms of actions or solutions; these questions generally contain "should" statements.
3. Keep the question short and the language simple.

Careful wording of your questions for a group discussion will pay big dividends. Poorly worded questions tend to create confusion.

Looking Back: A Quick Review

KINDS OF DISCUSSION QUESTIONS

Fact	Questions about data
	Questions about definition
Value	Questions about goodness
	Questions about worth
	Questions about desirability
Policy	Questions about desirable action/new policy
	Questions about existing policy
	Questions about modifying existing policy

DECIDING ABOUT STRUCTURE

How structured does decision-making activity need to be for a group to do its job efficiently? There is no easy answer to this question. The group must weigh a number of factors to answer it.

Need for Order

Observation suggests that different people need varying amounts of order in their lives. Psychologists tell us this is a personality trait.

Consider your own experience in growing up. Did members of your family tolerate levels of clutter differently? The amount of orderliness needed differs from person to person. How about planning the family vacation? Did you discover various needs for organization? Maybe your mother needed to know when and where you were going—hour by hour—but perhaps your father would have been satisfied with just knowing that you would spend Tuesday at Gulf Shores.

This variety in need for orderliness and organization is experienced in groups. Experience verifies that some members are content to have a loosely structured agenda. Others thrive on more structure. They want to know what issues will be covered, the order in which these will be addressed, the specific role they are expected to play, and so forth.

Hirokawa and his associates (2000) have investigated this issue. They found that those who have a high preference for procedural order (PPO) do better in choosing among alternatives (solutions) when the group follows structured problem-solving agendas versus those with low PPO. High PPO people did not seem to think as clearly during loosely structured discussions. On the other hand, groups of low PPO people were comfortable with less structured discussion, but did equally well following either a highly structure or loose structured procedure. This research suggests that the low preference for procedural order people will do well using a structured problem-solving agenda, so that is the route to take.

On the other hand, some group members feel restricted and much less spontaneous under circumstances with too much structure. It may be difficult for these people to adapt. Task leaders should take these desires into account in planning agendas. If you are a task leader and have both types of people in your group, you may have to take the middle ground to try to satisfy these divergent needs. Yet there may be other determinants that, when considered, will cause you to introduce either more or less structure. These factors include the time available, the number of group members involved, the social climate of the group, and the nature of the task.

Time Considerations

Consider how time relates to a group's structural options—in this case, a neighborhood homeowners' association. The city council has decided to install new streetlights. It needs a recommendation from the residents as to locations for the lights by Monday of next week. The group has scheduled a Thursday night meeting. Do they try to set a specific agenda? Or do they let the group proceed without any plan? The time limitation may present a need for more structure. Most of the members are busy people and are not likely to want to meet several times. Group members may find it impossible to make a decision within a single meeting of reasonable length if they do not set a specific agenda. On the other hand, if they had several meetings to complete their task, the members might approach the problem in a spontaneous fashion.

Group Size Considerations

Consider again the meeting of the neighborhood association. Will there be 50 neighbors present? 20? 15? 10? 5? Certainly if members want to ensure the opportunity for participation when the group is large, they will want to provide more structure, thereby providing a greater chance for everyone to talk. Structure can limit the freedom to move to side issues and personal agendas. Formal procedures may restrict the amount of time any one member is permitted to talk, which can allow the less aggressive person to participate more fully. In a smaller group it is possible to allow for more lengthy comments and greater spontaneity. The larger group restricts this behavior.

A group of three members may feel constrained and tense because they may think their number of members creates a situation that requires them to speak more and contribute more than they are comfortable doing. On the other hand, members of a large group, 8 or more members, often experience uneven participation and difficulty saying all they would like to say. The leadership style required in a large group situation is more formal and may seem restrictive to some members. Their freedom to participate is affected. Research (Powers & Boyle, 1983) also indicates that member satisfaction and cohesiveness decrease in a large group, but competitiveness, aggression, withdrawal and fragmentation of work increase.

Group Members' Emotional Involvement

Groups whose members are emotionally involved in the task may need more structure. Suppose that an older member of the neighborhood association is terrified because his property is dimly lit. His emotional involvement in the topic may cause him to dominate the meeting. He may even try to obstruct progress if he is not getting his desired outcome. If others are also emotionally involved, the group may not be able to think rationally without some agreed-on agenda.

Hostility among group members can cause problems too. Members may move outside the task as they express hostility. This failure to come to direct contact can be disruptive to task completion, especially when the group has a deadline. Securing agreement to an agenda may limit this behavior. For example, the leader can remind group members that they have an agenda and can ask them to try to stick to it.

Focus on Research

WHAT IS THE APPROPRIATE SIZE FOR A GROUP?

Such a simple thing as the number of members in a group can have dramatic effects on the group's complexity. Robert N. Bostrom demonstrated the potential effect that adding members to a group might have on the complexity of the interaction. (Note: Your author is not interested in a two-person group, but that is where Bostrom begins.) He calculates that two interactions are possible in a two-person group: person A to person B and vice versa. In a three-person group, with members A, B, and C, there are nine possibilities: A to B, B to A, A to C, C to A, B to C, C to B, A to B and C, B to A and C, and C to A and B. As group size increases, the number of possible interactions increases exponentially. Thus, in a four-member group there are 28 possible interactions, in a five-member group there are 75, in a six-member group there are 186, in a seven-member group there are 441, and in an eight-member group there are 1,056.

How does this increase in size affect the group's decision-making process? Kessler pointed out that as size increases there are greater numbers of nonparticipants. Size also affects members' conformity and satisfaction. Bettinghaus and Cody suggest that members in smaller groups can more easily apply pressure to conform to majority opinion than members can when the group is large. Compared to members of larger groups, members of a smaller group are also more satisfied because they have greater opportunity to participate and influence.

What is the appropriate size for a group? This text suggested that a five- to seven-member group is about right for a decision-making group, assuming that members have appropriate information and skills. Bormann supports this contention but recommends a five- or seven-member group to avoid 3–3 split votes.

E. P. Bettinghaus & M. J. Cody (1987). *Persuasive communication*. New York: Holt, Rinehart and Winston.

E. G. Bormann (1990). *Small group communication*. New York: Harper & Row.

R. N. Bostrom (1970). Patterns of communicative interactions in small groups. *Speech Monographs, 37,* 257–263.

J. Kessler (1973). An empirical study of six- and twelve-member jury decision-making processes. *University of Michigan Journal of Law Reform, 6,* 712–734.

Nature of the Task

Tasks differ in ways that affect the need for organization. Marvin Shaw (1973b) used a step-by-step procedure to identify task dimensions within a set of 104 tasks. From this work, five task dimensions that are of interest can be identified: task difficulty, solution multiplicity, intrinsic interest, cooperation requirements, and experience with task (Hirokawa, 1990).

A *difficult task* may require considerable effort to complete. It may require more effort because it is complex and/or requires considerable knowledge. Some tasks involve less data, fewer causes, less complex solutions, and the like. The neighborhood association's consideration of the placement of streetlights might be such a task. But suppose that the association wants to deal with a problem of declining membership. This problem may require collecting data and analyzing complex causes. It may best be handled by a more structured approach.

The *number of reasonable alternatives* available affects the kind of structure needed. Some problems have many alternatives that cannot easily be demonstrated to be correct. Research findings bear directly on this issue. For example, Shaw and Blum (1965) studied solution multiplicity with respect to directive and nondirective leadership. They rated three tasks as differing on the basis of multiplicity. In the first, group members listed the five most important traits for success in our culture. In the second, the group selected one of five solutions for a politician with an alcoholic spouse. The third task required the group to play the game Twenty Questions.

These tasks are presented to show why research can be an indirect indicator. Notice that the three tasks are very different from what decision-making groups usually do. The first does not ask for a single decision. The second provides the answers and

Focus on Research

BARRIERS THAT KEEP A GROUP FROM SUCCESSFUL DISCUSSION

Do you need a little encouragement in your effort to study small group communication? Consider the findings of this research by Benjamin Broome and Luann Fulbright. They spent six years asking people who were members of discussion groups what kept them from achieving their full potential. Their answers are just the things you will study in the coming pages:

- Lack of structure.
- Insensitivity to cultural differences.
- Poor planning.
- Lack of resources.

- Key people not involved.
- Pressure for immediate results.
- Misunderstandings, inattentiveness, and dominance by subgroup.
- Lack of support, cohesiveness, trust.
- Negative attitude toward project or each other.
- A focus on solutions before defining the problem.

B. J. Broome & L. Fulbright (1995). A multistage influence model of barriers to group problem solving: A participant-generated agenda for small group research. *Small Group Research*, 26, 24–55.

asks for a selection process. The third is a parlor game. But the findings might general-ize to other tasks. Based on task completion time, Shaw and Blum found that directive leadership was more effective in groups with low solution-multiplicity tasks, but nondi-rective leadership was more effective on the mid- to high-range multiplicity tasks.

The *interest level* members have in the task affects structural need. This level of interest is related to attraction and motivation for the group. Leonard Berkowitz (1953) studied preferences for shared leadership in small decision-making groups. He found that members who were extremely involved in the task—high attraction and interest—were more interested in sharing procedural control. On the other hand, members preferred strong procedural control by the leader when tasks were less interesting.

Consider again the neighborhood association and its decision about streetlights. Suppose you have a strong interest in the issue. Would you want the leader to dictate the agenda and procedure? Or would you want to have a part in deciding how the group will proceed? Very likely, you would want to be involved in this decision.

Cooperation requirements are defined by the degree of coordinated effort necessary to complete the task. Much of the group work we experience in our professional lives fits this category. Suppose that a management team of a company that manufactures elec-tronic equipment is trying to make decisions about moving into manufacturing tele-phones. The complexity of the problem and the need for a coordinated effort are both inherent in this task. A published agenda for the discussion of this issue will give members the best opportunity to come to the meeting prepared to provide input and coordinate their efforts. A meeting that follows a published plan can lead to greater productivity and efficiency than one that doesn't follow a published plan.

Task experience is the extent to which the group is familiar with a task. Groups that are highly familiar with a task tend to do better with it (Davis, 1969). But there is also a very clear danger with high task familiarity. Groups with long experience are likely to be less critical and less creative because of that experience. You can imagine a member saying, "Oh, I see. This is the same problem we settled last month. I know exactly what to do." Because of this tendency, high-familiarity groups probably need procedures to ensure that members look carefully at the uniqueness of the problem.

Looking Back: A Quick Review

CONSIDERATIONS REGARDING STRUCTURE

Order	How much order is needed?
Time	How much time does the group have to complete its task?
Group size	How many people will be present to process information?
Group sentiment	How strongly do members feel about the topic and each other?
Task	How does the nature of the task affect the need for structure?

They must be prepared to go beyond the usual solutions. Brainstorming (addressed in Chapter 3) is a procedure that is effective in combating such tendencies (Osborn, 1993).

Should groups follow structured decision-making agendas? It depends. You can see this question has no easy answer. The guidelines will help you to weigh these factors and decide.

CRITICAL THINKING AND DISCUSSION

Part of planning and preparing to talk about some problem or topic is becoming informed. This is, of course, an ongoing process in a group that meets regularly.

The need for research and critical analysis of the information seems obvious. Amazingly, though, some individuals appear to believe that knowledge of a subject is not a relevant qualification to discuss that subject. In one group discussion observed in an executive workshop, a well-paid junior executive made this remark:

> I am surprised that I have always done so little to study questions before we sat down to discuss them. I suppose I thought the purpose of a group meeting was for others to inform me so that I could offer my opinions. Of course, I always try to know what I'm doing when I have to make the decision, but I really have not made much effort to know what I'm doing when a group is deciding. I can see now that the group decision suffers.

This individual's statement received quite a bit of support from others in that workshop. Consider these fragments from their tape-recorded conversations:

> Yeah. I can't say that I leave it all to other people, but I sure have done that, too. Once I went to a meeting—last week, I think it was—when I didn't know much more about the subject than that the company was thinking of working on it. I guess I didn't understand what I was supposed to accomplish at that meeting. I wasted my time by not being informed.

> I don't always have much time . . . [chuckles from the others] . . . I don't always take time to look into things. In fact, I guess that I depend on the group members to do my initial thinking for me. Of course, when I get involved, I try to study the matter. . . .

Such comments suggest that some individuals in responsible positions attend group problem-solving meetings without preparation.

What do you do to get ready for a problem-solving discussion? How do you identify and find information? Answers to these questions follow.

Securing Information through Research

Assess what you already know   Review what you know in some systematic fashion. Have you taken courses related to the subject? Have you had life experiences in the area? Have you written papers on the subject or related to the problem? Have you read books or articles? Have you had conversations about the subject? Make some notes as you work through these questions. Organize this information using one of the problem-solving agendas in Chapter 3.

Gather additional information *Interviews* provide a useful source of information and expert testimony. A knowledgeable person may well be able to provide you with pamphlets, brochures, and books directly related to the subject, as well as his or her expert knowledge. An individual who knows about the subject area may be able to help you clarify the issues and may lead you to sources of information that would require hours of exhaustive research to find.

At a second level, we recommend careful planning of each interview so you have a clear focus. Get an appointment at a convenient time, try to agree on a specific amount of time for the interview, be punctual, and end the conversation within the allotted period. During the interview, try to keep the conversation on the subject. Use the problem-solving agenda to help plan your questions. Let those questions provide the agenda for the conversation. You might submit the questions to the informant in advance so that you can find out if he or she knows enough to provide useful information.

Be selective in the people you interview. Not everyone on the staff of the chamber of commerce knows enough to be a good source of information about the community. Not every person who works at the local bank knows about the economy. Not every police officer knows about the incidence of drug abuse. Temper your conclusions on the basis of the information you receive and the person's ability to know.

Your group may want to collect data using a *survey*. This is a structured interview in which each respondent is asked the same set of questions, with the responses then pooled to draw conclusions. A scientifically designed sample of the overall group being polled is a must if the results are to be valid. If you do collect data through a survey, it is wise to consult someone who has been trained in survey research to help.

Library research provides information that may be unavailable from interviews. For example, an expert may not be able to give you time for an in-depth interview. Or perhaps it is too costly in time and other resources to interview enough experts. In many cases another major source of information is library materials.

Books, magazines, brochures, pamphlets, a variety of government documents, computerized databases—all are sources of information. Reference works (encyclopedias, both general and topical) can provide ideas. They can identify other sources of information (a bibliography or bibliographies). They can give you precise definitions of a wide range of complex and technical terms (dictionaries, both general and topical).

You may be able to find help in locating sources of information by consulting bibliographies of bibliographies. Among the ones you are likely to find are *A World Bibliography of Bibliographic Catalogues*, *Bibliographical Index*, and *Bulletin of Bibliography and Magazine Notes*. Of course, bibliographies are found in books and research articles.

You can consult indexes to locate information in magazines, journals, and newspapers. The word *index* indicates an alphabetized listing of names or topics. An index gives you access to articles by subject and sometimes by title or author. Each entry provides complete bibliographic information. These, of course, are useful in developing a working bibliography. Some common indexes are *Reader's Guide to Periodical Literature*, *Applied Science and Technology Index*, *Education Index*, *The New York Times Index*, and *Social Sciences Index*.

Many topics that may be of interest to your group are also of interest to the government. Most libraries keep a collection of government documents. This collection is one of the most difficult to access, so we recommend that you talk with the government documents librarian.

Magazines come in general form (*Reader's Digest, The New Yorker*) and in more specialized form (*American Photography*). There are academic and professional publications (*Quarterly Journal of Speech, Academy of Management Journal, American Journal of Sociology*) and also special-interest magazines (*Business Horizons, Mechanix Illustrated, Consumer Reports*). Indeed, for every subject that bears on any relevant subgroup in our society, you will be able to find specialized publications.

Your library may have the capability to conduct a computerized database search. The databases are searched using key words that identify your subject. The more specific the key words, the more likely the material identified will be of interest to you. These databases provide citations, with or without abstracts or summaries of the material. The searches are generally limited to periodicals, books, and documents. A computer database search can be expensive and time-consuming if you do not use rather specific key words.

Special-interest groups and special-interest agencies within larger organizations publish an enormous number of pamphlets and brochures. Of course, the largest publisher in the world is the federal government of the United States. The Government Printing Office has almost certainly published something on any subject you wish to discuss.

You also will want to consult the library's online catalog to locate additional sources and to discover which of these sources you have located are in the library's collection. An **online catalog** is a database of materials the library holds. A menu will drive the computer-accessed system and will provide specific instructions for use.

Most online catalogs have access to their list by author, title, and subject. The subject category is likely to be the most useful. If you do not know the obvious subject headings for your topic, check the *Library of Congress Subject Headings* for help.

Securing Information through Direct Observation

Sometimes *direct observation* is the appropriate kind of information gathering. If a group is about to discuss some condition in the local community—for example, the willful littering of the highways and byways—knowledge of that subject may mean taking photographs.

Direct observation has three common pitfalls. First, untrained observers may not see things accurately or objectively. An individual observer may record a distortion simply because he or she was not at the scene long enough to get a complete understanding. Also, observers may place themselves in a location that may create a distorted image. A well-traveled highway is likely to have more roadside trash than a barely traveled country lane. Observation of only one of these may yield distorted conclusions.

A second pitfall is inaccurate reporting. Careful use of descriptive language (as suggested in Chapter 4) is the most obvious single security against false reporting. Descriptive language uses specific rather than general words. If a reporter says "The city council was in disarray today," she leaves an impression of a problem but gives very little information. If she chooses to be more accurate in reporting her observation, she might say: "I spent two hours observing the city council meeting today. The president began by asking members to add to an already-published agenda. Then he shuffled the agenda so that an issue that was to be considered later was considered first. Consequently, those who wished to speak about it were not present. Then he allowed discussion of a seemingly minor issue to go on for almost an hour. The result of the apparent disorganization and lack of control was completion of only half the agenda items."

Biased reporting is the third and perhaps the most dangerous pitfall. The major problem is often not evil or deceptive intent—it is that inexperienced reporters tend to see what they want to observe. Consider the city council illustration a final time. An individual who has developed an antagonistic relationship with the city council chair is likely to report observations of the council meeting in more biased and stronger language. We might read: "The city council meeting was disorganized and out of control today. Again the council president lost perspective when. . . ." When information is couched in this kind of bias, the group's recommendations may reflect this bias too.

Securing Information through Interviews

An excellent source of information is questioning an expert or other knowledgeable individual. This information would generally not be the only source of information your group would use, but it is an excellent supplement. The expert can provide answers that might be difficult to find. It is generally wise to interview several individuals, asking each the same questions. That approach allows you to compare their responses.

It is wise to work as a group, or at least as a subset of the group, to generate a list of interviewees and questions you will ask. If your group members are students at a college or university, you might consider the various academic departments that concern themselves with the topic. The faculty is a readily available group of experts.

After you have generated a list of interviewees and questions, you are ready to arrange and carry out the interviews. Here are five considerations that will allow you to achieve the best from your interviews:

1. Learn as much as you can about the topic and issues related to the questions prior to the interview.

2. Call ahead to make an appointment for a specific amount of time and be on time for the interview.

3. Take notes but also tape-record the interview if the interviewee will allow this.

4. Conclude the interview within the time agreed upon with the interviewee.

5. Be sure to thank the interviewee and do so in writing if that seems appropriate.

Be sure to allow time to ask follow-up questions to each planned question. Listen carefully; often the follow-up question is one that asks for additional information.

Securing Information through Surveys

Gathering the same information from different people often provides data that reflects the experiences or opinions of the larger group to which they belong. Surveys are excellent for establishing the extent of a problem being experienced.

The first step in developing a survey is to figure out the overall purpose. Suppose you were looking at crime on campus. Your purpose might be to discover how aware students are of safety measures to protect their property and person. You, then, would develop a series of questions that ask what campus safety measures the students know about, how often they use these measures, and how effective the students judge them to be. In addition, you would want to collect demographic information (year in school, age, sex, and so on) about the respondents. Of course, you would want your group to generate the survey questions. Also, it is wise to order your questions so that those easier to answer come first and the more difficult questions later.

Here are four specific guidelines for conducting survey research (Wilson & Goodall, 1991):

1. Randomly select a sample of the group about which you wish to know (the population).

2. Pretest your survey on several people who will not be part of the survey. The results will allow you to refine your survey if these people have difficulty with it.

3. Ask the respondents whether they will participate, indicate the amount of time it will take, and don't press them if they say no or seem reluctant.

4. Be sure to ask each respondent the same questions, tabulate your data carefully, and carefully draw your conclusions.

Securing Information through Electronic Resources

You will probably want to look at some electronic resources for information. A good starting place is an encyclopedia on a compact disc (CD). This will allow you to access a good deal of basic information. You will undoubtedly find one in your library.

Reference materials   Two popular encyclopedias are *Encarta* and *Compton's Encyclopedia*. You can go to a free online multimedia encyclopedia that contains 25,000 articles by logging on at www.funkandwagnalls.com.

There are several other standard reference sites that can be useful for you. They are

1. An online dictionary with over three million entries at www.onelook.com.

2. The U. S. Census Bureau at www.census.gov.

3. Online telephone number information for white pages at www.555-1212.com and for the yellow pages at www.bigbook.com.

4. An online atlas at worldatlas.com.

5. An online encyclopedia at www.encyberpedia.com.

Internet searches   Your web browser will allow you to access one of the many **Internet search engines.** Some of the most popular are Google, Yahoo!, Excite, Infoseek, and

Lycos. If you type http://www.yahoo.com in the search bar of your browser, you will get to Yahoo!. If you enter more than one word for a search, such as University of Alabama, you will want to link the words with "AND," such as "University AND Alabama." This type of search eliminates a number of entries you do not want. You also can use the word "NOT" to eliminate possibilities you know will produce entries that are not of interest, such as "adoptions NOT private."

Electronic databases   You may find the information you want by consulting an **electronic database.** You will find these on compact discs or online in your college library. Databases you are likely to find in your library are ERIC and LEXIS-NEXIS. **ERIC** is a database of citations and abstracts to journal articles as well as research papers and reports on educational issues. **LEXIS** provides legal documents such as legal briefs and court decisions. **NEXIS** provides news reports by publishing several nationally recognized newspapers, such as *The New York Times,* and news magazines, such as *Newsweek,* as well as transcripts of network news broadcasts. Your library may subscribe to specialized databases, such as **Dow Jones News/Retrieval** and **Burelle's Broadcast Database,** which includes transcripts of television and radio programs. Some of these databases are password-protected so you cannot use them without permission, and some require payment for their use.

Other databases that may be of use in your research are

1. Psychology at www.apa.org.

2. National Center for Education Statistics at www.ed.gov/NCES.

3. An international database at www.census.gov/ftp/pub/ipc/www/idbprint.html.

4. The International Earth Science Information Network at www.ciesin.org.

5. U.S. Federal Statistical Agencies at www.census.gov/main/www/stat-fed.html.

6. Social science information at www.sosig.ac.uk.

7. International Communication Association at www.public.asu.edu/~corman/infosys.

Electronic journals   You may want to search an **electronic journal** from a particular academic field. The introduction of these journals has been growing over the past several years. One journal of interest to the communication field is the *Electronic Journal of Communication/La Revue Electronique de Communication.* The entries include the editor's introduction to each issue and all abstracts published in English and French.

The Internet is perhaps the easiest way to secure information, but it also poses some difficulties as a research tool since sources can be difficult to identify and the credentials of authors difficult to verify. We provide in Figure 2.1 a series of questions you can use to evaluate the validity of what you find on a particular site.

Fortunately, Internet search engines are becoming increasingly user-friendly. Most college libraries provide on-line search capabilities. Your librarian can help you become familiar with one of these if you are not already using one. In addition, an ever-increasing number of electronic journals are available. Check with your professor or librarian about possibilities for your research. Finally, check out the home page of any governmental

1. How did you find this page? Can you trust the source if someone referred it to you?
2. Are there any signs that call into question the credibility of this page? Does it look like someone took the time and effort to create it? Are there misspelled words? Are there graphics that are incomplete or "under construction"?
3. From what domain is it coming? If it is an educational or government source, the information may be more reliable.
4. Does an individual or organization sign the Web page? Do you recognize this individual or organization as trustworthy?
5. Does the author and/or organization supply credentials or affiliations or supply an "about us" or "who we are" link?
6. Is there a link to a home page you can examine or can you backtrack the URL to find out more about the author or group?
7. What do you think the motivation is for putting up this page?
8. Does the information appear to have a particular slant or bias?
9. Does the author indicate the sources of the information?
10. Does the material seem to be factual information and data or mostly opinion?
11. Does the page indicate when it was created or updated?
12. Regardless of the creation date, can you tell if the information is current?
13. Is there some way to contact the author—perhaps an e-mail address or a physical address and telephone number?
14. What kind of links, if any, does this page have to other pages? Do these seem credible?

If your answers to these questions call into question the information's truthfulness or authoritativeness, you will be better off relying on printed library sources. Your reference librarian can help you in this search.

FIGURE 2.1
Questions to Help You Evaluate WWW Information

agency, organization, or commercial enterprise you may be researching. You will find a wealth of information as well as links to other sources of information.

Critical Evaluation of the Information

Clear thinking is an essential part of planning and preparing to talk about problems and topics. The quality of your thought depends on a number of variables, including the accuracy of your information and the logic you apply.

Concerns regarding quality   These are five standard concerns you should apply in assessing the quality of information.

1. *Is the information relevant?*   Does the information relate directly to the issue or point being made? A member may argue that spending more money on a pollution problem in San Francisco Bay will produce a greater effect than spending less. Close examination may suggest, however, that the amount of money spent is not relevant to solving the particular problem.

Looking Back: A Quick Review

SOURCES OF INFORMATION

Personal knowledge	Surveys
Observations	Electronic resources
Interviews	

---

2. *Is the information current?* When were these data collected? Information that has not been gathered close to the time of deliberation may no longer be valid. A group discussing a pollution problem in San Francisco Bay would want current information. Otherwise, members cannot be certain that their conclusions will be valid.

3. *Is the information representative?* Sometimes members reason from a single example or statistic. A group might argue that the bay is polluted because a sample showed bacteria at twice the level considered safe. You would want to know not only where the sample was taken but also whether that sample would be the same as other samples taken over a period of time in the same area.

4. *Is the information sufficient?* Important decisions generally should not be made on the basis of a single statement by a single individual. Ask whether other sources are available to examine. If they are not, then you hope that the information is of good quality. That may depend on the credibility of those who have collected and provided the information.

5. *Is the information credible?* Credibility of information that meets these first four standards depends on its source. Two questions will help you tell whether a source is credible. First, ask whether the source is qualified to make the statements. You need to consider this person's credentials to answer this question. It is not always easy to discover the credentials of a source. If you can discover the person's credentials and use these to assess the qualifications, that is what you should do. When this information is not available, you may have to rely on the credibility of the publication where the information was published. A credible publication generally will investigate the credentials of its writers. If an article is an account from another source, you may have to make some telephone calls to check out the source.

A second issue of credibility is bias that may result from a person's viewpoint or special interest. Ask whether the source has some relationship to what is being reported that might bias the statements. A developer may report that his or her testing of San Francisco Bay water shows that it is safe. This information may or may not be true, but it is obvious that a developer might be biased and would have an interest in reporting safe water. You would want reports from other sources before deciding to accept this report as reliable.

Concerns regarding the logic you use   You will want to be sure you avoid errors in logic. Here are some concerns about logic to consider.

FACT VERSUS INFERENCE   A **fact** is a statement about an observation that can be demonstrated to be true. It can be verified. Statements about past events cannot be verified directly, so a different kind of test is applied. Such statements are assumed true if several independent observers report the same information.

An **inference** is a conclusion that is made on the basis of some observation. The conclusion is one person's opinion, based on his or her analysis of the situation and, perhaps, evidence about what is or has been observed. Our confidence that an inference is correct is often a function of the credentials and training of the person making the statement and the number of other people who share that opinion.

Clearly not all information presented as factual is true. Likewise, some inferences aren't carefully drawn. Answers to these questions can help you evaluate information:

Can you verify the information being reported as fact?

Have the facts been reported similarly by several witnesses?

Have the facts been reported by someone who has expertise that gives the information credibility?

Have the facts been reported by someone who is without bias?

Consider these questions when the task is evaluating inferences:

Is the person making the statement recognized as an expert?

Is the person making the statement in a position to observe the situation and know the facts?

Do other experts agree with this person?

Does the person have some vested interest that might bias the opinion?

Can you identify facts that support this person's position?

If the information collected from one group is to represent a larger group, is the smaller group actually representative of the larger group? Is the sample group large enough? Is it really similar in its makeup? (Note: It may be impossible to answer this question unless the information is being reported in an academic journal where the researcher reveals how data were collected.)

Does the person's reasoning make sense?

ERRORS IN REASONING   This last question leads us to a discussion of **fallacies,** or typical errors in reasoning. Be alert for errors such as these:

1. *Overgeneralizing*   A generalization is a conclusion. An **overgeneralization** occurs when the data for some reason are not strong enough to support a conclusion.

A good example of this error can be seen in the reasoning of a person who reads of several incidents of teenage crime and concludes that the crime rate among teens has increased. Obviously a few articles about teen crime do not provide a basis for this conclusion. How can you test a generalization? A generalization is an inference, so the questions presented above apply. In addition, ask

Is the generalization based on a sufficient number of cases?

Are the cases used to make the generalization representative of other cases that might be cited? (Are there other cases that contradict the conclusion?)

2. *Causal fallacies*   Sometimes a causal relationship is suggested that might be in error. A **causal relationship** between two events is present when one circumstance provides the basis or impetus for some other happening. The following questions can be asked to test this kind of reasoning:

Does the causal link seem reasonable?

Are other circumstances present that might also account for the current happening?

Are circumstances present that are strong enough to discount the alleged link?

Suppose, for example, someone argues that low pay is causing low morale. It seems reasonable to suppose that low pay might cause low morale. Yet there are certainly other possible causes that we would have to investigate and rule out. Perhaps management has been mistreating its subordinates, for example.

3. *Personal prejudice*   Sometimes people make the **personal prejudice** error in reasoning when an argument is dismissed because of some inappropriate characteristic of the person making the argument. A person might say, "You can't believe that argument. Look at the person making it. He is a _____ [the name of a class of people who may not be respected]."

4. *Either-this-or-that reasoning*   **Either-this-or-that reasoning** supposes that there are only two possible choices in a situation and that one of them must be selected. This type of thinking is represented in the statement "You are either for us or against us." Or perhaps "Either parents will take charge of sex education or the task will fall to the schools." Obviously, the reasoning is faulty in both these situations because it ignores the middle-ground positions.

5. *Faulty comparisons*   A final error in reasoning occurs when an analogy is used to make a **faulty comparison.** Frequently, when groups are engaged in problem solving, two events are compared as a basis for arguing a solution to a problem. Members look for a situation like the one they are considering to discover solutions that might work. The reasoning goes something like this: If the solution worked in the other situation, it is likely to work in this one. You might read an analysis of a problem that argues, "They solved the parking problem at Northern by building a parking garage. We should do the same thing here at Western."

This kind of reasoning can be appropriate if the two situations are similar in all important aspects. Often, however, it is difficult to find situations that meet this requirement. When you encounter this kind of reasoning, ask yourself whether the situations are enough alike to make the comparison.

Looking Back: A Quick Review

EVALUATING INFORMATION

Quality	Relevant
	Current
	Sufficient
	Credible
Logic	Inferences carefully drawn
	Overgeneralization avoided
	Fallacies avoided
	Prejudice avoided
	Either-this-or-that reasoning avoided
	Faulty comparisons avoided

STRAIGHT THINKING   In a group situation two features of straight thinking are especially important. It is important to think for yourself and to think tentatively.

Thinking for yourself means that you avoid following a group that is not thinking carefully and critically. Some groups get caught up in a solution and stick with it even though members have misgivings about it. These members keep their doubts to themselves for the sake of group unity. This phenomenon is *groupthink*.

Thinking for yourself also means that you watch for the tendency to accept uncritically ideas and opinions of individuals who claim expertise. And, more subtly, individuals tend to accept a basic orientation toward the world—an orientation that derives from family and friends and from the mores and attitudes of such influential organizations as the church and the local school. If a general climate of opinion prevails somewhere, the people who live there are likely to conform to it, and they often do so without consciously thinking about it. Clearly, thinking for yourself implies avoiding these pitfalls. You might ask yourself the following questions as you consider the information you have gathered:

1. Do I have any built-in bias about this information? From family? From friends? From school? From church? From some special other person?

2. Have I accepted this idea because the information justifies it? Or have I accepted the idea because I trust the individual who gave it?

Without clear thinking, the individual who engages in discussion runs the serious risk of accepting wrong conclusions. Beyond that, there is always the risk that an uncritical thinker may influence the group toward a wrong conclusion.

Thinking tentatively means remembering that the entire purpose of group discussion is for members, collectively, to supply a better base for their work than any individual. If you go into the discussion with your mind made up, you cannot contribute productively. It follows that thinking tentatively means holding final judgments in abeyance. It means that as a good discussant, after you have considered the matter, you will submit that thinking to the scrutiny and evaluation of other members. Do not commit yourself to a conclusion. Keep your thinking tentative.

Preparing the Material for Use

You must prepare the information you have collected so that it is in a form you can easily retrieve when you are interacting in a group. The most effective approach is to integrate the information into a tentative outline that follows the agenda you plan to use.

Consider the major headings and subheadings in your outline as main issues that the group will take up. Major issues might be "those affected by a problem," "seriousness of the harm," "contributing causes," and so forth. Now mark in the margin of your notes the issue to which the material pertains. Group the material for each issue and record it on your outline. The outline will prepare you to make significant contributions.

A final important preparation you can bring to your group's deliberations is good listening skills. The concluding section of this chapter provides practical advice to help you know how to avoid listening problems and hone your listening skills.

LISTENING

Personnel managers rated listening as the most important group communication skill (Hawkins & Fillion, 1999).

Listening is a more complex skill than most of us imagine. Listening is an especially difficult problem in groups because of the ease with which a member can actually tune out and not be noticed. Certainly, in a one-on-one situation the attention is directly on the listener—a fact that makes it difficult for that person to fake listening. On the other hand, a group situation requires that attention be divided among the several members. So it is much easier for members to fake attention. Watson (1996) notes that since there is less social pressure to listen in groups, ineffective listening goes unnoticed. The result may very well be less vigilance in listening and unnoticed errors in the group's decision-making process.

We can all be better listeners if we gain a better understanding of the process, understand what problems we may encounter, and take on some strategies to improve our ability. Let's start by looking at each component of the process.

The Components of the Listening Process

The four components of the listening process are sensing, attending, understanding, and remembering. An examination of each will help you understand the part it plays.

Sensing   Sensing is the act of receiving stimuli through the five senses. It is not necessarily a conscious act. For example, any sound that has sufficient intensity to reach the ear may be heard. You may ask, then, why you are unable to hear the ticking of a clock when you are working. The answer is that in fact you *can* hear the clock. The sound has sufficient intensity to reach your ears, but it is blocked by our attending.

Attending   You may not be selecting a particular stimulus—the ticking of the clock—to be part of your consciousness. In other words, you are not **attending.** Theoretically, you might sense and attend to hundreds of stimuli at a time, but you cannot. Therefore, you select those that are important to you and ignore others.

Perhaps you failed to notice footsteps as someone entered the room because you were paying attention to a book you were reading. You filtered out the irrelevant. But if the footsteps had been those of your boss, who wandered in to talk with you, you would have filtered out an important sound. Filtering of this kind also happens when you are listening to someone talk. You may filter out important pieces of information.

Understanding   The third component of listening is **understanding**—interpreting and evaluating what comes in through the senses. Blaine Goss (1982) presents an information-processing model of listening in which he suggests this pattern: signal processing (understanding the segments and structures of what we hear) → literal processing (understanding the meaning and simple implications of what we hear) → reflective processing (understanding a deeper meaning through critical analysis and coming to appreciate what we hear). Understanding is an important part of listening.

Remembering   Like attending, **remembering** is selective. To explore this idea, talk with someone about a movie you both have seen. You may discover that you have remembered the things most interesting and useful to you and have forgotten others. Your friend will have remembered what he or she found interesting. Comparing notes, you'll probably discover that you have remembered different details. You select not only what to attend to but what to remember.

Listening Problems

Each of the four components—sensing, attending, understanding, and remembering—gives rise to certain problems. We will examine the problems before considering techniques to overcome them.

Problems with sensing   Two problems are related to sensing, *physical impairment of the sensing mechanism* and *external noise.* Obviously, not being able to sense adequately makes it difficult to listen—and a trip to a professional would be in order. Once the problem is solved, you can train yourself to take maximum advantage of your sensing ability.

The second problem is noise, or interference. Everyone who has attended movies can recall the experience of someone nearby talking or joking. The talk made it more difficult to hear accurately. But talking is not the only kind of noise; the sounds of people passing by or automobile or airplane sounds are other examples. Inadequate light may impair your sight and also be "noise." Temperature may be another.

Problems with attending   Attending difficulties are more numerous than sensing problems. Five aspects of attention inhibit listening.

SELECTIVE PERCEPTION AND ATTENDING   People perceive and attend selectively. On the basis of past experience, we select what we believe worth perceiving and attending. Because things are always changing, we nearly always need to adjust our sense of what to attend to.

POOR ATTENDING HABITS   Ralph Nichols and L. A. Stevens (1957) cite three poor attending habits. Some people learn to *fake attention*. They sit as if they are listening carefully but are in fact thinking about something else.

A second poor attending habit is to *avoid difficult listening*. In other words, people who do not expose themselves to difficult listening situations do not gain practice in attending to difficult material.

The third poor attending habit is to *listen only for facts*. This kind of attending may cause the listener to miss important cues about the message. Tone of voice and variations in the rate of speaking are two auditory factors that often reveal a great deal about the message. People who have trained themselves to listen for and jot down facts may miss these nonverbal cues and thereby misunderstand the message.

LISTENER ATTITUDES AND NEEDS THAT INTERFERE   Attitude will have a significant impact on how people attend to a message. For example, if you were forced by your company to attend a seminar, your attitude might impair your listening. Status can be a problem, too. If you think it is inappropriate for group members to be offering you advice, you may pay less attention. The same attitude-perception mechanism works when a co-worker has a different perspective on how to do a job.

In addition, people attend to messages that satisfy their needs (Thayer, 1968). We hear what we *think* was said because our needs and values cause us to ignore disconfirming stimuli.

LOW INTENSITY OF THE MESSAGE   Some messages may be presented in such an unenthusiastic way that they are difficult to attend to. You may have discovered how difficult it is to listen when an instructor drones on and on. Nichols (1957) suggests that deciding early in the listening task that you have some use for the material helps you attend to it. Active listening, discussed later in this chapter, also will help.

UNACCUSTOMED LENGTH OF THE MESSAGE   Donald Campbell (1958) found that the longer the message, the greater a person's loss of information. People have a natural tendency to shorten, simplify, and eliminate detail when listening to a long message. In addition, people tend to drop the middle of a long message.

Problems with understanding   Understanding and agreement are different concepts. Some people say they don't understand when actually they don't agree. Problems of understanding can be attributed to four sources.

DIFFERENT FIELDS OF EXPERIENCE   You know what words mean from your experience with them. Your past experience with the words in this text, with this context, and with this content will all be relevant to your interpretation. For example, if you have read another author's definition and discussion of the concept "field of experience" and it differs from this one, you may have trouble understanding this passage.

INABILITY TO EMPATHIZE   Since people have different fields of experience, they may hold different values. People are likely to disagree some of the time—maybe most of the time—if their orientations are very different. This tendency sometimes makes it difficult to see another's view. (Sometimes it is difficult to imagine another's view.) A frequent result is that people mentally criticize another person's view, constructing arguments to refute his or her ideas and not listening carefully.

Empathizing is an activity in which participants attempt to put themselves in another's mental and situational framework. Empathy requires a more active mental commitment to what is being said. Consequently, empathizing facilitates understanding.

POOR USE OF FEEDBACK   People can create problems for themselves because they do not get and give adequate feedback. Almost everyone has stopped at a service station to ask for directions. What can you do to be sure you understand the directions? One technique is to repeat the directions back to the person and ask for correction of errors.

MENTAL SETS   The fourth problem related to understanding is alluded to by terms such as *closed minded, overly critical,* and *polarized viewpoint.* Mental sets such as these can cause listeners to assume that they know what is right and can prevent them from understanding another's view. This is not to say that you should not have opinions. You do need to acknowledge that others also have something to say. You may not hear what they are saying unless you can momentarily put your opinions aside.

Problems with remembering   How long will you remember what you have heard? Tony Buzan (1991) has suggested that you will forget 80 percent of the details in 24 hours. The curve that Buzan plotted is based on data he collected with students who had memorized word lists (Figure 2.2). Buzan discovered that we are not 100 percent efficient at remembering, even when we have just heard the information. Notice the rise at the end of receiving information—the mind keeps working and making connections. Remembering is more efficient for a short period after we've completed a listening task than it is *during* the task. Researchers have been aware of this forgetting curve for a century. Herman Ebbinghaus (1885) did basic research with forgetting.[1] Compare the Ebbinghaus curve with Buzan's. Notice that the retention problem seems to be the general rule.

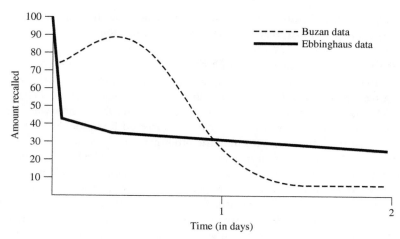

FIGURE 2.2
Forgetting Curves

Source: Adapted from Tony Buzan (1983). Reprinted by permission of the publisher, E. P. Dutton.

Gender Differences in Listening

The act of listening has different meanings for men and women, so they behave differently (Tannen, 1990). Men rarely listen for a lengthy period without interrupting. Supposedly an uncomfortable feeling motivates this behavior because listening is seen as a one-down, low-status behavior. Women, on the other hand, see listening as an opportunity to connect with the other person on a personal level. Listening for a lengthy period is seen as an attempt to show interest, confirm the other's ideas, and show appreciation for the information. Women see interrupting to take the floor as being insensitive to the other's feelings.

Men interrupt mixed-sex conversations more than women do (Borisoff & Merrill, 1992), and they usually do it for conversational control (Mulac et al., 1988). Women, on the other hand, interrupt most of the time to communicate assent, elaborate on an idea of another member, or participate in the topic of conversation (Stewart & Stewart, 1990).

Developing Listening Skills

Work hard at listening   Becoming a better listener requires the *belief* that listening can be hard work. It involves making an effort to get the information you need.

For example, suppose a member of your group seems to talk too much. "He has an opinion about everything," you say. You have developed the habit of discounting his opinion. During one meeting he says: "I've found some important information on the problem. . . ."

Given your experience with this member and your attitude about his contributions, you may find it very difficult work to stay with him and to get his point.

Paraphrase the content   The technique of paraphrasing helps you to attend more carefully and know whether you understand. By paraphrasing the content, a technique also called **active listening,** you say back to the speaker in your own words what you believe he or she said. This forces you to concentrate. When you paraphrase, you'll know whether you understand. You can continue if you do; you can be corrected if you don't.

You may argue that paraphrasing everything the other person says would drive anybody mad. You are right. Paraphrasing is a special technique that is used when the information being given (1) is particularly important to you or the organization, (2) is complex or involves several steps, or (3) involves a problem and the person has come to you. Routine talk and information sharing do not usually require this attention.

You may find that paraphrasing seems artificial. But that artificial sound of the talk will disappear if you practice its use. Paraphrasing sounds different because people use the same lead-in to active listening every time. They may say, "What I hear you saying is. . . ." This is a good lead-in, but if overused it can sound artificial. Learn a variety of ways of saying, "Here is what you've said."

Check your inferences   It is often difficult for people to say directly what they are feeling, needing, or wanting. Thus it becomes a useful listening technique to verify your inferences when the other person is not being particularly clear. This skill requires a high degree of selectivity in responding to the other's talk. Inferences about negative feeling, for example, ought to be carefully weighed before responding. In this regard, plan and practice saying, "What I'm guessing you mean [feel, need, or want] is. . . ." Otherwise the usefulness of the checkout technique will be limited by the sound of artificiality.

Remember: It is difficult for many people to communicate the feelings associated with the content of their talk. If underlying feelings are clearly evident, it is probably better to respond to them. Carl Rogers (1942) suggests that responding to the feeling facilitates the expression of related feelings and helps the listener and the speaker understand the surrounding feelings and assumptions, needs, or other thoughts.

Empathize with the speaker   *Empathizing*, that is, getting into another's frame of reference, is a most useful listening technique. Jack Gibb (1961) suggests that one of the six characteristics of a supportive climate is empathy. Carl Rogers (1962) tells us that accurate empathic understanding of his clients' private worlds is an essential part of the client–therapist relationship.

Empathic listening involves suspending evaluation. **Evaluative listening** is a deliberative activity and is, therefore, different from empathic listening. Charles Kelly drew this distinction clearly in his comprehensive dissertation research on listening:

> The difference between empathic listening and deliberative [evaluative] listening is primarily motivational. Both listeners seek the same objective: accurate understanding of communication from another. . . . The empathic listener lets his understanding of the speaker

determine his modes of evaluation, which are automatic; the deliberative listener's understanding of the speaker is filtered through his predetermined modes of selective listening, and he actually spends less time as a communication receiver. The empathic listener is more apt to be a consistent listener, and is less prone to his own or other distractions. (Kelly, 1984, p. 297)

The deliberative listener pursues an evaluative orientation. In contrast, the empathic listener tries to withhold evaluation long enough to understand the other person.

Work on remembering   It is possible to prevent the sharp drop in the amount of content remembered after an exchange, but not to prevent some drop. Three important techniques aid memory: organization, repetition, and association (Deese, 1958).

In his useful and well-written book *Use Both Sides of Your Brain,* Tony Buzan suggests ways to intervene in the forgetting process. Study his graph of the forgetting curve, pictured in Figure 2.3. He suggests that you take notes during the listening activity whenever possible to provide a basis for the review process. We recommend that to you also.

The Complexity of Listening in Groups

Listening is a more complicated in groups than in a one-to-one communication. Sources of information change rapidly. There are multiple sources, sometimes talking over each other. Topics change rapidly. Members are monitoring both verbal and nonverbal messages to discover task and relational information as participant-analysts. A great deal is going on in an effective, working group. This activity makes listening a challenge.

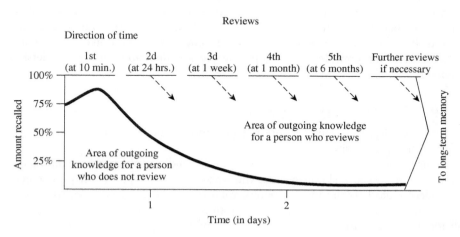

FIGURE 2.3
Spacing Organizing and Practice Sessions to Aid Memory

Source: Adapted from Tony Buzan (1983). Reprinted by permission of the publisher, E. P. Dutton.

Looking Back: A Quick Review

LISTENING PROBLEMS AND SOLUTIONS

Problem	Solutions
Poor attending	Give special effort.
Different experience	Talk about your experience.
Inability to empathize	Empathize with the speaker.
Poor use of feedback	Paraphrase the content.
Mental sets	Check out your inferences.
Remembering	Organize and review to remember.

Remembering under these circumstances is difficult. Therefore, an important key to effectiveness in the listening process is note taking. Note taking functions very much like the active listening technique in that it forces concentration on the message. The task of taking careful notes requires careful attention and provides an opportunity to review what you heard. Careful attention enhances listening. Careful attention enhances your ability to remember, too. Your skill in listening is tied to group effectiveness.

Given the complexity of effective listening, you might wonder if it is worth the effort. One study provides a reason for making the effort. Belcher and Johnson (1995) found that members who were rated "most like the leader" also were rated "good listeners." On the other hand, those seen as "poor listeners" were more likely to be eliminated from leadership consideration. So people see a connection between leadership and listening.

Listening in Electronic Meetings

The listening activity when members are not face to face, but communicating through electronic means, is different.

Listening may become reading if it is not a video/audio hook-up, which means the communication moves at a slower pace as the written message appears on your screen. If it is a video–audio hook-up via computers, then there is some delay from speaker to speaker. There is sort of a hopscotch pattern of turn-taking. Since it is turn-taking and difficult for the speaker to know you have something to say (it is more difficult to recognize nonverbal cues), your listening may be hampered by the frustration of not being easily able to make your point in a timely fashion.

If you find yourself in a computer-assisted meeting with group members in the same room, you will find the interaction more like a conversation. As you sit at your concealed keyboard, you can type in your idea instantly. You can piggyback on another person's message at any point by typing it in reference to the number assigned to that message. Turn-taking is determined by the order in which the transmissions appear on the screen.

You will discover that the flow of ideas is not as rich and full in an electronic meeting as in face-to-face communication. Ideas that appear on your screen in written form will not reveal the feelings and nonverbal cues you normally receive. If your hook-up is video and audio, you may find the technology limits the richness of the communication. Listening under these circumstances may require extra effort.

SUMMARY

An initial step in planning for a meeting is selection of participants. You can identify certain participants by looking at special qualifications or expertise. Other participants may be invited because of the political sensitivity of the subject matter. Check also to see whether any unnecessary duplication in the membership could inhibit or inadvertently undermine the group's deliberations.

Next, consider the discussion issue. Is it an issue of fact, value, or policy? Issues of fact are answerable by securing needed information and, therefore, are rarely issues for decision making. Issues of value are questions about the goodness or worth of something. These call for a group to make a judgment. Issues of policy are questions that invite the group to some action. These issues provide the richest opportunity for groups to work toward some common goal. Whatever the nature of the issue, the group must focus it into manageable limits before it proceeds.

The decision about how much structure is needed in a decision-making group is a complex one. When deciding, the leader—or perhaps the group itself—must consider several questions: (1) How much order is needed to allow group members to feel comfortable? (2) How much time does the group have to carry out the task? (3) How large is the group? (4) How many people will be present to give input? (5) Do the group members have strong feelings about the topic or about one another? (6) What is the nature of the task? Tasks can be classified by their difficulty, solution multiplicity, intrinsic interest to members, cooperation requirements, and population (member) interest.

A final step in preparation is securing information. First, conduct an inventory of what you know. Next, gather additional information to supplement your knowledge through interviews, surveys, library research, direct observation, and electronic search. Finally, evaluate and organize the information. Asking appropriate questions can help you in the evaluation process.

There are four components of the listening process: sensing, attending, understanding, and remembering. Each of these presents a potential area of difficulty for a listener. If your sensing mechanisms are faulty, you will not receive the message. If you are distracted and do not attend, you will not know what is said. If you do not understand, you may assume one message when the speaker means another. If you cannot remember the message that you processed, your listening effort is wasted.

Sensing problems may be related to actual defects in the mechanisms or to noise from the environment. Attending problems emerge from a greater range of difficulties. These include selective perception, poor attending habits, the listener's attitudes and needs, low-intensity messages, and messages that are too long. Difficulties related to understanding can be attributed to four sources: different fields of experience, inability to empathize, poor use of feedback, and various mental sets. Finally, as forgetting curves demonstrate, people forget much detail unless they learn to intervene in some way.

Important listening skills must be practiced if they are to be acquired. Five suggestions are

1. *Work hard at listening.*   Avoiding distractions is hard work.
2. *Paraphrase the content.*   Active listening will force involvement.
3. *Check your inferences.*   Checking will allow confirmation or denial.
4. *Empathize.*   Empathy helps you understand the speaker's view.
5. *Work on remembering.*   Note taking, association, and review help memory.

Women and men behave differently when listening because the act of listening has different meanings for men and women. Men see listening at length as a one-down, low-status behavior. Therefore, they interrupt frequently to maintain control. Women see listening as an opportunity to connect with the other person. They see interrupting to take the floor as insensitive to the other person's feelings.

KEY TERMS AND CONCEPTS

20 percent rule
active listening
attending
Burelle's Broadcast Database
causal relationship
DowJones News/Retrieval
either-this-or-that reasoning
electronic database
electronic journal
empathic listening
encyclopedias on disc
ERIC

evaluative listening
fact
fallacies
faulty comparison
home page
inference
internet search engines
LEXIS
NEXIS
online catalog
overgeneralization

personal prejudice
question of cause
question of definition
question of fact
question of policy
question of value
remembering
sensing
thinking for yourself
thinking tentatively
understanding

EXERCISES

1. Select an unsuccessful group experience. Prepare a written analysis of the experience using the five criteria presented under "Deciding about Structure," pages 43–47. Which of these factors contributed to the problems you experienced? Briefly describe how these factors contributed to the problems. Share your analysis with the class.

2. Check your understanding of wording a discussion question by critiquing these:
   a. The federal government should provide help for job training.
   b. What should the fraternity do for its spring event?
   c. How much money should be provided for repair of storm-damaged buildings?
   d. What can be done to improve the student health service?
   e. Should students who have an A in a course be required to take the final exam?
   f. What should be done to promote worldwide racial harmony?
   g. The state government should provide a credit voucher to parents who send their children to private schools.

3. Select a topic to use for a discussion later in the term. As a group, identify sources of information. Be specific.

Experts	Scholarly journals
Government agencies	Periodicals
Newspapers	Professional organizations
Online searches	

4. Observe a small group discussion. Make a list of instances in which members present information. After each item of information, write C for credible, NC for not credible, or U for uncertain of credibility. Total your ratings for the discussion. What do your ratings tell you about the "information pool" this group used to make its decision?

5. Norms often seem "invisible" to participants. Here is a way to get in touch with some group norms. Describe member behavior in two very different groups to which you belong regarding: starting times, patterns of who talks to whom, amount of the communication that is goal communication versus relational communication, the ways decisions are made. What similarities and differences do you find?

RECOMMENDED WEBSITES

The home page for the International Listening Association, which discusses effective listening skills and techniques, can be found at www.listen.org/. The site has great listening exercises, resources, and even a section called "listening factoids."

Enhancing Experiences of Group Work by the Institute for Interactive Media and Learning at www.iml.uts.edu.au/learnteach/groupwork/ gives a background on how to manage and motivate student groups. It even includes a section on forming effective groups.

The site www.viha.ca/hr/leader_resources/pdf/mr_gath_info.pdf is devoted to gathering information and has an easy-to-use table which details how to collect information using different types of methods, such as interviews and focus groups.

This site has several listening exercises with varying degrees of difficulty for individuals who are speakers of English as a Second Language (ESL): esl.about.com/library/quiz/bllisteningquiz.htm.

Communicating at work: Listening strategies and skills gives examples of individual and group activities to test listening skills and give suggestions for listening: slincs.coe.utk.edu/gtelab/learning_activities/21evej.html.

RECOMMENDED READINGS

T. Adams & N. Clark (2000). *The Internet: Effective online communication.* Fort Worth, TX: Harcourt.

E. Babbie (2000). *The practice of social research,* 9th ed. Belmont, CA: Wadsworth. See the chapters on survey research.

B. N. Moore and R. Parker (1995). *Critical thinking,* 4th ed. Mountain View, CA: Mayfield Publishing.

G. L. Wilson and H. L. Goodall Jr. (1991). *Interviewing in context.* New York: McGraw-Hill.

NOTE

1. Interest in researching this phenomenon has begun to pick up in the last few years in relation to split-brain studies and their offshoots. In all the research, the retention curves look about the same as the two presented.

chapter
3

PARTICIPATING IN GROUP MEETINGS

A steering committee for the annual financial pledge campaign of a local church was meeting to organize. Carl, finance committee chair, is leading this group. Other members of the committee are Dan, Gail, Marta, and Calvin. Notice this interaction:

> CARL: I guess we are all here. Let's get started. It seems to me that our first task is to lay out a plan to get ourselves organized. We have to kick off the program by November 1. Some of you worked on the campaign last year. Let's list the tasks that need to be accomplished.
>
> GAIL: We will need to recruit captains to lead groups to visit members.
>
> MARTA: I believe we also had co-captains. We'll need to recruit these people too.
>
> CARL: Right. And what else do we need to worry about?
>
> DAN: We'll need to work up material describing the church's plans for its program.
>
> GAIL: And we need a budget and discussion about the areas of increase.
>
> CALVIN: As I remember, we worked up some examples of ways of answering questions that people might have about the program. We'll need to get someone from programming to work on this right away.

You can tell by the direction that Carl is leading this group that he has begun the process of organizing. He has asked group members to define what it is they have to do. We can imagine that Carl will continue the process of defining the task and then set agendas for a series of meetings. This kind of planning is important if the group is to accomplish its goals in a timely manner and to be successful. Understanding how to set and follow an appropriate agenda was a key factor in the group's success.

This chapter begins by discussing individual versus group decision making. Then we consider several agendas. Each is useful under certain circumstances, so we explore how each agenda might be used and also adapted to meet a group's needs. Next, vigilant interaction theory suggests how groups can improve their work by careful attention to the decision-making process. Following this, five special discussion techniques are examined. Included here is a discussion of technology as an aid to group process. Finally, decision-making methods are presented, along with the circumstances under which each is useful.

INDIVIDUAL OR GROUP DECISION MAKING?

Every problem requires a judgment about who should make a decision. Should the decision be turned over to an individual or to a group? This complex question does not have a simple answer. In fact, Victor H. Vroom and Arthur G. Jago (1988) developed an elaborate plan for making a judgment about who should make a decision. Here are some important questions to consider in making the judgment about who should wrestle with a problem. The discussion is based on Vroom and Jago's work as well as that of others.

1. *Is one person in the group truly an expert?*
   If so, the expert should probably make the decision.

2. *Is there a severe time constraint on making a decision?*

   Turn the problem over to an individual who possesses the information and expertise to decide if there is a time constraint. Groups usually move more slowly than individuals. If the problem is given to a group, a leader can help the group move more quickly by imposing structure and time limits.

3. *Is the problem complex?*

   If the problem is complex it may require a variety of views and expertise. A group is more likely to have the knowledge and expertise. Turn the problem over to the group, provided there is no time constraint. If the problem is simple and non-controversial, turn it over to an individual who has the expertise to decide.

4. *Is it important that the group accept the decision?*

   If the problem is straightforward and the group is likely to accept the decision, turn the problem over to an individual. If the group has to live with the decision and/or must implement it, and especially if the issue is controversial, it will be important for them to accept the decision. Turn the problem over to a group that has the knowledge and expertise to make a decision.

Social Facilitation

If the decision is made to turn over a task to a group, the process may benefit from social facilitation. **Social facilitation** is the effect that comes to a group's effort because members are working in the presence of each other. Social facilitation is the tendency for individuals to work harder because there are other people present (Zajonc, 1965; Gagne & Zuckerman, 1999; Geen, 1991). This effect is thought to come about because the presence of others creates a situation where social evaluation can take place. The social evaluation motivates members to work harder to find the best possible solution (Kameda, 1996).

Although other research findings indicate both positive and negative effects on performance and learning from the presence of others, considerable evidence suggests that working in cooperative, interdependent work groups—teams—enhances learning and individual performance (Schmitt, 1981). In addition, research by Deutsch (1990) indicates that cooperative, as opposed to competitive, groups facilitate performance.

The key to achieving the benefits of social facilitation appears to be gaining skill in working together, having a cooperative spirit, and being interdependent.

AGENDAS FOR GROUP MEETINGS

An Agenda for a Business Meeting

Tradition has set an agenda for a business meeting that you may want to adopt if you are to lead one. The agenda includes categories of business, and the content varies from meeting to meeting. An agenda for a business meeting is displayed in Figure 3.1.

---

1. Meeting is called to order.
2. Minutes of previous meeting are distributed.
3. Minutes of previous meeting are approved and corrected.
4. Standing committee reports are given.
5. Special committee reports are given.
6. Old business is considered (from previous meetings).
7. New business is considered (business not previously discussed).
8. Officers and members give announcements.
9. Adjournment is called.

FIGURE 3.1
Typical Business Meeting Agenda

The rules require members to be recognized and to make proposals in the form motions—formal proposals. The proposal must receive the endorsement—a "second"—of another member, who indicates by the action support for the proposal. Debate of the merits of the proposal is then permitted, with the chairperson formally recognizing speakers. This discussion may continue until all have spoken as much as they wish, or it may be curtailed by a vote. Members may also set aside an issue for later consideration by voting to "table" it, that is, to end the discussion. They may take the proposal from the table and consider it at some future meeting.

An Agenda Based on Reflective Thinking

Suppose that you are enrolled in Professor John Dewey's philosophy class at your college or university. He is interested in how people think when they solve problems. So he asks your class to describe the steps you take in solving problems.

Professor Dewey collects all your statements and analyzes them for common characteristics. Dewey (1910) finds enough similarities to be quite confident that he is onto something. He decides that the similarities are so significant that he will write a book, *How We Think*, to let others know of his discovery.

Dewey believed that thinking reflectively obligates a person to adopt an attitude of "active, persistent, and careful consideration of any belief or supposed form of knowledge in the light of the grounds that support it and the further conclusions to which it tends" (Dewey, 1910, p. 6). Dewey is suggesting that the person must be committed to "active, persistent and careful consideration" of beliefs. Also, the person must carry this commitment to an examination of the "support" and "conclusions." All the while, group members must remain flexible in applying the decision-making process.

Below is a decision-making sequence which flows from the ideas of John Dewey (1910). This type of agenda has the advantage of a systematic and usually thorough analysis of the problem and solutions. Some caution is advised. Jarboe (1996) found that, although a standard agenda like this is ideal, some groups have difficulty following the steps and therefore find it impractical. What this means is your group may need to gain some practice so that a "standard agenda" will work for you.

The steps of Dewey's agenda, highlighted by italic print, are illustrated below, each with an outline used by a housing authority to consider security in one of its buildings. Read through this illustration twice. First, scan the italicized sections. Then, go back and read the full text.

I. *What is the nature of the problem?*
 A. *What are the particulars of our problem?*[1]
  1. *What is the problem?*
   There has been a 10 percent increase in crime in the Hillsdale Building. There were five burglaries, one rape, and two cases of vandalism in the past three months.

  2. *Do we understand the terms?*
   What is meant by burglary?
   Breaking and entering the premises and taking possession of another's property.

  3. *What outcome is expected of our group?*
   (Discussion of problem? Recommendation of possible solutions? A decision?)
   We are to analyze fully this problem, discuss solutions, make a decision, and present a plan for implementation.

 B. *What harm is present in the current situation?*
  1. *What is the harm?*
   The pain and suffering of the individuals.
   Loss of property valued at $4,500.
   Image of the housing authority as not providing safe living arrangements for the citizens of the county.

  2. *Who is affected?*
   The residents of the Hillsdale Building.
   The employees of the housing authority who work in the building.
   All the housing authority board members and employees, indirectly.

  3. *How serious is the harm?*
   Crime is on the increase.
   The loss and the personal injury involved are substantial.

  4. *How widespread is the harm?*
   People on nearly every floor have been victims or know victims.
   Residents of other buildings have complained of an increase in security problems.

    C. *What seems to be causing the problem?*
        1. *What factors seem to be causing the harm?*
           Vacant apartments seem to attract vandalism and crime.
           Residents do not report suspicious people who hang around.
           Residents often leave doors unlocked.
           Many residents do not have telephones, so they have no good way to call for help.

        2. *What are the obstacles to successfully removing the causes of the harm?*
           It may be difficult if not impossible to rent all the units in this building. Residents do not have funds to have telephones installed, and board policy prohibits payment for private installation.

II. *What criteria, or standards for judging an effective solution, should we set?*
    A. *What important conditions—criteria—must an effective solution meet?*
        We cannot break existing board policy.
        We cannot spend more than $5,000, the amount allocated for this project.
        We must not approve a plan that advantages particular residents of the complex over other residents.
        We must be able to implement the plan in other buildings where security problems are beginning to surface.

    B. *Are some criteria more important than others? If so, rank-order them.*
        Yes. We must treat all residents equally. We cannot go over the $5,000 allocated. Board policy might be changed but only if absolutely necessary.

III. *What alternatives might meet the causes of this problem and alleviate the harm?*

        1. Install an emergency alert system on each floor.

        2. Increase outside lighting.

        3. Replace locks on doors with double-bolt-type locks.

        4. Install peepholes in doors.

        5. Offer incentives for residents to move to empty apartments, closing off the top floor temporarily.

        6. Organize a crime watch among the residents, offering cash rewards for making a report that results in apprehension and conviction of criminals.

        7. Hire a private security system.

        8. Attempt to get increased county police surveillance.

IV. *What is the best solution for this problem?*
    A. *Which of these or what combination of these solutions seems most likely to counter the causes of this problem?*
        Better locks and peepholes would help keep criminals out.
        Elimination of empty apartments would allow for more people to be around to discover the crime.

A private professional security service would provide the most reliable protection.

Increased outside lighting would most certainly discourage crime.

B. *Of the solutions that seem likely to be effective, which ones meet the criteria that were set?*

Moving residents might not be fair. Some residents have lived in their apartments for 15 years.

Cost is a factor. The funds will not allow for a private security company. Perhaps county police are an alternative.

Cost of the other items is probably within the $5,000 limit.

C. *Given solutions that are likely to counter the causes, and meet the criteria set, what seems to be the best solution?*

All the solutions seem likely to work except moving people and the crime watch. Residents are unlikely to respond to an effort to organize. They haven't been known for community responsibility and pulling together.

V. *What plans will we set in order to implement our solution?*

A. *What needs to be done?*

Turn the plan over to the executive director for action.

B. *In what order?*

Ask the director to begin lock installation immediately.

Contact the county police department and ask how it can provide increased patrolling of the Hillsdale Building.

Contract to upgrade the lighting.

C. *By whom?*

The executive director will carry out these plans and report back to us within 30 days.

VI. *How will we evaluate the effect of our solution?*

A. *What observable evidence will we monitor to evaluate the effect of our solution?*

We will collect crime reports and residents' complaints.

B. *Who will be responsible for follow-up evaluation?*

The executive director.

Looking Back: A Quick Review

REFLECTIVE THINKING AGENDA

Nature of the problem	Possible solutions to the problem
Harm created by the problem	Evaluation of possible solutions
Causes of the problem	Selection of a final solution
Criteria for judging an effective solution	Implementation of final solution

---

Vigilant Interaction Theory

"Be cautious in your decision making" advises Randy Hirokawa. The scholar believes that decision quality rests with the agenda and its application. His **vigilant interaction theory,** or **functional theory,** is based on the idea that the quality of group performance is directly influenced by the quality of the interaction (Hirokawa, 1996; Hirokawa & Rost, 1992). Vigilant interaction theory is based on the work of Dennis Gouran (1986), who linked critical thinking and communication to high-quality inferences. Randy Hirokawa found higher-quality outcomes in groups he studied when they were vigilant (that is, thorough and careful) than in groups that weren't vigilant.

Four issues are important to *vigilant interaction theory* (Hirokawa & Rost, 1992):

1. *Examining the problem* Is there something about the current state of affairs that requires improvement and change?

2. *Clarifying objectives* What do we want to achieve or accomplish in deciding what to do about the problem?

3. *Developing available choices* What choices are available to us?

4. *Examining potential consequences* What are the positive and negative aspects of these choices?

Notice that this approach to decision making is very similar to that presented in the agenda based on reflective thinking. Hirokawa found that productive groups usually take up these issues in an organized sequence, though the sequence may vary from group to group. He concluded that the biggest error groups make is the omission of one or more of these steps (Hirokawa, 1983; Poole & Doelger, 1986).

This research argues for careful attention to the group's decision-making process as it works through the problem. This means the group must thoroughly and accurately understand the problem, consider a variety of acceptable alternatives, and evaluate each alternative carefully. Careful evaluation means considering both positive and negative consequences associated with each alternative. Thus the importance of critical thinking cannot be overestimated. Further research by Randy Hirokawa (1985) concludes an additional step after a solution is reached. Vigilant decision making requires retrospective questioning and asking, "What if we implemented our decision? How would it play out?"

Adapting the Agenda to the Group's Needs

A wise group leader will modify an agenda to fit the group's needs. Galanes, Adams, and Brilhart (2004) present a useful scheme for modifying agendas according to problem characteristics. They suggest tailoring the agenda for a particular problem characteristic by adjusting the problem-solving emphasis and agenda steps. These suggestions are presented in Table 3.1.

TABLE 3.1   Problem Characteristics Matched to Agenda Steps

Problem	Problem-Solving Emphasis	Agenda Steps
1. Intrinsic interest in problem is high.	1. A period of ventilation before systematic problem solving.	1. A problem-solving agenda with which the group is familiar.
2. Difficulty of problem is high.	2. Detailed problem mapping with many subquestions.	2. Problem mapping, as presented in single question format. Ideation, step III of the reflective thinking format, with brainstorming.
3. Multiple solutions to problem are possible.	3. Brainstorming or nominal group process.	3. Include a criteria step, as in step II of the reflective thinking format.
4. Cooperative requirements for solving the problems are high.	4. A criteria step, creating and ranking explicit standards.	4. Include a criteria step, as in step II of the reflective thinking format.
5. High level of acceptance of the solution is required.	5. Focus on concern of persons affected when evaluating solutions.	5. Include step II of the ideal solution format.
6. High level of technical quality is required for a decision.	6. Focus on evaluating ideas, critical thinking; perhaps invite outside experts to testify.	6. A reflective thinking sequence may be most suitable.
7. Members are responsible for one or a few of the stages of problem solving.	7. Shorten agenda to include only the required steps.	7. Emphasize the steps of any sequence that will allow the group to meet its charge.

Source: Adapted from Brilhart & Galanes (1982); Galanes, Adams, & Brilhart (2004).

In addition to the special needs that might be presented by the characteristics of the task, you should consider the nature of your group. Ask these two important questions about the group to help you decide on your agenda: "How long have members been working together?" and "Do they have experience in working with this kind of task?"

Groups that have been working together for a long time very often develop a particular way of working with problems. If their agenda works and if it allows reasonable consideration of problems, then it may be a mistake to change.

But how do you know whether an agenda allows reasonable consideration of the problem? There are two tests to apply. First, do the decisions the group implements seem to work? Do the decisions alleviate the harm? Are the people who are affected by the decisions satisfied? Second, does the group have difficulty coming to decisions? Some problems are difficult and very controversial. We expect groups to engage in conflict about their ideas in these cases. But if the group has difficulty with decision making on a regular basis, then the difficulty may be a function of the agenda.

Perhaps the problem needs a more careful analysis. Sometimes too few solutions are considered. At other times the group's membership is so diverse that it needs to recognize and consider the ideal solutions for the different subgroups. Decision-making difficulty can be a function of failure to discuss criteria—especially if the problem involves values. A group might modify its agenda to take one of these problems into account.

Using the Agenda Effectively

Five important guidelines will help your group make more efficient use of an agenda.

Tailor the agenda to the specific problem   You should formulate specific questions for the agenda in terms of the problem. These questions help focus the group's attention in a way that would not be possible if the agenda were published with more general questions.

Do not keep the agenda secret   Some leaders bring their agenda to the group's meeting, and members see it for the first time. This procedure does not allow group members to prepare. Informed preparation is usually better than uninformed preparation. Publish the agenda several days before the meeting.

Ask the members at the start of the meeting if they wish to modify the agenda   Permit group members to change the agenda. When they seem satisfied, get verbal agreement. This step constitutes "public agreement" to a rough statement of the group's goals.

Send an abbreviated form of the agenda to the group   This agenda helps keep the group oriented, and it serves to remind the group of its progress.

Use the agenda to check on the quality of the process and discussion   Did the group conduct a careful analysis of the problem? Does the solution seem to eliminate the causes? Does the solution meet the criteria? Does the group's plan allow for careful monitoring of the implementation of the decision? Has the group considered contingencies to be put in place if necessary?

DISCUSSION TECHNIQUES

Consultants to various organizations have developed a number of group techniques (Seibold, 1979). Brainstorming, focus groups, and buzz groups have as their goal generating information and ideas. Further, the buzz group addresses the problem of increasing member participation in the idea-generation process. Nominal group process and Delphi are decision-making processes formulated to overcome certain situational problems.

Brainstorming

Brainstorming is a procedure in which ideas are posed and recorded without discussion or critique. It is used to foster creativity. The underlying assumption is that criticism of ideas causes members to be cautious about suggestions and interrupts creative idea generation. Therefore, members are required to hold their criticism and discussion until all ideas have been heard and recorded. Further, members are encouraged to present all ideas that occur to them and to hitchhike on each other's ideas. (In **hitchhiking** a member uses an idea of another member to stimulate his or her imagination, thereby creating an idea that is a variation of the first idea.) A further assumption is that a large number of ideas will include many good ones.

Alex Osborn (1959), co-owner of an advertising agency, first discussed this procedure in his book *Applied Imagination.* Osborn sought a way to help his staff become more creative in developing marketing strategies. The assumptions about generating ideas and creativity yielded four rules to guide a group toward this goal:

1. All evaluation and criticism of ideas are forbidden.
2. Wild and offbeat ideas are encouraged.
3. Quantity, not quality, of ideas is the goal.
4. New combinations of ideas are sought.

Brainstorming can be used in a variety of ways in a decision-making task. For example, a group might use this technique to answer any of these questions:

Where can we find information?

What kind of information do we need to solve the problem?

Which solutions might we consider?

Which criteria are important to us?

What are the various ways we might implement our decision?

A group can use brainstorming at many points, especially in generating solutions.

Groups that are using brainstorming may experience problems. One problem comes from the tendency for people to support their own ideas. A person who presents an idea may want to elaborate on it. Someone who thinks that her idea is better wants to tell why. So a group using brainstorming needs a leader to gently enforce the no-discussion rule.

Groups may also get stalled after they have a list of several items. Encouragement is needed. The leader might say, "Can we think of three more ideas?" Sometimes it helps the group to get started again if the leader reads the list. The leader might say, "As I read this list, try to think of ideas we have missed."

Allow enough time for brainstorming to achieve its full level of productivity. Brief pauses are normal. Encourage people to continue. Researchers who gave some groups four minutes were productive, but not as productive as those that had more time (Kelly & Karau, 1993).

Another problem is the tendency for some members to stifle the flow of ideas through their nonverbal communication. For example, a member may frown with disapproval at an idea and thereby discourage the contributor's willingness to provide ideas. The leader may need to caution members about this tendency and perhaps invoke some prearranged signal if these nonverbal messages emerge.

Research has demonstrated that someone who is external to the group is most effective in the role of facilitator of a brainstorming session (Offner, Kramer, & Winter, 1996). In many circumstances, this arrangement will not be practical. If the leader understands the process, is committed to the rules, and gives the group opportunity to practice, this disadvantage of not having an external facilitator can be mitigated.

Brainstorming can also have an effect on group cohesiveness. The effect appears to come from the active involvement of more of the members and the obvious group productivity that comes from the process (Pavitt, 1993). Members seem to enjoy the brainstorming process. One study reports that members enjoyed the creative process they realized from building on each other's ideas (Kramer, Kuo, & Dailey, 1997).

Focus Groups

A **focus group** meets to share about experiences with a particular idea, product, or problem by responding to questions. Generally, the group does not have decision-making authority; it meets to provide information and opinion. Focus groups are especially useful when seeking information about how a group of consumers is receiving something. Soda, cigarette, and movie companies, for example, rely heavily on focus groups to improve products. A facilitator, who is often not a member of the organization, prepares a list of questions about the product or service and competitive products or services. Members are generally paid and are part of the larger group of consumers. The facilitator introduces the topic and then poses the first question. For example, a facilitator working for a drug abuse treatment center talked briefly of the need for quality services and then posed the question, "What do you see as the components of a quality drug treatment program?" The facilitator encourages participants to respond and probes their answers for clarification. The interaction is tape-recorded for transcription and analysis.

Focus group meetings are not restricted to marketing research. Groups of employees or students or congregational members could be called together to share their experience with the organization or even to consider specific organizational problems.

Nominal Group Technique and Delphi

Sometimes more alternatives and higher-quality decisions can be achieved through the **nominal group technique (NGT).** It is a procedure for generating ideas and making decisions in which members work silently in a group. They then pool their ideas, clarify them, rank-order them, and also may move to a discussion and a decision. NGT is especially useful when a group has members who may be reluctant to suggest ideas because they are concerned about being criticized or about creating conflict.

This procedure has been labeled "nominal group" because it is not necessary for the members to engage in verbal interaction. In fact, in a version of this technique called **Delphi,** participants generate a decision without ever meeting face to face. Delphi requires that the process be conducted by postal mail or electronic mail. Participants mail a list of ideas and then rank-order a master list that was generated from this original list. A decision is reached by noting which ideas are most favored. Some scholars suggest that

Focus on Research

ELECTRONIC BRAINSTORMING

Here is a new twist on a technique that has been proven effective by researchers. Electronic brainstorming uses networked computers so that a group can brainstorm using the technology to connect. This technique is also similar to nominal group technique in that it asks members to generate a list of ideas prior to the sharing process. This then serves as a basis for members to brainstorm electronically. Members see the ideas as they are written, either on a big screen if they are in the same room or on their own monitor. They can piggyback off each other's work or pose new ideas.

Researchers investigating the effectiveness of this technique report the process generates more ideas than traditional face-to-face brainstorming (Roy, Gauvin, & Limayem, 1996). It even seems to make a difference if used as a supplement to include absent members. Sosik, Avolio, and Kahai (1998) studied the effect of using electronic means to include absent members in the brainstorming process. They report more ideas are generated and of higher quality than when using only a face-to-face group. Finally, researchers speculate that this advantage comes from the anonymity present when ideas are submitted electronically (Cooper et al., 1998).

W. H. Cooper, R. B. Gallupe, S. Pollard, & J. Cadbsy (1998). Some liberating effects of anonymous and identified electronic brainstorming. *Small Group Research, 29,* 147–177.

M. S. Roy, S. Gauvin, & M. Limayem (1996). Electronic group brainstorming: The role of feedback on productivity. *Small Group Research, 27,* 215–247.

J. J. Sosik, B. J. Avolio, & S. S. Kahai (1998). Inspiring group creativity: Comparing anonymous and identified electronic brainstorming. *Small Group Research, 29,* 3–31.

NGT can produce better performance than techniques involving group discussion (Kanekar & Rosenbaum, 1972). Here is how André Delbecq describes the procedure (Delbecq, Van de Ven, & Gustafson, 1986, pp. 7–16):

I. *Silent generation of ideas in writing.* The first step in NGT is to have the group members write key ideas silently and independently.

II. *Round-robin recording of ideas.* The second step of NGT is to record ideas of members on a flip chart visible to the group. Round-robin recording means going around the table and asking for one idea from one member at a time. The leader writes the idea of a member on the flip chart and then asks for one idea from the next member.

III. *Serial discussion for clarification.* The third step of NGT is to discuss each idea in turn. Serial discussion means taking each idea listed on the flip chart in order and discussing it for a short time. The leader points to item 1, reads it out loud, and asks the group if there are any questions, statements of clarification, or statements of agreement or disagreement. . . [The leader should] not allow discussion to: (1) unduly focus on any particular idea; or (2) degenerate into argumentation. [Note: The idea here is not to interact about disagreement, but to present the reasons for agreement or disagreement without engaging in a clash with other members.]

IV. *Preliminary vote on item importance.* The average NGT meeting will generate over twelve items in each group during its idea-generation phase. Through serial discussion, group members will come to understand the meaning of the item, the logic behind the item, and argument for and against the importance of individual items. In some manner, however, the group must aggregate the judgments of individual members in order to determine the relative importance of individual items. [One method of doing this is to have group members rank-order their choices in terms of acceptability. These can then be tabulated and the results tallied. An idea may clearly emerge from this process. If no idea emerges, the group can then engage in discussion and attempt to achieve an agreement.]

NGT has the advantage of minimizing status differences and ensuring relatively equal participation. It also may be a time-saver. Susan Jarboe's (1988) research suggests that NGT decreases the tension and hostility a group might experience. Delbecq and his colleagues suggest it is best used in meetings concerned with *judgmental* decision making. These are meetings that involve *creative* decision making, and NGT has significant advantages. NGT groups develop both more proposals and higher-quality proposals than groups using other procedures (Kramer, Kuo, & Dailey, 1997).

The type of questions that such groups consider are "What should be done about employee absenteeism?" "What activities should be planned for the fraternity?" "What marketing plan should we adopt for this new sport shoe?"

Delbecq makes the point that the technique is not suited to routine meetings. For Delbecq, the routine meeting is a "situation where members of the group agree upon the desired goal, and the technologies exist to achieve this goal. In such a meeting the focus is on coordination and information exchange, and the meeting is 'leader centered'" (Delbecq, Van de Ven, & Gustafson, 1986, p. 4). (These meetings are also called **programmed decision situations,** since no real decision making is taking place.) So a meeting to report on production quotas and to set new goals would not be suited to NGT.

Buzz Groups

The **buzz group** technique was conceptualized by J. Donald Phillips (1948). It is useful in large groups to ensure as much individual participation as possible. The large group is divided into subgroups of six persons. Each group discusses the same question for a specific length of time and reports its conclusions to the large group's leader. The leader collects the results and displays them for the membership. The technique is useful for identifying issues or problems, posing a list of solutions or ideas, and generating questions for study. An example of a question a service group asked its members is "What new projects shall we undertake in the new year?"

The technique involves six steps:

1. The chairperson of the group presents a carefully formulated question to the group. The question must be concise and limited in scope so that the groups will be able to manage it in a brief period.

2. Divide the large group into smaller groups of six members. These groups are provided tables if possible. If this is not possible, they must be given enough space to have some privacy. (Usually a large auditorium is used if available.)

3. Appoint a spokesperson for each group. This person will chair the meeting and report the results to the larger group. The leader should understand the rules: (a) All ideas are to be recorded, and (b) the group is to rank-order them according to the most preferred. Provide cards for recording ideas.

4. Ask the group members to follow this procedure: Propose ideas for five minutes; then devote one minute to deleting duplicates and ideas the group does not want to pass on; then rank-order the remaining ideas.

5. Notify the groups when five minutes have elapsed. Give the groups an extra minute to finish their listing; then ask them to evaluate and rank-order.

6. Ask each spokesperson to read his or her group's first suggestion in a round-robin fashion. The suggestions can be listed on a chalkboard or overhead projector for all to see. Of course, duplicates will not be read. Instead, the spokesperson should read the next item on his or her list.

The conclusions from this process may be evaluated by some appropriate subgroup of the membership, such as the group's executive committee or an ad hoc committee.

This technique is useful in a variety of contexts. Political, social, and fraternal groups can use it to get their members involved in decision making. It helps overcome problems with a too-large group engaging in decision making.

Looking Back: A Quick Review

Discussion Techniques

Technique	Use
Brainstorming	Idea generation Creative involvement
Focus group	Provide input Conduct research Explore opinions
Nominal group and Delphi	Idea generation Decision making Silent generation of ideas Sharing ideas Vote on importance of ideas
Buzz Group	Information processing Decision making Idea generation; decisions Large group technique Six-member groups discuss a question and report results

TECHNOLOGICAL AIDS TO GROUP INTERACTION

Technological advances in communication are a source of amazement to many people. The hardware and software range from the simple to the complex and from the expensive to the relatively inexpensive. Oper and Fersko-Weiss estimate that more than 400 products are available to enhance group deliberations (Coleman, 1992). Johnson-Lenz and Johnson-Lenz (1992) have coined the term **computer-mediated culture** to suggest technology and group processes can be bound together so each affects and alters the other. Aids are available to help members in writing and deliberating tasks. Group-writing systems permit co-workers to simultaneously create and edit a document. Here we discuss two technological aids: teleconferencing and group decision support.

Teleconferencing

Face-to-face meetings are not always possible in organizations where members are located throughout the country or the world. This circumstance makes the electronically mediated meeting, the **teleconference,** a necessity.

Several authors offer help to improve electronically mediated meetings (Johansen, Vallee, & Spangler, 1979). Larry Barker and his associates (1991, p. 210) suggest that "inexperienced audio conference participants often find themselves interrupting others, not knowing when to speak, failing to identify themselves, or nodding instead of responding verbally." (The many nonverbal cues we use to know these things are absent in the audio conference.) Beyond these, V. A. Ostendorf (1989) suggests that the most common problems encountered in an audio conference are delay or confusion in beginning, unclear meeting goals, lack of group interaction, difficulty in identifying speakers, and problems in obtaining the floor.

You can overcome these problems by employing certain procedures and setting guidelines. Here are some suggestions:

Appoint a moderator/gatekeeper to facilitate the meeting.

Provide a written notice of the calling time, including time zone and date, along with calling instructions.

Include with your instructions the duration and purpose of the meeting.

Request that members identify themselves by name when they speak.

Video conferencing increases somewhat a participant's ability to pick up nonverbal cues. Also, for some the prospect of being on camera is frightening. Some organizations have tried to overcome these problems by providing training for participants.

Here are some guidelines to help you manage a teleconference:

Appoint a trained conference coordinator/moderator.

Make sure all participants are aware of the beginning and ending times.

Appoint a person at each site to facilitate participation.

Provide written documents for participants to brief them on the purpose of the meeting and any information they might need related to the topic.

Many organizations are making increased use of teleconferencing. Their use is likely to increase as travel costs and time constraints increase and technology improves.

Group Decision Support Systems

Group decision support systems (GDSS) are computer hardware and software designed to enhance problem analysis and group decision making. These systems provide a structure for generating, storing, organizing, and evaluating information. Generally the program will move through a series of decision-making steps, for example, analyzing the problem, establishing criteria, generating solutions, making decisions, and creating an implementation plan. In actual use, however, members overlap, loop back, and leap forward as they work together in the decision task. So the decision-making structure provides a strategy as well as procedural guidelines (Broome and Fulbright, 1995).

Group decision support systems are sometimes called **groupware, computer-supported cooperative work (CSCW), electronic meeting systems (EMS),** or **group support systems (GSS).** Each GDSS is structured to meet certain needs—some may focus on the idea-generation process, whereas others may include the entire decision-making process. GDSS are often used along with face-to-face meetings. Most groups will require some practice with the system if they are to use it to full advantage.

GDSS meetings take place in a special computer-equipped room. The one we are familiar with is arranged in a U shape with the facilitator at the top of the U. The room also is equipped with a projection system and a screen, located where all members can view it. Once members' ideas are typed into the system, they can be projected on the screen for face-to-face discussion.

Research on GDSS suggests it is an effective tool. Olaniran (1994) found that computer-mediated groups produced more ideas than those meeting face to face. In addition, groups took longer to get to consensus than did groups not using this technology. Decision quality was highest when the GDSS groups also participated in face-to-face discussion. Jessup and Valacich (1993) concluded that computer-supported decision making is as good as or better than more traditional approaches. One thing GDSS does well is to keep members on the track. Also, members of *large* groups like the process because it seems to equalize participation and reduce the time they would normally spend. Poole and his associates (Poole & Holmes, 1995; Poole et al., 1993) report similar advantages to GDSS groups. They also note that GDSS seems to focus members' attention more on the decision-making procedures and improve the group's organization of the process.

Electronic meetings enhance some group activities. Research suggests that brainstorming is an activity that can benefit (Kramer, Kuo, & Dailey, 1997; Brown et al., 1997). On the other hand, certain kinds of group activities may be hindered by electronic links. In particular, complex problems and relationship issues are better considered in a group meeting face to face (Straus, 1996, 1997).

Some problems with the use of GDSS can be avoided. For example, training can reduce poor initial performance. Hollingshead and colleagues (1993) discovered that poor initial performance seems to be related to unfamiliarity with the equipment. Groups observed by Poole et al. (1993) did not demonstrate improved critical thinking. The researchers attributed this condition to the fact that these groups did not use a facilitator. A facilitator can help the members select the right technology and feel comfortable with it.

As this technology matures, we can expect more and more organizations to invest in it. Keep in mind these are support systems. Group decision support systems are not meant to replace more traditional face-to-face decision making.

Electronic Mail

Groups that are constituted to make decisions may effectively use e-mail when they are planning for their meeting and exchanging initial impressions and ideas about the assignment. It can cut back on the time they will have to spend in a face-to-face meeting, and is especially helpful if a lengthy meeting is anticipated (Adams & Clark, 2001). E-mail communication has been found not to be beneficial when a group is in the decision-making process (Palme, 1995).

Looking Back: A Quick Review

Techniques and Use of Technology in Groups

Technique	Use
Teleconferencing	Linking group members in remote locations
	Information sharing
	Decision making
Group decision support group	Enhanced problem analysis
	Enhanced decision making
	Instantaneous communication
Electronic mail	Member preplanning
	Member exploration of issues
	Member sharing of research
	Opportunity to chat informally

Focus on Research

ELECTRONIC MEETINGS VERSUS FACE-TO-FACE MEETINGS

Electronic meetings and other electronic collaborations have benefits and liabilities. One benefit is that people tend to be more honest when they see their contributions as anonymous (Siegel et al., 1986; Bordina, DiFonzo, & Chang, 1999). But it is not just anonymity, members are not subject to the possible nonverbal cues that indicate disapproval. Emotional displays can have a negative impact on the freedom with which members communicate (Straus, 1999). A liability is a lack of these nonverbal cues that may take away most of the emotional and relational information we get in a face-to-face encounter. It is difficult to gain an understanding of the subtle meaning when significant nonverbal cues are lost.

P. Bordina, N. DiFonzo, & A. Chang (1999). Rumor as group problem solving: Development patterns in informal computer-mediated groups. *Small Group Research*, 30, 8–28.

J. Siegel, V. Dubrovsky, S. Kiesler, & T. W. McGuire (1986). Group processes in computer-mediated communication. *Organizational Behavior and Human Decision Processes*, 33, 157–187.

S. G. Straus (1999). Testing typology of tasks: An empirical validation of McGrath's (1984) group task circumplex. *Small Group Research*, 30, 166–187.

METHODS OF DECIDING

The output of the decision-making process is often affected by the way the group comes to its decision. Member satisfaction, willingness to work toward carrying out the decision, and even the quality of the decision may be affected by how members decide. Here are five methods of deciding and their outcomes.

Consensus

Consensus means all group members agree. In decision making, however, we usually mean that all members *genuinely* agree. Groups often aim at achieving this kind of consensus. An important reason for doing this is that groups often have a part in implementation. If one or two members are opposed, implementation may be difficult.

Consensus does not mean that members are completely in favor of something. As you might imagine, such a position may be difficult to achieve. Imagine, for example, an office manager calling her workers together to decide on the allocation of a new computer. Tracy's involvement in the situation is quite understandable. As the senior department member, he is inclined to argue for the new computer because of his seniority. Sally believes just as strongly that she should receive a new computer. She has the oldest machine. Others have their arguments, too. In this case consensus is unlikely unless the group has a strong need for consensus. Such a need can lead to a norm—a standard for behaving—in this case, to agree (Gero, 1985). This group is likely to have to move to some other method of deciding, perhaps to compromise.

Compromise

Compromise decisions are those in which the people involved give up some of what they hoped for so that the group can come to a decision. Compromise represents the "best solution" the group can achieve given the diversity of opinion. In the case of deciding about the computer, Tracy may agree to wait for a year. But again, if Tracy thinks that he really needs a new computer, he may be unhappy with a compromise. Others, such as Sally, also may be displeased. If the implementation of your group's decision requires participation of all its members, the compromise may have created a problem—Sally and others may not help.

Majority Vote

Majority vote differs from compromise in that the majority will prevails. Most citizens of a democracy are quite willing to abide by what the majority decides; but if we put it in terms of the decision about the computer, the difficulty with this method of deciding becomes clear. Suppose the group has seven members. Four members vote to allocate the computer on the basis of seniority, and three members vote to give it on the basis of need. Sally believes that she is being held back by an old piece of machinery. How does she react? She says, "I've lost a big one. I have a knot in my stomach. And I'm really angry." Majority vote is a win–lose situation. The majority has "forced" its decision on the rest of the group. Sally and perhaps others are very unhappy.

In ongoing groups that make use of majority vote, different segments may win at different times. This makes losing somewhat easier. Most of us feel better about the situation if we get what we want some of the time. In contrast, if a segment of an ongoing group loses most of the time, cohesiveness and group morale may suffer. Julia Wood (1984) noted that people become anxious to take a vote and achieve closure on an issue. She concludes that the vote is often taken at the expense of group harmony and equal representation of differing points of view. Also, if the majority needs the minority to help implement the decision, the minority may not put much effort into helping.

Decision by the Leader

Sometimes, by virtue of the leader's position, he or she can impose a decision on the group. In these cases it may appear that the group is being given the power to make the decision, but the leader has actually retained that power. Usually the decision is announced after the group has discussed the problem and some solutions. Sometimes, though, the leader may argue in a way that makes it clear that only one solution is acceptable. The leader might say, "Joe, that's an interesting idea. But I don't see how I could recommend that to the boss. Let's consider this other suggestion again." In still other cases, the leader may merely thank group members for their efforts and then dismiss them. She might say, "I appreciate your ideas and input. Thank you for your help. I'll write up a report and make a recommendation."

Group members' reaction to a decision by the leader depends on the circumstances. If members have been misled into thinking that they have the power to decide, they are likely to feel betrayed. If they know that they are only providing input, and if they believe that they are actually being listened to, then they may engage in worthwhile discussion. If the group knows its interaction is only a show, the members may merely go through the motions of discussing the issue and resent the waste of their time.

Imagine again the group deciding about the computer. It reaches a decision, only to find that the computer has been pledged. Perhaps the office manager plays an active role in the group, objecting to every decision but the one she wants. The manager finally imposes a decision. The result is resentment and disillusionment.

Arbitration

Sometimes groups are unable to make a decision and do not want to take a vote on the issue. They would prefer to have some disinterested third party make the decision, a process called **arbitration.** Generally this third party makes a decision that allows each faction of the group to win some issues while losing others. Labor-management negotiations are typically subject to decision by arbitration when the two sides have reached a stalemate and they want to settle the terms of their contract. This method of deciding brings results, but also may create disappointment and lack of interest in implementing the decision.

Each of these methods has advantages and disadvantages. Probably the method with the most advantages is consensus. Beyond achieving consensus lie the other methods, each

Looking Back: A Quick Review

METHODS OF DECIDING

Consensus	All members discuss until they agree.
Compromise	Diversity of opinions forces members to make a decision to settle for less than their ideal.
Majority vote	The majority, through a vote, forces the minority to accept the majority view.
Leader decision	Leader receives input from group and then decides.
Arbitration	A person who is not a member listens to various positions members advocate, then makes a binding decision.

with advantages and disadvantages. Be aware of the differences and the consequences of the method your group comes to use in making decisions. When groups have neither the time nor the ability to achieve consensus, pay careful attention to the implementation of the decision. Not all members may support it enthusiastically.

SUMMARY

The first step in decision making is to decide whether a problem should be handled by an individual or a group. If one person is truly an expert and the group is clearly not or if there is a severe time constraint, then an individual may best make the decision. If the problem is complex or if it is important for the group to accept the decision, then a group should probably make the decision. Keep in mind that the decision might be enhanced by social facilitation of the group.

A second step is to decide which agenda will best suit the situation. John Dewey presents a five-step reflective thinking agenda. These five steps are (1) What is the nature of the problem? (2) What criteria should be set? (3) What alternatives might resolve the causes of this problem? (4) What is the best solution for this problem? (5) What plans will be set in order to implement the solution? We suggest a sixth step: (6) How will the effect of implementing the solution be evaluated?

A decision to use a particular agenda is based on certain characteristics of the task. If the task is difficult, the group may want a relatively complete agenda. If multiple solutions seem likely, the group may want to engage in some idea-generation technique. If high cooperation is needed to make a decision and carry it out, then the group should spend time in step 2 of the reflective thinking format. If the group is not very familiar

Focus on Research

CROWDING AND GROUP MEETINGS

You will have many decisions to make as a planner of a public meeting. One decision to be made is location. Suppose you find yourself in a situation where you are forced to use space that is too small. You expect a crowd that will fill your assembly room to overcrowding. Will the crowded room enhance or detract from your program? Research on crowding can help you know what to expect.

The classic study of overcrowding was conducted by John B. Calhoun in 1962. He established a colony of rats in a quarter-acre pen. The rats were allowed to breed freely. They were given plenty of food and water and were protected from predators. The population of rats stabilized at about 150. The rats mostly grouped in 10- to 12-member groups.

Next, Calhoun built a pen that allowed him to control a feeding area so that 60 to 80 rats had to congregate in a smaller area during feeding times. This high-density situation he created caused a condition he described as a *behavioral sink*. The condition disrupted courting rituals, nest building, mating, territoriality, and more. Conditions deteriorated, and members of the colony died off rapidly. It is obvious that crowding can have profound effects.

What effect does crowding have on people and their perception of an event? Jonathan Freedman's research suggests that high density will make a good situation even better and an unpleasant situation even more unpleasant. He crowded people into rooms where a speech was delivered. Freedman manipulated the situation so feedback in some groups was always positive and in others always negative. Density interacted with pleasantness so that the greatest pleasantness was in the high-density positive feedback situation; the greatest unpleasantness was in the high-density negative feedback situation. So the effects of crowding appear to revolve around the expected nature of the activities being conducted in the space.

J. B. Calhoun (1962). Population density and social pathology. *Scientific American, 206,* 139–148.

J. L. Freedman (1975). *Crowding and behavior.* San Francisco: Freeman.

J. L. Freedman (1979). Reconciling apparent differences between responses of humans and other animals to crowding. *Psychological Review, 86,* 80–85.

with the problem, then it might choose to map the problem carefully by step 1 of the single-question sequence. If a high level of acceptance of a diversified group is needed, then step 2 of the ideal solution sequence might be important.

Vigilant interaction theory suggests that group decision making is enhanced by the group's being thorough and careful (vigilant). Hirokawa recommends the following sequences of activities: examining the problem, clarifying objectives, developing available choices, and examining potential consequences.

A leader can make the most efficient use of an agenda by publishing it in advance, tailoring it to the specific problem, allowing the members to modify the agenda, posting an abbreviated version of the agenda where all can see it, and using the agenda to help group members check the quality of their decision.

Brainstorming, focus groups, nominal group technique, and Delphi are idea-generation techniques. Brainstorming, nominal group technique, and Delphi are ways of getting group participation by withholding criticism while members are listing ideas. Brainstorming is a group technique in that members interact. Nominal group technique and Delphi do not involve member interaction as the group generates ideas. A focus group meets to share ideas in response to questions posed by a facilitator. These questions seek to generate ideas about how people experience a particular idea, product, or problem.

Buzz groups are used to gain input from all the members of large groups. The group is broken into subgroups of six members, and each subgroup has six minutes to generate ideas. The leader of the large group gathers the ideas and presents them to the reassembled large group.

Technology can enhance a group's deliberation. If the members cannot conveniently meet, then they might interact through a teleconference. If the members are part of a network, they might use their computers to interact through a group decision support system (GDSS). The group might use the GDSS in a specially equipped facility. Both teleconferences and GDSS sessions are most productive when the facilitator and members know how to use the technology.

Groups can make decisions through consensus, compromise, majority vote, decision by leader, or arbitration. Consensus means that all members find the decision acceptable. Compromise involves giving up some of what members want so that the group can agree. Majority vote suggests the decision is made on the basis of what most of the members want. Decision by the leader means that the leader listens to the group discussion and then imposes the decision he or she favors. Arbitration is a method of deciding in which a disinterested third party hears each position and makes a decision. Each method of deciding has its advantages and disadvantages and must be carefully considered.

KEY TERMS AND CONCEPTS

arbitration	Delphi	majority vote
brainstorming	electronic meeting system	nominal group technique
buzz group	focus group	programmed decision
compromise	group decision support	situation
computer-mediated culture	system	quality circle
computer-supported	group support system	social facilitation
cooperative work	groupware	vigilant interaction theory
consensus	hitchhiking	

EXERCISES

1. View a videotaped problem-solving discussion. Analyze the structure of the group's problem solving. What were this group's strengths? What were its weaknesses? How could the members improve their problem solving?

2. Observe a classroom group making a decision about a problem. Write a critique to include these points:
   a. The group's organizing effort.
   b. The adequacy of the information shared.
   c. The climate of the group.
   d. The group decision making.
   e. The adequacy of each member's contributions.

3. Form a group of five to seven class members. Prepare for and conduct a problem-solving discussion. Begin by selecting a problem that interests your group. Conduct research regarding the problem. Using one of the agendas presented in this chapter, prepare discussion notes. Finally, using your agenda, conduct the discussion in class with other class members serving as observers.

4. Form a group of five to seven class members. Practice brainstorming with the topic "the good things about student life." Upon completing the brainstorming, answer these questions:
   a. How many ideas were you able to generate? Were you surprised by the number?
   b. How did the brainstorming process work for you? Was it easy to avoid commenting on the suggestions offered? Were any of you able to hitchhike on the ideas of others? How would you suggest the group might avoid problems it encountered?
   c. At what points in a problem-solving discussion would brainstorming be advantageous?

5. Plan a panel discussion on a topic of interest in your community. Specify who your panel members should be and why these people are qualified. Plan an agenda for this meeting and include the questions you would use. Submit a report and include a statement of the issue, names of panel members and their qualifications, and the leader's agenda for the discussion.

6. Recall a group situation where you met an ethical challenge. How did you resolve this? Speculate about other ways of resolving this challenge. Are any of these preferred over what you actually did?

RECOMMENDED WEBSITES

At www.mapnp.org/library/grp_skll/grp_dec./grp_dec.htm, Carter McNamara has assembled many links to sites about group decision making and problem solving. The site gives three categories of small group information: various perspectives, related library links, and online discussion groups.

The site www.hq.nasa.gov/office/hqlibrary/ppm/ppm17.htm is a bibliographical list provided by the NASA Headquarters Library Program/Project concerning small group decision making. The page also contains material on communication and interpersonal skills.

People and Planet is a comprehensive small group network that contains guides to being an effective group, including information on agenda and goal setting: www.peopleandplanet.org/groups/guide/default.php.

Basics of Conducting Focus Groups, www.mapnp.org/library/evaluatn/focusgrp.htm, details how to conduct and plan a focus group session and provides links to other focus group sites.

This site is devoted to links relating to focus groups, including several useful sites on how to conduct telephone focus groups. There is also a form to fill out to join their monthly newsletter: www.mnav.com/qualitative_research.htm.

This link is to the *American Arbitration Association* at www.adr.org/index2.1.jsp, which is a consortium devoted to dispute resolution; the website contains information and background to arbitration, as well as a list of arbitrators.

RECOMMENDED READINGS

R. Y. Hirokawa (2003). Communication and group decision-making efficacy. In R. Y. Hirokawa, R. S. Cathcart, L. A. Samovar, & L. D. Henman, eds. *Small group communication: Theory and practice,* 8th ed. Los Angeles, CA: Roxbury, pp. 125–133.

F. LaFasto & C. Larson (2001). *When teams work best: 6,000 team members and leaders tell what it takes to succeed.* Thousand Oaks, CA: Sage, pp. 1–32.

A. F. Osborn (1993). *Applied imagination,* 3d ed. New York: Scribner's.

S. Worchel, W. Wood, & J. A. Simpson, Eds. (1992). *Group process and productivity.* Newbury Park, CA: Sage.

chapter 4

COMMUNICATION PROCESSES

After reading this chapter you should be able to
- Draw, label, and explain Richard's triangle of meaning.
- Explain how these processes can lead to information processing problems: perception, ambiguity, and too much and too little information.
- Give examples of gender differences in language use.
- Explain differences in verbal behavior of people from low- and high-context cultures.
- Specify the functions of nonverbal messages and show how each function bears upon accuracy in group communication.
- Recall the six nonverbal codes and specify their uses.
- Apply the text's suggestions for improving nonverbal communication in groups.
- Provide examples of gender and cultural differences in the use of gesture, posture and bearing, eye contact, and facial expression.

Think for a moment about a community action group trying to influence the city council to provide better lighting in a west-side neighborhood. Perhaps you can imagine yourself as one of the members, drawn together from diverse backgrounds.

One such group, the Maryknoll Neighborhood Association, wanted funding included in the city's public works budget to double the number of streetlights in the neighborhood. Joe Valenza, the elected leader, suggested that participants list recent security problems and gather a group to go to the next council meeting to present their case. Further, he suggested that they arrive early and sit together. A number of those present spoke in favor of this plan until Sally Davis objected. Instead she argued that two or three of them should visit each council member to plead the case. Others joined her in opposition, and no decision was reached.

A talk with Sally after the meeting revealed that her difficulty with Joe's plan resulted from a misunderstanding. She knew the council had a reputation for not responding to large group pressure. She interpreted what Joe said to mean this type of show of power. Joe intended a small group to present a petition and make a carefully documented presentation.

Obviously, Joe and Sally did not understand each other. Why did they have this problem? What can they do to prevent it from happening next time? The answers to these questions are complex, but the knowledge gained in answering them is worth your time and effort. Knowing how to avoid common verbal and nonverbal problems when they occur in your groups and how to manage them are important skills.

Communication is the verbal and nonverbal processes by which individuals become a group, maintain the group, and coordinate their work. "Communication is the lifeblood that flows through the veins of groups. Communication is not just a tool that group members use; groups are best regarded as a phenomena [sic] that emerges from communication" (Frey, 1994, pp. ix–xiv).

This chapter can help you understand how to improve communication in groups. It begins by exploring verbal communication and some common barriers to it. The discussion of verbal communication concludes with suggestions for improving these skills. The material on nonverbal messages begins by describing their functions. Next, problems related to these functions are raised. The ambiguity of nonverbal communication and the "unintentionality" of it are factors that inhibit nonverbal messages. Finally, ideas to help you improve your nonverbal communication skills are provided.

UNDERSTANDING VERBAL MESSAGES

Imagine yourself as a member of a group appointed to provide suggestions for dealing with a growing drug problem in your community. The group has five members: the owner of the local store, the production manager of a cookie-manufacturing plant (he is from France and has been in this country three years), a pastor of a church (it has a drug counseling program), the principal of a high school, and you (a representative from the college).

The Concept of Meaning

How do you know what words mean as group members exchange messages? How do you know what a particular sentence means? For example, how do you know the meaning of

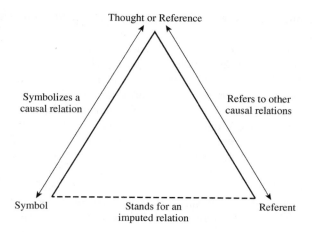

Thought or Reference

Symbolizes a
causal relation

Refers to other
causal relations

Symbol

Stands for an
imputed relation

Referent

FIGURE 4.1
The Triangle of Meaning

Source: Figure "Thought or Reference" from C. K. Ogden & I. A. Richards (1923). Reprinted by permission of Harcourt Brace Jovanovich, Inc.

the phrase *drug problem,* a central idea that your group wants to discuss? You will not be surprised to learn that numerous theories attempt to answer such questions. One explanation was developed by I. A. Richards (Ogden & Richards, 1923), whose characterization of meaning is referred to as the **triangle of meaning.** The diagram in Figure 4.1 shows how symbols, thoughts, and their referents are related.

One easy way to understand Richard's triangle is to think of it in terms of the drug problem your group is to consider. Suppose we turn back to the question "What is the meaning of the term *drug problem?*" You might imagine the production manager saying, "A drug problem is a situation where a significant number of people in a community are abusing drugs." The pastor might say, "A drug problem is the emotional trauma a person and his or her family feel as the drug begins to control the person's life and relationships." The high school principal might say, "Meet me behind the football stadium tomorrow at 4 P.M., and I'll show you people smoking pot and being wasted."

Each of these statements represents a different kind of meaning for the term *drug problem.* The first, "A drug problem is a situation where a significant number of people in a community are abusing drugs," is a *dictionary definition* of the *symbol* drug problem. It stands at the lower left corner of the triangle of meaning. The second meaning for the symbol drug problem is a report of a member's *thoughts,* "A drug problem is the emotional trauma a person and his or her family feel as the drug begins to control the person's life and relationships." This "thought" meaning stands at the top corner of the triangle. The third meaning for the symbol is an actual presence of the drug problem, the *referent.* A **referent** is the object or event to which the symbol (usually a word) refers. It is represented by viewing the actual situation, the problem, and is expressed by the school principal, "Meet me behind the football stadium tomorrow at 4 P.M. and I'll show you people smoking pot and being completely wasted." The triangle's lower right corner represents this kind of meaning.

At this point many students may ask, "So what?" The remaining markings on the triangle can help you to understand language and some misconceptions related to its use. Look now at the part of the triangle that shows the **symbol** (word) and the referent (thing). The breaks in the line show that there is no direct connection between words and objects they represent. For example, if you said "drug problem" to any of these committee members, would they point to the same situation you had in mind? Some would; others would not. If you move the other way, that is, from the referent to the symbol, perhaps you can see the problem. Suppose you took someone to the corner of Main and Spring at 9 P.M. Suppose further that you asked the person to tell you what he sees. He says, "This is the corner of Main and Spring with some people standing around." You are thinking "drug problem" because you see people smoking marijuana; he is thinking "geography." The same referent has produced different symbols. There is obviously some relatedness, but the relatedness is indirect.

Notice the solid line between the symbol and the thought (or referent) on the left side of the triangle. This line represents a causal relationship. Using symbols, "drug problem" does cause the person hearing it to recall his or her experience and meaning for it (as is the case for the person using it). Moreover, having the idea or thought requires the person to produce the term (symbol) in order to communicate or think about the situation. Thus there is a two-way relationship between symbol and thought. Keep in mind, though, that this meaning is associated with these *people's experiences*. And further, it is a "problem" because these people have organized what they observed and have constructed meaning *based on their own experiences*.

One very important relationship remains: the symbol to thought to referent relationship suggested. Meaning between a symbol and referent is achieved by means of the thought process. To say this another way, **meaning**—the relationship between symbol and referent—is a constructed reality in the head of the person using the symbol. The committee members investigating the "drug problem" may experience their first difficulty because of this notion and never know it. If you know how meaning is related to symbols and referents that essentially represent your own experience, you may be able to take some action to avoid problems. The degree of difficulty your group will experience is related to the degree to which members' experiences overlap and the degree to which they share and negotiate meanings. It also will depend on how skillfully members handle several common verbal communication problems.

PROBLEMS WITH VERBAL COMMUNICATION

Various difficulties in small groups prevent accurate processing and understanding of members' messages. Sometimes perception is a problem. **Perception** is the process of becoming aware of people, objects, and events by taking in information through the senses. A group member might focus your attention on a message in ways that cause you to be misled. At other times, the *ambiguity* of our language creates difficulties. For example, you may use abstract, difficult-to-define words in your group. Or perhaps the way people or things are labeled presents problems. And groups encounter two other problems. They sometimes gather so much or so little information that they experience information-processing problems.

Perceptual Difficulties

Perception occurs in a step-by-step progression. We take in information. We organize it. We interpret and evaluate what we have received. The process sounds simple, but it is not. Many perceptual problems grow out of three characteristics of perception: (1) Perception is a subjective process. (2) People strive for stability in their perceptions. (3) People assume that what they perceive is meaningful.

Subjectivity   When members observe their group interact, they are selective in what they notice. Members select what is important to them and omit what is not. Selectivity means they "tune in" to what they want to hear; they "tune out" what they do not want to hear. This selectivity can create problems in groups. Take this example. Suppose you are part of a training department. You and several other members meet to discuss a schedule of training programs. Several ideas are discussed, and the group ends up with five programs. As group leader you summarize what you think is the consensus. But Jean objects: "We said we would do career planning instead of sessions on computers." Who is right? After additional discussion you find you are correct and Jean "tuned out."

You can combat such an error in several ways. One is to say back in your own words what you think was said. In other contexts you also might check your perceptions with a friend who was present as well. Often these techniques help you discover differences that can be talked about. Finally, in a group meeting you may need to resolve differences by going directly to the leader of the meeting.

Stability   We usually expect group members to behave consistently over time. We know from past experience in the group how an individual behaves. We know what is important to that person, and therefore we expect things not to change. We expect stability.

For our purposes, **stability** is the same as predictability of behavior. We expect the president of the Kiwanis Club, who regularly starts meetings on time, to begin on time. We expect a classmate who seems always to be late to walk in late. We barely pay attention if our predictions are correct, but we notice if the president is late or the student is early. The trouble is that we develop biases on the basis of our expectations. If someone's behavior is not stable, you may distrust that person. Moreover, we tend to anticipate one another, sometimes wrongly, because we expect stability. If you *think* John is going to take a particular stand, you may *hear* that stand whether he takes it or not.

Beyond being aware of this bias, try to avoid it. Check out what a group member is saying—especially with those you know well. The members you know well are the ones you are most likely to anticipate and, therefore, perceive inaccurately.

Meaningfulness   We generally assume what is being said is meaningful. Even when something makes no sense, we try to find a meaning in it. The principle of **meaningfulness** means that you *may* perceive things in what a group member said that are not there—you filled in the "holes" to make the message meaningful.

Overcoming this perceptual problem is difficult, since you may not know you are filling in missing parts. So ask questions when something is not clear. Make it your general policy to go over the conclusions informally with a friend after a group meeting. If you are leading a group, summarize your group's progress and conclusions frequently.

Abstraction in Language Use

To understand the idea of abstraction, consider the terms that could be used to describe the leader of the chamber of commerce. A member might say, "Jamal conducts our meetings in an orderly fashion and with considerable skill and grace." The member could be more and more abstract, saying, "Jamal leads our group well." Or perhaps she says simply, "Jamal leads." Each time the member chooses some level of abstraction. In this case the speaker moves further away from identifying Jamal's leadership characteristics.

General semanticist S. I. Hayakawa (1991) suggested an "abstraction ladder" to help people visualize this process. Terms on such a ladder look like the representation in Figure 4.2. The lower on the ladder, the easier it is to visualize the detail. The higher up on the ladder, the more general the description.

How does understanding abstraction help us in group communication? **Abstractions** are generalizations that allow us to talk about the similarities among several objects. We can say the word *man* or *woman* and thus classify people into one or the other category. This allows us to generalize about a group of similar people. But the higher the level of abstraction, the more we must ignore the uniqueness that makes objects different. This can obviously lead to serious group communication problems.

Dale G. Leathers (1969) used confederates to introduce abstract language into the deliberations of discussion groups. **Confederates** are people working for the experimenter who pose as subjects. Suppose in a discussion about how to improve participation, a member interjected the terms *relational deterioration, tangential motives,* and *disparaging interaction*. Without definition and illustration, we may not know what the person means. The result may be frustrating and disruptive. Leathers found that these abstract statements disrupted the discussion. The more abstract the statements, the more disruptive. Discussants became confused, sometimes tense. Some members withdrew.

Labels and Language

The language we use in our talk about one another shapes the way we think about these people and also the way they think about themselves and our relationship with them. The use of racist or sexist language in interactions can seriously affect the relationships and spirit of cooperation that are so necessary in a group. Sexist and racist language usually define relationships as superior or inferior, which is counterproductive.

We all use language we learned as we were growing up. So our use of language may seem automatic. It is possible to change the language you use if you wish. The discussion

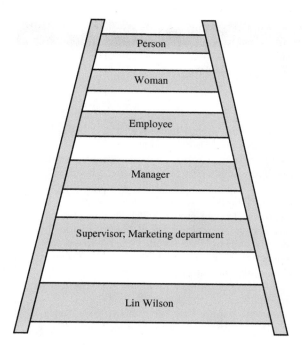

FIGURE 4.2
Abstraction Ladder

throughout this book illustrates a style of writing that reflects the author's view of equality. The text uses the sexually neutral plural (they), the he-or-she structure, and balanced references to male and female roles. Work on the labels you use if you need to do so.

Too Much Information

An employee of a public accounting firm said of a recent group meeting: "For me there was too much to remember. I tried to keep track, but there were so many things and some of them didn't pertain to me." That statement reflects **information overload.** Everyone can experience information overload—especially when meeting with a large group.

Information theorists have been studying overload for quite some time. George A. Miller (1965) has calculated that an individual can effectively work with seven plus or minus two items at one time. Thus if you have a group of seven and each member presents one idea, the members of the group may be at or near capacity.

The group situation is especially prone to overload because a group often considers multiple ideas. Wise leaders encourage members to generate many ideas. But the group may experience overload. Consider the problem a company that manufactures paper clips faced. It decided to run a series of advertisements to call attention to its company's name. It wanted the series to focus on imaginative uses for paper clips. Sanchez

A Question of Ethics and Responsibility

THE VERBAL ATTACK

The planning committee for educational activities of a large urban church is meeting to discuss adding additional church-school classes. Part of the committee's task is to find space for some new classes. This involves shifting some existing classes to smaller space so that larger space can be allocated to classes that are anticipated to be large. Harold Rodriguez is a member of one of the classes, "The Beginning," being considered for a change to a smaller room. Harold is also a member of the planning committee, but members of the committee are unaware of his membership in that class, and he is not volunteering the information.

Harold sees the move as a "slap in the face" for his class. The room that is being considered not only is smaller but also has less desirable furnishings.

He is vigorously opposing the idea of moving his class, although he is not stating the real reasons for his opposition. He also has chosen to verbally attack the chair of this committee, Lisa. Lisa is obviously stunned by the attack and is not coping well with Harold's tactics. She does not have much experience leading groups and is leading this one only because her pastor asked her to do so. She knows that Harold's behavior is highly inappropriate, but all that she can think to do is to quickly adjourn the meeting. An hour of seven people's time has been wasted without anything being accomplished.

Assume you are Lisa. What will be your strategy for dealing with Harold when you meet again? How will you deal with his verbal attack? Be specific.

Advertising believed that the way to begin such a project was to gather a group of people to generate ideas. Amazing as it sounds, the group generated 23 ideas. The group created a communication problem that it had to address. The group used some strategies we discuss in the next section for dealing with this information overload.

Too Little Information

Some groups operate with too little information. Perhaps the members do not possess the needed information. Perhaps members do not realize the need to present the information they do have. Stewart (1998) found that the amount of information the various members of a group are willing to share is important. It turns out that the more information shared the more likely a good decision will evolve from the group deliberation. Perhaps this is not surprising, but perhaps more interesting is that groups share information that most members know first (Larson, 1997). So it is important to encourage members to get beyond that which first occurs to them to share to information that others may not know. The advantage of having multiple inputs of information is lost if too few members participate. A study by John Oetzel (1998) demonstrated that better decisions were made when there was more equal participation in the effort.

This problem often has as its root the failure to ask appropriate questions. The questioning process often guides a group in the collection of information. So failure to have adequate information may be a result of not asking the right questions.

Asking questions can ensure that a group addresses the important issues in the discussion, has adequate information, and manages relationships effectively. Each aspect of asking questions is important to the effective processing of information.

Questions to guide the discussion   Questions that guide a discussion deal with group process. General questions that are useful in guiding group process make up the agendas in Chapter 3. These questions help orient and guide the group. Questions also are asked that seek guidance and orientation. You can get a grasp of what guiding means if you think of these questions as seeking procedures or orientation. Here are some questions that seek procedures:

How shall we attack this problem?

What agenda will we use to guide us in making our decision?

Do we move to solutions next?

Questions that seek orientation are like these:

What is our goal in this discussion?

Have we completed our work with criteria?

Have we all said what we wanted to say about the causes of this problem?

Questions to ensure adequate information   A group must have adequate information to perform its task effectively. This information takes the form of fact, opinion, or value. We made the distinction between fact and opinion (inferences) in Chapter 2. Recall that a **fact** refers to a piece of information that can be verified or that has been repeatedly reported as true. Here are some questions that seek facts:

How many incidents of vandalism were reported in the neighborhood?

Did the president say that she was aware of this spending problem?

Sally, what did you find out about eligibility requirements for this scholarship?

Questions of **opinion,** in contrast to questions of fact, ask for a conclusion, an inference based on someone's observation, or an interpretation. In the case of small group deliberations, these are questions about others' opinions, interpretations, and judgments about facts the group is processing. Examples of questions of opinion are

Does the department need additional secretarial help?

Does this candidate meet the needs of our church?

What would be the effects of shifting the hours of operation from 8 A.M. until 5 P.M. to 7 A.M. until 4 P.M.?

A question about **value** calls for members to offer their judgments about the merits of an idea. Asking for a value statement suggests that some comparison is being made to something else. Here are examples of questions assessing value:

Would it be more beneficial to add buses to shuttle people to the work site or should we build additional parking spaces instead?

Would it be better to plan just two spectacular events for the year rather than several smaller ones?

How well has the decision not to add a second family car served us?

Questions to maintain a productive climate and relationships   Questions that ask members to consider climate and/or relationships can be important. The relationships we develop can have a significant effect on our willingness to work productively. Tension can rise if signs of frustration, anger, boredom, or alienation are ignored. Showing concern

Focus on Research

GENDER AND RELATIONAL CONTROL

The language differences that we observe may result from the sex roles a person performs rather than from the person's biological sex. Research by Donald Ellis and Linda McCallister supports this idea. They identified experimental subjects as masculine, feminine, or androgynous. Next, they looked at the language the subjects used in group discussions to see if each of these types used a particular language pattern. They found that language use does vary among these three types.

One area that was particularly interesting was relational control. They found that the language used suggested dominance ("one up"), submissiveness ("one down"), or equivalence (mutual identification). Masculine-type subjects used significantly more dominance language than either the feminine or the androgynous subjects. Feminine-type subjects used language that was slightly more submissive and

more equivalent than the androgynous subjects. Finally, they found the feminine subjects' submissiveness and equivalence behaviors were much greater than the masculine subjects' were.

These three types also responded differently to a person's bid to control. Masculine types generally responded with a counterattempt to dominate the conversation—producing a series of one-up interactions. Feminine types generally responded to a bid for control unpredictably—producing a random use of dominance, submission, and equivalence behaviors. Androgynous types responded with a symmetrical interaction and then moved to equivalence, sometimes acting deferentially as they moved toward equivalence.

D. G. Ellis & L. McCallister (1980). Relational control sequences in sex-typed and androgynous groups. *Western Journal of Speech Communication*, 44, 35–49.

about them and bringing them out so they can be dealt with are functions of the relationship question. Some examples of relationship-oriented questions are these:

Now that we have had a chance to get acquainted, do we all believe as though we know one another well enough to move on?

Mike, you seem a bit on the quiet side today. Is something wrong?

Is anybody else upset with the way we are working together today?

There is great power in asking the right question at the right moment. Most of the time someone will try to answer the question, and the group's effort benefits.

Communication Apprehension in Groups

Communication apprehension is "an individual's level of fear or anxiety associated with either real or anticipated communication with another person or persons (McCroskey & Richmond, 1992, p. 368). You are not alone if you feel anxious about communicating. About 20 percent of the U.S. population experience very high levels of communication apprehension. About 75 percent experience apprehension when faced with the prospect of making a presentation (Richmond & McCroskey, 1995). And McCroskey and Richmond have reported "it is not an exaggeration to suggest that CA [communication apprehension] may be the single most important factor in predicting communication behavior in a small group (1992, p. 368). Communication apprehension can have a significant effect on the group too. When a member experiences high apprehension, he or she may be reluctant to participate in a group discussion. In this case the valuable knowledge and skill of the member are lost and the group suffers.

You probably know if you are a person who experiences high communication apprehension. So what can you do to help yourself join in and thereby help your group to a successful outcome?

Understand Your Situation Is Not Unusual   We hope the statistics we quoted provide a little perspective on your situation. Understand this is a normal feeling for many people. It is quite possible that others in your group are anxious about participating. We hope it provides some encouragement to know that you are not alone in this situation.

Try to Relax Physically   Advice we often give students of public speaking who are experiencing anxiety is to breathe several deep breaths in and out, slowly. Many of these students experience a slower pulse rate and are calmer. Perhaps you will too. Try, too, to focus away from your physical feelings on to the people and discussion of the group.

Be Well Prepared   Well-prepared members are those that have done their "homework." They generally have something to say regardless of the topic the group is addressing at the moment. We hope being well prepared will provide you a sense of confidence.

Preparation is a significant help because it goes a long way to eliminate the fear that you don't have much of importance to say about the issue.

Visualize Success   Success is, of course, what you are aiming for in this situation and the group. You can find a quiet place before your class and sit and relax. Try to visualize yourself communicating effectively as you have in other situations. Take the materials you have prepared for the discussion and rehearse saying them as you would if you were speaking in your group. Think positively and try to get yourself in a state of confidence.

Gender and Communication

The term **gender** refers to learned characteristics and psychological attributes of masculinity and femininity. In contrast, the term **sex** refers to the biological characteristics of a person. Of course, what we say about gender and language must be understood as tentative, because female and male gender roles have been changing dramatically.

Gender is a factor that affects small group communication. While research supports the idea that there are differences in the ways males and females use communication that come from biological gender, it also suggests the psychological differences may be at least as important (Stafford, 2000). Researchers conclude that gender differences "characterize women as using communication to connect with, support, and achieve closeness with others, and men as using communication to accomplish some task and to assert their individuality" (Woodward, Rosenfeld, & May, 1996, p. 260).

Lea Stewart and her colleagues (1990) provide a review of research on gender differences. The research report suggests differences in initiating behaviors, interrupting, and verbosity. Women initiate more topics than men, and yet more topics introduced by women are dropped from the communication. Women and men use questioning differently, too. Men ask questions to acquire information, whereas women do so to maintain conversations. Women also speak more tentatively and differentially than men. Finally, men talk more and interrupt women more often than women do. In one study 96 percent of all interruptions were men interrupting women (Zimmerman & West, 1975).

Looking Back: A Quick Review

VERBAL COMMUNICATION PROBLEMS

Inaccurate perception.	Too much information.
Abstract ideas.	Too little information.
Labeling things and people.	Gender differences.

Gender differences in communication behavior have been found in small group research. Findings suggest that both men and women are capable of similar leadership behavior in groups and that neither sex is more effective. Patricia Andrews (1992) concludes that gender is a less important consideration than are the uniqueness of the person and that person's skills. Findings reported by Georgia Duerst-Lahti (1990) support this conclusion. Contrary to earlier reports, she found that successful high-status businesswomen were not "frozen out" of conversations. Women, in fact, talked more often, gave more indications of verbal support, and challenged men freely. The ideas of the women studied were included in the final product, suggesting that they had real power in the group. The fact that these successful women had power may actually be a significant factor in these outcomes. Vivian DeKlerk (1991) found that the amount of power possessed by a man or woman seemed to explain the use of expletives, believed to be a male stereotypical language, better than the individual's gender did. Perhaps as the balance of power between men and women becomes more equal, the number of linguistic differences will shrink.

Unfortunately, men still have more status than women in mixed-gender groups. Information provided by a male member is more likely to be used in the group's decision than the same contribution by a female (Propp, 1995).

CULTURE AND VERBAL COMMUNICATION

Cultural diversity can provide a significant advantage to a group if it develops its own culture from the combination of cultures brought to it. The creation of unique norms and procedures becomes a basis for developing members' group-related values, beliefs, and attitudes. The convergence of member's values, beliefs, and attitudes serves to enhance their feelings of identity and cohesiveness. Race and culture are just two of the many factors that make groups diverse. People differ in age, profession, economic status, and social standing. The factor to take into consideration is how your group differs in ways that may affect important task characteristics.

This section addresses communication differences that result from one's culture and dysfunctional and functional responses to diversity. We begin with a discussion of cultural styles of expression.

How Culture Affects Communication

Language use in culture is classified as low-context or high-context (Hall, 1959). A **low-context culture** uses language primarily to express thoughts, ideas, and feelings as clearly and logically as possible. The meaning of what is communicated lies in the spoken words. On the other hand, a **high-context culture** uses subtle cues, often nonverbal, with the aim of maintaining social harmony. Communicators from these cultures learn what is meant by examining the nonverbal behaviors, context of the message, history of the relationship, and the social rules governing interaction. Table 4.1 presents some important characteristics of low- and high-context communication styles.

TABLE 4.1   Characteristics of Low- and High-Context Communication

Variable	Low Context	High Context
Information	Much of the information is in the explicit verbal messages. There is not as much reliance on the context in terms of relationship, time, and place.	Much of the information is in the contextual cues, such as situation, relationship, time, and place. There is not as much reliance on explicit verbal messages.
Aims	Opinions and needs are stated directly. Communicators may attempt directly to persuade. Self-expression is important.	Opinions and needs are stated indirectly. Communicators will abstain from directly saying no. Relational harmony is important.
Directness	Clear, eloquent speech is valued, and verbal fluency is important.	Ambiguity and silence are valued, and an ability to talk "around the point" is important.

Language varies on the basis of *directness*. Dominant cultures of Canada and the United States are low-context cultures. Most Asian and Middle Eastern cultures fall within the high-context designation. Where members of U.S. culture might resent the indirect approach, people from Asian cultures are likely to avoid clear communication if it threatens another person's ability to "save face." A group member's attempt to communicate effectively with a member from another culture can be enhanced by understanding this distinction.

Language also varies across cultures in its *succinctness* (Gudykunst & Ting-Toomey, 1988). For example, a speaker of Arabic will use language that is rich and expressive. A person from the general American culture will often engage in "talkativeness." In contrast, Native Americans and Asians may prefer more succinct language. A Native American would also probably handle an ambiguous social situation such as meeting a person by using more silence. The silence of a group member from another culture may not mean what one might think. Knowing about the idea of succinctness may help you communicate cross-culturally.

Finally, language may vary from culture to culture on the basis of *formality* (Gudykunst & Ting-Toomey, 1988). People from Canada, the United States, and Australia generally approach their relationships informally. Many parts of Africa and Asia, on the other hand, are careful to define the other person's position in a relationship by using distinctive grammar. For example, different language is used when speaking to a friend, an acquaintance, a stranger whose background is known, and a complete stranger. Language used may also suggest social status.

Be aware of these varying aspects of high context cultures when your group has diversity in terms of high and low context cultures. Knowing this makes it easy to understand why people from contrasting cultures might not understand each other's formality or informality. Respect for a member of another culture's notion of formality can be an important factor in establishing relationships in groups.

Dysfunctional Responses to Diversity

Larkey (1996) and Thomas (1995) suggest four dysfunctional responses to diversity. These may be familiar to you because all of us have been a minority at some time.

A first response is *exclusion*. The members who are the majority exclude the minority. This means that the majority members initiate communication with and respond primarily to other majority members. This means the majority may focus on topics of interest to them and direct conversation away from topics of interest to the minority. This also means that nonverbal cues of inclusion, such as eye contact, will be directed toward majority members and away from minority members.

A second dysfunctional response is to *maintain one's own communication style* when other styles are present in the group. There is no attempt made by majority members to accommodate or match other group member styles. For example, a member grew up in a part of the country where the phrase "you guys" meant both males and females. When he found himself in a different culture where this phrase was not used and was interpreted as meaning only males, he refused to change—even when the offensive nature of its use was pointed out to him.

A third response is to *refuse to consider ideas* that do not fit within the majority culture's perspective. This creates two problems. It limits the pool of ideas from which the group has to work and thus stifles creativity. It also limits the majority's understanding of those who make up the minority.

A fourth response is to *think and convey negative evaluations* of minority members. This is an especially dysfunctional behavior. This behavior will likely generate defensive behaviors from minority members and an unwillingness to cooperate. It is obvious that such a climate is extremely detrimental to effective group deliberations and goal achievement.

Functional Responses to Diversity

There are a variety of strategies suggested by the research literature for managing diversity effectively. We present six here.

First, learn about the cultures represented in the group (Triandis, 1995). You might set aside time early in your group's deliberations to talk about the cultures present. Ask individuals from each culture to talk about their language use—verbal and nonverbal, customs, and food, for example.

Second, discover and focus on similarities among the cultures (Triandis, 1995). Ask members to share how they have found their culture to be similar to that of other members. Talk about these areas of similarity. Learning about areas of similarity helps focus members and overcome perceived differences.

Third, talk about how differences can be an advantage for the group. Some of these advantages are greater creativity, more alternatives, a stronger end product, and even more interesting interaction.

Fourth, focus on interdependent or cooperative goals (Triandis, 1995; Wong, Tjosvold, & Lee, 1992). Spend time discussing what your group is trying to accomplish, why it is doing so, and what benefits can be gained from task accomplishment.

Looking Back: A Quick Review

RESPONDING TO DIVERSITY

Functional	Learn about other cultures.
	Focus on member similarities.
	Discover the advantages differences bring.
	Attempt to achieve interdependence.
	Attempt to set cooperative goals.
	Adopt procedures to promote equal status.
Dysfunctional	Adopt an attitude of exclusivity.
	Be unwilling to accommodate.
	Refuse to consider minority member views.
	Negatively evaluate minority members.

Talk also about how goal achievement will benefit individual members. Focus on the group's long-term goal and not its immediate, short-term goals. Long-term goals are often more general than short-term goals and, therefore, easier to agree upon.

Fifth, try to promote equal status by adopting group discussion procedures that balance the amount of talking. One such procedure is nominal group technique. Another is brainstorming. Discussion procedures such as these are covered in Chapter 3.

Finally, focus on the individuality of the other members and away from their cultural identity (Oetzel, 1995). Try to view yourself and others as unique individuals with unique personalities. You might set aside some time for social talk with refreshments to facilitate this process. You might even play a get-acquainted game that causes people to mix and get to know each other if that is appropriate. More equal participation generally results when group members are seen as individuals.

INCREASING VERBAL EFFECTIVENESS

Knowing the nature of language and how meaning is derived can help you avoid some communication difficulties. Problems of perceptual bias, language ambiguity, and information overload may all be treated by any group member who knows how. This section provides advice for handling these and other communication problems in groups.

PROBLEM   You aren't sure that your group understands you. What can you do?

LANGUAGE AND/OR SUGGESTIONS

1. Recall the ladder of abstraction. Try to keep what you have to say as concrete as possible.

2. Include examples and illustrations of what you mean. (This is what a public speaker does to increase clarity.) For example, if you are talking about the drug problem, you might recount a specific case.

3. Watch for nonverbal cues. If you see that people seem puzzled or distracted, clarify or give an example. You might say, "I'm not sure I was clear. I'll try again."

4. Ask someone to summarize the progress the group has made and/or ideas that have been presented so far. Or ask someone to paraphrase so that you can see if people understand. You might say, "I presented several ideas and want to find out if I've been clear. John, would you mind feeding them back to me?"

5. You may be experiencing an organizational problem instead of an abstraction difficulty. In this case, state one point at a time. Then be careful to organize what you have to say. You could follow this simple outline: (a) Show the relationship of what you are saying to the remarks of the last speaker(s), (b) state the idea, (c) explain the idea, (d) develop the idea through examples or evidence, and (e) show that what you have said relates to the topic.

PROBLEM   You're confused or not clear about what has just been said by a group member.

LANGUAGE AND/OR SUGGESTIONS

1. Ask the speaker to give an example or illustration. You might say, "John, I'm having trouble understanding your point. Could you give me an example?"

2. Paraphrase what the person has said in less abstract terms. Say, "I want to make sure I've understood. Let me see if I understand. You said. . . ."

3. Sometimes ambiguity is the problem when you do not understand the specific task the group is undertaking. Ask the group to focus briefly on where it has been and where it is going. You could say, "I'm trying to put Jill's comments into the context. Could we take a moment to review?"

4. Ask a direct question. Say, "Emile, I want to be sure I've understood you. Do you mean . . . ?"

PROBLEM   You want to guard against any perceptual bias that you may be experiencing with respect to what a member has just said.

LANGUAGE AND/OR SUGGESTIONS

1. Paraphrase the content back to the speaker to check for accuracy.

2. Check your interpretation with a colleague from your group.

3. Take notes. Often this focuses your attention and will help you to get more of the message.

4. Try to put yourself in the place of the person speaking. If you can empathize with the speaker you may "tune in" to what he or she is saying and thus avoid your bias. Imagine what the person was thinking and feeling when experiencing the event. Try to figure out how the speaker is connecting the ideas to what has been said.

5. Paraphrase the content of the person's message; then try to formulate a good question. Often the question might relate to the significance of the issue. You might say, "How does this relate to [the previous issue or decision]?"

PROBLEM   Information overload is hampering your group's productivity.

LANGUAGE AND/OR SUGGESTIONS

1. Combine related issues. Channel capacity can be increased by placing items into a larger class. To illustrate, group the causes of a problem under two or three categories. "I see these causes as falling under three categories. [Name the categories.] Could we group them under each category and then discuss the ideas in each?"

2. Try to eliminate solutions or ideas that do not seem relevant. You might say, "We've been working so hard on generating ideas that we have made a long list. Are there any that we might be able to cross off in favor of others?"

3. See if you can combine and reformulate the ideas or solutions. Perhaps the other group members can help. You might begin by pointing out the problems created by too many proposals and then talk about how to combine them.

NONVERBAL MESSAGES

Nonverbal communication pervades every message you communicate. Consider the vast number of nonverbal cues a group experiences—cues from the physical setting, seating of members, appearance and clothing, body movement and posture, eye contact and movement, facial expressions, and voice. These give group members information about how other members perceive them and the message sender (Leathers, 1979) and are important in group settings (Infante, Rancer, & Womack, 2003).

This section begins with a discussion of how nonverbal messages function. Next, problems related to these functions are raised. These include the ambiguity of nonverbal communication and the "unintentionality" of nonverbal communication. Finally, ideas that can help you improve your nonverbal communication are provided.

Understanding Nonverbal Messages

Consider the impact of the arrangement of seats in a college curriculum committee meeting. It is traditional for this group to elect a chairperson at the first meeting. Prior to this meeting, one member, Bob, decided it would be an interesting experience to lead the

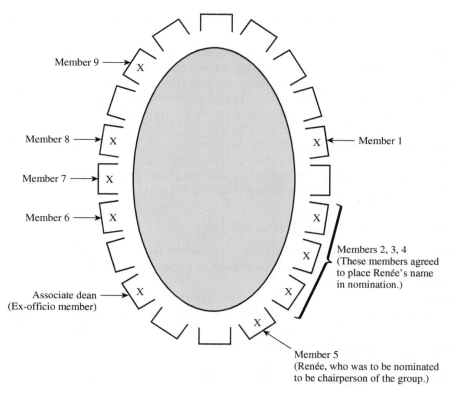

Member 9

Member 8

Member 7

Member 6

Associate dean
(Ex-officio member)

Member 1

Members 2, 3, 4
(These members agreed
to place Renée's name
in nomination.)

Member 5
(Renée, who was to be nominated
to be chairperson of the group.)

Where would you sit if you wanted to share in the leadership of this group?

FIGURE 4.3
Seating Arrangement of College Curriculum Committee

group. He approached a member to seek nomination. This person told Bob that she and two other members had decided to nominate Renée. Bob arrived at the meeting and noticed the seating arrangement in Figure 4.3. What do you make of what you see?

Renée had taken a central place near the table head. Those who intended to nominate her sat together on her immediate right. On the other side was a group of three members, 6, 7, and 8. Members 1 and 9 sat away from other members—isolating themselves. No one sat next to the associate dean. Where would you sit if you wanted to assume leadership? If the placement and seating of people do make a communicative difference, then observing the seating pattern could be useful. Where people sit may provide information about the group's role structure and influence patterns.

A person who wants to maximize his or her leadership contributions would sit in a central location. Three central seats are available: one at either end of the table and one to the right of the associate dean. Here good eye contact can be maintained.

In addition, the seats are as central as that taken by Renée. (Incidentally, she *was* chosen to lead.)

Other status and role considerations became apparent as the group met. It turned out that members 1 and 9 were isolates—they communicated less than any of the others. Members 6, 7, and 8 were acquaintances. Because they had different attitudes and expertise and because they rarely met elsewhere, they were active in the meetings but never acted in concert. Bob took the seat next to the dean. He tried to influence discussion in productive directions.

This example is presented to give you an appreciation of nonverbal messages. Of course, they work simultaneously with other nonverbal messages. We turn next to a discussion of how these nonverbal messages function. Some pitfalls are suggested, and some advice about how to improve your nonverbal behavior is given.

The Functions of Nonverbal Messages

Nonverbal messages serve four basic functions: *reinforcement, modification, substitution,* and *regulation.* The example of the seating arrangement of the college curriculum committee illustrates all four.

A word of caution seems wise. People do not use nonverbal systems uniformly, so much of what you sense of members' nonverbal communication may be somewhat ambiguous to everyone. These four categories, then, describe how nonverbal signals function, but they cannot describe how a particular member uses cues for particular meanings. Where another's nonverbal messages are ambiguous, it is best to ask for a translation into words. Now, let's consider these functions.

Reinforcement   Sometimes nonverbal messages reinforce the verbal message by *repeating* what the words say. The seating arrangement was described, and a picture of what it looked like was produced. You might describe the layout of a parking lot and also use your hands and arms to gesture in ways that will repeat the message. This repetition introduces redundancy into the communication, which helps the listener to understand.

Facial expressions, like gestures, also serve to reinforce. You use facial expressions to *elaborate* on meaning as you describe feelings or emotions. For example, a group member—in recounting the frustration she experienced in interviewing a reluctant expert—tensed the muscles of her nose, tightened the muscles of her arms, and gestured rigidly. Clearly understanding her emotional state was an important part of processing the message.

Nonverbal messages also reinforce the verbal by *accenting* important points. Certain words were emphasized as the seating arrangement of the college curriculum committee was discussed. Typesetters use italics for emphasis. You do essentially the same thing with your voice, face, hands, arms, and body. Group members emphasize the important aspects of a message by raising volume, setting words off by pauses, and gesturing with their hands. These reveal the organization and key ideas of the message.

Modification   Suppose that Renée, the chairperson nominee, sat in the central position she chose but avoided eye contact. Perhaps her face carried an expression of disinterest; maybe she even slouched. When asked if she would be willing to serve if elected, she said, "Well . . . uh . . . I suppose I would serve if elected." Would you believe her verbal message? Her physical behavior contradicts her verbal message. Sometimes nonverbal behavior is purposeful; sometimes it seems to slip out without the speaker's knowing it. But people generally believe and use it to modify what a person says. In this case, what is far more likely is that Renée's behavior, as described here, would not have been clear to everyone. Still the group's success may be in jeopardy if members did pay attention to the nonverbal component. Renée's cues of disinterest were overlooked. The group had elected her to do the important job of leading and could be buying trouble.

Focus on Research

NONVERBAL INDICATORS OF STATUS AND POWER

Nonverbal cues can be an important indicator of status and power (Leffler, Gilespie, & Conaty, 1982). People in a group may claim status and power through such cues as an unwavering gaze, a firm handshake, a relaxed poised posture, or an unsmiling face. Lee and Ofshe conducted an interesting study of nonverbal dominance cues. Subjects read a summary of a personal-injury lawsuit and estimated a monetary award of about $10,000. Next, subjects viewed a video of a man arguing that the plaintiff should receive only $2,000. The researchers held the content of this man's argument constant, but they varied the nonverbal behavior. The three nonverbal behavior situations are as follows:

1. *Deference-demanding condition*   The man spoke in a loud, firm, rapid delivery. His talk had few hesitations and little stumbling over words. His posture was relaxed, he dropped his eyebrows to make a point, and he looked up. He wore a tie and sport coat.
2. *Deferential condition*   The man spoke softly, hesitantly, and slowly. He used pauses, searched for words, and said "umm" and "ah." He sat rigidly but made wringing hand movements, and he looked down now and then. He wore a T-shirt.

3. *Neutral condition*   The man used a moderate speaking rate, did not mumble, and hesitated only occasionally. He had a relaxed posture but did not use facial cues such as raising his eyebrows or making extensive direct eye contact. He wore a sport shirt.

Subjects who saw the deference-demanding speaker lowered their initial award by an average of $4,273. Those who saw the neutral speaker dropped their award by an average of $2,426. Interestingly, those who saw the deferential speaker increased their award by $2,843. It seems obvious that how something is said nonverbally can have a powerful influence.

M. Lee & R. Ofshe (1981). The impact of behavioral style and status characteristics on social influence. *Social Psychology Quarterly,* 44, 73–82.

A. Leffler, D. Gilespie, & J. C. Conaty (1982). The effect of status differentiation on nonverbal behavior. *Social Psychology Quarterly,* 45, 153–161.

Substitution   If you knew that Renée had been approached about leading the curriculum committee and then you saw her take a chair near the head of the table, you might conclude that her behavior was a substitute for the words "I'm interested and willing to be chairperson." Consider some of the other ways group members communicate nonverbally. They fidget in their chairs; stand up to indicate adjournment; avoid eye contact to say, "I don't want to be involved"; frown to say, "I disapprove"; and the like. All these signs substitute for the verbal message, so all are important clues.

Regulation   Group members regulate one another's behavior by using nonverbal messages for words. To illustrate, it is common for group leaders to use eye contact, head nods, and gestures to encourage and discourage contributions. Members who begin to talk at the same time may look to the leader for a cue as to who should continue. A leader may maintain eye contact and give head nods to cause a speaker to continue, or perhaps to cause a person to elaborate. On the other hand, these behaviors may be withheld to discourage a talkative member.

Members regulate the behavior of the group by using nonverbal signals to indicate their desire to talk. One may lean forward and raise her hand slightly. Another may make a nonverbal utterance—perhaps an "uh" sound. Still another may suddenly lean forward and begin speaking. Finally, members use hand gestures to slow down and speed up speakers. Have you ever found yourself making small upward motions in an oval pattern in an attempt to cause a very slow speaker to talk faster?

There are many examples of the four functions of nonverbal messages. Members *reinforce* one another and their own statements with nonverbal messages. They *modify* their spoken words with nonverbal messages. They *substitute* nonverbal messages for spoken words, and they *regulate* one another nonverbally. Learning to do these things comes quite naturally, since nonverbal messages are a part of each person's fluency. But, like the use of language, fluent use of nonverbal messages is rarely conscious behavior. And since our use of these codes tends to be idiosyncratic and very subtle,

Looking Back: A Quick Review

NONVERBAL COMMUNICATION FUNCTIONS

Reinforcement	Cues that repeat, elaborate, or accent a verbal message
Modification	Cues that change the meaning of a verbal message
Substitution	Cues that replace a verbal message
Regulation	Cues that are used in place of words and have the purpose of controlling another's behavior

group members may generate confusion as well as understanding. The next section will focus your attention on ways to use nonverbal message systems on purpose.

USING NONVERBAL CODES

There is much to know about nonverbal codes in small group communication. We have examined four functions. But our goal is to be able to *choose* nonverbal messages. Here we look at four nonverbal codes and their uses: physical environments; gesture, posture, and movement; face and eye behavior; and use of time. After reading this section you should be able to put what you have read to deliberate use in groups.

Physical Environments

Where you hold a conversation has an effect on communication. Consider the effect of moving a conversation with colleagues from place to place. Suppose the conversation takes place in the cafeteria. Now suppose it is in a conference room. Now imagine having it in the parking lot. Each time you change the environment, you change the conversation. This principle of environmental effect holds for other groups, too.

One important environmental factor is the appearance of the meeting room. Abraham Maslow and Norbett Mintz (1965) investigated the effect environments have on group members' attitudes toward the task and the emotional states evoked. Subjects rated photographs in three settings: a room like a janitor's closet (the ugly room), a professor's office (the average room), and a living room with nice furniture (the beautiful room). Subjects gave more positive ratings to photographs, enjoyed the task more, and wanted to stay with the task longer when working in the beautiful room. The ugly room caused the group members to feel tired, irritated, and unpleasant.

What does this classic study tell us? Surroundings make a difference in the ways people behave. Of course, few meetings are conducted in living-room-like surroundings. Still it is possible to find a comfortable, appropriately illuminated meeting place, and much can be done to make any room attractive. For example, chairs can be arranged comfortably. People meeting in a very large room may want their chairs grouped. Of course, distracting clutter can be removed.

The seating preferences and arrangements that group members adopt affect both participation and leadership emergence. Researchers report an interaction pattern when people are seated across from one another. Steinzor (1950), Strodtbeck and Hook (1961), and Hearn (1957) have all found a strong tendency for communication to flow between members across the table more than between adjacent members. This effect can be negated by certain personality characteristics. For example, group members who are sensitive to rejection might not follow this pattern (Mehrabian & Diamond, 1971).

The quality of interaction also seems to be affected by seating arrangement. Russo (1967) presented diagrams of five different seating arrangements at a rectangular table with a single member at each end and the other four people seated two on each side (Figure 4.4). Subjects were asked to guess whether the shaded pairs were intimate/

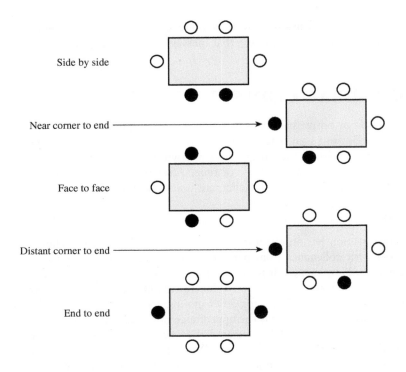

Blackened circles represent positions in the arrangements that Russo examined.

FIGURE 4.4
Seating Arrangement in Russo's Study

unacquainted, friendly/hostile, talkative/untalkative, and equal/unequal. Russo found the greater the distance between the two people, the less acquainted, friendly, and talkative they were thought to be (Edney & Grundmann, 1979). Of course, as you might suspect, seating preference is culturally based. For example, Chinese people prefer to sit side by side as opposed to directly across from each other (Dodd, 1997).

When you can do so without appearing to be manipulative, seat talkative members on the same side of a rectangular table with another person between them. This can provide greater opportunity for others to participate.

If it is not possible to control the seating of too-talkative members, the flow of talk may be controlled through eye contact, head nods, and so forth. Also, the fewer empty chairs at a meeting, the less interpersonal distance and the more the perception that the situation is friendly and intimate—and the greater the interaction.

The emergence of a person whom the group will accept as its leader is also affected by seating. When members identify their leader, the potential leaders generally are persons who interact with the group members easily. For this to happen, the person needs to maintain eye contact. L. T. Howells and S. W. Becker (1962) reasoned that the group member who could control the communication most—the person who could maintain face-to-face eye contact—would most likely emerge as its leader. They seated five-member groups at a rectangular table, two people on one side and three on the other, to test this hypothesis. The members on the two-person side would have the opportunity to maintain eye contact with more members, so Howells and Becker thought they would be the most likely candidates for emergent leader. This is in fact what happened.

If it is important to lead, you might take a central position to maintain maximum eye contact with members. If you want to decrease your chance of being selected as leader, then reverse this advice. If you want to equalize the seating advantage among the members, choose a circle.

Gesture, Posture, and Movement

Gesture and movement help regulate the flow of communication in groups. John E. Baird and A. Schubert (1974) reported leaders gave more positive head nods than nonleaders and they gestured more. Certain nonverbal behavior controls or directs interaction among group members. Later Baird (1977) demonstrated nonverbal participation is related to leadership emergence. Relatively high-status people tend to show more relaxed posture than lower-status members. On the other hand, such behaviors as uncrossing arms and legs, unbuttoning a coat, and general relaxation usually signal openness and a feeling of equality (Nierenberg & Calero, 1973). So using your body to communicate can have a very direct impact on the leadership you can contribute.

Gestures that people in the United States use include the thumbs-up gesture to suggest that everything is ready, the V-shaped sign with the first and second fingers pointing upward that stands for victory, and shaking the head from side to side to say no or nodding the head up and down to say yes. But gestures do not always have universal meanings. The familiar OK sign used in the United States, for example—made by joining the thumb and forefinger in a circle—is an obscene gesture that represents the female genitalia in some cultures. The same gesture has even different meanings in other cultures. In France it means "nothing," and in Japan it means "money" (Harrison, 1972).

Gesture, posture, and bearing differ on the basis of gender. Tables 4.2 and 4.3 summarize some very interesting findings from research in this area.

Be a student of the norms of your group in evaluating gesture, posture, and movement. Also, be aware that research suggests slouch and nonanimated gestures are not effective behaviors. Rather, erect and attentive posture will serve you better. Research also suggests that you should use animated gestures to illustrate your speech when it is appropriate.

Beyond urging you to maintain an alert posture, giving specific suggestions about posture is not possible. Nevertheless, you should follow your group's dominant norms.

TABLE 4.2   Kinesic (Gestural) Differences in Women and Men

Female Behavior	Male Behavior
Women use fewer gestures than men. Women discriminate in their use of gestures, as they use fewer gestures with other women and more with men (Peterson, 1975).	Men use more gestures than women. Men do not discriminate between male and female partners in their use of gestures.
Women tend to keep their hands down on the arms of a chair more than men (Peterson, 1975).	Men rarely keep their hands down on the arms of a chair.
Women use fewer one-handed gestures and arm movements (Shuter, 1979).	Men use more one-handed gestures and arm movements.
Women play with their hair or clothing, place their hands in their lap, and tap their hands more frequently than men (Peterson, 1975).	Men use sweeping hand gestures, stretching the hands, cracking the knuckles, pointing, and using arms to lift the body from a chair or table more frequently.
Women tend to cross their legs at the knees or cross their ankles with their knees slightly apart (Peterson, 1975).	Men tend to sit with their legs apart or with their legs stretched out in front of them and their ankles crossed.
Women tap their hands.	Men exhibit greater leg and foot movement, including tapping their feet (Peterson, 1975).

Source: From J. C. Pearson, L. H. Turner, and W. Todd-Mancillas, 1991. Reprinted by permission.

Face and Eye Behavior

Because facial cues are important indicators of a person's orientation, the face exerts a special influence. According to Dale Leathers's (1976, pp. 33–34) review of the literature on facial expression:

> The face communicates *evaluative judgments*—good and bad—through pleasant and unpleasant expressions that suggest whether the communicator sees the current object of his attention as good or bad.
>
> The face communicates *interest* or *disinterest* in other people or in the surrounding environment.
>
> The face communicates *intensity* and, hence, degree of involvement in the situation.
>
> The face communicates the amount of *control* the individual has over his or her own expressions.
>
> The face probably communicates the intellectual factor of *understanding* or lack of it.

One research group found that smiles and head nods enhance credibility (Woodall, Burgoon, & Markel, 1980).

TABLE 4.3 Kinesic (Posture and Bearing) Differences in Women and Men

Female Behavior	Male Behavior
Women tend to hold their legs close together.	Men tend to have their legs apart at a 10- to 15-degree angle.
Women maintain their arms close to their body.	Men hold their arms about 5 to 10 degrees away from their bodies.
Women rely on more closed body positions.	Men rely on more open body positions (Aries, 1982).
Women tend to engage in less body lean.	Men tend to engage in more backward lean (Aries, 1982).
Women walk with the pelvis rolled slightly forward.	Men walk with the entire pelvis rolled slightly back.
Women present their entire body from their neck to their ankles as a moving entity when they walk (Birdwhistell, 1970).	Men move their arms independently and exhibit a slight twist of their rib cage.

Source: From J. C. Pearson, L. H. Turner, and W. Todd-Mancillas, 1991. Reprinted by permission.

Compared to facial expression, eye contact usually produces less ambiguous messages. People make direct eye contact when they want to indicate they are open for communication or wish feedback (McCroskey, Larson, & Knapp, 1971). People use eye contact to decrease distance psychologically and sometimes to show hostility (Exline, 1963). Group members believe that eye contact is important. Judee K. Burgoon (1996) discovered that when student groups were allowed to arrange their desks any way they wanted, they adopted a U pattern. This arrangement allowed individuals to maintain eye contact.

Constant eye contact is a sign of confronting and can make people nervous. When you are listening to other group members, where is the focus of your attention? If it is not on the speaker, what do you think other members might conclude?

Eye contact differs on the basis of gender and among cultures. Women engage in more eye contact than men, regardless of the gender of the person with whom they are talking. The amount of eye contact also varies greatly among cultures. Michael Argyle (1991) reports that eye contact is high in Arabian, Latin, and American cultures. It is lowest among Indians and northern Europeans (Thayer & Schiff, 1975; Ellsworth, Carlsmith, & Henson, 1972; Muirhead & Goldman, 1979; Ellsworth & Ludwig, 1972).

Directness in eye contact differs culturally. A direct gaze is considered normal for speakers in Latin American and in Arab and southern European countries. In contrast, Indians, Asians, Pakistanis, and northern Europeans do not gaze directly at the listener, and sometimes they do not look at the listener at all.

Eye contact and facial expression vary on the basis of gender. Notice the differences uncovered by research and reported in Tables 4.4 and 4.5.

TABLE 4.4   Kinesic (Eye Contact) Differences in Women and Men

Female Behavior	Male Behavior
Women establish more eye contact than men (Thayer & Schiff, 1975; Rubin, 1970; Ellsworth, Carlsmith, & Henson, 1972; Muirhead & Goldman, 1979; Ellsworth & Ludwig, 1972).	Men establish less eye contact than women.
Women engage in a higher percentage of mutual looking than men (Exline, Gray, & Shuette, 1965).	Males engage in more mutual eye gazing as they age (Muirhead & Goldman, 1979).
Women avert their gaze more than men (Dierks-Stewart, 1979).	Men engage in staring behavior rather than in gaze aversion.
Women appear to value eye contact more than men (Kleinke et al., 1973; Argyle, Lalljee, & Cook, 1968).	Men do not appear to be disturbed by people who do not watch them.

Source: From J. C. Pearson, L. H. Turner, and W. Todd-Mancillas, 1991. Reprinted by permission.

TABLE 4.5   Kinesic (Facial Expression) Differences in Women and Men

Female Behavior	Male Behavior
Women use more facial expression and are more expressive than men (Mehrabian, 1972; Buck, Miller, & Caul, 1971).	Men use less facial expression and are less expressive than women.
Women are better at conveying emotions than men (Schiffenbauer & Babineau, 1976).	Men do not convey their emotions through their faces.
Women demonstrate superior recognition memory of their own facial expressions (Yarmey, 1979).	Men do not recall their own facial expressions.
Women smile more than men (Argyle, 1975; Dierks-Stewart, 1976; Frances, 1979; Parlee, 1979).	Men smile less than women.
Women are more apt to return smiles when someone smiles at them (Henley & Thorne, 1977).	Men are less likely to return a smile than women.
Women are more attracted to others who smile (Lau, 1982).	Men are not more attracted to others who smile.

Source: From J. C. Pearson, L. H. Turner, and W. Todd-Mancillas, 1991. Reprinted by permission.

Use of Time

Two aspects of time are important to a small group. The first is inferences people draw from starting meetings on time especially if they are taking time away from their work. Start at the designated time if you have control. If you are a member, arrange to be at the meeting place on time. Use of time is more than a matter of courtesy.

Second, when a meeting drones on, people become uneasy. People can maintain attention at a fairly high level for about one hour. Leadership in this regard means being sensitive to the group's needs. If the meeting is beginning to drag, suggest a short break. If you are the chairperson, begin promptly after the break.

Be aware though that use of time varies culturally. Edward T. Hall (1976) documented this fact dramatically when he described the Native American Navajo belief that the time to start a ceremony is when all the preparations have been made. Such an understanding of time would defy the expectations of certain North American industrialists. They would want to know what that means according to "clock" time.

Groups have different approaches to managing time and space. Ballard and Seibold (2000) report that groups they studied pursued one of three approaches: flexible, separation, and concurrency. Groups who pursued the flexible approach were characterized by fewer

---

Looking Back: A Quick Review

CATEGORIES OF NONVERBAL CUES

Environment	Attractiveness of space contributes to productivity. Seating affects participation and leadership emergence. Seating affects the quality of the interaction.
Gesture, posture, and movement	Help to regulate communication flow. Provide a sense of member involvement. Show state of relaxation.
Face and eyes	Communicate emotional states. Enhance credibility. Control the flow of communication. Are gender related.
Time	Can indicate attitudes toward group and its goals (being on time). Can cause people to become uneasy if "improperly" used. Varies culturally.

deadlines and more autonomy. Groups who operated in the separatist mode preferred to physically separate themselves from other groups and people by meeting behind a closed door. The concurrency groups were the multitaskers. They were likely to be doing several things at one time and to look for ways to combine projects or activities. Each of these styles might create problems you need to anticipate. You may need to monitor deadlines in a flexible group. You may need to guard against becoming so isolated that you lose sight of larger group goals in a separatist group. You may need to help your group track tasks and suggest structure in a concurrency group.

Problems in Using Nonverbal Messages

The very nature of nonverbal messages sometimes presents problems in groups. Suppose a member of your group rarely says anything. Her silence communicates—but what? Is that person shy? Does she have nothing to say? Is she preoccupied by a problem? Did she spend the last night working on a project? Silence does not communicate clearly.

Nonverbal messages are ambiguous   Ambiguity creates problems for small groups. Misinterpreting others' nonverbal expressions can be as damaging as misunderstanding what they say! People are unique. Their experiences are also unique. How they experience a group meeting can readily change the meaning they get. A smile may be a greeting in one context and "I put one over on you" in another.

Even cultural differences can affect how we communicate without words. The amount of eye contact expected and the degree of personal closeness permitted and many other nonverbal behaviors vary from culture to culture. For example, if a person from Thailand was in your group and you crossed your legs so that the sole of your foot was pointing at him, he would be insulted!

Nonverbal messages are often unintentional   When group members read an unintentional cue as intentional and act on it, interpersonal conflict can ensue. Suppose John, a group member, was concentrating on an idea that he was going to present and stared out the window as he thought. He may not have intended to create any impression by this behavior, so a conclusion of "disinterest" might lead you to the wrong conclusions. You might be embarrassed if you chose to act on such an interpretation.

Nonverbal messages can inhibit communication   Sometimes group members' nonverbal behavior inhibits communication. Consider the person who talks in a group while staring at the wall. By not adhering to the expected eye contact this person seriously inhibits communication. Other nonverbal behaviors might inhibit communication. Sometimes members attend meetings in inappropriate clothing, fidget in their seats, doodle too much on paper, and the like. These behaviors can inhibit communication.

Consider this nonverbal behavior observed in a planning session of a group of young professionals who were developing a fund drive for a nonprofit organization. There were

---

Looking Back: A Quick Review

PROBLEMS WITH NONVERBAL COMMUNICATION

It can be ambiguous.	It can inhibit communication.
It can be unintentional.	

---

four men in business suits and two women, one in a conservative dress and the other in a tailored suit. Fifteen minutes late, the final member, a man named Stan, bounded into the room saying, "I'm so sorry I'm late . . . " But probably no one heard the end of that sentence. The man was wearing blue jeans and a V-neck sweater. He had misread the situation and dressed down. Of course, he was embarrassed. Stan soon left the meeting.

So nonverbal messages can cause problems. You need to find ways you can address them.

INCREASING NONVERBAL EFFECTIVENESS

If you decide to improve your nonverbal communication, you'll want to know what needs improving. One way to identify areas for improvement is to isolate problems you have had in the past and then find ways of addressing them. This section points out common problems in nonverbal communication and suggests ways to overcome them.

PROBLEM   You find that some members talk too much and others talk too little.

LANGUAGE AND/OR SUGGESTIONS
1. Try to regulate the talk patterns by eye contact and head nodding. Avoid eye contact with talkers; increase your eye contact with silent members.

2. Examine the seating arrangement. Maybe the talkers are seated across from one another. In an ongoing group whose members value one another and the group's task, you may be able to approach the more active members and secure their agreement to sit in positions that will minimize the problem. Seat talkative members next to one another if possible. Seat less talkative members across from one another and in central positions. Be careful not to interpret the silent members' nonverbal behavior as a lack of interest. Bormann (1990) found that these members were often experiencing high-level primary tension.

PROBLEM   You want to be more influential in a new group.

LANGUAGE AND/OR SUGGESTIONS

1. Sit at the end of a table if possible. If this is not possible, try to sit where you can make eye contact with most of the group's members.

2. Make frequent eye contact with members and the group as a whole.

3. Pay close attention to the nonverbal cues. You can provide support, reinforce people, clarify, and the like when you are sensitive to the cues others are presenting. These help you to provide both social and task leadership. (Study Chapter 7, "Leading Group Meetings," carefully.)

PROBLEM   You believe ambiguous language is creating misunderstandings.

LANGUAGE AND/OR SUGGESTIONS

1. Check out your perceptions when you can comfortably do so. Use tentative language to let others know that you are checking out an inference. You might say either publicly or in private, "I noticed that you were [are] staring out the window. You are usually with us. I wonder if there is some problem."

2. Joseph DeVito (2004, p. 138–39) has said, "Nonverbal behaviors are normally packaged." That is, a nonverbal behavior is generally accompanied by other nonverbal behaviors that go along with and support the primary behavior. If you observe someone staring out the window, for example, study the facial expression, posture, and other cues to help you understand the meaning of the behavior.

3. Try to be aware of the context. Ask yourself, "How does this behavior relate to the person's contributions and to what others have been saying?"

A Question of Ethics and Responsibility

ACCOMMODATING DIVERSITY

Rachael, student government president at a major university, decided to appoint a task force to look for ways to promote understanding among the diverse ethnic and national student population. She envisions a first meeting that is mostly a social time. The task force will be composed of people from Caucasian, African American, and Hispanic cultures. Students from four international student organizations will join them. The groups are Japanese, French, African, and Arab. Rachael has been studying nonverbal communication and is concerned about violating expectations. She wants the setting to be comfortable for interaction among people from such diverse cultures. What considerations should she make regarding room arrangement and seating to accommodate these concerns?

PROBLEM   You believe some members think they are excluded.

LANGUAGE AND/OR SUGGESTIONS

1. Make eye contact with these people.

2. Ask yourself, "Am I being sensitive to these members' feelings and viewpoints?" If you answer no or you aren't sure, give them more attention.

PROBLEM   You are worried about giving off unintentional nonverbal cues in your group.

LANGUAGE AND/OR SUGGESTIONS

1. Ask a friendly group member privately, "I've been wondering how I'm coming off in the group. I want to do my best. How are you experiencing me as a member?"

2. Self-awareness is the only other answer to this problem. Since you cannot easily observe your behaviors, try to be aware of what you are doing as you observe others. Often their reactions may give you a cue to what you are doing.

PROBLEM   You think a member's nonverbal behavior is inhibiting communication.

LANGUAGE AND/OR SUGGESTIONS

1. The behavior might be unintentional. If you think the behavior is unintentional and the member values the group, approach the person privately. Be supportive. (Chapter 8 provides help on being supportive.)

2. If the disruptive behavior seems to be intentional, then the group leader may need to talk with the person. A decision about who should talk to the person depends on who is most likely to be successful. Supportive communication principles should enhance the likelihood of success.

3. The group may need to discuss this problem. Do not take the leader and group member by surprise with such an issue. Check it out with them before the meeting. Be as supportive as possible.

We have examined options for dealing with nonverbal communication problems. You must decide which of them, if any, is best suited to you and to a particular group situation. Be flexible. Incorporate them into your own style as best you can. And *practice*. Learning a new way to communicate is much, much easier when you rehearse.

SUMMARY

Interpreting verbal messages requires the application of your personal experience to the words being used by group members.

Verbal communication is affected by perceptual bias, ambiguity of language, the labels we use, and too much or too little information. Bias is experienced because perception is a subjective process in which people strive for stability and assume what they perceive to be meaningful. Ambiguous language causes communication problems because the more abstract words are, the less likely it is that members will be visualizing and understanding the same thing. Labels that we attach to people and things create problems because they can shape the way other people feel and think. Biased labels are particularly problematic. Finally, groups can suffer from too much or too little information. Too much information can create an overload situation that makes thought and processing of information difficult. Too little information may mean that a group is acting without full understanding. Suggestions are offered for each of these problems.

Gender is a word used to describe learned characteristics and psychological attributes of masculinity and femininity. In contrast, *sex* refers to biological characteristics. Research suggests that behavior differences in initiating behaviors, interrupting, and verbosity are gender based. Women initiate more topics, but more topics are dropped. Men ask questions to acquire information, but women do so to maintain conversations. Men interrupt more than women do. Women are as capable as men in leading groups and are not "frozen out" of decision making if they are high-status, successful businesswomen.

Group members may be of low- or high-context cultures. People from low-context cultures—for example, Canada and the United States—use language to express thoughts, ideas, and feelings as clearly and as logically as possible. People from high-context cultures—for example, most Asian and Middle Eastern cultures—use language with the aim of maintaining social harmony. Communicators from these cultures learn what is meant by examining the nonverbal behaviors, the context of the message, the history of the relationship, and social rules governing interaction.

Language varies in succinctness and formality cross-culturally. Some cultures use language that is rich and expressive—Arabs, for example. People from the United States are known for their "talkativeness" when they meet people. Native Americans may handle an ambiguous social situation with silence. People in the United States and Canada generally approach their relationships with informality. On the other hand, people from Africa and Asia are careful to define the other person's position in a relationship by the use of language. Obviously, culture has dramatic effects on group communication.

Nonverbal messages form an important part of the group communication event. They serve to reinforce the verbal message through repetition, elaboration, and accenting. Sometimes they modify words by contradiction. When this takes place, the nonverbal communication is generally believed. Some nonverbal messages serve as substitutes for the verbal message, whereas others may regulate the flow of communication.

The physical environment of a group—the attractiveness and appearance of the meeting room—can cause the members to view the task more positively and want to stay with it longer. Seating preferences and arrangements also affect groups.

Gesture, posture and movement, face and eye behavior, and use of time also communicate in a group setting. You can use gesture, posture, and movement to exert influence and to affect leadership emergence. Positive head nods and greater gesticulation help people to emerge as leaders. Face and eye behavior convey evaluation, interest, intensity of involvement, amount of control, and probably understanding. Finally, use of time is an important message system. Starting meetings on time and regulating their length can help the efficiency of any group.

Nonverbal messages are ambiguous, can be unintentional, and can inhibit communication. You must depend on the context to interpret the meaning of the message. Unintentional nonverbal messages, if not recognized as such, can be misleading. Messages like improper clothing, fidgeting, and doodling can distract the listener and create problems.

KEY TERMS AND CONCEPTS

abstraction	low-context culture	regulation
communication apprehension	meaning	reinforcement
confederate	meaningfulness	stability
fact	modification	substitution
gender	opinion	symbol
high-context culture	perception	triangle of meaning
information overload	referent	value

EXERCISES

1. In groups of six members, explore concepts that are important to verbal and nonverbal communication. Half the members should work on verbal; the other half on nonverbal. Create lists of concepts that are important to verbal and nonverbal communication in groups. Create a rating form that could be used to evaluate these concepts in groups.

2. Make an audiotape of one of your group's discussions. Analyze the verbal interaction. Identify the major incidents of functional and dysfunctional language use. Suggest steps members might take to avoid the language difficulties discovered in your analysis.

3. During a group discussion, have observers analyze the nonverbal behavior. Call "freeze" to stop the interaction. Members should try to maintain whatever nonverbal behavior they are doing. Observers should comment on what the behavior is saying about the person's relationship to the group and what the behavior says about the member's feelings about the group. After several observations, members and observers can discuss the implications.

4. Ask groups to meet at two very different locations while working on the same project. Each member should write a two-page analysis of the effect of the environment on the group climate and task productivity.

5. Suppose you are in charge of plans for a decision-making meeting, and you know that two powerful and aggressive members will attend. (This group has five members.) How can you arrange the environment to minimize this potential problem? Compare and contrast your answers with those of your classmates. Can the class agree on a plan?

6. Work in a small group to develop a description of an ideal member. Consider the member's interpersonal style, communicator style, and communication competence. In other words, what attributes does this person have?

RECOMMENDED WEBSITES

The site www.pertinent.com/pertinfo/business/exercises/SayItBetter.html helps you to "Say It Better in All That You Do." There is a 20-item quiz that asks you how well you communicate both verbally and nonverbally. The answers may surprise you. On a similar Web page, www.pertinent.com/pertinfo/business/exercises/nonverbal.html, there is a brief true-and-false quiz that asks, "How well can you interpret nonverbal cues in communication?"

Students from the University of Massachusetts at Boston developed the site www.geocities.com/SouthBeach/Shores/2339/nonverbal.html. The page contains great links to other informative nonverbal websites, including a site about the history of nonverbal communication and a site that gives tips on how to improve your nonverbal skills.

The site, www.uen.org/themepark/html/communication/verbal.html, is a theme park dedicated to nonverbal communication that includes links to other sites, ranging from nonverbal symbols in different cultures to Morse code decoders.

Communication beyond Words, at www.deltanetwork.org/skills/nct.htm, is devoted to nonverbal communication, identifying several factors. There is also a link to motivating teams.

The Northwest Regional Educational Laboratory has a site devoted to *Cross Cultural Communication* www.nwrel.org/cnorse/booklets/ccc/index.html and has several chapters covering various aspects of cross-cultural communication.

RECOMMENDED READINGS

J. K. Burgoon (2003). Spatial relationships in small groups. In R. Y. Hirokawa, R. S. Cathcart, L. A. Samovar, & L. D. Henman, eds. *Small group communication: Theory and practice*, 8th ed. Los Angeles, CA: Roxbury, pp. 85–96.

P. Eschholz, A. Rosa, & V. Clark, eds. (1994). *Language awareness*, 6th ed. New York: St. Martin's.

H. L. Goodall Jr. (1990). What you should know about communication in the small group. In *Small group communication in the organization*, 2d ed. Dubuque, IA: Wm. C. Brown, Chap. 3.

B. B. Haslett & J. R. Ogilvie (2003). Feedback processes in task groups. In R. Y. Hirokawa, R. S. Cathcart, L. A. Samovar, & L. D. Henman, eds. *Small group communication: Theory and practice*, 8th ed. Los Angeles, CA: Roxbury, pp. 97–108.

part

III

PARTICIPATING IN GROUP MEETINGS

ENCOURAGING GROUP DEVELOPMENT AND EVOLUTION

OBJECTIVES

After reading this chapter you should be able to
- Name and explain five motivations for belonging to groups; then specify how understanding these might be useful.
- Recall and explain Bales's, Fisher's, Poole's, and Gersick's explanations of group development; then specify how these might be useful in encouraging group development.
- Identify, define, compare, and contrast the two types of social tension; then explain how knowledge of these might be useful.
- Describe Scheidel and Crowell's notion of idea development in a problem solving group; then specify how this might be useful.

Suppose you were asked to serve on a committee to consider changes in general education requirements for all students at your college or university. You have ideas about general education and were flattered to be asked. The president selected eight members— five faculty and two other students. The first meeting is next week. You begin to think about what the meetings will be like. Can you imagine what will happen? Would you be able to make a sequential list? Stop now—and it's hoped that you actually will—and try to make such a list. How many items do you have?

How did you do at "crystal ball" gazing? Perhaps you were able to make some good predictions. Or perhaps you realized the difficulty of this task and did not try it. Your ability to operate productively in groups depends on your ability to wrestle with questions like these. Shortly, you will find some useful generalizations about group development provided by scholars who have investigated these issues.

Motivations for participation in groups are the first topic of this chapter. If you know why people belong to your group, you can help them to be more productive by giving attention to their needs. The phases of group development are considered next. Then the topics of task development, social tension, and idea development are addressed. Each of these processes happens with some regularity in its sequence. Knowing these sequences can help you to understand and make predictions about your group.

MOTIVATIONS FOR MEMBER PARTICIPATION IN GROUPS

Examine your motives for being a member of a particular group. Stop for a moment and pick one. Now think both of yourself and of the other members. A good question to ask yourself is, "What things do members of the group receive that keep them in the group?" See how many different motivations you can list.

Now check your list against the following to see how your ideas match. People are motivated to belong because of (1) attraction to others in the group, (2) attraction to the group's activities, (3) attraction to the group's goal, (4) attraction to being affiliated with the group, and (5) attraction to needs outside the group. We will take up each of these ideas, give illustrations, and provide suggestions for group development.

The motives for belonging to a group that a person brings affect the development potential and direction of the group. The leader can use these motives to develop members' motivations to participate. Specifics of how you can accomplish this will be presented at the end of this section—and when you affect a member's motivation to participate, you affect the group's development.

Attraction to Others in the Group

If you ask a group of people to describe why they are attracted to one another, you are likely to get a variety of answers. You can gain an appreciation of the complexity of this issue by considering someone you know in a group, to whom you are attracted. Take a moment to think of several of the reasons you like to be with that person.

Do you find the other person physically attractive?

Do the two of you have similar interests?

Do your attitudes and values seem to match those of the other person reasonably closely?

Are your important values a close match for the other person's?

Do the two of you see yourselves as having similar personality characteristics?

Are you two of similar economic status, race, and so forth?

Do you see the other person as having abilities similar to yours?

Count the number of times you said yes to these questions. You may have done so several times, because attraction is complex. People are attracted to groups for a variety of reasons. Pete Wells belongs to the Rotary Club because the members represent an image he admires. Yuka Ando belongs to a study group at her church because some members are interested in tennis. Sally Williams belongs to a group investigating computer needs in her department because she enjoys the people who volunteered. Motivations for being part of a group are varied, and they are not always related to the task.

Attraction is related to pleasing physical characteristics and to similarities in attitude, belief, personality, race, economic status, and perceived ability of the other person. Perhaps the strongest of these—and the most often studied—is perceived similarity of attitude. Theodore Newcomb (1961) conducted the classic study that demonstrated the strength of similarity. He invited 17 male students to live in a house rent free for two years. After they occupied the house, he gave them a series of tests to measure attitudes and values. He also checked the room assignments and likings of group members. He discovered that liking was based on proximity—how physically close to one another they were situated. Later, when he retested the interpersonal attractions, he found a shift. Those who perceived themselves to be similar in attitudes had developed attractions. Newcomb concluded that people initially got to know those closest to them. When they were able to know others, they were attracted to those who were similar. Similarity is a good starting place when you look at why members are attracted to groups.

Attraction is also related to personality similarity. Byrne, Griffitt, and Stefaniak (1967), for example, measured personality characteristics of subjects. Then they examined a stranger's response that agreed with their choices—25 percent, 50 percent, or 80 percent of the time. Next the subjects rated the stranger's attractiveness. The more the stranger agreed, the more the person was liked.

The details of these studies are presented for two reasons. First, it is useful for you to have an appreciation of how researchers examined these issues. Second, the kind of evidence that supports these generalizations is important. There is also support to show that attraction is related to economic similarity (Byrne, Clore, & Worchel, 1966), race (Shaw, 1973a), and similarity of ability (Shaw & Gilchrist, 1955). The findings related to ability are interesting. Initially people were attracted to those who had previously been successful at a given task. However, when they were allowed to shift from their initial choices, in time unsuccessful people chose unsuccessful partners.

Attraction to the Group's Activities

Sometimes people belong to a group because they enjoy some aspect of the task (Sherif & Sherif, 1973). This is not always the same thing as valuing the goal. For example, imagine an athletic woman joining the sorority softball team to participate in its athletic program, but not really embracing its primary goal of socializing. Some people belong to a civic group to socialize with its members rather than to work toward its goals. You can imagine how important it could be to realize that particular members are not especially interested in the group's goal. Your success in motivating them is likely to be minimal if you try to emphasize goal commitment. On the other hand, you may be able to link achievement of their needs to the group goal and be successful. For example, a sorority might show how other athletes are attracted to groups with strong social programs. This could give the woman who joined to participate in athletics a reason to support the social program, too.

Attraction to the Group's Goal

Perhaps the most important reason for a member to belong to a group is attraction to the goal. Goal attraction contributes more to a group than mere achievement of particular ends. Members who are committed to the goal also may work at being able to get along. They even may be able to put aside differences and hostilities because they value the goal. Sherif and Sherif (1973) vividly demonstrated this aspect of goal achievement in their famous boys' camp experiment. They created hostility between two groups of boys. For example, they invited both groups to a party in which half of the refreshments were badly damaged. They invited one group to arrive earlier than the other so that the first group had an opportunity to eat the undamaged portion of the food. This they did; the other group became predictably angry. Next Sherif and Sherif tried to manage the conflict by creating a goal to which they thought both groups would be attracted. They arranged a baseball game in which their camp would play a neighboring camp. The embracing of this attractive goal served to ease much of the hostility and created a new group loyalty.

Attraction to Being Affiliated with the Group

Groups allow people to interact and thereby fulfill a need to affiliate with others. You undoubtedly know people who do not care about the task of the group, are not interested in the group's goals, and may even not wish to get involved with the members, but who attend some of the group meetings. You might suspect that affiliation with the group per se is rewarding. These people like to say they are members. Perhaps they believe belonging to these groups gives them prestige. The aim of their attendance at a few meetings is to keep themselves in good standing so they can say they belong.

Need for affiliation when it is a member's sole attraction to the group presents a difficult problem. How do you interest the person in the group's goals? The member's presence may be disruptive if you cannot do this. Your group can suffer if you have several of these members. Imagine a PTA member who attends an occasional meeting. This person is uninformed. He or she may want to discuss an ongoing issue, but the effort is more disrupting than helpful.

Attraction to Needs Outside the Group

Finally, it is clear that people belong to groups for reasons that may have nothing to do with the group's task, goals, or members. Perhaps you know of a fellow student who has joined groups to bolster her or his employment résumé. Some people belong to religious groups merely because it is the socially acceptable thing to do. Sometimes businesspeople belong to civic organizations because they think it will be good for business.

You can imagine the problems it might create for your group if you have members like this who are pursuing goals primarily outside the group. They may be totally unreliable, may attend only rarely, and may even be disruptive when they do attend.

Encouraging Group Development: Applying Members' Motivations to Encourage Participation

People perceive their membership as satisfying some need, and this need can serve as an important source of motivation for those providing leadership.

The problem for members and leaders who wish to develop their group is finding out what motivates various members. If you find that you have a number of people who are motivated by a particular need (say, affiliation), you might try to get them to value the group members more. Perhaps you could invite them to a group social function. This approach may promote cohesiveness and may also develop their commitment to members and the group, thereby enhancing productivity.

Looking Back: A Quick Review

WHY MEMBERS JOIN GROUPS

They are attracted to other members.	They are attracted to the group's name and reputation.
They are attracted to the group's activities.	They see the group as a way to achieve personal goals, not related to the group's primary purpose.
They are attracted to the group's goals.	

Sometimes it is the activities of the group that interest the member, with goal achievement being of little concern. Of course, if the group's activities are only task related, this is not a problem. One method of using this attraction to motivate is to link the activities to goal attainment. For example, if the person's primary motivation is to participate in your group's philanthropic effort, you might make sure that you devote some time in each of your meetings to this issue. You might emphasize how important you think this activity is and tell the person how much you appreciate his or her contributions in this area. You would also want to show how accomplishment of this philanthropic activity is related to the overall task.

Still others may belong to your group to try to fulfill their need for affiliation with others. These people may not care much about the group's goals or task or even the particular attributes of its members. If this attitude is a chronic problem that disrupts the work of the group, you may need to make the problem an agenda item. The group's members need to affirm their commitment to the tasks and goal. The group might decide, for instance, that regular attendance and work on the task are necessary for continued membership in the group. If these people enjoy the affiliation with the group enough, they may be motivated to embrace and work on the task in order to meet that need.

Finally, some members may belong to a group for a goal that is outside the group's purpose. They wish to receive the benefits that outsiders might attribute to them because

A Question of Ethics and Responsibility

MOTIVATIONS FOR JOINING A GROUP

You found yourself elected to lead your neighborhood association. You have called the group together for its first formal meeting. You are meeting in the clubhouse. The room is arranged in such a way that people could decide to sit in a close circle or spread out. Members chose to spread out. You find it difficult to talk in this arrangement, so you suggest that they move into a closer circle of chairs. Members introduce themselves and tell what they do to occupy their time. It turns out that three members are close neighbors and socialize with each other frequently. Yuka, 24 years old, works as a speech pathologist at a local hospital. Carol, 60 years old, works in her home, while Isabel,

20 years old, works at a local bank as a marketing manager. Juan, 40 years old, is from a nearby state and owns a franchise for a fast-food restaurant. Doug, 50 years old, is coordinator of recreation for the Parks Department.

It appears that you have a diverse group. Some members know each other, while others do not. Age and place in life vary significantly. Some members have grown children, while others have youngsters. What problems do you anticipate in your attempt to develop this group? What strategies will you use to accomplish your objectives of completing some worthwhile tasks for the neighborhood and getting this group to pull together?

of their membership. If the members are not genuinely interested in the task and in this case may not even particularly value the members, then your group may have to make membership contingent upon maintaining involvement. This measure is hard to implement, but it is one of the more practical solutions to this kind of problem.

PHASES IN GROUP DEVELOPMENT

Suppose for a moment that you think the career for you is in medicine. Maybe you decide to specialize in pediatrics. Part of your task would be to guide children in their development. So you would be involved with parents, too. You watch for normal developmental processes and alert parents to normal expectations. You use your knowledge of how children develop to know how a child is doing and to help you spot difficulties. Sometimes you encourage parents to refrain from certain behaviors that may hinder normal development. On the other hand, you might encourage them to do things that would help develop motor skills.

Groups also develop in predictable ways. Understanding the developmental process allows you to make more meaningful contributions to groups.

Group Development

One of the most interesting findings about group development is that task groups pass through phases in evolutionary and decision development. Understanding this phase development is particularly important to you because, as Marshall Scott Poole (1981, p. 20) put it, the research suggests "a logically ideal format for decision making . . . (that) may well be the simplest effective path a decision-making group could follow." Although there have been many studies of this phenomenon, here we will examine three, which together will give you a firm understanding of group development. The first, from the research of Robert F. Bales, focuses on evolutionary development. The second, from the work of B. Aubrey Fisher, addresses decision development. The third, from research by Marshall Scott Poole, helps us understand what happens when the Fisher model doesn't fit a particular group.

Robert F. Bales   Bales (1976) conducted the first controlled study of group development. He identified two predominant concerns in groups. These concerns, **socioemotional** and **task,** are evidenced in interactions about interpersonal relationships and accomplishment of the task. Bales found that issues related to one or the other of these predominate at particular times. As a group is forming, for example, the issue of who the members are and how they will relate interpersonally is foremost. This does not mean, of course, that task concerns will not be addressed at all, but that relationship-related interaction predominates. As these interpersonal issues are settled and the group matures, task-related issues become prominent. Now the group focuses attention on production and thereby achieves maximal task effectiveness.

Issues of relationship and task cycle back and forth as the group situation changes. Thus each new meeting of an ongoing group may begin with relational talk being prominent as members reacquaint. Then the group might move to task issues. If a group takes in new members or member status changes, the group might move to a period of relationship talk.

Bales (1976) reported task and social leadership tend to be managed by separate individuals within a particular group. Since his work was done in the United States, scholars have conducted research to discover whether this situation holds in other cultures. Studies of British students and managers (Smith, 1963) and Dutch students (Koomen, 1988) found the task and social leadership division. A study of sports teams and student groups in the Soviet Union also replicated Bales's results (Krichevskii, 1983). Although not studied directly, we can speculate that this might be different for Japanese groups because work team research suggests flexibility in occupying these roles (Smith & Bond, 1999).

Aubrey Fisher   A communication scholar, Fisher has focused on the task dimension of decision making. Fisher (1970) analyzed audiotapes of ten groups, using task dimension categories. His focus was on the process whereby members' ideas are transformed into consensus. Thus he was interested in the number of favorable, unfavorable, or ambiguous opinions offered; the evidence presented; the support given to opinion; modifications offered; attempts to clarify; and agreement or disagreement with others' opinions. You can tell by the kinds of behaviors he identified that his concern was with contributions related to decision emergence. From this work, Fisher identified four phases that seem to occur consistently: orientation, conflict, emergence, and reinforcement.

The **orientation phase** is characterized by members' spending most of their time agreeing with each other, clarifying, and giving information. They often present ambiguously worded suggestions and tentative statements. For example, a member *might say*, "I think the problem *might be* that Nat is bored." Another member might say, "That certainly might be part of it, but outside factors also *may be* a problem." Notice the tentative language. They are testing the group and feeling their way, as they do not know what to expect. Usually members of a new group do not know one another well and are unwilling to risk assertive behavior. You would not be likely to hear, "This is the way it is and we should accept it." Ellis and Fisher (1994, p. 156) suggest that this behavior serves "to avoid disrupting the developing social climate."

Opinions about the decision are forming even in this first phase. For example, the member agreement above serves as a base for the future. Here tentative agreements have an impact on what follows. Often these preliminary opinions change in other phases to opinions favoring the proposal. Yet this agreement is hard to recognize initially, when ideas are expressed ambiguously and voicing of agreement is in a tentative form.

The orientation phase, then, is centered on behavior that allows the group to get acquainted, clarify the task, and suggest tentative ideas and attitudes. People are testing the group to find out where they stand and how they will be received. They avoid assertive behavior that might lead to disagreements and conflict.

Members eventually come to understand the group and task. They make up their minds by this second phase, the **conflict phase** and are willing to express their opinions assertively. Here a favorable proposal is frequently followed by the expression of an unfavorable attitude. Juan might say, "I think the department's production is off because there are so many people sick." Mary might reply, "Juan, there is no evidence to support that. In fact, we've had people out before and kept production up. Remember when. . . ." Through this process the key decision proposals become evident. In the conflict phase, members feel free to enter into arguments. They also bring out evidence to support their positions and may engage in debate.

Polarization of attitudes can take place as a decision proposal emerges. So groups often find themselves divided into two coalitions—one favoring each side of the proposal. The opposition here is genuine. Those members who do not participate in the debate at this point are considered deviates. The normative behavior in this phase is "dissent, controversy, social conflict, and innovative deviance" (Ellis & Fisher, 1994, p. 158).

The conflict stage ends as a decision begins to emerge. Two events characterize the **emergence phase:** dissipation of conflict and argument, and a return to ambiguous comments. We find more tentative language again. Words like "might," "perhaps," and "seems" reappear. If you were counting the statements of dissent, of unfavorable opinions, you would find fewer. Coalitions weaken as the statements that opposed the emergent decision become more ambiguous. You find less positive reinforcement of others' unfavorable attitudes. Perhaps Juan says to Mary, "I guess I can see your point. That's a good way to look at it." In addition, members expressing these ideas drop supporting evidence and reasoning that previously bolstered them.

This return to ambiguity of the initial orientation phase serves a different purpose. This represents a process of changing their stand. Opposition is now expressed through ambiguity rather than directly, but attitudes are being modified. As we observe more ambiguous comments from the coalition against, we also will see an increase of favorable opinions toward the decision. Polarization dissipates.

During the emergence phase many group members seemed to favor the decision, but consensus was not achieved. Consensus is achieved during the **reinforcement phase.** Evidence offered in favor of the decision serves a different purpose here. The evidence reinforces the decision. Juan might say, "I see that Mary's idea is right. I remember data we collected about a year ago that support it."

Ellis and Fisher (1994, p. 160) report, "Members constantly and consistently express opinions favorable to the proposals and positively reinforce one another's favorable opinions with expressions of agreement and additional social support." You might hear, "I'm so glad we were able to finish this today. I thought it would take two meetings."

The dissent that characterized the conflict phase—and to some extent the emergence phase—is nearly nonexistent here. Few negative attitudes toward the proposal are observed, and almost no social conflict is present. This lack of conflict reinforces the unity of opinion. There are other signs of this unity. The ambiguous comments of the emergence phase have lessened. Tension is replaced by jovial, loud, laughing behaviors. This phase increases commitment to the decision.

In summary, Aubrey Fisher discovered that groups go through four phases in making decisions. They orient themselves, engage in conflict, modify the opposition to allow decision emergence, and finally reinforce the emerging decision. Fisher's observation of this developmental process was helpful but incomplete. The work of Marshall Scott Poole adds to our consideration of phases in group development.

Marshall Scott Poole Poole views Fisher's phase sequence as the "ideal sequence" that groups follow. However, groups depart from the ideal under certain circumstances. Poole's work describes what causes these departures.

Poole's approach to investigating sequences differs from Fisher's in that he adds to the task-dimension consideration two others: relational and topic concerns. So for Poole three important dimensions of groups, what he calls **activity tracks,** are task, relationship, and topic (Poole, 1983). These ideas are not new to us, since we examined each of them earlier. **Task-process activities** have to do with the decision-making process. They are such things as *problem analysis, orientation, reflection on the group's process,* and *establishment of solution guidelines—design, evaluation, confirmation—and selection.* **Relational activities** focus on the social processes. These include activities in four relational areas: *work-focused relationships* such as *focused work without criticism* and, then, *critical work with criticism and repartee; conflict* such as *overt opposition,* and *conflict resolution of various kinds, integration* of members, and *expressions of ambiguity about relationships.* Different areas of content in the deliberations represent **topic activities.** These, of course, depend on the issue being discussed at the time.

ACTIVITY TRACKS When these activity tracks—task, relational, and topic—develop together and at roughly the same speed, we have the recognizable phase development represented by Fisher. The orientation phase, for example, interlocks activities of task and relationship. Thus the group orients itself toward the decision-making process and toward one another socially. The same is true for other elements of Fisher's phase formulation.

BREAKPOINTS Group activities are divided by **breakpoints.** These represent transitions in the development process. When a breakpoint interrupts all three activity tracks at the same time, the group is following Fisher's model.

Poole identifies three types of breakpoints. The **normal breakpoint,** the most common, occurs when the group moves from one topic to the next, from one activity to the next, or to plan a task. The **delay** is a breakpoint that occurs when a group doubles back to repeat the same analysis or activity. The group is in a holding pattern until it moves to its next activity. The final breakpoint, the **disruption,** can be of two types. One type has its roots in *major disagreement or conflict.* The issue is such that it requires the group to redirect its activity toward the conflict and maybe even reorient itself. The other type of disagreement has its root in *group failure.* Here the group discovers that its effort is not going to be sufficient. This too requires corrective action.

Poole (1993) introduced a **multiple sequence model** or **contingency model** of decision emergence. This multiple sequence model portrays groups as moving along the three activity tracts. Groups, however, do not necessarily proceed along each track at the same rate or in the same pattern. Some groups may devote more time to the relational (social) activities of the group before proceeding to the task activity.

Poole and Roth (1989a; 1989b) found groups move through one of three principal paths in reaching decisions. The first path, the **unitary sequence,** follows the phases described by Fisher. Breakpoints for topic, task, and relationship change—that is, break and move on—at the same time.

The second path, the **complex cyclic,** describes groups that engage in repeated cycles of focusing on the problem, then the solution, and then back to the problem, and then the solution, and so forth. This pattern would move the task track so its breakpoint does not line up with the topic and relationship track breakpoints. This is an *uncoordinated track.*

The third path, **solution oriented,** is one in which the group moves directly into a discussion of solutions with little or no focus on an analysis of the problem.

Poole and Roth discovered that the complex cyclic path was chosen most frequently, followed by the solution-oriented path, with the unitary sequence used less frequently.

Fitting Together the Models of Group Development

The Bales model of development helps us understand the formation process in a group. Members must have a need to "know" with whom they are working before they achieve maximal productivity. So a newly formed group will spend some time working on relationships before it moves to task issues. If the group is ongoing, it will likely return to issues of relationship at the beginning of each meeting.

Fisher's research provides conclusions about how a general pattern of decision making develops. This pattern may repeat itself each time the group moves to a new topic. Here is a summary of the five important conclusions from Fisher's research:

1. Most groups go through some kind of orientation. They need time to discover who is in the group and what the group is all about.

2. Groups generally experience conflict. The intensity of the conflict may vary with the task, but differences in members come out. This conflict may involve ideas, personal relationships, and/or authority and influence.

3. Successful groups solve their differences and manage the conflict. They move to a period in which polarization and argument diminish. Roles and norms stabilize during this period. Unsuccessful groups eventually dissolve.

4. Successful groups enter a more productive period. The portion of their energy that has been devoted to group concerns can now be focused on the task.

5. Groups go through a leave-taking stage. This may be evident in long-term groups, but it probably takes place in most groups. Often groups feel good about their effort and take time to congratulate one another.

Marshall Scott Poole presents a refinement of these ideas to account for the circumstance when the activities in a group are not in synchrony. In this case, Poole suggests that group development can be looked at through three major activities: task process, relationships, and topics. Movement from activity to activity within a track is defined by breakpoints. Decision sequences might follow Fisher's traditional unitary pattern, a complex cyclic path, or a solution-oriented path.

Encouraging Group Development: Application of Task-Group Development Theory

Imagine yourself faced with a group experience and armed with this information about how groups develop. What will you do with the information? What kind of applications can you make? There are important applications, so take time to read carefully.

Consider that researchers from different backgrounds have discovered similar phases in task groups (Caple, 1978; Bell, 1982). They used different terminology, but an analysis of their conclusions led to four steps.

These broad phases seem to develop naturally in many groups, although the specific content of each phase may differ from group to group. No one took these groups aside and taught them to move through phases. The phases are functional because most groups seem to sense particular needs at different times in their process and fulfill them. Thus it seems reasonable that these communication behaviors serve important functions.

Why do groups skip phases if they perform important functions? Here are two answers to this question. First, some leaders guide their groups away from these functions. For example, the manager who led a task force to investigate absenteeism began by saying, "What should we do about our attendance problem?" Through this question this leader bypassed the orientation phase. Instead the leader might have recognized the need for orientation. He might have said, "Let's focus on the problem for a minute. Could someone describe it?" Second, some group members assume that others in the group are sharing their understanding of the task and are as familiar with the task as they are. These people, too, may urge the group to bypass certain phases.

The problem for you is to decide whether a real need is being ignored. Considering the possible outcomes of bypassing each of the phases will help you do this.

Phase 1   The orientation phase allows members to understand the task and one another's frame of reference. If a group skips this phase, it may move directly to conflict. The intensity of the conflict may be increased if members do not understand each other's positions. Here are some key suggestions a leader might use to help a group:

Ask members to introduce themselves.

Ask members to tell how they are associated with the project and their experience with it.

Ask someone to verbalize the task.

Make sure members understand the task.

Phase 2   The conflict stage serves the function of testing ideas on the road to consensus. When a group skips this step, it may not have looked critically at the issues. This may produce an inferior decision. Here are some suggestions for helping a group:

Conflict can be useful, so be patient in dealing with it.

Clarify members' positions.

Pose a middle ground.

Pose alternatives that might be acceptable.

Compliment members who are managing conflict well.

Phase 3   The emergence phase serves the purpose of producing a decision, healing the wounds of conflict, and generating consensus. Some members may not be able to accept the decision if the group does not emerge from the conflict stage. Relationships may be damaged and polarization may remain. Here are some things you can do to help:

Compliment the group on its progress.

Verbalize consensus when you hear it.

Compliment members on their ability to work through disagreements.

Phase 4   The reinforcement phase calls attention to the good work a group has done and generates group satisfaction. Omission of this phase has implications for carrying out decisions. When the group must advocate a solution to someone in authority for it to be carried out, or when members must do so themselves, omission of this step may cause them to have less commitment and vigor. The leader and members of a group might reinforce the group's decision by

Complimenting the group on its effort.

Visualizing the implications of the decision.

Phase theory can help you anticipate what might happen next in your group. Sometimes members try to resist the conflict phase, for instance. They believe there is something wrong with conflict. Decision-emergence theory alerts us to expect this. If you understand phase theory, you will realize that conflict serves an important function.

Understanding phase theory can help you discover that your group has become stalled. We all have experiences with groups stuck in a particular phase. Often groups are bogged down in the conflict stage. If you have experienced this, you will want to move your group through conflict when possible. You will find some helpful techniques in Chapter 10, "Managing Conflict in the Group."

Since groups do move through phases, it is important to know what these are. You can facilitate your group's development if you are able to identify them. You can (1) discover whether your group has skipped a phase, (2) anticipate the group's movement through phases, and (3) know when your group is stalled in a phase. Discovering, anticipating, and knowing these things can help you to provide leadership.

Keep in mind that for some groups these phases are cyclic. Long-term groups that take on new members and new problems recycle to the orientation phase. As a member of a long-term group, you should expect such behavior.

How can we identify a group that might not conform to the traditional phase model? Poole and Roth suggest we look for contingencies. Three contingencies seem to be highly predictive: urgency, value-laden issues, and high power concentration. Both urgency and value-laden issues often suggest some sort of complex cyclic path. High power concentration often generates a solution-oriented path.

When you determine that the traditional phase model might not apply, track the task activity to determine what kind of decision sequence it follows. If not, continue your analysis. Does it repeat Fisher's phases? Does it follow a problem focus—solution pattern? If so, you have a complex cyclic path. On the other hand, if it doesn't follow these sequences, you might discover that it follows a solution-oriented path.

Continue your analysis if your group does not follow traditional phases. Use the preceding information to determine whether bypassing phases has created any problems. If you find unmet needs, then bypassing a phase has had an impact.

Social Tension

Social tension is the uneasiness group members feel when they are uncertain about members' relationships. It is a factor that exhibits a phaselike pattern. This tension can be graphed in relation to time and a threshold of tolerance. **Threshold of tolerance** is a point when the level of tension is so high it makes productive work difficult. If we could measure the amount of tension generated in a group as it meets over time, we might characterize this flow as pictured in Figure 5.1. If the level remains too high for too long, the group's productivity can suffer. Ernest G. Bormann (1990) distinguished between two types of social tension: primary and secondary.

Primary tension is a normal occurrence when people come together to work with one another. You may experience it on the first day of class because you are not acquainted with the professor and class members. This is usually characterized by long periods of silence, discussion of light topics, and tentative statements. Groups experience social inhibitions. Meeting for the first time means that members may not know how they will be received and how they are expected to act. Ongoing groups that do not meet for a time may reexperience primary tension when they gather for a meeting.

Primary tension is evidenced by a particular interaction. Members are usually very polite, and the intensity of the talk is very low. Sighing and yawning might be observed, as though members are bored or tired. People speak softly and try not to offend. Frequently you will notice long pauses as members seem not to know what to say.

Primary tension is nothing to be overly anxious about. It cannot be avoided. Just be aware that people may not be productive during this period. You can also give each person a warm, friendly welcome. Beyond this, primary tension may be broken by introduction of humor. Perhaps you can do this.

A group may engage in "small talk" in their efforts to manage primary tension. They joke, laugh, and chitchat about surface-level interests and experiences. In the process they get to know each other better.

Engaging in "small talk" may not be seen in the same way through the eyes of people of different cultures. In the United States, small talk is generally seen as something to be endured, but a waste of time. Asian cultures such as Japanese, Chinese, and Korean; Middle Eastern cultures such as Saudi Arabian; and Latin American cultures such as Mexican, Brazilian, and Chilian view small talk as a necessary ritual to be engaged in over many cups of coffee or tea and for several hours, or even several meetings, during which the group task may not be mentioned (Samovar & Porter, 1995). Keep these customs in mind if you are meeting in a cross-cultural group.

Secondary tension is to be expected also. It is different from primary tension in that it occurs later in the group's meetings and is created by topics different from getting acquainted. Members may be struggling to discover what roles they will play, to define their status in the group, and to secure esteem and rewards. They also may experience conflict over perceptions and personalities. Groups are likely to have members who have very different ideas about goals, what solution might fit the problem, who should fulfill what role in the group, doing one's part, and being absent or tardy. You can undoubtedly add more situations you have experienced. The potential is present for significant tension in groups. Figure 5.1 illustrates secondary tension.

Secondary tension is frequently marked by a departure from the group's routine. There may be an outburst from a member. Interchanges may be antagonistic and hostile. Secondary tension is marked by loudness. Two or more members may try to talk at the

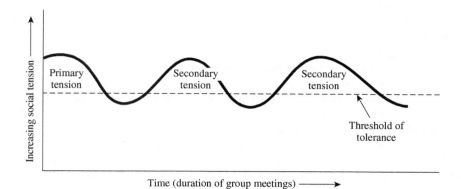

Display of Primary and Secondary Tension in a Hypothetical Group

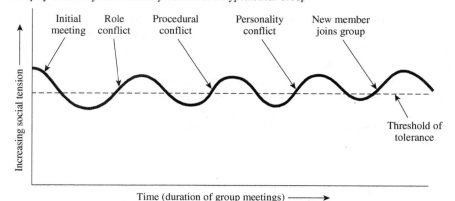

FIGURE 5.1
Phaselike Structure of Social Tension

same time. Generally, the group's interaction is monopolized by two or three members talking while others observe. Long pauses may be evident as members who are arguing try to gather thoughts. Extreme secondary tension is unpleasant and may damage the group if not controlled. Ideas about addressing this situation are suggested next.

Encouraging Group Development: Application of Social Tension Theory

You can provide leadership in dealing with social tension. Here are some examples of how the ideas presented above may be used. Suppose you expect primary tension because your group has not met recently. You might want to allow time for the group to get reacquainted. You should make sure that people understand one another and the task before you move ahead. You also can try to break the tension by introducing humor.

One of the difficulties in managing social tension is knowing when there is too much tension. Healthy groups experience tension within their range of tolerance. This keeps them alert, helps hold them together, and keeps them active. Healthy groups also experience tension above their tolerance level. This tension can overpower the group's productivity. These groups reduce tension and then move on with the task. But how much tension is too much? It is impossible to make any definitive statement. Too much tension can be measured by a group's inability to work and to maintain a satisfying climate. There is no absolute.

Another problem in managing social tension is related to stress-reduction techniques. What works for one group may not work for another. Members must monitor the situation and make decisions and take actions to manage it.

One role that develops in groups to manage social tension is that of the **tension releaser.** This person may help the group by making light of the situation. Phil Johnson, a member of a management group at a bank, was good at this role. One day, when two people who were locked in an argument finally agreed, he joked, "Wow! I'm so glad you settled that. I was about to break out the squirt guns so you could have at it." Sometimes, however, this kind of carefree joking behavior is unsuccessful. For example, persons experiencing a personality conflict may not find it easy to laugh at themselves or the situation. They are likely to resent an intervention of this type. Likewise, a serious dispute over leadership may not be appropriately met with humor. Members may find a person insensitive if he or she tries this approach.

An alternative to using humor is mediation. **Mediation** is a dispute resolution technique where both parties in the dispute negotiate with the help of a respected third party. In some situations this person is an appointed arbitrator. This works better than humor when members are experiencing interpersonal conflict. A person who is respected by both parties often can provide leadership. This intervention may take place either within or outside the group's regular meeting. The manager of a sales force for an office supply company resolved a disagreement over sales technique this way: "Joe, Jean, I see that you both are really involved in this issue—and I can tell you are dead serious. Maybe I can help. Would you consider this position?" (This topic receives careful treatment in Chapter 10.)

Another successful tension-relieving technique that can produce positive or negative results is scapegoating. **Scapegoating** is blaming others for one's own mistakes. Sometimes the scapegoat is an outsider. In the world of work it is often a boss; in the classroom situation it is generally the instructor. The group may label the blamed person the "enemy." A group of fraternity men found their funds for social activities depleted. Instead of placing the blame on themselves, the president released the tension through a long speech about dues they had to pay to "national." This treatment may be rather unpleasant for the scapegoat and thus, if this person has power, can backfire.

Finally, a successful technique for reducing tension is **direct confrontation.** This solution is often difficult for groups. Most of us do not like the pain of confrontation, but the outcome is often worth the effort. When a problem is such that it needs direct confrontation, it is generally too important to be ignored.

A large paper-manufacturing firm holds an annual weekend retreat for midlevel managers. Their leader poses management problems, and the group addresses them in a discussion format. During a recent retreat, Sue, a manager, produced considerable tension addressing the issue by rattling off a solution from a management course she was taking. This interruption was unnerving to members, and because of her rapid-fire delivery, the other managers were unable to understand her. She also usurped their opportunities to make contributions. On the second day, two members confronted her:

KENJI: Sue, we want to talk with you about something.

SUE: What do you mean?

KENJI: We think we are not getting as much out of the retreat as we should. I have come to this conclusion, and so have others. Usually, when John throws out a discussion question, you answer it immediately. But you not only answer it, you rattle off all the solutions from your class—and so fast.

SALLY: I agree. I'm not getting what I came for. I don't get a chance to talk.

KENJI: We appreciate that you have done your homework. And you certainly deserve a chance to talk. But we'd like to have our own chance, too.

Nearly every member had something to say. They did so in a direct, supportive manner. The result was an about-face. With the leader's help, the group was able to state specific behaviors that the member could change. She was willing to do so.

Confrontation will not always have such a positive effect. But avoiding problems does not mean they will go away. Usually they remain, and their presence causes destructive tension.

In summary, Bormann suggests that primary tension is related to the acquaintance process. Secondary tension results from perceptual problems, procedural disagreements, role development, and personality differences. Some methods for dealing with this conflict are humor, mediation, scapegoating, and confronting. Successful groups experience tension and manage it when it moves beyond their tolerance level.

Focus on Research

Fantasy and Group Development

When we think of fantasy, we may think of our creative thought that produces something fictitious or unreal. Perhaps we have a hope or dream for what we would like something to be. Small group researchers use the word to mean something different. Ernest Bormann (1986, p. 221) suggests that *fantasy* refers to "the creative and imaginative shared interpretation of events that fulfill a group's psychological or rhetorical need to make sense of their experience and to anticipate their future." This formal definition refers to periods in a group's interaction when members are telling stories, sharing anecdotes, and recounting past experiences. This talk may not seem to be directly related to the group's task, but it does serve a purpose related to task accomplishment. It serves to establish and reinforce the group's culture, and that culture has an impact on how the group operates and accomplishes its tasks. Members are not deliberate in their efforts to establish the group's culture; that is, they don't consciously set out to accomplish this aim.

When one member picks up on another's storytelling and adds to it, group storytelling that Bales (1970) refers to as a *fantasy chain* begins. Interaction during this period often changes dramatically as voices become louder, speed of interaction increases, and the tone turns to excitement. These fantasy chains may last as little as 30 seconds or as long as a half-hour. These chains are a rhetorical tool for establishing group identity and culture as members share images of the group and its environment. This storytelling also turns out to be a means of passing on the group's culture to new members.

Fantasies have themes—both obvious ones and those below the surface. The latent, or below-the-surface, meaning is where we most often find ideas about the group's culture, values, and norms. Robert Bales recommends that we look for sudden insights rather than doing systematic analyses of fantasy. Often, fantasies will have a plot line with heroes and villains. We also may find moral or psychological guidance that provides a basis for group action.

It is through these fantasies that a group constructs its shared realities that bond members to each other. As Linda Putnam and her colleagues (1991, p. 87) put it, this shared meaning "accounts for the creation and maintenance of group consciousness through shared motives, common emotional activity, and consensual meanings for events."

R. F. Bales (1970). *Personality and interpersonal behavior.* New York: Holt, Rinehart and Winston, pp. 105–108, 136–155.

E. G. Bormann (1986). Symbolic convergence theory and communication in group decision making. In R. Y. Hirokawa & M. S. Poole (eds.), *Communication and group decision making.* Newbury Park, CA: Sage, pp. 219–236.

L. L. Putnam, S. A. Van Hoeven, & C. A. Bullis (1991). The role of rituals and fantasy themes in teachers' bargaining. *Western Journal of Speech Communication, 55,* 85–103.

Idea Development

Thomas M. Scheidel and Laura Crowell (1964) found that idea development does not follow a straight line. Instead, groups develop a spiral of anchoring and reach-testing.

Scheidel and Crowell described idea development in terms of communication patterns rather than in terms of the task and social dimensions. Thus their work is limited to one aspect of group development—idea development—and does not give the broad picture.

Scheidel and Crowell studied five trained discussion groups that carried out two-hour discussions. The recorded discussions were then evaluated for type of contribution. These investigators were interested in the amount of initiation, extension, modification, synthesis, confirmation, clarification, or substantiation of ideas.

All these behaviors can be seen in the development of an idea. Follow, for example, the development of this idea in a city council meeting:

INITIATION: We ought to have an ordinance that will regulate businesses that come to town to sell their goods on a transient basis.

EXTENSION: Yes. And the ordinance should cover door-to-door salespeople and those that rent temporary space.

MODIFICATION: But it should be limited to people who come to town and sell. Not the kids who are selling for clubs or the farmer setting up a roadside stand.

SYNTHESIS: So we ought to have an ordinance that regulates businesses that set up temporary sales locations but not temporary business by local people.

CONFIRMATION: Yes. That is what we need.

CLARIFICATION: I want to make sure I got this straight. You mean those people who come to town and set up in motels and the traveling salesperson. I know these people. They can be real rip-offs.

SUBSTANTIATION: Yes. Last year we had 75 complaints to the chamber of commerce about inferior merchandise they sold. And they were no longer here to answer questions about the things they sold.

Scheidel and Crowell were also concerned about how people tested ideas. Assume for a moment that you are Tom or Laura. What kind of pattern would you expect to discover? Start with your own experience. Does somebody introduce an idea that is then discussed and tested by the group? Does a member voice disagreement that then causes the group to test and modify the idea? Does the group spend considerable time refining an idea before it goes on to the next? Would you expect some sort of linking behavior—like the speaker who creates a transition in a speech to link ideas to one another? What comes next will be more meaningful if you stop here and try to answer these questions. Take your pencil and jot the answers, yes or no, in the margin if you like.

If you are operating on the assumption that ideas develop in a step-by-step line, then you may have answered yes to most of these questions. Scheidel and Crowell assumed that a linear model would include a sequence that looks something like Figure 5.2. This chain of events would recur for each decision made by a group.

However, a typical sequence of response did not follow this pattern. These kinds of statements accounted for only about 22 percent of the total comments. Further, most of the comments with respect to what others said were quite positive: 25 percent of the comments were statements of agreement, and another 25 percent were devoted to

Initiation — — — → Extension — — — → Modification — — — → Synthesis

FIGURE 5.2
A Linear Model of Idea Development

rephrasing (clarifying) and providing evidence to support (substantiating). Not much extension, modification, or synthesis was observed at all.

Scheidel and Crowell observed a **reach-test cycle.** This pattern involved (1) the suggestion of an idea, (2) agreement by others, (3) presentation of examples to clarify the idea, and (4) affirmation that the information confirms the original assertion. Consider an interaction from a sorority meeting that illustrates this pattern:

> Let's make our spring social a beach party.
>
> That sounds like a good idea.
>
> Yes. I think so, too.
>
> Let's do it.
>
> We could go early—say nine. Spend time on the beach. Then go to an entertainment spot while it's hot. Then back to the beach by three.
>
> Yes. Good idea.

This reach-test motion of the group is sometimes followed by a member's criticizing the idea. Scheidel and Crowell found that disagreement was rare. But when it happened, it almost never took place immediately after the new idea was suggested. If the new idea has been rejected, then the group moves back to its previous **anchor point,** the point of agreement. If the reach-tested idea is approved, a new anchor point is established. Then a new idea is presented for the group to reach-test. This process looks like the illustration in Figure 5.3. Notice that the process involves cumulative and progressive movement in which the group introduces, confirms, clarifies, and substantiates ideas. When ideas are rejected, the group backtracks to the agreed-upon position and reconfirms its decision (Hirokawa, 1987).

This spiral pattern explains what seems to be an inefficiency in decision making. The linear model assumes not much backtracking. Thus, some who observe groups and discover that they are not moving in a straight line label groups as inefficient. It is not appropriate to describe the spiral movement as inefficient. Efficiency is related to more than doing a job quickly. If the spiral motion serves a purpose—suppose, for example, it helps the group to develop more commitment to its decision—then it may be the most efficient way to achieve a desirable end. It is quite possible that the spiraling has this effect, as much of it is devoted to voiced agreement.

Data that support this interpretation of the reach-test process were provided by a follow-up study on feedback in groups. Scheidel and Crowell (1966) focused on the

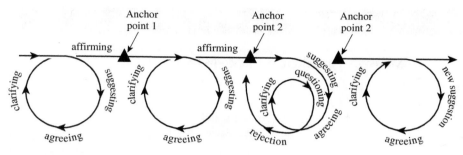

FIGURE 5.3
The Spiral Model of Idea Development

occurrence of feedback loops of the reach-test variety—an interaction pattern in which one person initiated a comment that was responded to by another and then was reacted to by the initiator. They found that 35 percent of the interaction consisted of these patterns. It is amazing that there were so many of these kinds of loops. The most frequently observed feedback response was the statement of agreement (34 percent). An agreement-type feedback consists of a receiver making a comment to the source of the idea that shows agreement or asks for clarification. The loop is completed by the source speaking again. The receiver's reinforcing comment seems to encourage the speaker, as he or she often speaks again.

A speaker in a service group might say, "I think our spring project should be to raise money to buy camping gear for the boys' home." Another member might respond, "That's a wonderful idea. We ought to do that." The first speaker would then continue, "We could sell doughnuts at the shopping mall on a couple of Saturday mornings." Thus the anchoring and reach-testing processes seem to serve the purpose of encouraging the members and developing acceptance for commitment to the task.

In a recent study, Pavitt and Johnson (2002) reported that the spiraling model is not found in all groups. The groups they studied showed a wide variation in amount of spiraling, from very little to a great deal more than found by Scheidel and Crowell (1964). In spite of this finding, the process is common enough that understanding it is very useful.

But what happens to ideas that are not reinforced? Suppose a person disagrees or presents negative modification of the idea. Dennis S. Gouran and John E. Baird Jr. (1972) observed that group members have a tendency to change the subject within two to four comments after the topic draws disagreement. So groups that do not find that they have an anchor of agreement drop the idea and pick up a new reach-test cycle.

Encouraging Group Development: Application of the Spiral Model of Idea Development

The spiral model performs an important function even though it may seem inefficient. Knowing this movement is normal may help you be more patient with your group. Remember that it is the process by which groups build consensus and commitment to their decisions.

Looking Back: A Quick Review

MODELS OF GROUP PROCESS

Phase models	Robert Bales: Task and relational concerns predominate at particular times
	B. Aubrey Fisher: Groups follow predictable phases in the decision-making process
Multisequence models	Marshall Scott Poole: Groups move along three activity tracks—task processes, relational, and topic
Punctuated equilibrium model	C. J. G. Gersick: Groups engage in stable behavior, then disruptive behavior, then stable behavior
Social tension model	Ernest G. Borman: Groups experience two types of tension—primary and secondary. Sometimes groups move beyond their threshold of tension toleration
Spiral model	Thomas Schiedel and Laura Crowell: Ideas develop in a pattern of acceptance or rejection that rests on anchor points.

This reach-test model also suggests there is a natural tendency in groups to avoid conflict. Recall that 25 percent of the comments about others' ideas were statements of agreement and that another 25 percent were remarks that either clarified or substantiated. Only very rarely did a member disagree with an idea. This seems to suggest a need for members to foster an attitude that conflict is useful and can be handled in a supportive manner. Members may need to make a special effort to analyze one another's ideas critically.

SUMMARY

Understanding the reasons people have for being part of a particular group is important. People belong to groups because of (1) interpersonal attraction, (2) attraction to the group's activities, (3) attraction to the group's goals, (4) valuing group affiliation, and (5) fulfillment of needs outside the group. Attraction is related to pleasing physical characteristics, similarity in attitude, belief, personality, race, and economic status, as well as to perceived ability of the other person. The reasons people belong to groups are related to needs that can be reinforced in order to develop commitment.

Groups, like people, move through phases. Robert F. Bales, B. Aubrey Fisher, and Marshall Scott Poole present evidence of this. Their work suggests that groups move through four stages: (1) orientation, (2) conflict, (3) emergence, and (4) reinforcement. Poole suggests three activity areas—task, relationship, and topic. Each may follow this phase cycle at a different pace. These phases seem to serve certain needs, and, when phases are skipped, problems may result. The orientation phase allows members to understand the task and one another. The conflict stage serves the function of testing ideas on the way to consensus. The emergence phase serves to produce a decision, heal the wounds of conflict, and generate consensus. The reinforcement phase helps members to believe that they have done good work, and generates satisfaction and commitment. The ability to identify these phases allows a person to discover whether the group has skipped a phase, to anticipate the group's movement through the phase, and to know whether the group has become stalled in a phase.

Social tension in groups is both beneficial and harmful. A group needs a certain amount of tension to help hold it together and keep it active. Too much tension can be more than a group is able to tolerate. Tensions experienced as a group is forming are called primary tensions. These result from uneasiness among the members and uncertainty about the task. Other tensions develop as the group is working out roles and norms. These might be about leadership and about perceptions regarding procedure, personalities, and values. This tension level exhibits a phaselike structure in the healthy group. Groups manage tension through tension releasers, mediation, scapegoating, and direct confrontation. It is important that groups manage tension to keep it at a level that allows productivity.

Thomas M. Scheidel and Laura Crowell suggest that idea development follows a spiral structure. A reach-test cycle consists of four parts: the suggestion of an idea, agreement to the idea by others, presentation of examples to clarify the idea, and affirmation that the information confirms the original assertion. Groups move from an anchor point, a point of decision, to the next idea. Rejection of the idea means that the group moves back to its last anchor point and suggests a new idea to be reach-tested. This four-part cycle probably serves to reinforce the group's commitment to its decision. Leaders should not be unduly concerned about the apparent inefficiency this creates.

KEY TERMS AND CONCEPTS

activity tracks	mediation	relational activities
anchoring	multiple sequence model	scapegoating
breakpoints	normal breakpoint	secondary tension
complex cyclic	orientation phase	socioemotional
conflict phase	primary tension	solution oriented
contingency model	punctuated equilibrium	task
delay	model	task-process activities
direct confrontation	reach-test cycle	tension releaser
disruption	reach-testing	threshold of tolerance
emergence phase	reinforcement phase	unitary sequence

EXERCISES

1. Consider your classroom group. Describe and analyze the factors that attract you and your members to the group. Decide how these factors contribute to task performance.

2. How often do group goals and individual goals match? Answer this question in writing based on your experience. Which group stands out as one in which your goals and its goals were most alike? Which group stands out as one in which your goals and its goals were most different? Describe your attraction to each group. Describe your participation in each group. How did your participation differ between the two groups? Compare your answers with those of members of a small group. Are your experiences similar? Is there a typical experience? What motivational factors are presented to the group when individual and group goals differ? What can be done to bring these differing goals together?

3. Consider this question as a class: If you could pick members for a decision-making group, what member characteristics would you want in order to create an ideal group? What characteristics would each member have? Give reasons for your choices. Try to construct an ideal five-member group.

4. Select a small group with which you have met. Based on Fisher's phase analysis try to identify phases through which the group passed. Describe the phases you identified. Were they easy to identify? How did member behavior differ from phase to phase? If the group you analyzed is part of your class, compare your ideas with other class members' sense of the group.

5. Analyze a meeting of your group to determine whether you can identify primary and secondary tension. Was there primary tension? If so, what was interaction like at this time? How long did it last? Was there secondary tension? If so, what was the source of the tension? How did this tension affect your group's effectiveness? If the tension was released, how was that achieved? Now suppose the tension was not released. How do you think this situation might affect your group if it continued for several meetings?

6. Using the experience of members of a small group, identify culture differences that have been observed. How did these differences affect the group's task and social dimensions? If any of these differences created problems for the group, how were they resolved?

RECOMMENDED WEBSITES

Miami University in Ohio has a *Leadership Handout* series with a section devoted to motivating group members, including great tips on how to keep them engaged and on task: www.units.muohio.edu/saf/sac/handout/motivatingmembers.html.

Motivating and Retaining group members is the main theme at www.cl.uh.edu/stuserv/leadership_development/Motivating_and_Retaining.htm. It includes ways to stimulate participation and improve involvement in small groups.

Developmental Sequence in Small Groups is a 20-page document devoted to Tuckmen's proposal of how groups develop and make decisions. The site contains an extensive list of references: all.successcenter.ohiostate.edu/references/GROUP%20DEV%20ARTICLE.doc.

Association for Information Systems has a link to the full texts of some of Marshall Scott Poole's articles in three languages: aisel.isworld.org/article_by_author.asp?Author_ID=1581.

Group formation and development are topics you can look into at the Web location www.san.orglip/cds/cmp/hwgroup.htm.

RECOMMENDED READINGS

B. A. Fisher (1972). Decision emergence: Phases in group decision making. *Speech Monographs*, 39, pp. 53–66.

C. J. G. Gersick (2003). Time and transition in work teams: Toward a new model of group development. In R. Y. Hirokawa, R. S. Cathcart, L. A. Samovar, & L. D. Henman, eds., *Small group communication: Theory and practice*, 8th ed. Los Angeles, CA: Roxbury, pp. 57–75.

R. Y. Hirokawa (1983). Group communication and problem-solving effectiveness. *Human Communication Research*, 9, pp. 291–305.

M. S. Poole (2003). A multiple sequence model of group decision development. In R. Y. Hirokawa, R. S. Cathcart, L. A. Samovar, & L. D. Henman (eds.), *Small group communication: Theory and practice*, 8th ed. Los Angeles, CA: Roxbury, pp. 76–82.

chapter 6

ROLES AND ROLE EMERGENCE

OBJECTIVES

After reading this chapter you should be able to
- Explain the concept of *role* as it relates to participation in small groups.
- Identify what is meant by *role stability*, including its impact on the functioning of a small group.
- Differentiate between formal and informal roles.
- Describe a model of role emergence that includes the concept of group reinforcement.
- Name and explain three types of *role conflict* and speculate about some typical outcomes of each type of conflict.
- List and describe the roles that fall under each of these categories: group task roles, group maintenance roles, and self-centered roles.

The program committee for the Parent-Teacher Association (PTA) met to plan activities for its six meetings for the year. The committee had seven members, including the president and secretary of the organization. The group had spent a little time just chatting and getting acquainted when Dan McDonald, the program committee chair, interrupted:

DAN: I think we are all here and have had time to say hello. Let's get started. We will have six meetings this year. Five of them will include a program we plan; one will be a program put on by the students in the school. What ideas do you have for our programs?

GROUP: (Silence.)

MIKE: (Finally, after a short silence.) I've been having trouble dealing with my son. How about someone to talk about managing behavior problems?

DAN: Okay. Let's put that one down as a possibility. What's another idea?

GROUP: (More silence, with Mona finally speaking.)

MONA: I think that handling homework is worth some good advice from an expert. Homework time at my house is awful. I'll bet others think that's a problem. How about you, Jonathan?

JONATHAN: Well, Mona, I haven't noticed much difficulty with homework at my house. My children generally finish their homework by the time I get home from work. But if it's a problem for you, let's get someone to give advice.

ELIZABETH: Homework is certainly a problem, but I'm more concerned with the trash on television. I'm worried about the violence and sex that my kids are exposed to on TV. I try to keep them from watching, but somehow when I'm not close by they tune it in. I'd like to have someone talk about this problem.

ROBERT: I'd like to backtrack on all of this, Dan, if I may. I think these are interesting ideas. But I think we need to understand more about what we're trying to accomplish. I'd like to talk about what programs were offered last year and how they were received, and then get back to suggesting ideas.

DAN: We could do that. What do others think about starting again?

GROUP: (Silence.)

DAN: Latashia, do you have a suggestion about what we should do?

Think for a moment about these people. You probably formed ideas about each. Your vision of these people probably allows you to make predictions about their behavior. The set of behaviors exhibited by each member is the beginning of a role definition. Role is a concept that is central to understanding groups. Role determines the structure of a group and its outcomes. The roles that are developing in this committee may allow it to plan a year of exciting programs. On the other hand, the roles may lead to conflict, disagreement, and programs that will not serve the organization.

The chapter begins with a discussion of role as a concept. Next, it suggests how roles develop. This topic leads to three related ideas: role strain, intrarole conflict, and interrole conflict. We explore these problems and how a group might address them. Finally, we examine a useful category system for thinking about roles.

THE CONCEPT OF ROLE

Your first contact with a role was probably in connection with an actor who played a character in a play. You also assume certain roles in everyday life. You are a student, a daughter or son, a friend. Perhaps you are an employee. You learn to play these roles through interaction with others. Your culture tells you what roles there ought to be.

A small group is also a culture. It, too, has a set of roles that reflect its members' views of the group's needs and the preferences of its members. A **role** is the set of behaviors enacted by an individual in relation to the expectations of the rest of the group members. A role is something that evolves out of the trial-and-error process—the members of a group teaching individuals which behaviors are appropriate and which are not by rewarding and punishing trials. The group has power to mold the individual's role to the extent to which the individual cares about membership in the group. Group members reinforce certain behaviors and extinguish others. Sometimes a particular set of behaviors follows a pattern that can be described by a single term. *Leader* is an example of a term used to describe a set of related behaviors.

On the other hand, an individual must agree to play a particular role. **Role stability** emerges when the individual agrees and the group positively reinforces performance of the role. The person will generally continue to play the role on a regular basis.

The concept of role can be more fully understood by differentiating between formal and informal roles. A **formal role** is assigned by the organization or group. It usually includes a title, such as president, vice-president, secretary, or chairperson. The assignment of this type of role may or may not be determined by a person's expertise or talent. For example, a man may be appointed to chair a group and not perform as we might imagine a chairperson should. A formal role, then, identifies a position and a set of behaviors that a person may or may not fulfill. The definition of this role remains roughly the same regardless of the person within it.

An **informal role** is regulated, often very subtly, between the group and the person fulfilling it. (The person must attempt role fulfillment and the group reinforce the attempt.) The role emphasis is on its function rather than a position. Benne and Sheets (1948) and Mudrack and Farrell (1995) describe these roles. Thus a person may provide leadership functions and thereby fulfill a leadership role without the formal designation.

The formal role structure in an ongoing group, usually constituted by the organization itself, operates in addition to the informal role structure determined by the group. A network of informal roles is highly idiosyncratic to any particular group. Because of people's idiosyncrasies, the number of roles that can emerge in a group is large. With the exception of leader, no role seems to be present in all groups.

The rest of this chapter examines the process through which informal roles emerge, the issue of role conflict, and several of the usual roles found in decision-making groups.

ROLE EMERGENCE IN SMALL GROUPS

Suppose the president of a campus group to which you belong invites you to work on a committee to plan a special event. Imagine yourself in the first group meeting. What will you do? What roles might you play? Will you lead? Will you be an important source of information? Will you be the person to challenge the group's ideas? Will you help other members to feel included? Perhaps you have served some of these roles for groups in the past. If so, you may do so again. The question of what role you will play in this group may be answered by considering how roles emerge.

Ernest G. Bormann's (1990) study at the University of Minnesota provides a model of how roles emerge in groups. He presents a stimulus–response model that points to role emergence as a function of reinforcement through the group's interaction over time. Figure 6.1 displays the options for the emergence of a role for a particular member. At a time T_1 a member performs a given role function (RF_1). A member or several members either give ambiguous feedback or encourage or discourage the member's role behavior. At time T_2, presumably the next opportunity the person has to perform the role, the person behaves on the basis of the group's reinforcement. If the group members have given ambiguous cues, the member may try the role again. He or she does so until a clear signal is received from the group. If the group approves, the member will try the function again—this time with greater confidence. If disapproval is shown, the member is likely to quit trying to perform the role. In cases where the role is important to the group, other members may attempt to provide it. This stimulus–response model operates for each role that emerges.

To show how a role might emerge through group interaction—and how powerful a group's ability to control the behavior of one of its members might be—suppose that you do join a campus group. You might imagine yourself in any of a variety of contexts—member of the student newspaper staff, member of a special-interest club, member of the executive committee in a social fraternity or sorority, member of an ad hoc committee of the student government association. Let's suppose you join an ad hoc committee of the student government association. Interested and excited, you approach the first meeting very well prepared to discuss the topic, which, say, is selection of the entertainers the student government will bring to the campus in the coming year. Because the bottom line seems like a very large sum—$350,000—you have given a good deal of thought to the variety of speakers and entertainers. You have asked friends to mention their interests. You have spent a night walking the floors of a dormitory to survey the students. You have even contacted a New York booking agency to ask about the fees charged by several entertainers.

The chairperson opens the meeting with a little speech about getting the most for the money and then asks for suggestions. You wait quietly for an opening. After several of the members—all of whom have been members of the committee before—speak, you discover that they have not put much thought into their proposals. No one appears to know how much money would be required or whether the individuals named would be available. No one seems to have surveyed any students.

You begin to make your presentation. You say something like, "Hmm, uh, I did a little thinking about this before the meeting. I went to a dorm and asked 120 people to mention entertainers they would like to bring to campus. I was surprised how easily their

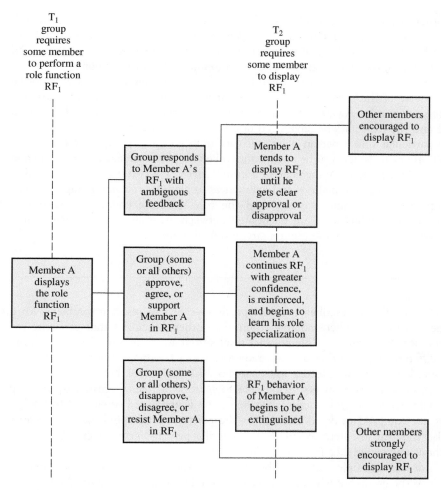

FIGURE 6.1
Model of Role Emergence by Ernest G. Bormann

Source: Figure from E. G. Bormann (1990). Reprinted by permission.

responses could be classified into categories. I'd be happy to say more, if you would be interested in hearing about it." You stop.

"Really?" "You did that?" "That's fantastic!" "Let's hear it." These responses seem to reflect the group's attitudes generally. People are interested. They are reinforcing your behavior. They are reinforcing your role as information provider.

"Yeah. Uh. There were really four categories. One was rock music. One was country and western. One was serious lecture. One was jazz music."

You are about to develop these categories further when one of the members says, "We tried jazz last year. No one came to the concerts."

Another member says, "That's that. No jazz." A discussion about the categories follows. They agree to jazz, and agree to try to get Grover Washington. In discussing your categories, the group has cemented your role of information provider. You have provided leadership that members have valued. They have reinforced your behavior.

The process of role development can be quite subtle. Often a member may not be specifically aware of the group's reinforcement pattern or even of the group's particular expectations for a role. Awareness usually comes *after* the role behaviors have been performed and the expectations have been developed (Ellis & Fisher, 1994).

The particular role a person plays will vary from group to group. If you think of the various groups to which you belong, you are likely to play a similar role in some and different roles in others. Each member of a group develops a pattern of behaviors that takes into account personal abilities and willingness to play the role *and* group approval. As a group meets over time, we may find the role structure changes as tasks and membership change. Thus roles are negotiated between an individual and the group's members and may change as the group's circumstances change.

ROLE PRESSURES

Joseph McGrath (1984) describes two role pressures that can result in problems for a group. These are role conflict and role strain. Two other difficulties that can arise are intrarole and interrole conflict. **Role conflict** results from an attempt to play two or more roles—in different groups—that are contradictory to each other. Under some circumstances social leader and task leader roles may produce such a conflict.

Role strain comes from not being able to perform a role. Occasionally a group member might experience role strain when he or she is appointed or elected to fulfill a role but is not equipped to do so. Sometimes the person has accepted the role because no one else will. An excellent example of this is the person who is elected to chair a group without any experience in such a task.

An additional example is provided by the person who is asked to collect information and bring it to the group but who has no access to the information or data-gathering skill. Role strain resulting from this situation—one in which the person fills a role reluctantly—can affect the social and task dimensions of the group. The person resents the imposition, and so the climate breaks down. If the person does a poor job, the task suffers.

Role strain also might result from gender stereotypes. Women, for example, might be drafted for the role of group recorder when they may not feel qualified or do not wish to take on the role. Men may be pressured to lead because some members think men ought to take the lead.

What might a person do when caught in this kind of role strain? Perhaps the best solution is to be direct with the group about your desires. For example, one woman came right out and said, "I don't enjoy the role of secretary. I'd rather not do it. Please find someone else." Another member took the role.

Intrarole conflict results from people in a group having different ideas about the enactment of a role. For example, some students may expect the teacher as leader to take charge in an autocratic fashion. Others may expect a more democratic style of leadership. Thus the teacher may experience intrarole conflict that may have to be explored with the students in order to come to some common understanding of the role.

Interrole conflict is most likely to occur when a person must take on an especially important role outside the group. Suppose, for example, that a prominent member of the community—say, the president of a local business—is appointed to a commission to study teenage delinquency. This president has had considerable experience with young people whom her company has employed over the past five years. She has come to believe that companies cannot afford to spend resources on irresponsible or delinquent youths. Now she finds herself appointed to a committee that is charged with finding ways of employing these people. The woman may be unable to fulfill the role because her role as president conflicts with the role of group member. She might not be able to seriously entertain the idea of integrating these juveniles into the business community.

What usually happens in a case like this is that a person will enact the role of greatest personal importance (Shaw, 1980). In the case of the president of the local company, she may try to block any programs that integrate juveniles into businesses.

Being alert to the potentials of role pressures is an important part of your participant–analyst role in groups. You can avoid role conflict in part through careful selection of participants. But when conflict has not been successfully avoided, a group may have to deal with the situation directly. (Chapter 10, "Managing Conflict in the Group," will be helpful in this situation.) Role strain can be minimized if group members are careful not to force a role on a reluctant person. Careful attention to the verbal and nonverbal cues a member gives off when a particular role is being suggested will aid in avoiding this difficulty. Interrole conflict may be minimized by making an effort to secure member commitment to the group's goal.

Looking Back: A Quick Review

ROLE PRESSURES

Role conflict	Result of a person's attempt to play two or more contradictory roles
Role strain	Result of a person's attempt to perform a role he or she is unprepared to play
Intrarole conflict	Result of a person's trying to play a role that is defined differently by various members
Interrole conflict	Result of a person's taking on two roles that are incompatible

FUNCTIONAL ROLES IN SMALL GROUPS

A common question asked by those who want to do their best in group meetings is "What do I do during meetings to make the best contribution I can?" In one form or another, that question has been asked for many generations. One of the most useful responses appeared in a classic essay written by Kenneth D. Benne and Paul Sheats (1948). These scholars studied the role behaviors that occurred in small groups engaged in

Focus on Research

ROLE STRESS ON THE JOB

Role ambiguity and conflict can take their toll on performance in the workplace. House, Schuler, and Levanoni (1983, p. 336) found that employees registered the following complaints related to job security:

I don't know what is expected of me.

I work under unclear policies and guidelines.

I find planned goals and objectives unclear.

I don't know how my performance will be evaluated.

Employees who were experiencing role conflict—an incompatibility between job, resources, rules or policies, and other people—had this set of complaints:

I work with two or more groups who operate quite differently.

I get myself into situations where there are conflicting requirements.

I'm asked to do things that are against my better judgment.

I do things that are accepted by one person, but not others.

I get incompatible requests from two or more people.

Research studies suggest that the negative outcomes of role ambiguity and role conflict on workers' morale and productivity are many. Kemery and colleagues (1985) found that job stress among accountants and hospital employees was linked to tension, decreased job satisfaction, and employee turnover. Other researchers (Fisher & Gitelson, 1983), in a review of 42 studies, discovered that these stresses were related to an increased desire to leave the organization and to a decrease in commitment, involvement, satisfaction, and participation in decision making.

So what is the solution to managing these problems? Suggestions include written job descriptions with the opportunity to discuss them, the opportunity for feedback, and moving potentially incompatible roles so that they are performed at different locations and at different times.

C. D. Fisher & R. Gitelson (1983). A meta-analysis of the correlates of role conflict and ambiguity. *Journal of Applied Psychology*, 68, 320–333.

R. J. House, R. S. Schuler, & E. Levanoni (1983). Role conflict and ambiguous scales: Realities or artifacts? *Journal of Applied Psychology*, 68, 334–337.

E. R. Kemery, A. G. Bedeian, K. W. Mossholder, & J. Touliatos (1985). Outcomes of role stress: A multisample constructive replication. *Academy of Management Review*, 28, 363–375.

problem-solving discussion. They divided those behaviors into three categories—goal achievement, group identity, and the needs of the members.

Interestingly, empirical research with the aim of discovering how well Benne and Sheats's three-category system describes typical member behavior from the viewpoint of the members themselves found that these categories still hold (Mudrack & Farrell, 1995).

Group Task Roles

In the first category, Benne and Sheats identified role behaviors that helped groups to achieve their goals. What behaviors help a group to accomplish its tasks? Someone tries to give the group some semblance of order, and undoubtedly someone will criticize and evaluate suggestions, and someone else will summarize what has been said. Typically, if the group believes its work to be important, someone will keep some kind of record of its work. These behaviors are what Benne and Sheats called **task roles.** In all, they identified and described thirteen such roles. Table 6.1 lists these roles.

1. **Initiator–contributor.** As the name suggests, this person initiates ideas and suggestions. The initiator-contributor comes up with new ideas and lines of discussion. You might hear "How about taking a different approach to this chore? Suppose we. . . ." If the contribution is related to an idea already being discussed, the role player will present a new or novel idea related to it. This person is the creative thinker in a group. He or she might begin, "You know, there is another way of looking at this that we might want to consider." This function is also performed by the leader when he or she introduces an issue.

2. **Information seeker.** Asking questions that seek information is an important function for all members of the group. But a group may not have any formal procedure to ensure idea generation. Group members also may be reluctant to provide the needed information. So the group must rely on certain members to sense the need for more information and actively seek it.

TABLE 6.1 Task Roles

1. Initiator–contributor	8. Diagnostician
2. Information seeker	9. Orienter–summarizer
3. Information giver	10. Energizer
4. Opinion seeker	11. Procedural assistant
5. Opinion giver	12. Secretary–recorder
6. Elaborator–clarifier	13. Evaluator–critic
7. Coordinator	

The information seeker asks for evidence that will allow judgment of the factual adequacy of ideas. This person might ask, "Does anyone have any data to support this idea?" The role player might, instead, ask for information or facts relevant to understanding the problem. Or perhaps this person will suggest that more information is needed before a decision can be reached. Perhaps the person might say, "I'd like to know more about what happened when they tried a play similar to this a couple of years ago. Let's find out and meet tomorrow to make a decision."

The information seeker also may seek information beyond what is available in the group. Seeking information from outside the group is important because members tend to talk about what they know, rather than seek new information (Schittekatte & Van Hiel, 1996).

3. **Information giver.**   The role of information giver is generally shared by members. It is obvious that the quality of a decision is related to the quality and quantity of information a group has. The information giver offers facts that are relevant to the task. The person who is playing this role well has the research skills, analytical ability, and knowledge to provide accurate and concise data. As part of the information given, you may hear the source of the information. The information giver might say, "I asked Dr. Jones, a specialist in this kind of thing. He said. . . ."

4. **Opinion seeker.**   Opinions differ from information in that they are inferences or conclusions, whereas information is the observed data. The opinion-seeker role is important because groups need members to offer conclusions about the facts they process. And, on the emotional side, members need to know how the others feel about the issues. If you were playing this role, you might say, "Does anyone else have an idea on this? Can someone clear up what this means?"

5. **Opinion giver.**   The opinion giver offers analysis of the information being presented. This means that the person states beliefs or opinions about suggestions. Perhaps you might hear, "I think we ought to go with the second plan. It fits the conditions we face in Concord best." The opinion giver might also indicate what the group's attitude should be: "We ought to take a hard line on absenteeism. We ought to let go people who miss work too frequently."

6. **Elaborator–clarifier.**   The person filling this role tests ideas and suggestions by elaborating on and clarifying what is being said. The person also may test understanding by asking questions. For example, "Do you mean that George actually said that he knew about the situation? I thought that that was your guess about what was going on." The elaborator-clarifier also may offer rationales for the group to consider. Perhaps a member will say, "I think we can tell Sue that we recommend this idea because. . . ." Finally, this person might try to help the group visualize how a suggestion would work.

7. **Coordinator.**   The coordinator tries to draw connections between what different members have said. This person might draw together information, opinions, and ideas or might check relationships among information, opinions, and ideas. For example, a coordinator might say, "John's opinion squares pretty well

with the research that Mary reported. Why don't we take that idea and see whether. . . ."

8. **Diagnostician.**   The diagnostician analyzes and identifies task-related problems. This person also poses issues related to the problem being discussed and, in doing so, may redirect the group. Typically, a person in this role might comment, "But I think you are missing the main point. The problem is that we can't afford to have unsafe. . . ."

9. **Orienter–summarizer.**   When the group moves too far off the task, the orienter-summarizer senses the appropriate time to bring it back. You might hear, "This discussion of . . . has been fun. Let's get back to where we were a few minutes ago." Or the orienter may ask a question about where the group is headed to allow members to see they have digressed: "I'm not sure where we are headed. What is the point?"

   This person also keeps the group oriented. He or she helps members understand where they have been and what conclusions they have reached by providing timely summaries. The summary may be followed by a question to check out the accuracy of the summary provided: "Is that what we've been saying?"

10. **Energizer.**   A member energizes the group when he or she raises the level of enthusiasm for its work. This is often accomplished by "upbeat" nonverbal behavior. Enthusiasm is generated by having one or more people in the group with an optimistic outlook. The energizer also may recognize the need for someone to challenge the group. You might hear, "Come on, folks. We're almost finished. I know we can be through in a few minutes if we work at it."

11. **Procedural assistant.**   The procedural assistant may take on a variety of tasks. He or she may organize such routine tasks as making seating arrangements, obtaining equipment, and handing out pertinent papers. This role is important because it fulfills functions that assist the leader in making sure that the group has what it needs and that meetings run smoothly. When the role is performed by several people, it can help to build a sense that members care about the group and about unity.

12. **Secretary–recorder.**   In many groups one person is assigned to take minutes of a meeting, serving as the "group memory." Obviously, keeping track of what is going on as a group is processing information requires skill and an ability to pay attention. This role presents a potential problem for the group, because the recording activity can limit other kinds of participation for some individuals. The person who takes the recorder role needs to be an individual who can record and participate otherwise.

   If the secretary-recorder also feeds back performance information, he or she can contribute to performance expectations. Research by Silver and Bufanio (1996) suggests a summary of progress is an important motivator when the group is being successful.

13. **Evaluator–critic.**   The person fulfilling the evaluator role is referred to as the "critical thinker." This role is important because the quality of a group's

decision is a function of how carefully and critically it evaluates ideas. The person in this role analyzes or causes the group to analyze its accomplishments according to some set of standards without causing members to feel threatened. You might hear an evaluator-critic say, "Look, we said that we had only $400 to spend. What is being proposed will cost at least $600. That's a 50 percent override."

This person also monitors the decision-making process to see that consensus has been reached. He or she may say, "What I hear people saying is that we must solve the attrition problem. Is that our first priority?"

This person serves as the **critical advisor** and suggests disadvantages to proposals, questions assumptions, sees errors in reasoning, and offers constructive criticism. Groups that have a member who performs this function make better-quality decisions because this person helps guard against several problems: faulty assumptions, poor information processing, and the single member whose view dominates the process (Schultz, Ketrow, & Urban, 1995). Keyton (2002) suggests someone other than the leader should take this role.

Several of these task roles are critical to the group's effectiveness: initiator-contributor, information seeker, information giver, opinion seeker, opinion giver, and evaluator–critic. Group members must initiate ideas and provide information and informed opinion. It is also crucial for some members to seek information and opinions if what is being offered is not sufficient to produce high-quality analysis and decisions. Finally, effective analysis depends on members' being willing to think critically—and to cause the group to think critically.

Group Building and Maintenance Roles

Group life includes moments of success and moments of failure. When times are bad, group members need to focus upon their relationships. Sometimes damaging conflict must be managed. At other times individual members develop problems that adversely influence the group. For example, when a task force is called, each person has been asked to meet because of personal expertise. If an individual suddenly stops making contributions to the group, the group loses the benefit of that person's input. Sometimes the tension levels in a group get so high that something must be done to break the tension. All these concerns and others are in the social, or relationship, dimension of group communication. When they occur, the role behaviors Benne and Sheats described as **maintenance roles** are needed. Table 6.2 lists the eight roles.

1. **Supporter–encourager.** The person or persons in this role offer warmth, solidarity, and recognition to the group's members. Support may take the form of praise, agreement, or signs of acceptance. A supporter-encourager might say, "I really like that idea, John." Or perhaps you might hear, "Priscilla's suggestion is attractive to me. Could we discuss it further?" This person-to-person encouragement is a valuable motivator and builder of cohesiveness. When offered by a high-status member, it can have even greater effect.

TABLE 6.2 Building and Maintenance Roles

1. Supporter–encourager
2. Harmonizer
3. Tension releaser
4. Compromiser

5. Gatekeeper
6. Feeling expresser
7. Standard setter
8. Follower

---

2. **Harmonizer.**   A harmonizer is the person who helps a group manage conflict. He or she works to reconcile disagreements, mediate differences, and reduce tension. The harmonizer is likely to be well acquainted with the conflict management techniques presented in Chapter 10.

   The person acting as harmonizer also may take on the role of tension releaser. Tensions are reduced by giving members the opportunity to explore their differences. Here are comments typical of a person in this role: "I don't think you two are as far apart as you think. Henry, are you saying . . . ? Benson, you seem to be saying. . . . Is that what you mean?"

3. **Tension releaser.**   The tension releaser's goal is to relax group members. This may be accomplished by poking fun at a situation so that members laugh at the situation. It even may require a diversion—perhaps a joke that is totally unrelated to the particular task at the moment.

   The tension releaser must be sensitive to the social demands of the group. Jokes that may be funny to an all-female group may not be funny at all in a mixed group. Making light of some issues is obviously in poor taste. When not played appropriately, the role may be viewed, instead, as a self-centered, playboy/playgirl role.

4. **Compromiser.**   This person offers to compromise when it is clearly necessary for group progress. "Looks like our solution is halfway between you and me, Loc. Can we look at the middle ground?" might be typical of the compromiser's comment.

   The nature of the group decision-making process often requires compromise if the group is to reach its goal satisfactorily. Thus, in the task dimension, many of the group's members often must play the compromiser role. Compromise will be necessary for some in the relationship dimension as well.

5. **Gatekeeper.**   The person fulfilling the gatekeeper role tries to keep communication channels open. One responsibility is to manage tactfully the time allotted to each speaker. If some members seem to be monopolizing the interaction, the gatekeeper might ask, "Does anyone else have an opinion on this issue?"

   This person is also skillful at drawing silent members into the discussion. The gatekeeper is careful to notice quiet people early in the session and to ask for their input. You might hear "Susan hasn't had the chance to say anything about this yet. Susan, I know you have been studying the problem. What do you think about . . . ?"

6. **Feeling expresser.**   The feeling expresser monitors the feelings, moods, and relationships in the group. The person articulates these group feelings, as well as his or her own, when doing so is appropriate. You might hear "Don't we need a break right now? I'm frustrated and confused and maybe we all are. I'd like to take a break so we can come back fresh to tackle this again."

7. **Standard setter.**   This role requires the person to suggest standards for the group to achieve. Recall from Chapter 1 that standards related to group process are called norms. The standard setter may challenge unproductive norms or unproductive behavior. For example, when a member is continually late, the standard setter might say, "John, we had to wait for you again. We won't get finished today. What happened?"

   Or the standard setter may be primarily concerned with setting criteria: "In my view, this decision doesn't measure up to our best. We really haven't set any criteria, much less tried to apply them."

8. **Follower.**   The follower goes along with the movement of the group. He or she listens attentively, accepting the ideas of others. Here is a typical comment from a person in the follower role: "I agree. Yes, I see what you mean. If that's what the group wants, I'll go along." In productive groups, members will usually not take on this role as their sole contribution.

Several of these building and maintenance roles seem to be especially important. Cohesiveness is generally important for productivity; thus the supporter-encourager performs a needed function. Conflict that is not managed effectively can destroy a group's effectiveness. The harmonizer works toward this end. Tension levels can rise above the group's threshold for tolerance. The group needs a member to recognize when tension has been too high for too long and to release it. Also, group members who are thinking critically about problems will undoubtedly have differing thoughts. Here the role of compromiser is crucial. Finally, a group must have standards for behaving and for deciding to be effective. Members must take the responsibility to help the group set and maintain standards. Thus five maintenance roles are critical: supporter-encourager, harmonizer, tension releaser, compromiser, and standard setter.

Some researchers believe behavior is either task- or relationship-oriented, but the distinction is not always that clear. Some acts obviously can affect both. For example, Mudrack and Farrell (1995) found the gatekeeper role, a maintenance role by this scheme, and the information-seeker role, a task role, fell into both categories.

Self-Centered Roles

Benne and Sheats described eight additional roles they believed are usually counterproductive. These **self-centered roles** focus on the individual's personal agenda. These role behaviors are not always counter to the best interests of the group, but self-centered roles often do inhibit group success. Table 6.3 lists the self-centered roles.

TABLE 6.3 Self-Centered Roles	
1. Blocker	5. Recognition seeker
2. Aggressor	6. Confessor
3. Deserter	7. Playboy/playgirl–clown
4. Dominator	8. Special-interest pleader

1. **Blocker.**   The blocker prevents progress toward the group's goals by raising objections, rejecting others' ideas, or taking a negative stand on issues. Issues that the group has already considered and decided may be reintroduced by the blocker. Blocking techniques are numerous, including emotional outbursts, filibustering, going on and on with procedural objections, and examining a solution or idea word by word to make sure each is exactly right. One blocker, whose presence was needed for the group to operate, declared, "Wait a minute! That's not right! That idea is absurd. If you take that position, I simply can't continue to work with this group."

2. **Aggressor.**   Some self-serving members struggle for status by trying to defeat one another. Their goal is to enhance themselves by lowering the status of others in the group. One aggressor exclaimed in a loud voice, "Wow, that's really swell! You turkeys have botched things again. Your constant bickering is responsible for this mess. Let me tell you how you ought to do this."

   People who are verbally aggressive are likely to have negative perceptions of their group's cohesiveness and degree of consensus. Group members who practice this "abusive pattern" may be less satisfied with the group's process (Martin & Anderson, 1997). They even may experience what Keyton (1994) refers to as a negative attitude about groups, or **grouphate.**

3. **Deserter.**   The deserter withdraws from the group's deliberation in some way. The person may act indifferent, aloof, and stiffly formal. Or the deserter might talk off the subject or engage in some sort of side conversation to avoid the issue. The person may merely sit in the group and daydream. A deserter may say to himself or herself, "Ho-hum. There's nothing in this discussion for me." But to the group the deserter says, "I guess I really don't care what you choose in this case. But on this other matter. . . ."

4. **Dominator.**   The dominator continually takes more than a fair share of the group's time. All members may dominate at some time or another, but this is not what the dominator role means. This person is a frequent monopolizer and may even interrupt and take the floor. The dominator might break in with, "Towana, you're just off base here. What we should do is this. First. . . ."

5. **Recognition seeker.**   The recognition seeker attempts to call attention to himself or herself in an exaggerated manner: "I think. . . . Don't you think I'm right? [Don't you think I'm wonderful?]" The role is played by boasting about present and past accomplishments, relating irrelevant personal experiences, and sometimes

attempting to gain sympathy. Here is a typical comment: "You guys wouldn't believe the bad day I had yesterday! It started when I woke up and went on and on. Let me tell you what happened."

6. **Confessor.**   The confessor role is played when a person presents personal difficulties to the group. These are not task-related issues; they are personal matters. The confessor is using the group for "therapy." Generally the group cares about the person, so members turn their attention to helping. A confessor might comment "This is not exactly on the topic, but I'm experiencing a problem with Rekha. Yesterday, Rekha and I had a fight about. . . ."

7. **Playboy/playgirl–clown.**   Some people love to be the clown. Humor can be an important part of group interactions, as it helps the group relax and attend to the task. Yet when the humor, horseplay, or cynicism is inappropriate, it can distract from the productivity. Members of the group may become caught up in the clowning and for the moment enjoy it. Later they may regret it, since the task remains incomplete. If members can play around without seriously damaging their productivity, then clowning is valuable. When a person distracts the group from its task, the role becomes self-serving. Most of us can recall a typical lead-in from the clown: "Did you hear the one about the. . . ?"

8. **Special-interest pleader.**   A member who speaks on behalf of an outside group, rather than the group of which he or she is a part, is pleading a special interest. When one group was deciding to whom it would award a contract, one member pleaded his special interest: "My friend Alan runs a company that makes this product. How about using his company? We might as well spend our money with people we know." The comment was a straightforward interest plea. No data were given to suggest that the firm offered advantages over others. The argument was merely on the basis of rewarding "a friend."

These self-centered roles are often referred to as deviant roles. A **deviant role** is one that detracts from the group's productivity because it focuses on the individual and away from achieving the group's goals.

When a member consistently detracts from the group's progress through this deviant behavior, the leader and members need to decide how to deal with the member in a way that can restore productive behavior to the group. Here is one suggestion:

First, members must clearly identify the role behavior—be specific—and decide if it consistently detracts from the group's progress. If it doesn't, the group may decide to wait and see how it plays out. They might ignore the behavior if this is the case. But a caution: Do not let this behavior go on and on. Early intervention is important because the longer this behavior goes on the more difficult it will be to deal with it.

If this ignoring does not stop the behavior, the leader and members may engage in functional conflict management using supportive communication behaviors. (Please refer to Chapter 10, Managing Conflict in Groups if this is the method chosen to deal with the deviant behavior.)

Next, the group needs to decide the best channel for communicating with the deviant member. A decision about what channel to use is based on which might be the most productive. One channel for communication is one member approaching the individual on a one-to-one basis and outside of the group meeting. The other channel is approaching the person in a regular group meeting. Use whichever channel you believe will produce the best outcome.

Finally, the group may need to "fire" the member if nothing seems to work. What this means is that the group should meet outside of the traditional meeting time and decide whether 'firing" is what is needed to bring back the group's productivity.

You will need to be direct in conveying this message, "[Name] you have been [describe the behavior] and this is seriously affecting our group's productivity and reaching our goal. We have talked to you about changing your behavior. We cannot see that anything has changed. So, we met and decided you can no longer be part of our group. There is no going back on our decision. So, you will have to accept it and leave this meeting." If the person does not leave, adjourn the meeting to allow all the members to leave the meeting place.

APPLYING YOUR UNDERSTANDING OF ROLE BEHAVIOR

You can see from studying these role behaviors that most groups have many more roles than they have members. Indeed, during the course of a single discussion, each person will contribute a variety of appropriate role behaviors.

A Question of Ethics and Responsibility

SELF-CENTERED ROLES

You are enrolled in an advanced small group communication course. The class has 15 members, so the instructor has decided to adopt a format that emphasizes individual participation. To facilitate the discussion process, your instructor has provided a list of questions for each class meeting that serves to focus the talk.

Over a period of meetings you discover a pattern of communication emerging that is quite disturbing to you. One member dominates most of the talk by quickly responding to whatever question is presented to the group before others have had the opportunity to respond. You have talked with others, and they say that they share your concern. One classmate said, "I paid my money too, and I want my share of the time to talk." Another member suggests that several

of you go to the instructor and ask that she intervene. One particularly upset member has volunteered to "ambush" the member after class and "lay it on the line." Others have additional suggestions. The professor is aware of the problem but has decided to let the group deal with the problem on their own. She believes that turning the problem over to them is justified because the topic of the class is small group communication. She sees this as a perfect opportunity for them to practice what they have been learning.

You are not quite sure what to do, but you do know that something has to be done quickly. Brainstorm on a sheet of paper about possible options for responsible behavior and then suggest a plan of action for dealing with this disruptive self-centered role.

Identifying the potential role behaviors allows you to do two things. First, it allows you to understand what is happening in a group while it is happening; in case something is causing the group to be unsuccessful, you can intervene. Second, the analysis of group role behaviors suggests ways of behaving that will help you achieve your own goals—and will help the group achieve its goals as well.

Ultimately, you are responsible for your own behavior in all groups you join. In a sense, as a participant analyst you are responsible for its success or failure. What you do to encourage the group to set and achieve appropriate goals is a mark of your worth to the group. What you do to encourage the group to become a more cohesive team and to establish a climate of trust in which communication can work well also establishes your worth to the group. Together, these two categories of behaviors constitute important aspects of group leadership, the topic of Chapter 7. And leadership is not confined to individuals who have been designated to lead. Each member of each group can and should contribute leadership.

SUMMARY

A small group is a culture with a set of roles that reflect its members' views of the group's needs and the talents and preferences of its individual members. A role is a set of behaviors that an individual member adopts in relation to the expectations of the rest of the group members. A member may take on a formal role that is assigned by the organization or group. This role usually has a title such as chairperson, vice president, or secretary. On the other hand, the person may take on an informal role. This type of role is characterized by behaviors that fulfill a function for the group. Such a function might be information provider, tension releaser, recorder, or leader.

Ernest Bormann describes role emergence as a trial-and-error process. This stimulus-response model suggests that members attempt roles and the group either reinforces or discourages the role behavior. Over a period of time, depending on the group's reaction, the member continues or discontinues the playing of the role.

Two problems that can occur as a member attempts to carry out a role are role conflict and role strain. Role conflict results from a person's trying to play two or more roles—generally in different groups—that are contradictory to each other. Role strain comes from not being able to perform a role. Sometimes gender stereotypes produce role strain. These problems can be addressed by selecting participants carefully and not forcing a role on a reluctant group member. Intrarole conflict comes from confusion about how to play a role. The role player's ideas may differ from the members' ideas.

Roles represent a wide variety of behaviors. Some roles are task centered, in that they help the group achieve its goal. Other roles are maintenance oriented; they focus on a group and its members, rather than on the task. Finally, self-centered roles focus on achieving the aims of individual group members and, therefore, are called deviant and often detract from task accomplishment and group maintenance. When a member consistently detracts from the group's progress through this deviant behavior, the leader and members need to decide how to deal with it.

KEY TERMS AND CONCEPTS

aggressor	follower	playboy/playgirl–clown
blocker	formal role	procedural assistant
compromiser	gatekeeper	recognition seeker
confessor	harmonizer	role
coordinator	informal role	role conflict
critical advisor	information giver	role stability
deserter	information seeker	role strain
deviant role	initiator–contributor	secretary–recorder
diagnostician	interrole conflict	self-centered roles
dominator	intrarole conflict	special-interest pleader
elaborator–clarifier	maintenance roles	standard setter
energizer	opinion giver	supporter–encourager
evaluator–critic	opinion seeker	task roles
feeling expresser	orienter–summarizer	tension releaser

EXERCISES

1. Describe and analyze the functional roles of the members of your group.

2. Think of a group with which you felt particularly frustrated. What roles did the various members play? Can you account for your frustration through an examination of the participation of the other members? What can you do if you encounter a similar situation in the future? Answer these questions in a two-page analysis.

3. Role-play a problem-solving discussion, perhaps a case study given to your group by your instructor. Assign two of the self-centered roles to two of the members. Attempt to complete this discussion within 20 to 25 minutes. Following the discussion of the case study, conduct an analysis of the group interaction. What effect did the disruptive role playing have on the group's decision making? What leadership behaviors did members employ to attempt to overcome these difficulties? How successful were they? If they were, why were they? If they were not, why were they not? What might have been done that was not done?

4. Which roles have you taken in groups? Think of at least five groups to which you have belonged. Based on the material presented in this chapter, identify what roles you have taken. How have the roles you have taken differed from group to group? How do the roles you have taken in these groups compare to those you have taken in this class? How could you expand your usefulness to groups by taking on new roles? What does your analysis tell you about your participation in groups?

5. With one or more of your classmates, observe a group. Independently, list the functional roles each member serves. Compare your findings with those of others who are observing the same discussion. Do you agree on the roles being played by each member? If not, how do you account for your disagreement? Now divide the behaviors among task, maintenance, and self-centered roles. Were the important roles played? What role functions might have improved the decision making if members had fulfilled them?

6. Think about a positive experience you had in a group discussion. Identify the informal roles each member took based on the category system presented in this chapter. Assess the role structure of this group. For example, how adequately did each member play the roles they took? Were there roles that were not played, but were needed? What effect did this have on the group's output? How adequate was your personal role playing? Are there roles you didn't take that you might take in future group interactions?

RECOMMENDED WEBSITES

The site Student Survival Guide to Managing Group Projects 2.0, at www.csc.calpoly.edu/~sludi/SEmanual/TableOfContents.html, is a small group manual complete with in-depth information by Stephanie Ludi in the Computer Science Department at California Polytechnic State University. The site includes sections concerning general group tasks and the evolution of group members, and a great section discussing problems students may have with other group members, such as laziness.

Ann Porteus's website, www.stanford.edu/group/resed/resed/staffresources/RM/training/grouproles.html, is a practical guide to the roles people play in groups. The page also tells what an individual in a group does to play each role, how he or she will play the role, and when he or she will take on the characteristics of that role.

Roles in Groups contains some common roles that are found in small groups. The site also has links to other group elements such as group size, group culture, and group developments, at www.dmu.ac.uk/~jamesa/teaching/roles_in_groups.htm.

Small Group Teaching has a useful list of forms and checklists devoted to all aspects of small group work, including planning and conducting sessions, at www.uchsc.edu/CIS/SmGpChkList.html.

Small group roles can be found at faculty.ed.umuc.edu/~prichard/crs_guid_gen/smlgrp_process.html. There is also a link to peer evaluation forms that can be used for assessing the roles of other group members.

RECOMMENDED READINGS

K. Benne & P. Sheats (1948). Functional roles of group members. *Journal of Social Issues*, 4, pp. 41–49.

D. G. Ellis & B. A. Fisher (1994). Behavioral standards: Roles and norms. *Small group decision making: Communication and the group process*, 4th ed. New York: McGraw-Hill, pp. 113–137.

M. S. Poole (1996). Group communication and the structuring process. In R. S. Cathcart, L. A. Samovar, & L. D. Nenman, eds., *Small group communication: A reader*. Dubuque, IA: Brown & Benchmark, pp. 85–95.

A. J. Salazar (1996). An analysis of the development and evolution of roles in the small group. *Small Group Research*, 27, pp. 475–503.

chapter 7

LEADING GROUP
MEETINGS

OBJECTIVES

After reading this chapter you should be able to
- Define and differentiate between these terms: *leader* and *leadership*, *designated leader* and *emergent leader.*
- Suggest and describe the five sources of power a leader or member might use.
- Describe the process of leader emergence, including the four scenarios identified by the Minnesota studies.
- Explain the characteristic features of the following ways of looking at leadership and suggest the utility of each: (1) the trait perspective, (2) the style perspective, (3) the situational perspective, (4) the contingency perspective, (5) the functional perspective, (6) the leader as medium, and (7) transformational leadership.
- Specify and explain the characteristics of an effective group leader.
- Recall the five major areas of responsibility that a successful group leader will attempt to manage, and specify how he or she might go about them.

A management group of a local department store met in the company training room. Poor leadership can be blamed at least in part for the way this meeting went. The time chosen for the meeting was poor—the middle of a very busy week just prior to a holiday. Moreover, the meeting was held—just after lunch and just before a 2 P.M. shift change. Several department managers were concerned because they had to check in employees at 2 P.M. A good leader carefully selects an appropriate meeting time.

The meeting included 15 department managers. The agenda for the meeting as published was to gather input about two questions: (1) "What problems might develop from changing store hours?" and (2) "If the hours were changed, what might the best hours be?"

There was also a hidden agenda. Indeed, there were two. One high-ranking manager was opposed to any change, but more than that, he appeared to be out to get another manager who favored the change. The senior manager clearly wanted to teach the lower-ranking manager a lesson—perhaps well intended or perhaps motivated by animosity. A wise leader would specify a clear agenda, taking the needs of members into account, and would do so well in advance of the meeting.

The meeting lasted well beyond the 2 P.M. shift change, and concluded with the store manager receiving plenty of input. But it also resulted in a set of unanticipated consequences. The lower-level manager who was opposed by the senior manager came away from the meeting feeling hostile. The management team sustained a deep fracture, mostly as a result of the store manager's inability to lead.

Many of these problems might have been avoided if the leader had planned carefully and if the goals and the objectives of the meeting had been thought through. As the meeting progressed, more skillful leadership could have managed the conflict—could have brought out, or buried, if necessary, the hidden agendas and made clear that they were inappropriate. Something could have been done about the relationship issues, too.

You can learn much by considering groups that have effective leaders. Think of the groups you've experienced that have had effective leaders. What have they taught you?

The chapter begins by making distinctions between *leadership* and *leaders,* and between *power* and *leadership*. Next it considers perspectives on leadership. Then the ideas of each perspective are considered with research on leadership to suggest characteristics of effective leaders. The chapter concludes with suggestions for improving leadership.

LEADERSHIP AND LEADERS

An early decision for any group is "Who will lead?" Sometimes the issue is decided by appointing a leader. For other groups, the group itself selects its leader. A single person may emerge to lead, or the leadership may be shared. This decision is crucial, for without adequate leadership the quality of the experience and the product are in doubt.

A student chapter of the Public Relations Council of Alabama faced the leadership question and found the answer was not easy. The group's meetings had been largely social, with guest speakers. Members felt no need for a leader. In their fifth meeting, they decided to produce a brochure for the local cancer society. This decision required task leadership.

Two members, Linda and José, saw themselves as capable leaders, and both wanted to lead. A struggle ensued. Sometimes Linda was in control, and some members accepted her. Then José would get the floor and try to move the group in his direction. One group member in particular would follow. Then Linda would reverse the process. It took several meetings for Linda to emerge as the accepted leader of the group.

The group's answer to who would lead detracted considerably from the task. They devoted so much energy to the leadership question that their productivity suffered.

Leaders and Leadership Defined

A **leader** is a person who directs and influences a group to move toward a group's goal. This person may be formally designated or may emerge informally from the group's interaction. Leadership, on the other hand, is an influence process. Marvin Shaw (1981, p. 317) defined *leadership* as "an influence process which is directed toward goal achievement." Notice that this definition takes into account all kinds of leadership and goals. For example, Linda might influence her group to socialize when it ought to be working. Her influence would qualify as leadership, but not in the desired direction. Again, a group member—say, Marc—might influence another to leave the group's meeting early. This, too, would be leadership by Shaw's definition, although it would be counterproductive to the group. Shaw's definition might be modified to take into account problems created by situations like these and to include the idea of communication behaviors. Insert the word *group* before *goal* and the words *through communication* in the definition so that it reads: "**Leadership** is an influence process through communication which is directed toward group goal achievement."

This definition of leadership omits specific reference to a leader. The term *leader* refers to a person who either is appointed or emerges to lead. A person who is appointed is generally referred to as a **designated leader.** A department head provides an example.

When leaders are appointed, an interesting problem may occur. This problem is often illustrated in classroom discussion groups with a designated leader. Perhaps this leader has never led—and furthermore doesn't ever intend to do so. Maybe the group senses this. This person may be a leader in name only—not accepted by the group as its leader or willing to try to carry out the role. In such a case the group may appoint its own leader—a designated leader. Sometimes a group has a designated leader and an emergent leader. An **emergent leader** is a group member who enacts behaviors that are accepted by members and leads the group toward their goal. The leadership responsibilities are divided. The designated leader may call the meetings and provide the agenda. The emergent leader influences the members in their effort to carry out the task.

Sometimes a member other than the designated leader might wish to lead, and the group might perceive this person as more desirable than the designated leader. Or perhaps there is no designated leader, and two members wish to lead. This situation could set the stage for a leadership struggle if these people are not willing to share leadership.

Focus on Research

GENDER AND LEADERSHIP

A series of studies have examined the possession of dominant qualities—forceful, self-confident, articulate, persistent, responsible, and logical—and being designated leader (Fleischer & Chertkoff, 1986; Nyquist & Spence, 1986). These studies suggest that when there has been little or no opportunity to interact in same-sex groups—where presumably gender is not an issue—the dominant person is named leader approximately 70 percent of the time. If there is no gender bias, then we would expect that the most dominant person in mixed-sex groups that have not had an opportunity to interact would be named at a figure near this number. Research, however, suggests that designation of leader is related to gender. When the dominant person was male, that person was designated 84 percent of the time in these groups; when the dominant person was female, that person was designated only 41 percent of the time.

This bias was substantiated in research by Porter and Geis (1981). Traditionally the person seated at the head of the table has been the person most likely to lead. When raters were shown photographs of same-sex groups, they picked the person at the head of the table to be the person most likely to lead. When the same people were pictured in mixed-sex groups, the males at the head of the table were designated as most likely to lead. In contrast, females at the head of the table were not designated as likely to lead.

Carli and Eagly (1999) indicate men seem to have a leadership advantage over women in that they have a greater tendency to talk in task-oriented groups, behave in more authoritarian and powerful ways, be task-oriented, and show more visual dominance.

Research reports provide evidence that women are as effective leaders as men (Kolb 1999; Eagly,

Karau, & Makjijani, 1995). One study reports female managers often have higher work motivation than men (Donnell & Hall, 1980).

These gender biases seem to break down when groups are allowed to interact before designating a leader. For example, Goktepe and Schneier (1989) found that 28 groups that met for 6 to 15 weeks were equally likely to pick a male or a female leader. In spite of what some research might indicate, it is likely that female and male leaders are relatively equal in their leadership performance (as found in the meta-analysis of leadership studies by Eagley, Karau, & Makijani, 1995).

L. L. Carli & A. H. Eagly (1999). Gender effects on social influence and emergent leadership. In G. N. Powel (ed.), *Handbook of gender and work*. Thousand Oaks, CA: Sage, pp. 203–222.

S. M. Donnell & J. Hall (1980). Men and women as managers: A significant case of no significant difference. *Organizational Dynamics, 8*, 60–76.

A. H. Eagly, S. J. Karau, & M. G. Makhijani (1995). Gender and the effectiveness of leaders: A meta-analysis. *Psychological Bulletin, 111*, 3–22.

R. A. Fleischer & J. M. Chertkoff (1986). Effects of dominance and sex on leader selection in dyadic work groups. *Journal of Personality and Social Psychology, 50*, 94–99.

J. R. Goktepe & C. E. Schneier (1989). Role of sex and gender roles, and attraction in predicting emergent leaders. *Journal of Applied Psychology, 74*, 165–167.

B. Haslett, F. Geise, and R. Mae (1992). *The organizational woman: Power and paradox*. Norwood, NJ: Ablex Publishing.

J. A. Kolb (1999). The effect of gender role, attitude toward leadership, and self-confidence on leader emergence: Implications for leadership development. *Human Resource Development Quarterly, 10*, 305–320.

L. V. Nyquist & J. T. Spence (1986). Effects of dispositional dominance and sex role expectations on leadership behaviors. *Journal of Personality and Social Psychology, 50*, 87–93.

N. Porter & F. Geis (1981). Women and nonverbal leadership cues: When seeing is not believing. In C. Mayo and N. M. Henley. eds., *Gender and nonverbal behavior*. New York: Springer-Verlag, pp. 39–61.

Shared Leadership

Occasionally, no single person takes on the responsibility to lead, and two or more members share leadership. For some groups **shared leadership** is quite satisfactory. One member might fulfill the task of managing conflict. Another might help the group move through the decision-making process. Still another might encourage reticent members to participate. Groups can function well without a designated leader.

On other occasions a designated or emergent leader may fill many, but not all, of the necessary functions. Here, too, leadership might be shared by perceptive members. In this case people who are not willing to lead might help. This willingness to help might be crucial to group success. Think carefully about how you make leadership contributions as you read this chapter, even if you do not want to be completely in charge.

When might shared leadership be appropriate? Here are some basic questions you can ask to guide you in this decision:

1. If there is a designated or emergent leader, is that person fulfilling the necessary leadership responsibilities to ensure an effective group? If the answer is no, then shared leadership is called for if the leader is willing to have it.

2. If there is no designated leader, is the group task such that relatively quick action is necessary or is the group meeting for a short period of time—say one meeting? If the answer to one of these questions is yes, then it might be wise to appoint a willing leader because of time constraints.

3. Are several group members, who are skilled in the tasks necessary to lead your group, also willing to share leadership? If so, share leadership. This situation is an excellent environment for shared leadership, especially if the group is not too large. Large groups may require a single leader.

LEADERSHIP AND POWER

Leadership is an influence process—a key concept in the definition of power. **Power** has been defined as the ability or potential to influence others (Franz, 1998). Power is group-centered. It is dependent on the relationship the leader has with the followers. Leaders can only influence the behavior of members to the extent that members perceive and acknowledge their power. But power is not just a leader to member phenomena. Group members have power and no group member is totally powerless. The interdependency that members have for each other and the leader has with the group provides some influence for every member.

Uses of Power

We generally think of power that is used to *dominate* others. This is the power we think of leaders exercising when they direct the activities of others. It flows from either hierarchy or status—hierarchy when the person is given authority over a group by its

TABLE 7.1   Uses of Power

Type of Use	Directed to	Characteristic
Dominance	Members	Active
Prevention	Leader	Reactive
Autonomous	Self and others	Proactive

organization or status when members allow a leader to emerge to take charge. This kind of power is often centered in a single individual, although it can be shared. It can be the impetus for conflict if there is competition for who will lead. This power use is seen as *active* in that it presses the goals of the leader and organization.

A second use of power is to *prevent* others from dominating us. Preventive power is used to resist leader domination. Members compete with the leader for the right to control. This power use is seen as *reactive* in that members are reacting to a leader's attempt to dominate.

The third use of power is *autonomous* action or self-control. This is also referred to as being *empowered*. This is the power to accomplish your own goals and/or help others achieve their goals. Members share in this power when the group is empowered. Generally, this power is given to the group by the larger organization or its leader. Leaders who follow a delegating style practice empowerment. This power use is characterized as *proactive*. This signifies the positive action members take to assist themselves and others.

Dominance is undoubtedly the major use of power in our society. There is a wide variety of enactments of dominance. Some are intolerable, but others are not. Autonomy is an alternative that each leader might consider to practice when appropriate.

POWER RESOURCES

French and Raven (1981) are scholars who are responsible for the classic typology of sources of power. Folger, Poole, and Stutman (1993) call these *power resources*. They define these as "anything that enables individuals to move toward their own goals or interfere with another's actions" (p. 100). These sources are reward, punishment, legitimate, referent, and expert. We will add a sixth, persuasion.

Reward and Coercive Power

Reward power is the influence that comes from a person's ability to provide or withhold benefits that another person values. A leader might provide compliments, special attention, personal favors, or even an increase in salary. Reward power becomes punishment when rewards are withheld. Withholding benefits or subjecting the person to unpleasant

TABLE 7.2 Using Power	
Power Resource	**How to Develop and Maintain the Resource**
Reward or punishment	Reward what members value. Reward with liberal praise when deserved. Reward and punish fairly and justly. Punish only if absolutely necessary. Punish swiftly and with certainty.
Legitimate authority	Earn the right to be the authority. Adhere to the group's norms and standards. Be honest and fair in your treatment of members.
Reference	Maintain the qualities that are attractive to members. Communicate effectively the vision.
Expertise	Maintain your knowledge currency. Be trustworthy and credible. Communicate knowledge so members can use it. Avoid a superior attitude.

situations uses **punishment** or **coercive power**, so it is rarely thought of as the opposite of reward power. A leader might frown or show disapproval or threaten to (or actually) withhold pay, demote a worker, or use some other coercive tactic.

Punishment should be used as a last resort. The coercion of punishment power often results in resentment or worse—sabotage and rebellion. Effective leaders try to avoid these tactics to gain compliance if they can. Punishment is a negative statement, rather than a positive one. It tells the person what they should not do, "Stop doing (something)." It usually does not tell the person what he or she should *do* to perform better. Punishment generally produces defensive, angry, and hostile attitudes. It produces preventive reactance that tends to lead to some sort of resistance. The person may even try to convince other members that he or she has been treated unjustly and urge them to join the resistance. Sometimes this member is successful and group takes on a resentful attitude toward the leader. This situation can escalate into very ugly conflict.

Those in a group who feel powerless often attempt to resort to coercive strategies (usually aimed at other "powerless" members) to try to achieve their aims. These strategies may not work because the targets, themselves, feel powerless and respond with defensiveness or rebellion (Bugental & Lewis, 1999).

There are three important principles that guide the use of threats and punishment. First, the punishment must be fair and just. Withholding pay for a minor infraction generally would not be seen as fair and just. Second, the individual believes that the punishment will be administered. Third, the follow-through with the punishment should come soon after the infraction is observed.

Rewards can be an effective use of power if the reward is something the individual values. There are two kinds of rewards a leader can offer. One of these is an external reward such as increased pay, grades on a student's work, recognition for achievement, and the like. The second is an indirect reward that would enable a person to be successful in their work, perhaps giving them more autonomy. This provides internal motivation and satisfaction. A word of caution is in order. Rewards need to be connected to behavior that suggests they are deserved and commensurate with the performance. It would be unwise to reward all members the same when some did little or nothing to deserve a reward.

Legitimate Power

Legitimate power is the influence a person has because of being elected, appointed, or selected to direct others. This power is generally considered inherent in the position or office. The leader has a right to call a meeting and expect members to attend and come prepared. The leader also has the right to make assignments related to the task.

A leader gains maximum power from his or her position only if the members of the group see this person as legitimately their leader. A leader who was appointed for his or her competence would gain more position power than a person who was appointed because he or she is related to someone higher up in the organization. A leader who does not conform to rules and norms of the group may not be seen as legitimate. A leader who asks members to do things that they see as inappropriate may not be seen as legitimate. The group confers the power, and if it does not think the person deserves to lead it may not readily comply with the leader's wishes.

Referent Power

Referent power is the influence a person has because others identify with or are attracted to that person. It is based on the principle that we are likely to be influenced by those we find attractive and admire. When the attraction is strong, when the power is strong, the person is said to have *charisma*. Charismatic leaders are also referred to as transformational leaders. (We will speak more about transformational leaders shortly.) Referent power may cause members to work harder to please the leader. It may cause members to want to be like the leader and to emulate this person's behavior. The more the leader is admired and respected, the more power the person has.

Charismatic leaders often have fiercely loyal and committed followers. Members have a strong identification with the leader and his or her vision of what needs to be done to accomplish their task. Members take on the values and the goals of their leader. What makes the group identify with this person so strongly will differ from group to group. Generally, they are effective speakers. Beyond this, what makes this person attractive is based on what the group values in their leader.

Carli's research (1999) supports the notion that women often possess greater referent power than men because it is not dependent on position power, but on liking. Further, Carli (2001) found that women are generally viewed as warmer and more supportive than men and, therefore, are better liked.

Expert Power

Expert power is influence based on what a person knows and/or on the person's abilities. For example, a leader might have power because he or she is good at organizing the task and has a great deal of task knowledge. The power comes from the fact that the leader or member has an expertise that is important to the group and he or she is able to communicate it in such a way that the group can use it productively. Of course, the group confers the power by accepting the person as an expert because they believe he or she has skill, knowledge, and ability in an area where they need it.

Persuasive Power

The final area of power is persuasive power. **Persuasive power** is influence based on a person's ability to create credible arguments. The term *credible* suggests that the group has to accept the argument as legitimate and the speaker to be trustworthy, and perhaps be willing and ready to act on it if necessary. This, of course, is an area of power that all of us can cultivate by study and practice of persuasion.

A leader or member will almost always have more than one source of power to draw upon. The greater the sources of power, the greater the potential the person has to influence others if that person chooses to exercise that power.

Powerful members communicate differently than the less powerful. These members talk more, issue more challenges, introduce more new topics, and respond to more questions. These behaviors are obviously ones that control the direction of the group's consideration of their topic. If less powerful members want greater involvement, they may work to increase their power base to achieve more control (Sillince, 2000). Conflict may ensue when this happens.

Power and Gender

Women have been portrayed as being more easily influenced and having less power than men. Often, women are seen as using less powerful speech. However, despite some mixed reports, research does not tend to support these stereotypes (Proff, (1995); Grob, Meyers & Schuh, 1997).

One research study found that when women were placed in positions of power, they were just as likely as men to use strategies associated with power (Sagrestando, 1992). Perhaps the stereotypes continue because men typically find themselves in roles that have higher power associated with them. Thus, the opportunity for men to use power strategies is greater than that of women. This observation led Sagrestando to conclude that the unequal distribution of power results in an illusion of gender differences. The conclusion, then, is that apparent gender differences must be understood within the context of status (position) and power. So, how is this playing out? Of course, the situation is changing. Here is some relatively recent data that suggest this change.

Women are poised to advance in the business and professional world. Consider the research. In 2010, women held more than half (51.5%) of all managerial and professional positions in the United States ("Women in U.S. Management, 2011). Women dominate 13 of the 15 job categories that are projected to grow the most in the decade (Rosin, 2010). More than half of all accountants are women, and women hold about half of all banking and insurance positions in the United States. Roughly a third of all physicians and most pediatricians are women, and 45% of associates in law firms are women (Rosin). This trend is very likely to continue, even to grow, because women are receiving more education than men in preparation for the developing job market. Women earn 60% of all bachelor's degrees, 60% of master's degrees, about half of all law and medical degrees, and 42% of MBAs. They also earn more than half of all doctoral degrees (Rosin)

LEADERSHIP EMERGENCE

All of us have participated or will participate in a group meeting in which there is no designated leader. In some of these situations no leader emerges, and instead, members make leadership contributions that move the group along toward its goals. In other situations a leader is designated, but members turn to another group member to supply leadership. Research suggests that groups with an emergent leader outperform groups where there is none (De Souza & Klein, 1995). So this is an important issue. Situations in which a leader emerges from the group have raised an interesting question for communication scholars: "How does a leader emerge in a group or team?"

The Minnesota Studies

Ernest Bormann (1990) and his students studied this issue. Bormann refers to this process as the method of residues. **Method of residues** suggests that the process is one in which members are gradually eliminated as potential leaders until one person emerges. This series of studies reported the process generally goes through two basic stages. The first phase is relatively brief; it usually takes no longer than the first meeting to eliminate half the group from consideration. These members seem to be eliminated because they are low contributors, seem uninformed, seem irrational, or are extremely dogmatic.

The second phase of leadership emergence is a "struggle" for leadership among those who remain in contention. Bormann found four distinct emergence patterns, or scenarios as he called them. **Scenario I** is a pattern relatively free of conflict. The leader candidate picks up support from a group member. This "lieutenant" provides a great deal of emotional support for the leader candidate. If no other potential leader picks up this kind of support, this candidate emerges.

Scenario II takes place when a second leader candidate picks up a lieutenant. This situation can produce intense conflict because they both seem to have the skill to lead and both have support. The author witnessed a group in which this leadership struggle was not be resolved. First, one person was leading with the lieutenant supporting; then the other person gained the floor and led with the support of a lieutenant. The leadership rotated like this throughout the whole meeting, with each candidate attempting to lead the group in a different direction. The result was a group that made no progress toward meeting its goals. On the other hand, if one leader does emerge, this person faces the serious problem of the losing candidate bringing strong opposition to ideas the leader supports. One strategy is to enlist the loser's support by giving that person an important job that recognizes his or her talents. If the rival candidate is of good will, this approach might work. If not, the person may disrupt the group.

Scenario III was witnessed by Bormann in groups that were confronted by a crisis. If a group without an appointed leader has to deal with a serious problem, the person who has the skills and knowledge to deal with it is likely to emerge quickly. If some internal situation causes a crisis, perhaps a social conflict among members, the person who solves the problem is likely to emerge. The urgency of the crisis issue is the driving force

Looking Back: A Quick Review

CONCLUSIONS OF THE MINNESOTA STUDIES ON LEADERSHIP EMERGENCE

Scenario I	Leader candidate picks up support from a group member and goes on to lead.
Scenario II	Two leader candidates each pick up a "lieutenant." One leader emerges to lead after intense conflict. The loser continues to be powerful and may present a problem.
Scenario III	The leaderless group experiences a crisis. A leader who has the skills and knowledge to deal with it emerges.
Scenario IV	The group fails to achieve its goal. Two leaders each pick up a "lieutenant." Neither emerges as leader. The group experiences extended conflict.

in forcing leader emergence. This crisis is sensed by group members and allows the person with the expertise to guide the group.

Scenario IV is somewhat like scenario II, but a leader does not emerge. This scenario describes paths to group failure. It differs from scenario II in that there are no clear candidates for leader. Sometimes the group realizes the problem and elects a leader. In the Minnesota studies this "leader" was most often a relatively weak or neutral person who was not in contention for leadership. In spite of the election, the leader was not followed and so made only brief attempts to lead. Another variation on this pattern was the emergence of a series of leaders, each of whom served only briefly. The problem here is that each potential leader has some important "defect."

Gender and Leadership Emergence

Jerie M. Pratt (1979) compared female leadership emergence to that of males in mixed-sex groups. She found that women were emerging on a basis approaching equality with men in the mixed-sex groups. Pratt's work substantiated the two phases identified by Bormann. Leadership emergence for males and females also exhibited the same three scenarios. A possible fourth pattern seemed to be predominately taken by women. In this pattern two women shared leadership, providing much of the information and becoming a dependable, responsible, and dedicated power core for the group.

Once the leader emerged and the role was established, behavior of male and female leaders differed only slightly (Chemers & Murphy, 1995). Yet, in spite of the fact that research demonstrates males and females can be effective leaders, stereotypes persist (Eagley, Karau, & Makhijani, 1995). When women occupy positions of authority, they face more resistance than men if they attempt to assert this authority. One research group suggests this is because members do not see their authority as legitimate (Atwater, Carey, & Waldman, 2001). Hawkins (1995) suggests that use of an effective communication strategy is helpful in overcoming this kind of stereotype. One such strategy would be to communicate task-relevant communication behaviors. These are messages related to task accomplishment, such as initiating an analysis of the group's task or problem, or other task-related problem-solving steps discussed in Chapter 3.

Does being a man mean a greater chance of emerging as leader? No. Biological sex is not the key factor. It is the style that increases likelihood of emergence. People who are independent, assertive, risk takers, and self-reliant—traits often identified with males—are more likely to emerge (Kolb, 1997).

Other Factors That Affect Leadership Emergence

Marvin E. Shaw and G. H. Rothchild (1956) concluded that leadership emergence depends on the person's place in the communication network. Those who occupy a central position in the communication network frequently emerge as leaders. At a table a central place is one where all members can be seen by this person. This position is often the end of a rectangular table. The person seated there will more often emerge as leader. Emergent leaders seem to create an early perception that they are able to get the job done. They help their group make sense of the information, set expectations for the group's success, and help them feel capable (Pescosolido, 2001).

Finally, Cal W. Downs and Terry Pickett (1977) showed that an interrelated set of variables affects leadership emergence. Leadership style, group compatibility, and the nature of the discussion situation are key variables. As you might imagine, both from our discussion and from your experience, leadership emergence is a complex process. There are no easy answers to how it operates, but research appears to offer hope that we will someday understand how to manage the emergence of leadership. Even given the limits of research, it is possible to suggest some practical applications.

If you wish to emerge as a leader in a group, follow the advice research suggests:

If you wish to emerge as leader, say so.

Talk often, and to all the group members.

Locate yourself physically toward the center of the group or assume a position that will give you ready access to all the group members. For example, take a position at the head of the table.

Know what you're talking about.

Katherine Hawkins (1995) reported her study of leadership emergence identified task-relevant communication as the only significant predictor, regardless of gender. Bryan Bonner (2000) adds commitment to the group's goals to task ability. Beyond this, Hawkins's study found no significant differences in the production of task-relevant communication attributable to gender. Hawkins's research suggests that the key factor for any person who wishes to emerge as leader is to engage in task-relevant communication.

PERSPECTIVES ON LEADERSHIP

Research has produced a number of leadership perspectives—each of which allows us to discover something useful about leadership. These perspectives, taken together, provide insight into characteristics and behaviors that can help you become a more effective leader.

The **trait perspective** is characterized by the question "What personal traits would set a leader apart from others in a group?" The second perspective relates to **style**. People interested in this approach would ask the question "What particular patterns of behaviors can be observed in various kinds of leaders?" A third way of viewing leadership focuses on **functions**. This approach is characterized by questions like "What might a leader do to manage task and social aspects of the group?" The fourth perspective—the **situational perspective**—is characterized by questions such as "What kind of leadership is called for

Looking Back: A Quick Review

FACTORS THAT AFFECT LEADER EMERGENCE

Gender	Task-relevant behavior helps women emerge. Women sometimes emerge in a shared leadership position.
Network place	People who occupy a central position emerge to lead.
Communication	Frequent task-related communication can lead to emergence. Being knowledgeable and communicating that knowledge can lead to emergence. Having and demonstrating task ability can lead to emergence.

by a particular circumstance?" Another approach combines some of the others. It is often referred to as the **contingency perspective.** People who are trying to understand leadership from this view might ask, "Given this task, what kind of leadership will be most effective?" Finally, two additional leadership approaches are addressed: the **leader as a medium** and **transformational leadership.**

Trait Perspective

The phrase *born leader* describes a person who is believed to possess characteristics needed to be a successful leader. This view supposes that certain individuals inherit unique leader characteristics that allow them to be successful. The *trait perspective* is based on this idea. It assumes that leaders have characteristics that set them apart from nonleaders.

The trait perspective is illustrated by the recent experience of a nominating committee at a local church. Ron Jenkins was proposed for a leadership position. The suggestion was met by "I don't think Ron will work out. I've known his family for years. They are not leaders."

Imagine how important this perspective might be. A corporation might identify people who have desirable leadership traits and then put those people into positions of power. But does this approach, which seems to make sense, actually work?

There are some traits that correlate reliably with leadership. Ralph Stogdill, after carefully reviewing 163 studies, concluded that leaders, relative to followers, rate higher in achievement orientation, adaptability, energy level, responsibility taking, self-confidence, and ascendancy (Bass, 1981). Deborah Baker (1990) who conceives of verbal style as a trait-like quality, found that it, along with communication content, contributed to leadership emergence. Studies also have revealed that leaders tend to have higher IQs, greater verbal facility, and more knowledge than their followers. They are also more flexible, sociable, persistent, and innovative (Stogdill, 1981; Shaw, 1981). Finally, David Kenny and Stephen Zaccaro (1984) lend support to the concept that some traits do make a difference. They speculate that, rather than specific traits, the ability to perceive the needs and goals of a group and to adjust one's approach to the group based on that assessment is a key to leadership emergence.

Style Perspective

Russell Hanna, a bright and capable management trainee, decided that in order to be successful he would have to learn to lead groups. In spite of his ambition, he was a little reserved, which caused him to hold back when it came to assuming leadership. But Russ decided he must overcome this problem. He reasoned he ought to study carefully the most effective leader-manager he could find.

So Russ modeled his leadership style after the leader he perceived as being most effective. This person's approach was to keep firm control.

About six months later Russ was assigned the task of leading a group that was reviewing his company's dress policy. Since he believed that productivity comes from careful, close control and a "take charge" attitude, he adopted that style—the **autocratic style** of leadership.

On the other hand, Russ might have adopted a different style. If he believed that people need to be involved in decision making and that people appreciate procedural help, then he probably would have adopted a **democratic style.**

He could even have come to believe in a third philosophy. If he thought that attempts to guide groups closely were likely to lead to negative consequences and if he felt uncomfortable trying to influence people, he might have adopted a style that lets people operate on their own. This style is called **laissez-faire.**

Autocratic and democratic leadership styles have received a great deal of attention from scholars. Keep in mind that most of the research compared "pure" examples of each style. You are unlikely to find a purely democratic or a purely autocratic leader in real-world groups.

Much of the interest in the study of leadership styles began with Ralph K. White and Ronald Lippitt (1960), who studied groups of boys as they responded to the various leadership styles. *Democratic leaders* allowed participation in policy decisions. The boys were free to select alternatives and to work with whomever they chose. *Autocratic leaders* determined all policy, dictated techniques, and usually dictated work partners. Style accounted for clear differences in behavior. Boys who experienced autocratic leadership demonstrated thirty times more hostility and eight times more aggression than boys who experienced democratic leadership. They also did more scapegoating, and their work was judged to be qualitatively inferior to the work of democratically led groups. We must be careful in making judgments about these data, however. The information was collected at a summer camp; thus it may be tied to the situation. Also, it involves the behavior of boys, which may not parallel that of adults. There is evidence in research with adults that shows these styles do produce differences. Sargent and Miller (1971) found that autocratic leaders tended to rush through the question-and-answer process. Democratic leaders, on the other hand, attempted to encourage participation. Rosenfeld and Pax (1975) discovered that autocratic leaders made fewer attempts to encourage members to participate, gave more negative reactions, and asked fewer questions.

Recent research on the link between democratic leadership and satisfaction reveals it is not as strong as once thought. Foels and his colleagues (2000) discovered that satisfaction depends on a number of factors. They found that:

- The relationship is strong in laboratory groups.
- The relationship is strong in large groups.
- The relationship is strong for males, but only in laboratory groups.
- The relationship is strong for women in all groups.

So the alternative preference for men, when it is not democratic, is autocratic leadership. Males in real-world groups prefer this style, presumably because they are accustomed to a more task-oriented, directive style.

Letting a group lead itself might mean a disaster. If someone does lead, then that can be described as some kind of leadership style other than laissez-faire. The laissez-faire leadership style encompasses the art of knowing when to stand back and let group members take charge. When the group has the talent and does not really need the help, this may be an appropriate strategy. For example, some groups whose goal is learning do best if the teacher-leader allows participants to take charge.

Some researchers have examined the amount of structure a leader brings to a task. William E. Jurma (1979) has labeled this behavior **leadership-structuring style**. A highly structuring leader will pay attention to group interaction procedures, will help set goals, and will stress equality. You might imagine a structuring leader spending time doing the following: (1) setting goals and steps leading to their attainment, (2) clarifying task alternatives, (3) urging self-direction among members, (4) volunteering task-related information, and (5) urging members to treat one another with equality.

Contrary to what you might expect, participants who were low in task orientation were more satisfied than highly task-oriented participants when led by a highly structuring leader. Moreover, members of structured groups rated their tasks as more interesting, valuable, and important than those who participated in low-structured groups.

A group of people representing a countywide literacy council was called together to discuss program ideas. This group was led by Michael Mirkovich. He thought he knew how to be a good leader. Using a structuring style, he didn't realize that members of his group were resenting him. They perceived themselves as peers. They appreciated the structure but believed that Mike's autocratic leadership was inappropriate.

Perhaps members who are task oriented do not depend as much on the leader as non-task-oriented participants. If this is the case, then it might explain Jurma's findings. But beyond this inference, as a leader you need to be aware of two important principles. First, if you are confronted by a group of participants who are not task oriented, it would be wise to pursue a structuring style. Second, a democratic structuring style generally *produces higher satisfaction and better task performance* than the nonstructuring and/or autocratic styles.

Situational Perspective

Support for the situational view had its beginning in the 1930s and the 1940s. Emory Bogardus (1931–1932, p. 165) suggested "a person may be generally consistent [in leadership traits] in some situations and inconsistent in others." Similarly, Albert J. Murphy (1941) argued that the traits a person demonstrates may change from situation to situation. A person who is assertive in a familiar situation may be reticent in an unfamiliar one. The situational perspective was given convincing support by the Office of Strategic Services (OSS) Assessment Staff Report (1948).

The OSS trained people to carry out secret missions in enemy territory during World War II. Staff members trained candidates to respond to general situations and assessed their general aptitude for leadership. Staff members solicited ratings of the people they trained from area commanders and fellow returnees, and with that information they calculated a leadership score based on performance. The correlation between leadership traits and leadership was discouragingly low (+.11). Because the trainees were exposed to specific leadership situations in the overseas areas, researchers concluded that situational factors influence the emergence and behavior of leaders.

Other researchers have attempted to discover how situational variables affect leadership. For example, Ralph M. Stogdill and his colleagues (1956) investigated the effect of transferring navy officers to new assignments. The researchers found that an officer's style of interpersonal behavior did not change but that patterns of work performance did according to the new situational requirements. Contrast the difference in performance that an impersonal style might make here. An officer is in charge of a unit of recruits. His pattern of handling the task is close supervision. He is transferred to an administrative unit. His interpersonal style does not change, but now the task-handling pattern is more permissive. The adjustment was obviously needed.

Contingency Perspective

Imagine you are reporting for a job as supervisor in a 10-person department. You are in a relatively weak power position, since they do not know you well and you've had little experience with them. In addition, your job is to supervise a sales force, and you know that selling represents a fairly unstructured task. Finally, you recall that you met several of the sales representatives and basically got along. Therefore, you believe that word has gotten around that you are a pleasant person, and you suspect that people assess your relationship with them as good. Thus your position on a situational-control dimension is like this:

Leader-member relationships: Good

Task structure: Unstructured

Position power: Weak

Once you know these things, can you know what approach to leadership is suggested? Research by Fred Fiedler suggests you can. He believes leadership is contingent—depends—on these three factors.

Fred E. Fiedler (1967) identified situation-control dimensions that involved a leader's position power, the task structure, and leader–member relations. Then he ordered these into a continuum of favorableness of the situation to the leader. Table 7.3 displays this ordering. For example, the highest favorableness of the situation for a leader would be when the leader–member relations were good, the task was structured (a step-by-step procedure could be followed), and the leader was powerful (strong).

Next Fiedler measured the effectiveness of two leader orientations—task and relationship—on the basis of group productivity. He assumed that an orientation toward task suggests the person sees the job of leader as especially involving task management. Likewise, an orientation toward relationships suggests the person sees the job as emphasizing relationships—that is, finding acceptance for self and members. Such a leader might be somewhat more concerned with relationships than with task.

Fiedler found that leaders who are highly task oriented function best in highly favorable situations (represented in Table 7.3 by octants I through III) and the highly unfavorable situation (represented by octant VII). In the most favorable situations (I and II), the leader can be task oriented and even somewhat controlling without arousing negative reactions because of the good relations and the structured nature of the task. The

TABLE 7.3   The Situational-Control Dimension

Favorable Situation Control					Unfavorable Situation Control		
Octant	I	II	III	IV	V	VI	VII	VIII
Relations	Good	Good	Good	Good	Poor	Poor	Poor	Poor
Structure	Structured		Unstructured		Structured		Unstructured	
Power	Strong	Weak	Strong	Weak	Strong	Weak	Strong	Weak

Source: Adapted by permission of *Harvard Business Review.* Exhibit from F. E. Fiedler (September–October 1965), p. 118. Copyright © by the President and Fellows of Harvard College. All rights reserved.

Looking Back: A Quick Review

PERSPECTIVES ON LEADERSHIP

Trait perspective	Identifies characteristics of successful leaders.
Style perspective	Studies and identifies different leader styles and the effects of their use.
Situational perspective	Examines situations and uses the results to guide decisions about appropriate leadership.
Contingency perspective	Identifies variables that guide in decisions about appropriate leadership.

situation in octant III is somewhat different, but the leader can still take on a task orientation because of the good relations and power, regardless of the fact that the task is unstructured. The leader can rely on the strength of the relationships and power to ensure cooperation in structuring the task. On the other hand, in the most unfavorable situation (VIII), when things are going badly, directive task-oriented leadership is required to keep the group from coming apart. Fiedler suggests that the leader place the emphasis on task, allowing for maximum effort in that direction.

Relationship-oriented leaders were more productive under both moderately favorable (octant IV) and moderately unfavorable (octants V through VII) conditions. In the moderately favorable situation (IV), the task is unstructured, and the leader generates the willingness and creativity of the group members to accomplish their goal by attention to the relationship. In the moderately unfavorable situations (V through VII), the task is structured, but the leader is not well liked. Here the relationship-oriented leader demonstrates care for the emotions of the group members and is successful in generating productivity. A task-oriented approach would presumably not meet these social needs and thus would not be as successful.

Why would a task-oriented leader do well in an unfavorable setting? Why would a relationship-oriented leader do poorly under favorable leadership conditions? Several years after the original formulation, Fiedler explained this relationship with his **motivational-hierarchy hypothesis** (Fiedler & Chambers, 1974; Fiedler, 1978). This hypothesis assumes that people are motivated to attain more than one goal at a particular time. For example, on graduation, a student may wish to marry, take on a full-time job, begin work on an advanced degree, and so forth. However, he or she cannot pursue all these goals at the same time and with the same amount of determination. Therefore, the student decides which goals to pursue first, second, third, and so on. The student could arrange these in a motivational hierarchy.

Fiedler suggests that leaders arrange goals into categories—perhaps "extremely important," "very important," "important," and "not very important." Since there is not time to work on all these goals, the leader works on the ones at the upper range of the hierarchy first and with the most vigor. Further, the leader's hierarchy ought to differ depending on the person's motivational orientation. Thus a task-oriented leader would be likely to place task goals high on the list, whereas the relationship-oriented leader would give relationship goals a high placement.

Consider this idea of hierarchy in terms of unfavorable situations. The task-oriented leader would work hardest on moving the group toward completion of its task. The relationship-oriented leader would concentrate on trying to reestablish good interpersonal relationships before concentrating on task goals. On the favorable side of Fiedler's continuum, the task-oriented person can guide the group through its task without much effort. This situation allows the leader to focus more on being interpersonally supportive. For the relationship-oriented leader, the reverse is the case: The person can focus more attention on task goals. Presumably the person is at a disadvantage as far as quality of task production by being less skillful at handling structured tasks (Forsyth, 1990).

Hersey, Blanchard, and Johnson's Situational Model

Hersey, Blanchard, and Johnson's (1996) approach to situational leadership states that the leader needs to be flexible enough to change his or her style as a group changes over time. They conclude that the leader's approach should be based on the group's readiness. **Readiness level** is defined in terms of three components: the group's ability, motivation, and education or experience. Hersey, Blanchard, and Johnson define four levels of readiness: low, R1—members are unable and unwilling to do the task or insecure about it; low moderate, R2—members are unable to do the task, but willing or confident about it; high moderate, R3—members are able to do the task, but unwilling or insecure about it; and high, R4—members are able and willing to do the task and confident about it. Leadership behavior is determined by readiness level. Readiness level is described in terms of relationship behavior (giving socio-emotional support) and task behavior (coordination, instruction, advice). A leader must adapt his or her behavior to be high or low on each orientation, depending on the readiness of the group. Hersey, Blanchard, and Johnson place these dimensions in the model displayed in Figure 7.1.

This model suggests that when readiness of members of a group or team is low (R1), a telling approach is needed. The **telling approach** (high task, low relationship) provides specific instructions and close supervision of performance. It is the best-suited leadership when members are unable and unwilling to take responsibility for performance of the task. The telling leader is very careful to give clear and specific directions for the task. The leader will need to take charge by clarifying the goal, structuring the group's task (by indicating steps in the process if necessary), and assigning duties to members. Of course, the leader does not ignore the relationship dimension. He or she is careful to be supportive in his or her approach.

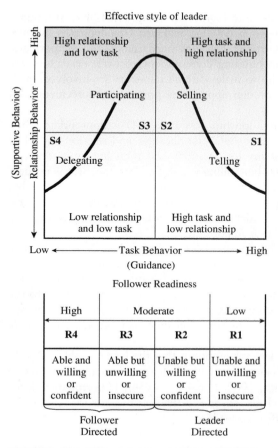

Effective style of leader

FIGURE 7.1
Hersey, Blanchard, and Johnson's Situational Model

Source: Adapted from P. Hersey, K. H. Blanchard, & D. E. Johnson (1996).

The **selling approach** (high task, high relationship, R2) is appropriate when the readiness level is low/moderate. Here members are willing, but unable to take responsibility. The members may be enthusiastic about accomplishing the task, but do not know how to do so because it is new to them. The leader involves the group in the process by asking for input—information, suggestions, feelings, and attitudes. This kind of leader is an encourager in that he or she exercises gentle persuasion. The primary job of this leader in the task dimension is to ask questions, guide and encourage, help the group identify solutions, and sell these as important goals. The primary task in the relationship dimension is to be supportive and help generate a supportive climate.

The **participating approach** (moderate to high relationship, low task, R3) requires the leader to share ideas and facilitate group decision making. This approach assumes that the group has demonstrated task knowledge, but needs emotional support and encouragement. This leader focuses on building commitment to each other and the group's decisions. This requires the leader to make sure all members are involved, facilitate the task effort, encourage effort through appropriate positive reinforcement, and create an open and supportive climate.

The **delegating approach** (low relationship, low task, R4) is appropriate when members are willing and able to take responsibility for the task and relationships. The leader turns over most of the responsibility for decisions and their implementation to the group. These members are confident, but willing to ask for assistance if it is needed. The primary task of the leader is to monitor group performance and be ready to do what is necessary to meet member and group needs. This involves listening, asking questions, and understanding. This leader must be available when the group needs help, so creating the understanding that access is available is important.

This delegating approach is like that taken with **self-directed work teams.** These teams are mature groups that are given the authority to manage and accomplish a particular task. This team provides its own leadership and manages its own resources. Scholars have directed their attention to discovering what elements are essential to the success of these groups. One of the necessary elements is autonomy. Another is empowerment. The third element is competence. The fourth element is motivation (Guzzo & Dickson, 1996).

Hersey, Blanchard, and Johnson's key assumption is that the leader is able and willing to adapt to the group's situation. Evidence suggests that effective leaders are able to adapt (Wood, 1977; Sorenson & Savage, 1989; Drecksell, 1984). Unfortunately, some leaders cannot or will not do so. Research on leader effectiveness suggests that those who are not flexible are judged to be less effective leaders.

Looking Back: A Quick Review

Two Contingency Models of Leadership

Model	Contingencies
Fiedler's model	Leader-member relationship
	Task structure
	Position power
Hersey, Blanchard, and Johnson's model	Task ability
	Confidence level
	Willingness to do task

If you have been thinking carefully about these three contingency approaches, you may be discouraged by the idea that a leader has a particular style and thus will be effective only if the particular group situational constraints happen to come together. There may be some truth to this idea, but it is far from being an absolute. Convincing evidence shows that effective leaders are adaptable. Wood (1977) has demonstrated that effective leaders adapt their behaviors as the situation changes. The leaders in her research changed their behavior from meeting to meeting according to how they perceived the group's goals. Develop sensitivity and flexibility as a leader to be able to make these kinds of adaptations.

Functional Perspective

Recall Russ Hanna, the management trainee mentioned earlier in this chapter. Perhaps you thought it unwise of him to select a single effective leader and take on that person's style. You might have suggested instead that he observe several leaders and ask what functions these effective leaders perform for their groups. He could make a list and then concentrate on learning how to provide these. This is a functional perspective.

The functional view is represented by the question "What activities might a leader do to help a group achieve its goal?" Asking such a question invites a long list of activities. Such a list can be both helpful and confusing. A person might discover from such a list some things to do as a leader. The list also might be useful in providing guidance to develop leadership skills. But if the number of items is great, it may be more confusing than helpful. One way to cope with this problem is to divide leadership behaviors into functional categories such as task, procedural, and social.

Task leadership functions facilitate group processing and thinking about the task, such as generating ideas and information, processing that information, thinking critically about decisions, and clarifying ideas. These functions help the group to process information. Productivity here is dependent on quality of thought. Securing the appropriate information and carefully processing it are key. A skillful leader will help the group be more productive by helping systematically analyze and decide about the task.

Five especially important task functions are suggested by research (Gouran & Hirokawa, 1983, 1996; Gouran et al., 1993; Hirokawa, 1982c, 1988; Hirokawa & Scheerhorn, 1986). These are

1. *Understand the problem.* The group should discuss the issue until it believes members have an accurate understanding of the problem: its nature, its seriousness, its causes, and the consequences if nothing is done.

2. *Understand what constitutes an acceptable resolution of the problem.* The group needs to achieve an accurate understanding of the objectives or specific standards that need to be satisfied for a solution to be acceptable.

3. *Seek and develop a set of acceptable alternatives for managing the problem.* The alternatives, of course, must be realistic. A wide range of alternatives should be explored in coming up with this set of acceptable alternatives.

4. *Assess the strengths of each of these alternatives.*   Here members assess the merits of the elements of a potential proposed solution to their problem.

5. *Assess the weaknesses of each of these alternatives.*   Of course, proposals that seem meritorious may have disadvantages. Sometimes the disadvantages outweigh the advantages. For example, the best way to improve the profits of a business might be to reduce the workforce. However, the serious morale problems caused by such a reduction might make it undesirable as a solution. So, both the strengths and weaknesses of each proposal must be weighed.

The reflective thinking agenda, presented in Chapter 3, focuses on these desirable task functions.

In problem-solving groups the talk of men and women is predominately task related, and this tendency intensifies with the leader. Nearly 91 percent of a male leader's communication is devoted to task behavior, and about 88 percent of a female leader's behavior is task behavior (Anderson & Blanchard, 1982). Females place a high emphasis on production whether they are task or relational leaders. They continue their strong contributions to tasks even when the group is doing well. On the other hand, males reduce their task contributions under this circumstance (Millard & Smith, 1985). A similar pattern holds for problem-solving groups. A study of actual leadership behavior in problem-solving groups demonstrated that female leaders devoted a greater proportion of their total communication to task issues than did the male leaders (Wood, 1981).

Procedural leadership functions guide a group or help the group members work together smoothly and efficiently. A procedurally aware leader focuses on setting an agenda, regulating participation, summarizing group progress, and verbalizing consensus. These functions make a difference for most groups but are difficult for some leaders. Since they do not pertain directly to the task, they are often overlooked. The skillful leader realizes the need for such guidance and carefully gives it. In addition, some differences in procedural suggestions seem to be based on gender. For example, Carrocci (1985) found that women made twice as many procedural suggestions as men when managing a conflict situation.

Social leadership functions encourage and promote aspects of the social dimension and are critical to a group's success. Social leadership can cause a group to be diverted from its task. Although social leadership serves an important purpose for the group, it is not directly task related. Robert Bales (1958) demonstrated that the task and social-emotional leadership functions are generally performed by different persons.

Anderson and Blanchard (1982) found that when social leadership behaviors between men and women do differ, women are more likely to meet these needs in the group. In addition, female leaders have been rated as more interpersonally warm during group interactions than are males (Goktepe & Schneier, 1989; Spillman, Spillman, & Reinking, 1981). Social-emotional leadership behaviors are important to the group because they contribute to more group satisfaction than task behaviors (Schriesheim, 1982).

The Leader as Medium

As our understanding of leadership advances, scholars have uncovered additional variables that affect it. An approach to understanding leadership is that one important leader function is to manage complexity—an approach supported by the ideas of Karl Weick (1978) and B. Aubrey Fisher (1986).

Complexity is viewed as "a property of leadership itself—a characteristic of communication, of functions, and of the social process called leadership" (Fisher, 1986). What does this mean in terms of leadership? Karl Weick (1978) answers this question by presenting a contrast. He suggests that a leader facing a complex problem can confront it in one of two ways: simplify the information-processing load or meet the complexity with complexity. This first approach is used when members reduce information complexity by selective attention, form quick judgments, and reduce alternative solutions to a manageable few. The second approach is to help the group manage the situation. Here the leader helps the group organize the variety of inputs, challenges them to consider a number of possible interpretations, encourages them to look for a wide range of alternatives, and helps them sort through and integrate these into a tentative conclusion. He or she does all this while helping the members avoid becoming confused. How is a leader capable of all this? A good leader is more cognitively complex than an average member and exhibits a wider range of communication behavior. In Fisher's words:

> Leaders are not necessarily leaders because they perform functions unique to leadership. They are more likely to be leaders because they are themselves complex and perform functions which exhibit complexity. They behave differently with different people; they behave differently at different stages of group development; and they behave differently when the task situation differs. (Fisher, 1986, p. 205)

Leaders performing this function are able to take in a variety of information from group members, weigh a number of ways to interpret it, integrate differing ideas, and draw tentative conclusions. When new information is uncovered, these leaders are able to integrate that information and come to new tentative conclusions or reject it. In the relationship dimension, these leaders sense the complexity of the group composition and adapt their communication when interacting with different members. Weick (1978) captures this functional perspective in the metaphor of **leader as medium.** In other words, the leader is the mechanism through which an organizing scheme of rules and procedures for problem solving is created.

How do people develop this kind of complexity? Although Fisher does not address this issue, we can speculate that it results from study and practice. One of the goals of this book is to help you understand the complexity of group process and decision making. Armed with that understanding, practice applying these ideas in the groups. Beyond this, early in the book you were challenged to become a participant-analyst. Notice what kinds of things work well for you and the group and what kinds of things don't and under what circumstances. This information will help you grow in your ability to adapt to changing conditions as you lead.

Transformational Leadership

A **transformational leader** elevates, motivates, inspires, and develops his or her team or group. Bass (1990) contrasts a transactional leader with a transformational leader. **Transactional leaders** manage within the existing norms of their organization; transformational leaders realign the organization by restructuring its assumptions and norms to fit the new vision. Transactional leaders exchange rewards for performance; transformational leaders help members obtain goals and fulfill needs and, in doing so, fulfill the vision and goals of the group and organization. The transactional approach does not emphasize the motivational, creative, and empowering aspects of transformational leadership (Barge, 1994).

Transformational leaders produce leadership behaviors that fulfill four functions that are sometimes referred to as "the four Is:"

> *Idealized leadership* provides vision and a sense of mission, instills pride, and gains respect and trust.
>
> *Inspirational motivation* communicates high expectations, uses symbols to focus efforts, and expresses important purposes in simple ways.
>
> *Intellectual stimulation* promotes intelligence, rationality, and careful problem solving.
>
> *Individualized consideration* gives personal attention, treats people individually, coaches, and advises. (Bass, 1990)

Transformational leaders help their group move from "what is" to "what is describable" to "what ought to be" (Rosenthal & Buchholz, 1995).

The Bass (1990) research found that transformational leaders, when compared to transactional leaders, had better relationships with their supervisors and had subordinates who worked harder. Other researchers, Howell and Avolio (1993), in a similar comparison discovered that transformational leaders positively affected performance; in contrast, transactional leaders negatively affected performance.

Bass and Avolio (1993) discovered that leaders who were perceived as transformational were more highly evaluated by their subordinates than those who were not in Canada, Germany, India, Italy, New Zealand, Singapore, Spain, and the United States. Other researchers studied leaders in 62 cultures and found transformational leaders were thought to be contributing, outstanding leaders (Den Hartog et al., 1999). Contributing leaders were described with these attributes: integrity (trustworthy, just, honest), charismatic (encouraging, positive, motivational, confidence building, dynamic), and organizers (team builder, communicative, coordinators).

Transformational leadership has the many benefits presented above. However, it is not without a potential adverse effect. Conflict can result from the passion engendered by the leader. What this means is that members of a group led by a transformational leader may feel more strongly about their positions on particular issues and fight harder than members who are under a transactional leader (Kotlyar & Karakowsky, 2006). The transformational leader must be prepared to effectively deal with this potential problem.

Looking Back: A Quick Review

ADDITIONAL LEADERSHIP PERSPECTIVES

Functional perspective	Seeks to identify important behaviors successful leaders perform—task, procedural, and social.
Leader as medium	The leader serves as organizer in developing a scheme of rules and procedures designed to meet the complexity of the problem.
Transformational leader	The leader elevates, motivates, inspires, and develops his or her group members. This contrasts with a transactional leader, who manages within existing norms and exchanges rewards for performance.

Visionary Leadership

We believe that all effective leaders have a vision for what the group's overall goal should be. This might be termed the group's end goal. It might also be called the long-term goal. This goal is the guiding vision that the leader uses to guide for the group. Of course, there are also short-term goals or intermediate goals that lead to the accomplishment of the vision.

The leadership style that embodies this notion of vision is best seen in the transformational leader. But, we believe all leaders who are successful must have a vision. Those leaders who do not have a vision do not know where they are going and when they get there.

The functional perspective is an attractive one because it links behaviors with leadership. It answers the question of what a person needs to do to cause a group to be successful. "While the transactional leader motivates subordinates to perform as expected, the transformational leader typically inspires followers to do more than originally expected" (Den Hartog, Van Muijen, & Koopman, 1997).

CHARACTERISTICS OF THE EFFECTIVE LEADER

Suppose you are convinced that you would like to lead groups, and now you are ready to begin a program in earnest toward the goal of improving your leadership. Where would you start? There are certain things you can do to build skill. This section of the chapter builds on ideas that have already been presented to support seven general characteristics of good leadership.

A Question of Ethics and Responsibility

ETHICS AND LEADERSHIP

Few would question that a leader ought to be ethical. But it is difficult to define what constitutes ethics. When we are asked to judge a leader to be ethical, we might find it difficult to label, beyond simple words like *honest* and *fair*. Michael Z. Hackman and Craig E. Johnson have given us one approach to answering this question in their book *Leadership: A Communication Perspective*. Here are their six items that represent an ethical leader:

1. A leader should not intentionally send deceptive or harmful messages.
2. A leader should place concern for others above concern for personal gain.
3. A leader should respect the opinions and attitudes of members and allow them the freedom to consider the consequences of their actions.
4. A leader should stand behind members when they carry out policies and actions approved by the leader and the group.
5. A leader treats members consistently, regardless of sex, ethnicity, or social background.
6. A leader should establish clear policies that all group members are expected to follow.

Identify a group where you felt uncomfortable. Use this list to see whether that feeling might have come from leadership that did not live up to these ethical standards. How often do you think members' frustrations with a group is a function of the ethics of the leader?

M. Z. Hackman & C. E. Johnson (1991), *Leadership: A communication perspective*. Prospect Heights, IL: Waveland Press, p. 129.

Effective leaders are well informed   Some leaders seem to ignore this idea. Consider a man who was appointed to head a policy committee in his department. He spent the first 20 minutes of each committee meeting discovering "what we ought to do today." Since there was no published agenda when he was finally ready to work, neither he nor the other members had the information necessary to approach the task. Sometimes he got lucky because one or two members were well informed, but frequently they struggled. Do not let this happen to you. Do your homework if you are to be successful—investigate the topic, consider alternatives, and perhaps even lay out a complete analysis. Studies consistently show a high correlation between task ability and effective leadership (Palmer, 1962).

Effective leaders provide direction and structure for the group   In most groups you will need to organize and direct the task. But directing is more than giving orders. Good leaders are generally good planners. You must be able to organize a task before you can organize a group. A leader often uses an agenda to accomplish this end. A leader should circulate that agenda—that plan—so that group members can use it while they prepare.

Effective leaders are skillful communicators   Leaders are, first of all, active participators. Research suggests that leaders have a tendency to talk more than the average member (Stogdill, 1981; Stein & Heller, 1979). Not only do they talk more than the average member of a group, they also communicate better. Leaders tend to be more fluent and more confident, and to speak more frequently, than the average member. They are also typically more effective listeners (Johnson & Bechler, 1998).

Being a skillful communicator also means being sensitive and adaptive to the changing needs of members. Leading successfully necessitates being aware of where group members are at any particular moment. This is accomplished by careful observation and evaluation of verbal and nonverbal cues. Wood (1977) is among those whose research supports this need. You may recall that she discovered that effective leaders were sensitive to the changes in a group and adapted to them. For example, you might discover through careful attention to feedback that your group is experiencing tension. Perhaps it is frustrated with a particular member. You might take time to talk through this issue with the group. Chapter 10 provides help for working through differences with members.

Effective leadership is an interactional process that helps members in three ways (Barge & Hirokawa, 1989). First, the leader takes active steps to reduce task uncertainty and manage the complexity of the task. In other words, the leader helps members overcome the barriers and obstacles they face in understanding their task and achieving their goal. Second, the leader establishes productive relationships with and between group members through verbal and nonverbal communication. Third, the leader demonstrates the appropriate level of communication competency necessary to be effective.

Research by Ludwig and Geller (1997) found that groups whose leaders waited for team members to present their ideas instead of leading with their own ideas generated more and better ideas than when the leader spoke first.

Effective leaders adapt their leadership style to meet the needs of the group   Fiedler points out the need for different kinds of leadership based on three contingencies: leader–member relationships, task structure, and power position. Recall that a highly task-oriented leadership style seems best under conditions of high and low favorableness for the leader. The relationally oriented leadership style works best in situations of moderate favorableness for the leader. A leader can take on the appropriate style as the circumstance changes. A good leader will be sensitive to the group's current situation and adapt to meet changing needs.

Effective leaders provide consideration in addition to structure   Most members want their leader to be considerate of them, to pay attention to climate. Charles Pavitt and Pamela Sackaroff (1990) discovered that experienced members expect leaders to be enthusiastic and well organized, to encourage participation, and to suggest procedures. Dominic Infante and William Gordon (1991) add that employees preferred a communication style they described as affirming (friendly, attentive, and relaxed) and low in verbal aggression.

Effective leaders adopt a "democratic" style   There are quotation marks around *democratic* for an important reason. Pure democratic style is unlikely to exist. There are likely to be degrees of democracy. The idea that a democratic leader tends to be more effective is supported by extensive research (Shaw, 1981). Autocratic leaders have a tendency

Looking Back: A Quick Review

EFFECTIVE LEADERS

Are well informed.

Provide direction and structure.

Are skillful communicators.

Adapt their style to the needs of the group.

Convey consideration to members.

Adopt an appropriate style. A collaborative, democratic style is often appropriate.

Are able to manage complexity.

to impose their will upon the group, thus creating a decision-making situation of pseudo-discussion. You have probably attended meetings in a work context where the boss called the group together "to make a decision," but meant instead "to announce a decision and discuss it." No real decision making is taking place.

Much of what is known about decision making suggests that autocratic leadership violates the aims of small group discussion. Groups make decisions to secure their commitment to the decision. Groups are called so members can feel included in the group and in the organization. Groups are called so the members of the organization will know that they are being taken into account. These are group- and organization-centered goals. Autocratic-style leaders often pursue leader-centered goals.

Some people confuse autocratic leadership with the desire for structure. So one final point remains to be made. Autocratic leadership and structuring behavior are not the same. Although leaders generally have a need to control, there is a very important difference. Autocrats generally *impose* their control. Democrats generally approach the matter of control by careful planning of a structure—either by presenting a plan and asking the group to ratify that plan or by asking the group to evolve a task structure on its own.

Autocratic leadership is directive leadership; democratic is largely participative. Research by Chen, Gordon, and McIntosh (1996, p. 1) found "significantly lower quality decision arose from groups with directive leaders rather than participative leaders."

Effective leaders manage complexity   Both group process and the decision-making process are complex. The interpersonal dimension also can be characterized by complexity. Complexity requires an effective leader be equipped with a large repertoire of communication functions for interacting with members. In addition, the effective leader will help the group understand the complexity of the issue and will guide members through a process of using that information to arrive at conclusions. So the group participates in the structuring process.

Given these leadership requirements it is very likely that the effective leader has high cognitive complexity. **Cognitive complexity** is a mental operating state that allows a person to process complex information effectively. This person will be able to successfully interpret many facets of a situation or problem, integrate these and create a complex solution that will meet the multiple causes of the problem. Members and leaders who are high in cognitive complexity tend to use more complex arguments, integrate their goals with those of others in their argument, and are better at building on others' feelings and beliefs during discussions (Kline, Hennen-Floyd & Farrell, 1990). Cognitive complex people also ask more questions and provide more objective information during a discussion.

So, what can you do if you do not think your cognitive complexity is high? The answer seems to be to assume less, ask more questions, and check out what you think others want, feel, and think.

PROVIDING LEADERSHIP

We do not think that these characteristics apply only to a leader. All members can supply leadership when it is needed. Because of that, these apply to you even if you are not in a leadership position. Research by Hirokawa, DeGooyer and Valde (2000) confirms this. Members who helped the group succeed were knowledgeable, skillful, highly motivated to complete the task, willing to listen, willing to share information, and expressed pleasure as well as fear about the task.

LEADING PUBLIC DISCUSSION

The leader of a public discussion will be more successful if he or she keeps several guiding principles in mind. Of course, you will find situations in which one or more of these will not apply, but generally they will.

Limit the number of topics.   A focused discussion will be easier to follow and more meaningful for the listeners. Generally no more than three or four main topics or issues should be addressed within an hour's discussion. Of course, the main issues are generally divided into subtopics. Usually a session should not continue beyond an hour and fifteen minutes.

Plan a series of open-ended questions to guide the discussion.   Open-ended questions call for a general response and allow respondents the freedom to express their views more fully. In contrast, a closed question asks for specific information. An open-ended question might be followed by more specific questions, but open-ended questions are important if you hope to stimulate a lively discussion.

A Question of Ethics and Responsibility

LEADING A PUBLIC FORUM

The Local Emergency Management Committee (LEMC) is planning a series of public meetings to help residents know what to do if the siren sounds because there is an accidental release of toxic chemicals. The LEMC includes concerned community members as well as members from a variety of industries that deal with toxic chemicals. The public meetings are viewed as information-sharing sessions that will teach people how to shelter themselves in place if the siren sounds. A second goal for the meetings is to answer questions and address concerns that residents might have. In order to answer most questions, panel members must be experts. Thus expertise is available from professionals in these industries and from the Civil Defense director. There is a concern that the panel of experts might be viewed as biased because they work for industries that handle toxic chemicals. Panel members do not represent their companies but, rather, the LEMC. There is a fear, too, that some community activists may attend the meetings and try to impose their own agenda on the meeting. Folks who are angry with a particular firm might try to get even.

A respected member of the clergy from the neighborhood where the plants are located has been selected as an impartial moderator. Assume that you are the selected moderator. Plan strategies for leading this meeting. Include a plan for dealing with community activists if they attend and try to shift the agenda to their own issues.

Attempt to keep discussants on the topic. Of course, you cannot and would not want to try to keep members directly on the topic all the time. Some diversion is likely and not unreasonable. But listeners may soon become bored or perhaps even disappointed if too many long diversions from the issues are permitted. Some specific advice about keeping members on the topic will be presented shortly.

Try to regulate participation so that all members have an opportunity to speak. There is a good chance that you will discover some members seem to have more to say than others. You will not want to be too heavy-handed in regulating, but you also will not want one or two members to monopolize the discussion. Again, refer to and use suggestions found later in this chapter for managing this problem.

Reward group members for their cooperation and participation. You should compliment both the group and individual members on their good work. You will, of course, want to thank them at the end of the discussion. But you also may find times during the discussion where praise is appropriate. Perhaps at the end of the discussion of one of the main topics you might say, "I appreciate the willingness of each person to speak on this issue. The lively discussion of it has been interesting to me and, I suspect, to our listeners, too."

Looking Back: A Quick Review

TIPS FOR LEADING PUBLIC DISCUSSION

Limit the number of topics to be discussed.

Plan open-ended questions to guide the discussion.

Keep discussants on the topic.

Regulate participation so all can speak.

Reward members for their participation.

IMPROVING YOUR LEADERSHIP SKILLS

The suggestions presented here are most easily implemented if the leader understands the major responsibilities involved and has a plan to implement them. There are five major areas of responsibility that a successful leader will attempt to manage:

1. Preparing for the meeting.
2. Structuring and guiding the group activity.
3. Stimulating creative and critical thinking.
4. Managing conflict.
5. Promoting cohesiveness.

Two of these responsibilities—managing conflict and promoting cohesiveness—are addressed in separate chapters, Chapter 9 and Chapter 10. The remaining issues are addressed here.

Preparing for Leading a Meeting

It would be unusual to find a successful leader who did not prepare. Most leaders prepare, of course, but some are more successful than others because their preparation is thorough. Consider the new manager, Carl Cooper, who called his supervisors together to prepare a request for his next year's budget. Some prepared a 15-minute talk that laid out what they needed. Others did the same but provided justifications and had supporting documents. Those supervisors went away with what they needed. This outcome might have been different if the unsuccessful managers had a planning checklist like the one that follows. Careful preparation involves formulating a statement of purpose, gathering information, soliciting input about purpose and agenda, contacting members, and setting the meeting place. Here is a checklist and comments:

___ 1. *Make a clear statement of purpose or purposes.*
Often people think they know their goals, but really do not have a very clear picture. Writing a statement of purpose tends to fix goals more firmly. You can circulate the statement and ask for feedback from members. This step will give them the opportunity to ask for clarification and should lead to a more focused and productive meeting. Sometimes a group might spend a whole meeting clarifying goals. For example, task forces or ad hoc groups often undertake complex, perplexing problems. A meeting or two to lay out goals is clearly in order. A group should always be involved in goal setting if views may differ. Solicit opinions about the agenda. State a tentative goal and ask for feedback. Ask, "Are there any ideas in this statement that seem unclear?" "Is this the direction in which we should move to handle this issue?" Sometimes circulating members' comments with the agenda provides a context for goal planning (Locke et al., 1981).

___ 2. *Take time to do research on the subject or subjects.*
One of the distinguishing characteristics of effective leaders is that they know more about the issues than the members do. Do you? If you do not—and sometimes even if you do—you need to get informed. Formulate questions that, when answered, will allow you to be informed. Ask experts; read; do some observation in the field. Get informed, whatever it takes.

For several years your author has been observing the college academic program planning committee. This committee is constituted anew each year. Sometimes uninformed members get selected to lead. They fail miserably. What happens is that a more informed member usually emerges as the leader. You see, being well informed is impressive and a source of influence.

___ 3. *Construct an agenda for the meeting.*
Publishing an agenda is an essential part of being a good leader of groups. A leader who does not announce an agenda creates a problem. Ill-prepared members suffer a good deal of discomfort and cannot contribute in any meaningful way.

The agenda may be a brief list of the topics to be covered. However, if it is expected that a group will be involved in decision making about a complex problem, or will be considering a situation about which members are not informed, wise leadership will include questions under each area of a problem-solving agenda. But be sure to adapt the agenda to your group's needs. Chapter 3 provides help in selecting and adapting an agenda. The agenda should be circulated a few days in advance. Bring additional copies to the meeting for members who forgot theirs.

___ 4. *Select members on the basis of their expertise, and secure their commitment to attend.*
A group of five to seven people is usually a good size for productive meetings, although a somewhat larger group whose members have experience working together can be productive, too. Expertise and ability to get along are important criteria for selection. Asking two people with similar experience and expertise may

duplicate effort unwisely, especially in business contexts. On the other hand, such duplication may be wise. The point is that the matter of duplication ought to be considered. As a general principle, it is important to find willing participants. Tell them directly what they will be doing and listen to what they say. If a person seems reluctant, try somebody else. Look to Chapter 2 for assistance.

—— 5. *Review the comments of the participants, revise the agenda, and select a meeting place.* Review the comments of the participants about your plan and take their comments into account. This step can save much group time later.

Once the agenda is set, you are ready to select a meeting place. Be sure the room is appropriate in size. If your group is small, pick a room that will accommodate it. Too much space and empty chairs detract from a sense of "groupness." Discover whether the group needs work space. If members will need to spread out papers, you need adequate space. Location also can be important. It might be wise to hold the meeting in a certain building if most of the group members work there. Occasionally you may have a member in a wheelchair. Can that person gain easy access? If it is a long meeting, is there an area for a coffee break? Is the room well lighted and comfortable? Are rest rooms close by?

Structuring and Guiding the Group Activity

Observers rate groups whose leaders are skillful at task structuring as better than groups that do not have such leadership. Structure is necessary for planning and coordinating the effort. So the leader should circulate an agenda, write a clear goal statement, secure group agreement about the agenda, and take responsibility for initiating and maintaining the discussion. Initiating and maintaining the discussion involves such activities as keeping goal oriented, introducing new agenda items, encouraging people to talk, regulating participation, summarizing group progress, and verbalizing consensus (Hirokawa, 1980).

There are big payoffs in successfully achieving these ends. For example, Street (1997) found that keeping a group task (goal) committed meant it was more likely to search for and assess alternative courses of actions than when groups were not kept committed.

Beatrice Schultz (1986) predicted, for eight of nine groups, who would become leader on the basis of the communicative functions performed. Leaders were more goal directed, direction giving, summary giving, and self-assured than others. So it seems that members need to cultivate functional behaviors if they are to emerge as group leaders. Further, Gregory Dobbins and Stephen Zaccaro (1986) found that members of groups with leaders high in initiating structure and consideration were more cohesive and satisfied than were members of groups whose leaders were low on these behaviors. These behaviors mark the difference between successful and less successful groups. They are behaviors that any member can contribute. Certainly every leader should be able to perform them, and the best way to learn how is to practice.

Some useful language and strategies for structuring and guiding activities follow.

1. Keeping the Group Goal Oriented

PROBLEM   Group is digressing too much into social conversation.

LANGUAGE AND/OR STRATEGY

1. Comment on the social issue being discussed and then say, "Now, let's move back to our discussion of [name what group was discussing]."

2. "I don't understand how this idea is relevant to our task. Is it? If not, we need to get back to the topic."

PROBLEM   Member persists in an effort to digress from the agenda.

LANGUAGE AND/OR STRATEGY

1. "I've noticed that we seem to keep getting off the track and haven't been making our usual progress. I'm concerned that we might not meet our goal. I'm wondering what the group thinks about this."

2. "How is it we get sidetracked? What can we do about it?"

3. "What should I do if we get off the subject again?" Then guide the group back.

2. Introducing New Agenda Items

PROBLEM   Group is ready and needs to move on to the next agenda item.

LANGUAGE AND/OR STRATEGY

1. "So, we've agreed . . . [Summarize.] Let's take up the next item."

2. "So, we've agreed . . . [Summarize.] Are we ready to take up the next item?"

3. "The next item asks us to determine what, if anything, should be done about. . . ."

3. Encouraging Members to Participate

PROBLEM   Member doesn't participate because of shyness or reserve.

LANGUAGE AND/OR STRATEGY

1. "Recently I was talking with [name of reticent member], who had an interesting [or useful, or insightful] comment. [Name], would you be willing to share your idea?" You need to be sure to discuss some aspect of the issue with this reticent person before the meeting.

2. "[Name], you heard Susan. Do you agree or wish to add to her comment?"

3. If you are apprehensive about communicating, here is a strategy: First, limit your group experiences to those where you feel most comfortable. Then, as you gain experience, broaden the group experiences. Your reaching out will allow you to broaden your range of group skills (Rubin, Rubin, & Jordan, 1997).

Focus on Research

SOCIAL LOAFING: AN INTERESTING PHENOMENON

Social loafing is a concern to people who value effective groups because many tasks require the pooling of individual efforts to achieve excellence in task achievement. **Social loafing** refers to the tendency of members to reduce their contribution. It generally happens in groups where individual contributions are difficult to identify.

Why do people engage in social loafing? Burn (2004) bases her explanation on Porter and Lawler's expectancy-valence theory (1968). This theory predicts people's motivation to perform will be high when they believe their effort will lead to increased performance (expectancy), their increased performance will be recognized (instrumentality), and they value the reward for the performance or outcome of the performance (valence).

Group members may believe their performance will not contribute much to the effort, so "Why bother?" (expectancy). Group members may believe their performance is not seen as important by more dominant group members (instrumentality). Group members may not desire whatever reward comes from participation (valence). According to Porter and Lawler, motivation will be low if any one of these is low. The result is social loafing.

An alternative explanation for the loss of effectiveness is sometimes referred to as the **sucker effect** (Burn, 2004). The sucker is the member (or members) whose effort has made up for the effect of the social loafer. This member decides to reduce his or her effort so that he or she is no longer carrying the freeloader. The group effort suffers, of course, but the member no longer feels taken advantage of and may view this as teaching the freeloader a lesson.

Some scholars argue that there are gender differences in social loafing. They attribute this to the fact that females are often socialized to be more friendly, cooperative, and concerned for others.

Males, on the other hand, are socialized to be assertive and competitive (Burn, 1996). Women, because of their greater interest in group harmony, group success, satisfaction of other members, and concern about how other members evaluate them, should loaf less. Karau and Williams (1993) analyzed data that turned out to be consistent with this prediction. They found greater social loafing in groups that were all male. In addition, the social loafing in all male groups increased as the size of the group increased.

Karau and Williams (1993) also investigated the influence of culture on social loafing. They reasoned that groups in individualistic cultures, the United States, for example, would display more social loafing than groups in collectivist cultures—China, Japan, and Taiwan, for example. They reasoned that groups in the more group-oriented cultures would have members who would place more value on being a good group member and would loaf less. Their analysis proved correct. Participants in groups in China, Japan, and Taiwan loafed less than research participants in groups in Canada and the United States.

S. M. Burn (2004). *Groups: Theory and practice.* Belmont, CA: Wadsworth.

S. J. Karau & K. D. Williams (1993). Social loafing: A meta-analytic review and theoretical investigation. *Journal of Personality and Social Psychology,* 65, 681–706.

L. W. Porter & E. E. Lawler (1968). *Managerial attitudes and performance.* Homewood, IL: Dorsey.

PROBLEM   Member doesn't seem to be "with" the group and is allowing others to do the work (social loafing); member may be distracted or working on some private agenda.

LANGUAGE AND/OR STRATEGY

1. "I think it would be a good idea to take stock of where we are. [Name], will you agree that we've. . . . [Summarize.]"

2. "[Name], what do you think about [the topic of discussion]?"

3. "[Name], you seem to be off somewhere. I was wondering whether. . . ."

4. Stop and summarize the group's progress. Then discuss where the group is heading in its discussion. Try to involve the nonparticipant.

5. Take some time to evaluate the group using some of the rating forms found in Chapter 11 of this book. Include some individual ratings, too. Discuss the results and goals for improving the group's interactions. We know that members often identify more strongly with their group than their supporting organization (Barker & Tompkins, 1994). So peer evaluation can be a powerfully motivating force.

PROBLEM   Member appears not to be informed, is fearful others will discover lack of preparation.

LANGUAGE AND/OR STRATEGY

1. "[Name], will you help me [or recorder] record these ideas? We want to be sure we keep a group memory. [Name], will you review. . . ."

Note: Usually you will not be able to know why people avoid involvement, so proceed with caution. Your goal is to involve these people right from the beginning. Often they will not contribute anything if you do not involve them in the first few minutes. Be alert and do something right away. Be careful to encourage without embarrassing. For example, if you ask someone what he or she knows about an issue—and the person doesn't know anything about it—you may not be able to get him or her to participate at all. If you anticipate the problem and are able to control seating arrangements, seat that person across from you. Eye contact can encourage participation.

4. Regulating Participation

PROBLEM   Member monopolizes the interaction.

LANGUAGE AND/OR STRATEGY

1. Avoid excessive eye contact with talkative person. Establish eye contact with others to encourage them to talk.

2. Ask group members to agree to make only one point when they get the floor.

3. Break in and say, "That is an interesting idea. Let's consider . . . first, John. Then we will come back to your other idea."

4. Approach the talker in private. Tell the person you are concerned about some of the quiet members. Ask the person to help draw them out.

5. Bring it up directly in the group. If the problem persists, you may have to deal with it straightforwardly. Try to be supportive but make sure that the group knows it must come up with an answer.

5. Summarizing Group Progress

PROBLEM   People get caught up in the interaction and lose track of their progress.

LANGUAGE AND/OR STRATEGY
1. Summarize. "Let's see what we've done so far. . . ."

PROBLEM   Group needs encouragement.

LANGUAGE AND/OR STRATEGY
1. Summarize.

2. Point out the agreement the group has had thus far. Congratulate the group on its progress.

6. Reducing Tension Levels

PROBLEM   Tension in the group is high.

LANGUAGE AND/OR STRATEGY
1. "We've been working pretty hard. Let's take a break."

2. Use humor, if you are skillful at humor, to divert the group and lighten the mood.

Some leaders attempt to use humor in their effort to guide the group. If they make this choice, they need to give attention to the type of humor employed. A study by Christi McGuffee Smith and Larry Powell (1988) found that the target of the humor made a difference in its effect. When the leader chose himself or herself as the target, the humor was perceived as more effective at relieving tension and encouraging participation, and the leader was seen as being more willing to share opinions. Leaders who targeted their superiors were seen as less helpful to the group and less willing to share opinions. Leaders who targeted subordinates received lower ratings on social attractiveness and lower ratings as tension relievers and summarizers.

Stimulating Creative and Critical Thinking

Creativity requires us to bring originality of thought to the discussion. **Critical thinking** suggests a thought process based on sound evidence and valid reasoning that joins information to conclusions in an acceptable way. There is no magic you can perform to cause people to think creatively and critically. You can only encourage them.

Cady and Valentine (1999) found that insights and sensitivities brought by people with differing backgrounds, based on gender, ethnicity, and functional knowledge, increased flexibility and promoted high-quality innovations. Other research suggests that homogeneous groups may perform better initially, but over time heterogeneous groups perform better in problem solving and innovativeness (Harrison, Price, & Bell, 1998; Knouse & Dansby, 1999). Aim for diversity in membership, if possible.

Chapter 2 addressed critical thinking when it discussed logical fallacies. Chapter 9 will say more, when we examine the notion of groupthink.

1. Stimulating Creativity

PROBLEM   How to stimulate creativity.

LANGUAGE AND/OR STRATEGY

1. Urge people to go beyond the normal constraints of their thinking. Much of our thinking seems to be boxed in by our private perceptions of an event.

2. Encourage people to listen to others' ideas and to try to expand on good ones.

3. Divide the issue and consider each part separately. This approach often promotes a more focused and in-depth investigation.

4. Talk members through the process of formally engaging in brainstorming. Using the procedure gives people permission to step out of their normal roles.

5. Try to encourage members to provide several alternatives. Actually ask them to say more. Point out the benefits of considering a variety of viewpoints.

2. Promoting Critical Thinking

PROBLEM   How to promote critical thinking.

LANGUAGE AND/OR STRATEGY

1. Agree with members that each person has the responsibility for helping to evaluate the information.

2. Spend some time asking the group to generate a list of "how" questions. Such a list might include:
   a. How do you know this is true?
   b. How does this information apply to the problem?
   c. How does the source of the information know this?

d. How were the statistics collected?

e. How well do our criteria apply to these solutions?

f. How well will this solution work when we try it?

Once the questions are formulated, you might place them on a flip chart.

Obviously you should not memorize the language used here. Instead, use these suggestions to develop your own language and strategies.

SUMMARY

Leadership and leader are not the same thing. *Leadership* is an influence process directed toward group goal achievement. On the other hand, a *leader* is a person who directs and influences a group toward its goal. A significant concept for understanding this influence is power. A leader can influence the behavior of members to the extent that members perceive and acknowledge the leader's power. Sources of power include reward, punishment, legitimacy, referent, expertise, and persuasion.

The leader may be appointed or may emerge. Sometimes leadership is shared among several people. Bormann suggests the emergence process is one of residues in which members are gradually eliminated as potential leaders until one person emerges to lead. Bormann offers four patterns, or scenarios, of leadership emergence.

Women have been portrayed as being more easily influenced and having less power than men. Often, women are seen as using less powerful speech. However, despite some mixed reports, research does not tend to support these stereotypes.

Leadership perspectives have developed historically, with each emerging perspective seeking to correct "faults" of and/or build on the other. The trait perspective attempted to identify characteristics that are common to leaders. The style perspective demonstrates the effect of a particular style on several variables. The situational/contingency perspectives point to particular variables that help determine leadership effectiveness. The functional perspective focuses on behaviors leaders perform to guide a group. The leader as medium suggests the need to manage complexity. The transformational leader elevates, motivates, and inspires as he or she develops the team or group.

The examination of these various perspectives yields six conclusions regarding effective leaders:

1. Effective leaders have experience and skill with the task.

2. Effective leaders provide direction and structure.

3. Effective leaders are skillful communicators.

4. Effective leaders are adaptive.

5. Effective leaders generally adopt a democratic style.

6. Effective leaders are able to manage complexity.

Finally, some straightforward suggestions are offered for improving your leadership. Checklists are presented for preparing for a meeting with language and strategy examples for coping with common leadership problems. Topics include keeping the group goal oriented, introducing new agenda items, encouraging participation, regulating participation, summarizing group progress, reducing tension levels, and stimulating creative and critical thinking.

KEY TERMS AND CONCEPTS

autocratic style
coercive power
contingency perspective
cognitive complexity
delegating approach
democratic style
designated leader
emergent leader
expert power
functions
laissez-faire
leader
leader as medium
leadership
leadership-structuring style

legitimate power
method of residues
motivational-hierarchy
    hypothesis
participating approach
persuasive power
procedural leadership
    functions
punishment power
readiness level
referent power
reward power
scenario I
scenario II
scenario III

scenario IV
self-directed work teams
selling approach
shared leadership
situational perspective
social leadership functions
social loafing
sucker effect
style
task leadership functions
telling approach
trait perspective
transactional leader
transformational
    leadership

EXERCISES

1. What is your personal definition of leadership? Share your thoughts with others in a small group. How are the definitions of your group members similar? How do they differ? Now write a definition of leadership that satisfies the group. Present this definition to your class.

2. Describe and analyze your group's leadership. You might find the Barnlund-Haiman Leadership Rating Scale (see Table 11.3 in Chapter 11) useful. Include a discussion of task leadership, social leadership, leadership style, leadership adequacy, and suggestions for improvement.

3. Your author has suggested that every member can contribute to the leadership of a group. Think about your leadership contributions to a group in this class. Describe your leadership strengths. Describe your weaknesses. What goals can you set for yourself as a leader?

4. In a small group, role-play the following leadership problems. Rotate the role of leader among group members and role-play each situation twice using a different leader. After each role-playing experience, discuss the effectiveness of the leader's approach. Here are the situations:
    a. A leader is trying to involve a nonparticipating member.
    b. A member is continually moving the group away from the task.

c. A leader wants to discourage an overly talkative member.

d. A leader wants to resolve an interpersonal conflict and get on with the task.

e. A leader wants to help members who are engaged in ideational conflict understand one another.

f. A leader wants to motivate an apathetic group member.

5. Work with your instructor to invite to your class several professional people from the community who are in leadership positions and work with small groups. Prepare a list of questions that will allow them to talk about their leadership experience. The goal of the interviews is to gain insights into how these people handle leadership problems.

6. Interview two people you know personally who lead groups. Ask and record the answers to these questions: How did they come to be in this position of leadership? What are the most important leadership functions they perform? What do they see as the three or four most important of these functions? Why? What is the biggest leadership challenge they face? How do they meet this challenge? Compare the answers of your leaders in a three-page report.

7. Analyze your personal leadership ability. Make a list of leadership behaviors you see yourself providing. Now identify your skill level on a scale from 1 to 10. What are your strengths? What are your weaknesses? How can you build skill in your weak areas?

RECOMMENDED WEBSITES

At www.princeton.edu/~oa/manual/sect9.html is a group dynamics and leadership site by the Outdoor Action Program at Princeton University. This page contains information on group dynamics and leadership and includes information on the functions and behaviors performed by a leader, as well as leadership and communication styles. It also gives a brief look into situational leadership theory (SLT).

The leadership site www.hope2help.com/team/skill.htm, by Dick Wulf, gives great examples of ineffective leadership and what to do to handle the inefficiencies. Wulf contends that one of the shortfalls in leadership is the leader's "not leading the team as a group."

Leadership Skills for Communication, Group Facilitation, and Action, at www2.hawaii.edu/~jharris/leadership.html, contains links to materials such as handouts and workbooks that Jeff Brooks-Harris is developing with colleagues at the University of Hawaii to train student leaders to use different types of leadership skills.

Experienced Based Learning, Inc., at www.ebl.org/examples.html, has a list of exercises for teamwork and team-building activities to help improve leadership skills and other issues such as trust.

Big Dog's Leadership Link Page, at www.nwlink.com/~donclark/leader/leadlnk.html, is a great source of links to leadership topics, including motivation and assessment instruments such as surveys. It also includes topics such as contingency theory and strategic planning.

RECOMMENDED READINGS

R. Foels, J. E. Driskell, B. Mullen, & E. Salas (2000). The effects of democratic leadership on group member satisfaction: An integration. *Small Group Research, 31,* pp. 676–701.

B. A. Fisher (1986). Leadership: When does the difference make a difference? In R. Y. Hirokawa & M. S. Poole (eds.), *Communication and group decision making.* Beverly Hills, CA: Sage, pp. 197–215.

D. D. Gouran (2003). Leadership as the art of counteractive influence in decision-making groups. In R. Y. Hirokawa, R. S. Cathcart, L. A. Samovar, & L. D. Henman (eds.), *Small group communication: Theory and practice,* 8th ed. Los Angeles: Roxbury, pp. 172–183.

S. B. Shimanoff & M. M. Jenkins (2003). Leadership and gender: Challenging assumptions and recognizing resources. In R. Y. Hirokawa, R. S. Cathcart, L. A. Samovar, & L. D. Henman (eds.), *Small group communication: Theory and practice,* 8th ed. Los Angeles: Roxbury, pp. 184–198.

chapter

8

RELATIONAL COMMUNICATION IN GROUPS

OBJECTIVES

After reading this chapter you should be able to
- Explain Schutz's concept of inclusion, control, and affection as needs.
- Specify how a group member can use Schutz's ideas in a group.
- Define and explain the terms *empathy* and *trust,* and show how each bears upon group communication.
- Name and explain the implications for group discussants of each quadrant in the Johari window.
- Name and explain the six defensive climates and the six supportive climates described by Gibb.
- Describe the behavior and suggest strategies for dealing with difficult people.

"I do OK with the day-to-day business of communicating," said Eric Mitchell, a trouble-shooter from the engineering staff group. "What gives me problems is the difficult situations of meeting with a group of engineers from one of our plants to solve a problem. They don't know me, and I don't really know them. And what we have to talk about is a problem that they have been unable to solve. They are feeling defensive. They see me as the enemy. I really have to rely on my relational skills."

"Yeah." Linda Kerr's eyes lit up. "That's a big problem for me too. And when I try to point out where the difficulty lies, people seem to want to attack me. But in the end, I'm responsible for getting the problem solved and convincing them to implement the solution. When I leave the plant, it's up to them."

Sung Woo, another engineering group member, offered a suggestion. "What I think would be helpful for us is instruction on managing these difficult people situations."

Bernard Jenkins, the group manager, had one final comment, and a good one: "The kind of thing you're talking about is not just a problem that we experience with the plant engineers we work with. It's a problem any time someone is faced with leading a group. It's just intensified because of the nature of our role in this operation."

This short transcript from an actual conversation of a group of engineers focuses on the theme of this chapter. What it all comes down to is that all groups are composed of individuals. Sooner or later some very fundamental notions about managing climate and relationships must be addressed.

This chapter examines four aspects of communicating with group members. First, we look at how group members can meet each other's needs. Many people spend as much time with their work colleagues as they do with their families. Consequently, the quality of life on the job is essential to an individual's personal and interpersonal health and growth. This is important not only to the individual but also to his or her colleagues, the group and, ultimately, to the organization. Second, we address the issues of self-disclosure, empathy, and trust. Next, we examine defensiveness and supportiveness and the communication behaviors associated with each. Finally, we discuss managing difficult people.

MEETING INTERPERSONAL NEEDS

The first question we want to look at is "How can individual group members meet each other's interpersonal needs?" Knowing what needs people bring to groups seems necessary, since a major reason for joining groups is to satisfy personal and interpersonal needs. The second question we want to answer is "How do self-disclosure, empathy, and trust contribute to member relationships and group process?" Finally, we will ask, "What can individual members do to create a positive group climate?" Learning how to provide this kind of atmosphere is a central skill for anyone who wants to improve interpersonal communication. This third question bears directly on the first and second. A group that manages to generate a supportive climate is able to meet the interpersonal needs of its individual members and to facilitate self-disclosure, empathy, and trust.

The Ideas of William Schutz

William C. Schutz (1958) published an influential book called *FIRO: A Three-Dimensional Theory of Interpersonal Behavior.* The letters **FIRO** in that title stand for "fundamental interpersonal relations orientation." Schutz argued:

1. Every individual has three important interpersonal needs: affection, control, and inclusion.

2. An individual's interpersonal behavior will be similar to the behavior he or she experienced in his or her earliest relationships.

3. Interpersonal compatibility—defined in terms of inclusion, control, and affection—is essential to the efficient operation of a group, increasing both the desire to communicate and the cohesiveness of group members.

4. As a group develops, it passes through stages that may be identified as inclusion, control, and affection; as it disintegrates, the group retraces its passage from affection through control and inclusion behaviors.

Schutz's theory has particular application to group communication. He believed that all people have these three interpersonal needs to some degree or another and that these needs are interconnected and "fit" along continuums described in Figure 8.1.

		Affection				
Complete commitment	Greater love needed Originating and initiating much love	Overpersonal	Personal	Underpersonal	Less love needed Never initiating affection	No affection
Strong control	Greater effect upon and power over others needed Controlling all of own and/or another's behaviors	Autocrat	Control Democrat	Abdicrat	Less effect on and power over others needed Controlling none of own and/or another's behaviors	No control
High interaction	Greater affiliation needed Always initiating interaction	Oversocial	Inclusion Social	Undersocial	Less affiliation needed Never initiating interaction	No interaction

FIGURE 8.1
The Interpersonal Needs Continuums According to Schutz

The **need for affection** is reflected in the desire to like and be liked by others. It is fulfilled by how personal or close those in the relationship are to each other. When little of this need is present, the group members will be distant and neutral toward each other.

Schutz refers to people who have a low need for affection as **underpersonal.** This person may be aloof to other members, avoiding anything more than a superficial relationship. On the other hand, a person who has a high need for affection is seen as **over-personal.** This person may go to great lengths to avoid being disliked by anyone. A group member who is overpersonal may be too concerned with the social dimension and thus spend far too much time talking about personal issues. A **personal** individual holds the middle ground. He or she can balance situations in order to be liked when affection is desired but also can maintain distance when affection is not needed. This balance allows group members to manage their relationships more productively.

A second need, **control,** is the desire both to exercise power and authority and to be controlled. The need to control is based on two principles: We have the need to control our environment and the destiny of our relationships, and our partners in relationships have the same need.

The individual who has a low need to control is called an **abdicrat.** The person abdicates all power and responsibilities to his or her group members. On the other hand, the person who needs to overcontrol, the **autocrat,** can cause serious problems in groups. The autocrat might try to control everything and everybody. The person who takes the middle ground is the **democrat.** This person can either take charge or allow other members to be in control, depending on the situation and the needs of the group.

The **need for inclusion** refers to the desire to be accepted, to feel wanted, and to be a part of a group. It also includes the need to accept others. Clearly, not all group members experience this need in the same way. Some may want more inclusion, whereas others avoid closeness and want less.

Members who feel little need for inclusion may behave **undersocially,** isolating themselves from group involvement. **Oversocial** people seek to join and be part of many groups. **Adaptable-social** people often allow the context of the group to motivate their degree of involvement.

Interpersonal Needs in Groups

But what do Schutz's ideas mean for communicating with other group members? In each of his categories, what is at issue from your perspective is not motivation but behaviors. A member can choose how he or she will interact with others, and making the appropriate choice is the key to successful interpersonal communication.

People act in certain ways because they believe that they will get a payoff greater than the price they have to pay. If a person's most valued payoff is interpersonal—and that is the basis upon which we usually interact with others—then the payoff most people are looking for will fall into Schutz's three categories. Thus a group member is always in a position to offer other members the payoffs they want. A member can provide evidence to another person that he is included and can choose to affiliate with him. A group member also can acknowledge the efforts of others to affiliate with him and can confirm them in doing that. As a member of a group, you can assure others that their membership is valued by the group and that their participation is wanted and important.

Similarly, if individuals need, as Schutz suggests, to be in control of their lives and also to exercise some control over others, you can provide them with payoffs that are valuable to them and to the group. For example, when another individual makes a contribution—say, an argument that appears to contradict the emerging group consensus—you can acknowledge and value that contribution. Given the tendency of some groups toward conformity to one another's views, the individual's contribution really *is* valuable. Even if the group ultimately decides in a way that is contrary to the person's arguments, your treating that person seriously can contribute to the individual's sense of control. You may be able to think of other ways to help individuals to satisfy their need to control. At their best and healthiest, such interactions—which treat substantive ideas seriously and thoroughly while valuing the individuals who make those arguments—are the essence of democratic decision making.

So as one individual communicating with another, you can provide payoffs in the dimensions of inclusion and control. It must be obvious, too, that you can do that in the dimension that Schutz called "affection."

Learning to talk about our affections may be easier if you translate affection into words like *valuing* or *liking*. Shows of valuing and liking are absolutely essential to every person, and can be critical to every human relationship.

Group members can give one another signs of affection. A member might approach another upon his arrival at the group's meeting and say, "It sure is good to see you tonight, Joel." Or perhaps a member might address the whole group at the end of a meeting: "I'm really glad that everybody could be here tonight. It's fun to work with you." Finally, a group might express its affection more freely through attention to the social dimension. Perhaps someone will say, "Let's go for a pizza now that we have finished."

SELF-DISCLOSURE, EMPATHY, AND TRUST

Self-Disclosure

In his important book *The Transparent Self*, Sidney M. Jourard (1971) posed a concern that **self-disclosure**—revealing information about yourself—is discouraged, especially in our culture. We teach individuals to close themselves. Jourard believed that it would be far better for individuals to become transparent. He said that people ought to tell others who they are—how they feel, what they want and expect, what their intentions are, what images they have in their heads, and the extent to which they are open to topics and persons. But, he said, we learn to distrust one another early on.

In task groups a person can be too open or not open enough. The appropriate degree of self-disclosure depends upon the nature of the group and its norms. Still, as you will see, learning to manage self-disclosure is very important to the group.

	Known to self	Not known to self
Known to other	I Open area	II Blind area
Not known to other	III Hidden area	IV Unknown area

FIGURE 8.2
The Johari Window

Source: J. Luft (1990).

How can you know what a group member wants if she will not tell you? Her telling you what she wants is part of disclosing herself. If what she wants is important to the climate of the group and she is feeling frustrated because you are not giving it to her—and if she will not communicate that want—then what is to become of the group? The group cannot know what she wants unless she discloses herself to the group.

Joseph Luft (1990) was concerned about the importance of self-disclosure to the success of working groups when he wrote his influential description of what he called the **Johari window.** Figure 8.2 illustrates his ideas. You will see that the window has four areas, each of which may be larger or smaller than the others, and each of which may change size.

The **open area** includes information that is known to the individual and also known to the individual's group. At first, perhaps only a person's name and other demographic information would be included. A group member can *see* how tall a person is, so he does not have to ask. He can *see* what color a person is. He can *hear* the person's tone of voice and accent. The other group member does not have to verbalize this information. Thus the information is known to the individual and known to the group. It would be part of the information in quadrant 1.

That is not very much to go on, is it? More information is needed to know the group member—information that is in quadrant III. The **hidden area** contains information that is known to the person, but not known to the group. For example, included here might be that the person is very knowledgeable in an area of concern. Unless the person brings that information to the open area, the group simply cannot take advantage of his knowledge and he loses opportunities to contribute.

We can imagine that there would be information that the person would need, too. Perhaps he needs information about how the group is experiencing him. That kind of information, information that is known to the group but not to the individual, is in the **blind area** of quadrant II. To illustrate, Chaz had just been appointed to a committee to study how to reduce energy costs at Teledyne Continental Motors. He had been at Teledyne for a year and considered this an important assignment. A colleague, Joe, the committee chair, approached him when it was time for the first meeting:

JOE: I'll walk with you to the meeting, Chaz. Are you ready to go?

CHAZ: Sure. Let me finish this little chore, and I'll be right with you.

JOE: I decided to meet informally for our first meeting, Chaz.

Joe steered toward the cafeteria across the street, rather than to the conference room in their own building:

JOE: I want to introduce you to some of the people who are going to be working on the committee with you. They haven't met you, but they've heard you're a bit of an opportunist, and they're feeling threatened. I think it would be a good idea for you to spend a little time chatting with them to see if you can't do something about that image.

That statement came as a surprise to Chaz, who received it with mixed thoughts. How could they have formed an opinion without ever meeting him? And what could be done about it, if anything? For that matter, what *should* be done about it?

JOE: Just be yourself, Chaz. They'll like you when they get to know you.

Information from quadrant II in the Johari window is difficult for the person to discover, but it can be very valuable. You might say Joe was disclosing himself in an effort to shrink this area and to increase the size of the known area, quadrant I. Chaz listened, heard the message, and was grateful. Joe began the meeting by asking members to introduce themselves and to describe their experience and expertise. He was causing them to enlarge the relevant area of open self by moving information from the hidden self. Helping the members know one another is important to the group's success (Honeycutt, Knapp, & Powers, 1983).

The point about disclosure is that in any group appropriate disclosure norms are important. A wise group member will attempt to monitor the known and the unknown and to adjust the Johari window according to his or her own needs and the needs of the group. That cannot happen without empathy and trust.

Empathy

Empathy refers to understanding another person well enough to understand what the person is feeling and saying from that person's point of view. Individual group members need to make an effort to empathize. If they do so, then other members can come to know and understand them. If members do not do so, then the others cannot know and understand them.

Suppose, for instance, that Joe had been unable to empathize with Chaz. Without empathy, Joe might not have "understood" how important the others' perceptions of Chaz were to Chaz. Joe might not have been able to put himself in Chaz's shoes. He might never have determined to introduce Chaz to the members of the important group he was to join. Joe might never have been able to anticipate or understand what the expressions of distrust he'd heard from the others about Chaz could mean to Chaz.

Beyond all this, empathy serves to counterbalance power in interpersonal relationships (Howell, 1982). The counterbalance allows people to trust one another and to work together. Without empathy, group members would be unable to give weight to other colleagues' interests as well as to their own.

Empathy, then, like self-disclosure and trust, is very important to the success of a group. It is nearly impossible to imagine a group having any cohesiveness if the members cannot listen empathically. When groups are cohesive, their members display themselves to one another, intellectually and without much censoring of their emotional selves. Even if an individual is presenting a string of facts and proofs, the group needs to be able to hear the tone of voice, the phrasing, and the pausing—all of which say "This is important to me. I feel strongly about it. I want your approval and support." Beyond this, it seems reasonable to suppose that empathy is a key to effective group activity.

To illustrate, if you imagine a group at the local YMCA working in a brainstorming session, you can readily see empathy at work. One member offers a suggestion—a half-baked idea at best, but a suggestion. A second member hitchhikes on the idea of the first. A third member tunes in to the emerging idea and offers a new facet. The first member, feeling support and now in better control of his own idea, adds a phrase or two. Someone from the group jumps in with another statement, and so on. The group members create a puzzle of idea fragments out of their own experiences. The members have become a single working unit whose creative task is shared because they are able to empathize. But they could not work together without trust.

Trust

Trust refers to the confidence we have in other people, so that we believe we can predict their behavior to be honorable and can rely on our prediction. Trust develops among group members over time. Members will generally be careful how far they go in revealing their thoughts and beliefs until they have had some experience with members that allow the trust to strengthen. Altman and Taylor (1973) suggest that we begin with a relatively nonthreatening disclosure, since it is the least risky, and stay at that level until we sense we can trust to go deeper. When we think we can go deeper—more personal and intimate—we will do so and stay at that level for a while. If our trust is violated, we will probably retreat to a less intimate level or not disclose at all.

Trust is central to cooperation because once people begin to cooperate (and the more they do so), they build the bond that trust provides. On the other hand, some are not so ethical in their relationships. Sometimes their *individual* gains can be maximized by *not* cooperating rather than by cooperating! Of course, this is a violation of the trust. Deutsch illustrates this argument by describing a group of men who agree to build houses for one another. Once the first house is completed, the individual whose house it is has no physical reason to continue to cooperate. His payoff (completion of his house) is a reality. If his only reason for cooperation was to get his house built, he has no reason to continue. Deutsch speculates that if he quit the group at this point, then no other houses would be completed. Moreover, if the group had foreseen that he would quit, it is unlikely that any of the houses would have been built.

The agreement to build houses by mutual cooperation, then, is an act of trust. Each participant puts himself into a position in which he can both suffer damages and gain

---

Focus on Research

GENDER DIFFERENCES IN SELF-DISCLOSURE AND EMPATHY

We have said that knowing your group members and being able to see their viewpoint as they are seeing it and experiencing it are important factors in group interaction. Let's pause here to see what researchers have to say about how these behaviors differ on the basis of gender.

The conventional stereotype is that women self-disclose more than men. On the other hand, men are stereotyped as strong and silent. These stereotypes are supported by research findings. Greenblatt, Hasenauer, and Friemuth (1980) reported that women disclosed more and received more disclosure than men. For men the researchers found that disclosure depended on the recipient. Men disclosed more often and more openly to women than to other men. Interestingly, women disclosed more often and with more depth to other women than to men. Perhaps the reason for this is that women are seen as more accepting than men—a notion borne out by the research of Derlega and colleagues (1985).

Research seems to be more mixed regarding empathy. One group of researchers (Brehm, Powell, & Coke, 1984) found no significant differences between men and women related to empathy. When researchers focused on the idea of gender differences rather than on differences based on sex, they found some interesting results. Bem (1975) found that

participants who were identified as traditionally feminine demonstrated more empathy than less traditionally feminine participants. Later, Fong and Borders (1985) identified masculine, feminine, and androgynous psychological types of participants. (*Androgynous* is a term used to describe individuals who transcend traditional role definitions and no longer depend on these to determine their behavior.) These researchers found that androgynous individuals were more empathic than masculine or feminine types, regardless of their sex. So research suggests that these are the people in our groups who may be better able to empathize with other views.

S. Bem (1975). The measurement of psychological androgyny. *Journal of Consulting and Clinical Psychology, 42,* 155–162.

S. S. Brehm, L. Powell, & J. S. Coke (1984). The effects of empathic instructions upon donating behavior. Sex differences in young children. *Sex Roles, 10,* 415–416.

V. J. Derlega, B. Winstead, B. Wong, & S. Hunter (1985). Gender effects in initial encounters: A case where men exceed women in disclosure. *Journal of Social and Personal Relationships, 2,* 25–44.

M. L. Fong & L. D. Borders (1985). Effects of sex role orientation and gender on counseling skills training. *Journal of Counseling Psychology, 32,* 104–110.

L. Greenblatt, J. E. Hasenauer, & V. Friemuth (1980). Psychological sex type and androgyny in the study of communication variables. *Human Communication Research, 6,* 117–129.

benefits. Typically, in trust situations, the risk is that the potential for damage from betrayal is greater than the potential benefits to be gained if betrayal does not occur.

After reviewing the extensive literature on trust and cooperative effort, Elmore Alexander (1977) concluded that careful communication makes a big difference in people's willingness to trust. Alexander knew that in order to gain the maximum benefits that communication can contribute to the evolution of cooperative efforts, individuals need training in communication. "Individuals should be complete and credible in their communication," he said. "Likewise, they should emphasize messages intended to coordinate action and to communicate positive affect or trust. Messages which communicate negative affect or distrust or threaten should be avoided."

We quickly put up our defenses if we cannot or do not trust one another. **Defensiveness** refers to a feeling of being threatened, dominated, or afraid. If we are feeling defensive about others, we may stop listening as we plan what we will say. We may become rigid in our positions on issues we were talking about. We may try to find some way to get even. Sometimes, if the situation is important enough, we end up regretting that we let things get out of hand. Let's explore this notion of defensiveness in greater detail.

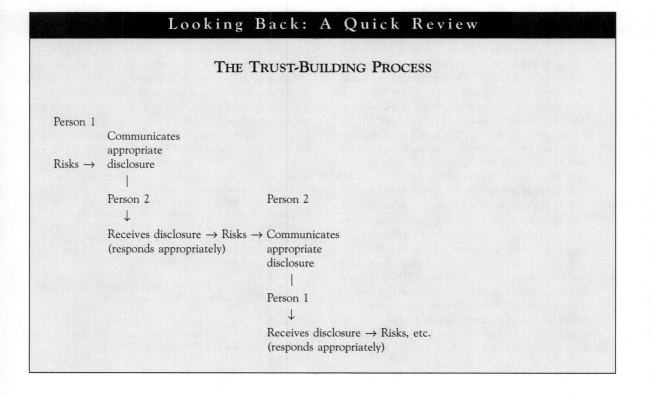

Looking Back: A Quick Review

THE TRUST-BUILDING PROCESS

Person 1

    Communicates
    appropriate
Risks → disclosure
       |
    Person 2   Person 2
     ↓
    Receives disclosure → Risks → Communicates
    (responds appropriately)   appropriate
                            disclosure
                               |
                           Person 1
                            ↓
                           Receives disclosure → Risks, etc.
                           (responds appropriately)

CREATING AN EFFECTIVE COMMUNICATION CLIMATE

Your first response will probably be to defend yourself if you feel threatened. You defend yourself if someone is attacking your self-concept or denying your personal worth (Rogers & Roethlisberger, 1952). If you suspect that either of these is happening in a group setting, or worse, that they are both happening at the same time, the situation becomes intolerable. You defend yourself. At least, you defend yourself unless you make a conscious decision not to do so. And that is a key idea. You *can choose* whether or not to defend yourself. You also can choose whether or not to discount others. Creating a climate in which communication can occur involves making choices about how you will talk with others and about how you will interpret what they say.

You can use a number of available strategies when you determine consciously or unconsciously to defend yourself. You can simply avoid eye contact. You also can confront the other person: "Barry, I'm wondering why you come late to our meetings. We don't like to start without you. Our meetings are almost always 15 minutes late." You can attack the other person, believing the popular wisdom that a good offense is the best defense. Perhaps Barry follows this strategy: "Sue, you're always on my case. You aren't such a hot-shot member yourself! You always get us off track and waste time." Sometimes, of course, it is sensible to avoid the other person. Barry might quit coming to the meetings. It will not be worth worrying about if the other person's judgment is unimportant or insignificant. Perhaps Barry responds as if Sue hadn't said anything at all: "Well, let's get started." Or perhaps he says, "Well, that's one opinion. I can't see that it's a problem." So **defensive behavior** consists of acts designed to ward off what is perceived to be an attack by another.

Sometimes you tend to avoid when you might more wisely choose another strategy. For example, you may tend to avoid others when you do not like what they are saying or when you do not want to hear their judgment. But if that judgment is important, it might be wiser to listen, even if the other person is not very tactful.

Sometimes you may attack others in order to win in a situation you define as competitive. In fact, this is a common method of defending, but we do not recognize it in every communication event. A student vividly illustrated this strategy in a paper she wrote to analyze a communication problem. She had been dating a group member. As she reported it, on one of their study dates they had been arguing about "some aspect" of her participating in their group meeting. She was offended by one of his remarks:

> When James came on so strong about me being lazy I knew I had to do something. He was wrong, and beyond that, it hurt. Well, I couldn't think of anything else to do, so I went for his jugular. He was attacking me, so I attacked him. I went for his self-image. I told him that both his jokes and his conversation are boring, not only in group but also on dates. I pointed out that he's not nearly as charming as he tries to be. Then the knife! I told him that he didn't even measure up to average men. Actually, I didn't have anybody to compare him to. Of course, he was very hurt. I "won" something, but I also lost; it was our last date.

The passage is an illustration of behaviors that Jack Gibb (1961) recommended against in his now-classic essay on defensive and supportive communication.

Defensive Climates

People have a natural tendency to react to the "argument context," rather than to the actual disagreement. Stephen Alderton and Lawrence Frey (1986) suggest that people react more to the "argument" than to the actual arguments. They become defensive when they perceive they are having a difference and stop listening.

Gibb studied what happened when people in groups get defensive, and he discovered six behaviors. The first of these is **evaluation.** When James suggested to his friend that she was lazy, he engaged in evaluation. When she told James that he was not nearly as charming as he tried to be, she was evaluating him. When she told him that both his jokes and conversation were boring, in group meetings and on dates, she was evaluating him. When she suggested that he did not even measure up to average, she was evaluating him. She was talking about James's ideas about himself.

A second category of behaviors, which Gibb called *control,* includes all those behaviors that occur when one individual attempts to manage what the other person believes about himself or what the other person believes about the world. You will surely recall that Schutz's theory of motivation included the idea that people have an inherent need to control others as well as their own destinies. If he is right, then we have some level of need to control what others believe. And it must be obvious from your own experience that if someone is trying to control you, and you become aware of it, you will surely try to resist. That resistance is defensive behavior.

Was the student who wrote about James trying to control his behavior or self-image? We suspect that she was. Indeed, she says, "When James came on so strong about me being lazy I knew I had to do something." Then she says, "I went for his self-image." This is a very clear and straightforward example of Gibb's control category.

Gibb also found that indifference tends to generate defensiveness. He called this third category **neutrality,** by which he meant treating people without consideration for their personal identity or uniqueness. You may have experienced neutrality in situations where someone else treated you as though you did not matter.

In a group situation, neutrality occurs when someone makes a contribution that the others just ignore. For example, an accountant in a training session complained about his group experience: "Heck with the group I'm in. I want *out* of there! Every time I say something, they just pay no attention. I can't possibly continue in that group."

The demand to be removed from the group is a clear example of one kind of defensive behavior—withdrawal. The accountant could no longer tolerate being ignored—he could no longer tolerate the group's neutrality.

A fourth category of behaviors occurs when someone takes on superior airs. **Superiority** implies behaviors that suggest a person is better than others—wiser, perhaps, or stronger or more creative. If you pretend that you can overrule another, you are acting superior. If, to illustrate, a member of a group repeatedly plays the game of "Yes, but . . ." he or she is acting out superiority. "Yes, but my way will work more efficiently." "Yes, but you have overlooked this information." "Yes, but don't you see that your argument breaks down at that point?" "Yes, but how do we know that this evidence is reliable?"

Certainty is fifth category of behaviors that create defensiveness. It implies or frankly states that a behavior or idea is unequivocally right. It implies that the other is wrong. "I am certain that I am right, and therefore, since you disagree, you are certainly wrong." Such behavior leaves no room for negotiation. It eliminates the possibility that anyone else's notions have value. The other group members usually defend themselves and their ideas in the face of certainty.

Imagine how James felt when the woman he was dating made it clear that he was below average. If he had any doubts about himself, her apparent confidence in her statement must have been very threatening. How could he ignore such an attack? His withdrawal from the relationship was virtually guaranteed.

Gibb identified a sixth category. **Strategy** includes any attempt by one person to manipulate another in order to implement a plan. If someone in your group tries to manipulate your behavior, and if you discover that, you will almost certainly have the urge to become defensive. The idea that others would try to trick you instead of just asking for what they want ought to be enough to build distrust. Such a behavior clearly contributes to a climate in which effective group communication will just not occur.

Consider a group in which one member was using a strategy on another over a two-month period. Audiotape recordings of their group meetings and journals that the members wrote clearly show that one member, Jess, was determined to strategize his way through the group assignment. Here are three excerpts from his journal:

> January 18. If it's true that these people are having difficulty in selecting a topic—and that's what [the professor] said today—then maybe I can trick them into discussing the bookstore pricing problem. Anyway, that's what I am going to try for the next several meetings.

> January 19. It works! And, it's easy! I set out, in this afternoon's meeting, to manipulate Kip's thinking—he seemed least interested and involved in the group, and I thought he'd be easiest. So I arranged to "bump into" him outside the building. Told him I was frustrated that our group wasn't getting anywhere, and that I thought he could really make a contribution by suggesting a solid topic that everyone could run with. He asked what, and I told him the bookstore price policy. I said I couldn't bring it up because it would look like I was trying to run things, and that, anyway, he hadn't said much yet, and that put him in an excellent position to have clout. He brought it up almost immediately, and with surprising force, given that he never talks much in the group. And the group bought it.

> February 9. Kip is so easy! Today I talked him into going along with Janice's idea about forming a student government bookstore, even though his first inclinations were that the SGA couldn't possibly support it. I am amazed at how easy some people are to manipulate.

But ignoring any moral judgment for the moment, Jess's strategic successes were not entirely without cost. Consider this entry from the journal that Janice wrote that day:

> February 9. Jess is such a phony—and so slick. Today he got Kip to back me. Poor Kip—no mind of his own. But, Jess, UGH! He's a snake, and you can't trust him for anything.

TABLE 8.1   Categories of Behavior That Generate or Reduce Defensiveness

Behavior That Generates Defensiveness	Behavior That Reduces Defensiveness
Evaluation: Judgments or assessments of another that imply the other's "not okayness"	*Description:* Statement that is an objective report of the situation. It is a report of the person's own observations and inferences. It avoids any evaluations or judgments and often employs first person singular language
Control: Behaviors that attempt to manipulate others—to impose upon them a point of view or attitude or some behavioral restraint	*Problem orientation:* Behaviors that make clear to the other that you wish to collaborate in defining a mutual problem and seek its solution; cooperation, not competition, in approach to others
Neutrality: Behaviors that show little or no concern for others and that treat the other as a *thing,* capable only of functions, rather than as a person capable of choices and emotions	*Empathy:* Behaviors that show an attempt to identify with the other's thinking and feeling and that show respect for the other's value-belief system and affirm the other's human dignity
Superiority: Behaviors that expressly state or imply a "one up" position and that discount the other; behaviors that state or imply, "I'm okay, but you're not okay"	*Equality:* Behaviors that expressly state or assume, "I'm okay and you're okay, too"; behaviors that minimize differences in status, ability, power, and the like
Certainty: Behaviors that show rigid commitment to a point of view and that suggest or imply that the other's ideas are wrong if they don't conform to that point of view; behaviors that create a win–lose definition of the situation	*Provisionalism:* Shows of one's own willingness to be tentative, to suggest that additional information might result in change of mind; behaviors that show willingness to cooperate in problem solving and that create a win–win definition of the situation
Strategy: To preplan a goal and then manipulate the other into believing he or she is making the decision; to imply caring that does not exist	*Spontaneity:* Straightforward, candid expressions of one's own attitudes, beliefs, and feelings

Source: Adapted from J. R. Gibb (1961).

These six categories, then, define the kinds of behaviors Gibb found in groups that experienced defensiveness. Looking closer at the interacting groups, Gibb came to believe that there must be an equal number of categories that would reduce defensiveness. Table 8.1 presents the two contrasting lists. They are presented in this fashion to help you compare, contrast, and remember the behavioral categories.

Supportive Climates

Behaviors that tend to diminish defensiveness in groups are those that suggest the individual is okay, although this does not necessarily imply agreement with the other's ideas. Members are more satisfied with groups where there is a supportive, cooperative climate

(Anderson & Martin, 1999). A supportive climate promotes cooperation, while a defensive climate promotes competition. Members feel safe in the supportive climate—safe to share their ideas, to show caring, to promote the group's well-being and task accomplishment. This climate produces a number of benefits. These include increased cohesion and increased productivity (Johnson & Johnson, 2000), people working harder and longer at tasks (Tyler & Blader, 2000), reduced friction and increased coordination of member efforts (Podsakoff, Ahearne, & MacKenzie, 1997; Tyler & Blader, 2000), and more satisfaction and cooperation (Anderson & Martin, 1999).

An effective team generally works in a supportive climate. LaFasto and Larson (2001, p. 68) describe this atmosphere. "The team is relaxed, comfortable, informal, fun, warm. Teams that are good at problem solving have a way of making their members feel accepted, valued, and competent." These team members also listen carefully, pitch in to help other members, and attempt to encourage others. They care very much about the group and its performance. So, they will challenge each other's ideas, but do so within a supportive climate. Research supports the link between this supportive climate and productivity (Tandy, 1992).

You can describe only what you can observe. You cannot observe such things as "beautiful" or "intelligent" or "correct." You could describe what you see as beautiful. What you can observe is behavior or existence. What constitutes beauty? What constitutes intelligence? What constitutes correctness? These are judgments. You might be able to make these judgments, of course—we all can—but presenting them as judgments tends to create defensiveness. A better strategy is to attempt, rather, to describe the behavior or the reality being observed. Then, if it seems appropriate, describe as well the evaluative criteria against which the observations led to the conclusion.

To illustrate, consider the following exchange, which occurred in a group meeting. Notice how Bill's response to Rick's evaluative statement not only softens the blow but is probably also far more accurate:

RICK: Honestly, Danielle. Sometimes I think you're spaced out. That question didn't make any sense at all—you weren't even listening to what I said.

BILL: Wait a minute, Rick. That doesn't seem fair to me. You may think her question wasn't any good, but I bet she thinks it was! It seems to me that any question about something she doesn't understand is a good one. Danielle's question seemed to me to be relevant to what you were saying.

Notice, also, that Bill's comment is descriptive. **Description** is an objective report of an observation and inferences. It uses first person singular language. When he makes any judgmental statement, he labels it as such (". . . doesn't seem fair to me," ". . . I bet she thinks it was!" ". . . her question seemed to me to be relevant"). He respects Rick but challenges Rick's ideas. There is no attack in Bill's remarks; that is, Bill does not attack Rick, although he does confront him. Bill defines what he thinks "fair" means (". . . any question about something she doesn't understand is a good one"); thus to label the question as not making sense and to brand the speaker as "spaced out" are unfair.

Gibb saw a problem orientation as the opposite of control. When some people engage in conflict, take on a win–lose posture, and set out to win, they are trying to control others. They show **problem orientation** when they make clear that they want to cooperate rather than to compete, and when they show that they want to share in identification, definition, and solution of a mutual problem, they are taking on a problem orientation.

Once you have experienced the difference, you will see immediately how the problem orientation is likely to reduce defensiveness. Suppose you were in this finance committee meeting with Carl, a fellow who truly believes that the world is hostile and competitive. Suppose further that the topic on which you are working is the budget for the coming year. You say, "Well, it is clear that there just isn't going to be enough money to do everything that we want to do. How will we solve this problem?"

If Carl tries to control, has already made up his mind about how the money should be spent, and has set out to have his way, he might say, "There doesn't seem to be any problem to me; we've got to meet our number-one goal as best we can. That means we've got to spend whatever it takes. We've already said that our first goal is to get a personal computer. So let's get on with it."

If Carl wanted to take a problem orientation, he would make clear that he had a mutuality of interest and wanted to work with you. He might say, "Well, we have listed some priorities, but that was when we didn't know our budget. This low figure might change things. Should we reconsider our priorities?"

Carl's first statement—his attempt to control—may cause the other members of the group to become defensive, especially if they had some other priority for spending the limited funds. Carl's second statement offers collaboration. It invites redefinition of a problem the whole group shares and suggests that Carl is thinking more of the group than his private preference. Group members are far less likely to become defensive.

Notice also that Carl's second statement shows empathy. **Empathy** implies an attempt to identify with the other group members' thinking and feelings and to respect what they value. Moreover, it clearly implies equality and provisionalism. **Equality** is the presentation of ideas in such a way that others see the presenter as acting like them in status. The speaker uses a tone of voice that shows interest and concern, rather than superiority. **Provisionalism** is behavior that suggests tentativeness in presenting ideas.

Carl's first statement, on the other hand, discounts the others. There is little evidence in that first alternative that Carl cares about the others. Moreover, the first alternative clearly implies that Carl thinks he is right. He is committed to the point of view, and he implies that any disagreement from the other members would mean that they are wrong. His second statement makes clear that Carl does not believe he has any more prerogatives, and any more claim to the limited budget, than anyone else in the group. That is, the second statement shows equality (Ellis, 1979). Moreover, the statement shows that Carl is willing to be tentative and eager to create a win–win situation.

Consider the differences between strategy and spontaneity. Imagine a little more of the conversation from this group meeting. Recall that strategy suggests an attempt to manipulate. **Spontaneity,** on the other hand, is a straightforward candid expression of attitudes, beliefs, or feelings. Consider the following exchange:

SUSAN: Well, it is clear that there just isn't going to be enough money to do everything that we want to do. How will we solve this problem?

CARL: It was pretty easy to list priorities when we didn't know how much our budget would be, but this low figure might change things. Should we reconsider our priorities?

REBECCA (thinking to herself, Hmm . . . I know Carl wants to buy a computer, and I'd like that too, but I don't want to be the one to suggest spending all our money on one thing): But Carl, didn't you have something in mind the other day? Seems to me you said we ought to be careful not to water things down and I thought that was a pretty wise suggestion. With a limited budget we can't be all things to all people.

A Question of Ethics and Responsibility

THE OFFICE WORK GROUP

Sue Angelino reported this situation, which she is experiencing in her office work group. She was looking for some advice about how she might handle it.

Over the last several months, Sue has noticed changes in the climate of her office. Specifically, she has noticed more arguments. Two employees, Stan and Rita, have been having heated arguments about things that seem to be insignificant. The other day they were arguing about who would make coffee. Stan stomped off and hardly said a word for the rest of the day. When Sue tried to approach them, both were quite defensive and even engaged in name calling. Sue reported this behavior to her boss, Max Moskowitz, citing this as one example of the decline she has noticed in the office climate.

Some members of the office staff had complained last week to Max about Sue. Sarah said that she often felt "put down" when she had to deal with Sue. Sarah commented, "Sure, she is the boss. But she doesn't have to have such a superior attitude. She's no better than the rest of us." Peter Alexander also visited Max to complain about Sue. He reported, "She just tossed work on my desk as she passed the other day with no comment or explanation. That seemed very rude to me."

Max wonders whether all these issues are related. Perhaps they have something to do with climate and the way people manage interpersonal relationships in the office. Max determines that something has to be done to reverse this climate problem.

Don't focus for the moment on the issue of conflict. Think now about the climate. Speculate what might be causing the climate problem. What would you suggest about dealing with whatever problems you uncovered?

Here is a clear case of pursuing a strategy. Rebecca has set out to manipulate Carl. She suggests by implication that she cares about Carl. She encourages him without taking a position of her own. A far more spontaneous comment would have made clear that Rebecca was speaking for herself:

> REBECCA (speaking as she is thinking in a game-free expression of her position): Well, I'm not sure that we ought to try to be all things to all people. I mean, I don't think it's a good idea to water down anything. I'd like to buy a computer, but I wouldn't like to buy a cheap computer just so we can also do other things.

Rebecca's second statement, far more open and more honest than the first, might bring out some controversy, but it is less likely to create defensiveness. Her first comment might not call attention to itself, and she might be able to pull it off. But if Carl or anyone else ever got the notion that Rebecca was strategizing the group, their defenses would go up immediately. That, of course, is the risk that Gibb was talking about.

If your group is composed of culturally diverse members, you will want to be especially mindful of maintaining a supportive atmosphere. This atmosphere is best for integrating the diverse views you may discover in your effort to achieve congruence and a decision. This is important because diversity can be a resource and advantage for the group (Adler, 1986; Cox, 1995).

Once you have analyzed the appropriateness of the communication for a situation, you will know whether to do something about it. If it is your own behavior

---

Looking Back: A Quick Review

DEFENSIVE AND SUPPORTIVE COMMUNICATION BEHAVIORS

Defensive	Evaluation
	Control
	Neutrality
	Superiority
	Certainty
	Strategy
Supportive	Description
	Problem orientation
	Empathy
	Equality
	Provisionalism
	Spontaneity

and it seems counterproductive, then simple determination to change, and some practice, will make the difference. If the person's behavior is problematic, then you have to make choices among tolerating, withdrawing, confronting, or attacking the behavior. Attack is often not a good strategy. Sometimes, of course, withdrawal or merely ignoring the behavior makes the greatest sense; but in those difficult cases where confrontation seems to be in order, you will be most successful if you have already been working to develop a climate in which effective communication can take place.

When defensiveness is the most likely outcome of a communication event, the climate will make confrontation difficult. Jack Gibb's classic research on group behaviors that produce defensiveness suggested six dichotomous categories of behaviors. Learn those behaviors that tend to minimize defensiveness and learn to avoid those that tend to maximize it.

SOCIALIZING NEW MEMBERS

Your group has a history. That is, it has been meeting long enough to have established norms and roles. So now you have a new group member in our group and you want the person to feel welcome and also believe that he or she is truly a member of the group in that his or her participation is welcome. The problem is, of course, how do you accomplish this?

The answer is to help the person fit into the group. This is not really a complex process, but an important one if you want to get the new member "up to speed" and be both a happy member and a productive member. **Socialization** is a two-way process of influence and change whereby group members use verbal and nonverbal messages to integrate a new person into their group.

What do we want to accomplish from the prospective of existing group members and the new member? Here is a list of goals:

- Mentor the new member.

- Help the new member feel included in group activities.

- Provide an orientation, often a responsibility of the leader, to help the individual understand group goals and where they stand in relation to those goals. Also, include information of the make-up of the group, how he or she fits into the group and the group's norms.

Goals for the new member:

- Learn what is and is not important to the group.

- Gain a sense of how you fit into the group, regarding skills, knowledge, and appropriate roles.

- Work to understand and embrace the values, norms, and behaviors of the group.

- Evaluate your efforts to fit into the group and contribute toward its goals on a regular basis.

One activity that is often neglected, but is one that will fulfill many of these goals, is mentoring. A **mentor** is a person who works with a new member of an ongoing group to facilitate his or her socialization. This experienced person establishes an interpersonal relationship with the new member thereby allowing for periodic meetings where the mentor can be a "sounding board" for the new member. The mentor also provides advice when the person seeks it. It is this advisor's job to facilitate the person's professional and social development within the group.

It is useful to ask a final question before we leave this topic. What is the outcome of a failure to socialize a new member into the group? Steven Worchel's (1994) answer to this question is loneliness. In the task dimension, a member who is not socialized to the group may feel powerless because he or she is not able or allowed to have influence and participation in the group process. In the social dimension, the person does not feel valued and included and he or she does not sense the warmth of relationships with other group members, like other members have. Of course, knowing this allows you to carry out positive socialization, so the group has the asset of a happy member who does not feel lonely and makes positive contributions to the group.

WORKING WITH PEOPLE WHO SEEM DIFFICULT

Most of us understand that our efforts to be supportive and sensitive to others, to encourage them to be productive participants, will not always be met with the response we would hope to have. Some people just don't seem to embrace this goal.

The person's difficult behavior can take several forms. Perhaps the person just won't contribute his or her share to the group effort. Perhaps the individual is irresponsible in his or her participation. Perhaps the person has some personal agenda and sidetracks the group. Or the person dominates the interaction. Occasionally, the person may be just plainly despicable. Fortunately, you will not find these problems with members surfacing in most groups, but when they do they have great potential for harming productivity. Here is a description for each of these types of members and some suggestions for managing their behavior.

The Nonparticipant

The **nonparticipant** may exhibit a variety of different behaviors depending on the motivating source. These behaviors might include doodling, staring out the window, focusing eye contact away from the group, looking bored, or just saying very little. These behaviors may suggest a shy person or, perhaps, an unprepared member. If gestures or a tone of voice that suggests negative feelings accompanies the behaviors, the person may be withdrawing because he or she is angry with another member or the group.

The first step in trying to help this member become more productive is to determine whether the problem is shyness, unpreparedness, or displeasure with a member or the group. You might *reach out to include the shy member*. You might ask for this person's opinion or ask a question to which you think he or she will know the answer. You also might try to *spend some time getting to know the member better*. You might suggest an opportunity for the entire group to meet for social time and make a special effort to draw this person into the socializing. You might *make specific assignments to group members* if you think it a matter of being unprepared. Often such a member will respond to a specific assignment by preparing. The preparation may serve as a basis for including the member.

If the participation problem is related to negative feelings, it will need to be carefully managed. We suggest using the conflict management method we describe in Chapter 10 to manage this problem person.

The Irresponsible Member

The **irresponsible member** is the one who is regularly late for meetings, doesn't do his or her share of the work, or doesn't show up at all. This is a most difficult person to deal with, especially if the problem has been going on for some time. Often the person will have an excuse or may display an "I don't care" attitude if confronted about the behavior. The reason this is such a difficult problem is that it may be the way the member deals with other aspects of his or her world; it's a habit.

First, you need to decide if it would be best to approach the person individually, perhaps privately, or to approach this as a group problem. If you decide to *approach the person directly*, you might focus on telling the person how valuable he or she is to the group. You might talk about how you need the person there to work on your task. You might ask if there is anything that you can do to help. Encourage the person. See whether the behavior improves. You might, instead, or as a second step to the first strategy if the first attempt doesn't work, *confront the member in the group*. Since this is a group conflict, we'd recommend you manage it with the approach outlined in Chapter 10. Basically, the group needs to *explain how important the member's input is to the group*, *explore the problem*, *ask for suggestions for solving the problem*, and *implement the plan*.

Two less desirable alternative strategies for managing this problem are available. You can *ask the person who constituted the group or the person's boss to intervene* or *you can "fire" the member*. The first of these will likely generate hostility and may make the member even less productive. The latter may short the group a member and that person's input. If you need this person's expertise, then this is an undesirable solution.

The Sidetracker

The **sidetracker** pulls the group away from the task. He or she may clown around with jokes, humor, and teasing when the group is hard at work and doesn't really need the diversion. Sometimes a diversion is important if the tension is high and the group needs to relax, but this person doesn't seem to understand when this behavior is appropriate. Consequently, the person's humor breaks the group's concentration.

Sometimes the sidetracker takes one of these different approaches. This person may get into personal story telling about events in his or her life. Or, perhaps, the member may pick fights or try to egg others on. Or this person may take offense regarding something that another said and go into a monologue about how he or she is mistreated. Or the person may pout or act disgruntled. All these behaviors are self-centered behaviors that draw attention to the person and away from the task.

One approach to dealing with this person is to *give a gentle reminder* that you need to get back to the task. This may be effective if the sidetracker's behavior is well meaning. You might say, "It has been pleasant to hear about _____. I'm getting a little nervous about finishing on time. Can we get back to our work?" Or, "H. B., I really enjoy your humor, but it seems to me that we need to try to stick to the task if we are going to finish. When we finish we can get a soda and enjoy each other."

The kind of disruption that involves attempts to pick a fight and/or anger requires a different approach. These behaviors can tear apart your group if carried to an extreme. The intervention needed here is a *careful confrontation* using the conflict management process described in Chapter 10.

The Dominator

The **dominator** holds the floor beyond his or her share of the time. This person also may attempt to dominate through aggressive communication behavior such as speaking with a loud voice, interrupting others, using categorical language that suggests his or her view is the only "correct view," and/or controlling by trying to dictate the agenda. The person might even try to "keep people in their place" with personal attacks.

Any intervention should address the specific behavior of the dominator. If the behavior is holding the floor too much, you might *appeal for a more even distribution of the talking time.* For example, you might say, "I'm feeling as though I haven't had enough time to state my view. I'd like a few minutes to lay out my plan and then I'll turn the floor over to someone else." If the problem is constant interruptions, you might say, "John, I'm not quite finished. Could I finish?" If the problem is different, perhaps one of making unsubstantiated statements, you might *ask for the evidence.* Say, "John, I'm wondering how you know this. I'd like to hear your evidence."

On the other hand, if the behavior is of the bullying type, you will need a carefully drawn confrontation of the type described in Chapter 10. This involves *carefully phrased descriptive statements that indicate the behavior* and *exploration of what is going on* when this happens. Then the group might be able to *talk about alternative behaviors* that might be more goal oriented.

The Despicable Member

The **despicable member** is consistently deplorable. He or she may be nasty, sexist, bigoted, plotting, dishonest, and/or unethical. This person may constantly belittle others' intellect, sex, race, economic status, and the like. The person may be constantly attempting to manipulate others or to put them in a bad light, or may use insulting or offensive language. This type of person rarely comes along, but when it happens, being a member of such a group is often painful.

We recommend that you *confront the behavior* without becoming defensive and being drawn into it. Don't laugh at the jokes. Challenge unethical acts. Help protect and defend people who are attacked. State your preference for taking a constructive approach, free of personal biases and attacks.

You also may need to *formally confront the despicable member* either privately or within the group. The group may, as a group, tell the member that this behavior is totally unacceptable and that they expect a more polite and respectful approach. Then listen carefully to what the person says. If the person cannot agree to change his or her approach, you may need to move to an alternative resolution. This approach might be to *ignore, ostracize, or dismiss the member.*

You probably realize at this point that there is a range of difficult people that you may find as a member in your group. Some problem types are more disruptive than others. We have given you guidance to help you deal successfully with the various types. Keep in mind, though, that there is a balance between ignoring these people and spending too much time dealing with them. Time you spend dealing with them is obviously time you do not have to work on your group's task.

Looking Back: A Quick Review

HOW TO WORK WITH DIFFICULT PEOPLE

Nonparticipant	Attempt to determine the source of problem. Try to involve the person by asking questions. Spend time with person outside of group. Make specific assignments to members.
Irresponsible member	Decide how to approach the person—privately and individually, or in the group. Let the person know the group needs him or her. Ask how you can help. Confront the person in the group if necessary.
Sidetracker	Gently remind the person (or the whole group) of the need to get back on track. Be direct, if necessary. Express your fear of not meeting your goals.
Dominator	Address the specific behavior of the dominator. Appeal for more equitable division of talking time. Set a rule to limit time for holding the floor.
Despicable member	Confront the person's behavior while remaining supportive. Tell the person that the behavior is totally unacceptable. If necessary, ignore, ostracize, or dismiss the person.

SUMMARY

Members meet one another's needs through communication behavior. William Schutz describes three interpersonal needs all people have that are met by members of a group: inclusion, control, and affection. Members have needs at various levels. When group members recognize these needs and meet them through communication, they provide satisfaction for group members and enhance the group experience.

Self-disclosure, empathy, and trust are important variables that contribute to group climate. Telling each other who we are, what we want and expect, what our intentions are, what images we have in our head, and the extent to which we are open to topics are all appropriate self-disclosure in most groups. Self-disclosure allows members to understand each other well enough to empathize. Empathy enables people to gain a deeper understanding of each other. Self-disclosure and empathy provide the basis for trust because group member behavior becomes more predictable. Trust can develop when the disclosure of group members is seen as appropriate. Trust is central to the cooperation that is essential to effective group processes.

Beyond meeting the group members' needs through communication, members' communication behaviors affect the group climate. A member can behave supportively by adopting behaviors that demonstrate descriptiveness, problem orientation, spontaneity, empathy, equality, and provisionalism. On the other hand, a member can generate defensiveness by adopting an alternative set of behaviors. These include evaluation, control, strategy, neutrality, superiority, and certainty. As group members talk to one another about relational problems, this communication can be more productive if the members follow the suggestions offered by Jack Gibb for creating a supportive climate.

New group members generally need to be oriented if they are to be productive members. This process is called socialization. The goal is to help the new member feel include in the group. It is the responsibility of the leader *and* the members to accomplish this task. Of course, the new member needs to participate in the process too, through seeking relevant information.

Working with people who seem difficult can be a challenge. A person's difficult behavior can take different forms. Perhaps the person won't contribute his or her share to the group effort. Perhaps the individual is irresponsible in his or her participation. Perhaps the person has some personal agenda and sidetracks the group. Or maybe the person dominates the interaction. Occasionally, the person may be plainly despicable.

The *nonparticipant's* behaviors might include doodling, staring out the window, focusing eye contact away from the group, looking bored, or just saying very little. If gestures or tone of voice suggests negative feelings, the person may be withdrawing because of anger with another member or the group. The *irresponsible member* may be late for meetings, may not do his or her share of the work, or might not show up at all.

The *sidetracker* pulls the group away from the task. This person may clown around or tell stories. Or, perhaps, the member may pick a fight or try to egg others on. This person may take offense and go into a monologue about how he or she is mistreated.

The *dominator* holds the floor beyond what is his or her share of the time. This person may also exhibit aggressive communication, use categorical language that suggests his or her view is the only "correct view," and/or control the meeting by trying to dictate the agenda. The person might even try to "keep people in their place" with put-downs and personal attacks. This person may constantly belittle others' intellect, sex, race, economic status, and the like. The person may be constantly attempting to manipulate others or to put them in a bad light, or may use insulting or offensive language.

Strategies were presented for dealing with difficult people. The less volatile behaviors—nonparticipation, irresponsibility, and sidetracking—can usually be dealt with through direct appeals or even humor. Often talking to the person when other members are not present relaxes the climate and provides a productive atmosphere for encouraging the member to change. More potentially volatile behaviors—those of the dominator and the despicable member—are best addressed with a carefully planned conflict management strategy.

KEY TERMS AND CONCEPTS

abdicrat	evaluation	personal
adaptable-social	FIRO	problem orientation
autocrat	hidden area	provisionalism
blind area	irresponsible member	self-disclosure
certainty	Johari window	sidetracker
control	mentor	socializing members
description	need for affection	spontaneity
defensive behavior	need for inclusion	strategy
defensiveness	nonparticipant	superiority
democrat	neutrality	trust
despicable member	open area	underpersonal
dominator	overpersonal	undersocially
empathy	oversocial	

EXERCISES

1. Complete the Postmeeting Reaction Questionnaire, Chapter 11, Table 11.9, for your discussion group. Describe and analyze your group's communication climate using information from this questionnaire and your personal observations. Include both defensive and supportive behaviors you observed. Speculate about the effect your group's climate had on its effectiveness.

2. Consider the idea of meeting members' needs. In a small group generate a list of ways members might meet one another's needs for inclusion, control, and affection. When all groups are satisfied with their lists, write the suggestions on the chalkboard. Which suggestions seem to be the most effective? Try to come up with a list of five of the best suggestions for each category.

3. Ask an international student to describe communication customs in his or her home country that are different from those in your culture. Bring these descriptions of these experiences to class. Discuss in small groups how other cultures differ in communication customs from your own. How might these customs affect your group's interpersonal communication if it were to have people from these other cultures as members?

4. Observe group discussion and rate group members on the supportiveness—defensiveness dimensions. Create a rating form for each participant that looks like the one below. Place a check mark on each continuum to describe where you believed the member of the group was on the dimension.

Evaluative	__:__:__:__:__:__	Descriptive
Controlling	__:__:__:__:__:__	Problem oriented
Strategic	__:__:__:__:__:__	Spontaneous
Neutral	__:__:__:__:__:__	Empathic
Superior	__:__:__:__:__:__	Equal
Certain	__:__:__:__:__:__	Provisional

Evidence for my evaluations:

Write a two-page report giving your evaluation of the impact of supportive and defensive behaviors on this group.

5. This experience is also suitable for use with Chapter 10. Role-play the following incidents in a small group to which you are assigned. Be sure to apply the communication skills presented in this chapter. After each role-playing situation, evaluate the communication about the particular situation.
   a. A member is continually late for group meetings.
   b. A member displays superiority when talking to other members.
   c. A member's need for inclusion is not being met by the group.
   d. A member's need for affection is not being met by the group.
   e. A person believes the group moves off the topic too much; the person wants more control.
   f. A person resents the childlike behavior that another member adopts when talking to her.
   g. A person resents the fact that one member wants to play, rather than work.

6. Focus on the climate in a recent group situation. Write a two-page paper describing the supportiveness, or lack of, in the climate. Provide examples that support your conclusions. What would you recommend members do to improve this climate?

7. Identify two groups: one where the trust was high and another where the trust was low. Write a three-page paper describing the trust levels. What factors account for the particular trust levels? Give specific examples to support your conclusions. How did the trust level affect the group's effort to complete its task?

RECOMMENDED WEBSITES

The site www.ac.wwu.edu/~mgmt311b/FormalGroup/cycle_ii_diad_group_reading_assi.htm gives a summary about self-disclosure, including "rewards" and "blocks" to self-disclosure. The site also contains a diagram of the Johari window and a section on perception.

You can learn more about interpersonal relationships in groups by exploring the site www.umr.edu/~flsp/group.html.

Doing CL (Collaborative Learning) addresses several elements of group processes, including improving relationships among group members by promoting and encouraging various forms of self-disclosure at www.wcer.wisc.edu/nise/CL1/CL/doingcl/groups.htm.

Dr. Fargher's *Growth-works.com,* at www.growthworks.com/library/nonfiction/defense.htm, is a detailed and thorough listing as well as a description of the types of Gibb's defensive communication climate.

Working with Different People in Groups, at www.wendwell.co.uk/Resources/Difficult%20People%20in%20Groups.htm, has a listing of roles and characteristics that individuals may exhibit if they are hindering the relationship or task processes of a group.

RECOMMENDED READINGS

C. C. Clark & R. W. Sline (2003). Teaming with emotion: The impact of emotionality on work-team collaboration. In R. Y. Hirokawa, R. S. Cathcart, L. A. Samovar, & L. D. Henman (eds.), *Small group communication: Theory and practice,* 8th ed. Los Angeles: Roxbury, pp. 158–168.

J. R. Gibb (1961). Defensive communication. *Journal of Communication,* 11, 142–148.

R. J. Lewicki & C. Wiethoff (2000). Trust, trust development and trust repair. In M. Deutsch & P. T. Coleman, (eds.), *The handbook of conflict resolution.* San Francisco: Jossey-Bass, pp. 21–40.

G. L. Wilson, 2000. *Let's talk it over: Interpersonal communication in relationships.* Needham Heights, MA: Pearson Custom Publishing.

PROMOTING GROUP COHESIVENESS AND SATISFACTION

OBJECTIVES

After reading this chapter you should be able to

- Describe the nature of cohesiveness in terms of its attributes and determinates.
- Explain the benefits of cohesiveness.
- Describe the relationship between cohesiveness and productivity.
- Specify how each of these bears on cohesiveness: leadership style, effective participation, commitment to doing one's best, commitment to the good of the group and its goals, commitment to cooperation, and commitment to careful listening.
- Explain the fundamental idea of Janis's groupthink.
- Recall and describe the conditions from which groupthink emerges.
- Specify and explain the symptoms of groupthink.
- List the consequences of groupthink and specify how to prevent them.

"The best people in our organization are not necessarily the ones we want to call together to solve a problem. Being good is not enough. We need people who can also work together—team players. I mean people who feel good about one another and want to put together the best answer to the problem they are facing." John Jacobson, a production manager for a midsized manufacturing firm, was speaking about what we will call "cohesiveness." He recognized it as being more important than being "the best people." Certainly he would say that expertise with the situation is important, but experts who cannot pull together are not his notion of an ideal group.

Your own experience and intuition surely verify this notion. A cohesive group or team, whether in school, government, business, or any other context, can perform better than a collection of highly talented individuals. But what attitudes and/or phenomena are at work in cohesive groups? What is missing from groups that are not cohesive?

Recall working in groups that you enjoy. Undoubtedly those groups are cohesive. The individuals like one another. They feel committed to the group's goals. They are willing to work together—to share their successes and their failures. They talk about themselves in collective terms saying "we" instead of "I" and "our group" instead of "my group." Those characteristics describe cohesiveness (Shaw, 1981; Ellis & Fisher, 1994, pp. 34–35). The purpose of this chapter is to describe the determinants of cohesiveness and to suggest how individual members of groups can build cohesiveness.

An important duty of the leader and members is to build a cohesive group from the raw talents of the members. When they do this successfully, the group has an improved chance of success. You are likely to receive the benefits of success in groups if you know how to build a team.[1]

The chapter begins by describing the nature of cohesiveness and the factors that determine its development. This is followed by a discussion of the benefits of achieving cohesiveness. Then we consider what leaders and members can do to promote it. Finally, we explore the negative impact of too much cohesiveness and groupthink.

THE NATURE OF COHESIVENESS

Cohesiveness is for many an elusive and mysterious group property. It is seen as some sort of social "chemistry" that some groups have and others do not. It is a highly significant group phenomenon that transforms a set of individuals into a team. Most of us know intuitively whether our group has it or not, but we may not know much more.

Cohesiveness is the bond that links group members to the group, the degree to which the members are attracted to one another and the group, and the unity a group has toward its members. A cohesive group has a special *esprit de corps* that is seen in their high morale. Members feel connected to the group and tend to remain in the group for long periods of time.

Cohesion binds group members   The word *cohesion* comes from a concept in physics. In physics, it is the binding force that attracts molecules to each other and holds them together. Cohesion is applied to groups to describe the bond that links members to one another and their group. Cohesiveness must be present to some degree if people are to become a group and remain a group. Members drift away from one another without it. Sometimes people never form these bonds but occupy the same space. These folks might more accurately be labeled an aggregate of individuals rather than a group.

Cohesion is a special kind of interpersonal attraction   Members of a cohesive group usually like each other. Their attraction has two sources: personal and social. Members are attracted on a personal level because of their relationships with other members. Members are attracted on a group level when their focus of liking shifts to group qualities. They like members because they possess qualities that they see as important to the group. This second type of attraction is more important than the first in keeping members.

Cohesiveness is the unity that members feel   The ideas of "we-ness" and "belonging" are seen by many as an attribute of cohesion. Members identify in terms of their group membership. Perhaps they may see themselves as a "family" or "community." They are willing to sacrifice their own personal desires for the good of the group because of their unity.

DETERMINATES OF GROUP COHESIVENESS

The evolution of cohesiveness in a group is an enormously complex process. People are attracted to groups for such diverse reasons as the other individuals in the group, the activities in which groups engage, their own personal need for affiliation, and the like. For example, John very much wanted to join the Junior Chamber of Commerce in the town to which he had moved. It is easy to understand that there are good reasons for John to join that particular service and social group. But what is of concern here is why, after joining, he developed such a group loyalty. The explanation lies in the group's cohesiveness, and an analysis of this group's attraction is instructive.

Similar Attitudes

First, John knew that he shared *similar attitudes* with the members (Terborg, Castore, & DeNinno, 1976). He had shared a dormitory room with someone who was already a member. He spent a good deal of time at social events with members of the group. He was able to identify similar values that he and most Jaycees shared—enjoying music and theater, being rather strongly opposed to violence, placing people and relationships high on their priority lists, and believing that "it's worth working for if it's worth having." Research bears this out. Barnard and his associates (1992) found the higher the cohesion among members, the more likely they were to stick together in their attitudes.

Successful in Achieving Goals

John knew that the group was *successful in its efforts* (Blanchard, Weigel, & Cook, 1975). The Jaycees were known to be leaders. One was vice president of a local bank. One was sports editor of the daily paper. One had just been elected president of the local ministerial alliance. The Jaycees seemed successful to John. They staged a very popular fund-raiser each year called "Blackouts," in which the members sang, played, and danced in a series of variety acts. All the parts, all the music, all the scripting, and all the scenery design and directing were carried out by members. And Blackouts was one of the social high points of the year in that small town. The Jaycees were successful, and John wanted to be a part of that success.

Clear Sense of How to Achieve Goals

Closely related to success, the third characteristic of the group that held John's interest was its *clear sense of how to achieve its goals* (Anderson, 1975). The members of the group made no bones about their goals. They wanted to be the best service club in town. In order to accomplish this, they focused their attention upon high-visibility activities that produced evidence of popular judgment—trophies, perhaps other kinds of awards. Whatever they could do to get local media coverage was considered important. So was influence in local government if that could be managed. So was mandatory team sports practice. Blackouts was a measure of group popularity because the members could tally the number of people who purchased tickets. The members of that organization had a very clear notion about how to accomplish their goals.

Clear Sense of Progress in Achieving Goals

It seems obvious that people in groups must believe their membership is paying off. This was true of the Jaycees for John. He had taken on their goals as his goals and the perception of progress in achieving these goals was a sense of personal achievement for him. His admiration of their goals was one of the reasons he joined the group.

Of course, it is easier to perceive progress when progress is being made than when it is not, but either way the perception may be more important than the fact. The perception depends to large extents upon the conversations that go on in the group. Since the Jaycees had wise leadership, frequent attention was called to the group's progress. All it took was a simple statement like "Consider all that we have accomplished" and then a summary of what had been achieved to that point.

Perceived Freedom to Participate

John knew that each individual member's participation was valued and welcome. He didn't always enter into the discussion, but he knew he could and that people would listen and value his input. The point is not that he did or did not participate, but that he knew he could. People tend to be more satisfied in groups in which they can actively participate (Bonito, 2000). One study determined that cohesiveness is positively related to group size that provides the opportunity to interact with other members (Mullin et al., 1994).

Perhaps you have experienced a similar situation. A group to which you belong appears to be making appropriate progress. You think that you have very little to contribute to the particular conversation, and so you sit there quietly. You might be very content about your place in the group, and you might very well believe that both the group and you are being successful. You are satisfied, even if you do not say anything.

But let the climate change. Suppose that you cannot talk in this group. That is, other members take control and monopolize the floor. Suppose the group climate is such that you do not think that you are free to participate. At that point, you will experience resentment and dissatisfaction. As soon as the option to participate is removed—or appears to be—you become dissatisfied.

Freedom to participate derives from an environment in which individuals experience themselves as "okay" and, if not equal, at least respected for their views. The most important part of that environment, its climate of trust and acceptance, comes from the ways members talk with one another. They reveal information about themselves. They empathize with one another. They are straight with one another, never deliberately misrepresenting themselves or their information. These are functional behaviors that can be learned. It is likely that you have learned them.

Status Consensus

Status consensus is the group's agreement that the roles and relative status of members are correct. Most groups evolve a status hierarchy, as did the Jaycees. Some members strive to achieve high status. Some members prefer not to be heavily involved—perhaps because they have made commitments to be heavily involved in other groups. Some members do not wish positions of leadership, a high-status position, but care very much about the group goals. These people may take on helping roles that assume responsibility but very little leadership. The point is that every Jaycee wanted to believe his or her place in the group was right and that the other members of the group saw it as right. So status consensus was a source of cohesiveness for the Jaycees.

The problem is that in a power struggle within a group, if two high-dominant individuals are competing for status, sooner or later one of them will win and the other will lose. Should this happen, the winner, who has thus emerged in the position of higher status, has an immediate leadership problem. The task is to help the loser accept and adjust to the second position—a status that flows from lack of success in the power struggle. Since the loser in that contest may be the second-most-powerful member of the group, if that individual does not accept the new position, he or she may be a significant potential threat.

Again, for a member to be satisfied with the group, status consensus must occur. Any member can help that to evolve, for status consensus is a function of the talk that passes back and forth in the group. Thus it is reasonable to say that every individual in a group has a responsibility for this important communication function.

Well-Managed Conflict

Perhaps less obvious than similarity of attitudes, success, and clarity of goal path, the Jaycees were attractive to John because of the way they *managed conflict* and because of the kinds

Looking Back: A Quick Review

FACTORS THAT DETERMINE COHESIVENESS

Similar attitudes.	Members believing they are free to participate.
Success in goal achievement.	Members believing their place (status) is right.
Knowing how to achieve goals.	Well-managed conflict.
Seeing progress in achieving goals.	Members positively reinforcing each other.

of conflict they had (Wheaton, 1974). The members of the Junior Chamber of Commerce mostly agreed upon principles. Their conflict almost always centered on the means to the ends and not upon the ends themselves. Thus the regular meetings of the organization included a fairly freewheeling norm. The members debated with one another, using as much evidence and argument as they could. Their Wednesday noon meetings gave them an opportunity to reinforce one another in the important things—the principles and values they shared—and at the same time to learn about new ways to accomplish their goals.

Members Reinforcing Each Other

Finally, the Junior Chamber of Commerce remained attractive to John because the members *reinforced one another.* They talked to one another. They gave one another frequent and positive feedback (Deutsch, 1968; Schaible & Jacobs, 1975). They supported one another's personal goal achievements, and they pitched in as individuals to help the group achieve its goals. After each success they staged a well-planned party to provide positive feedback to the members in a symbolically significant and socially pleasant way.

These eight determinants of cohesiveness—similarity of attitudes, group success, clear sense of how to achieve goals, perceived progress toward goals, perceived freedom to participate, status consensus, managed conflict, frequent and positive reinforcement—are all applicable to small groups. Individual members who contribute these functions contribute directly to the cohesiveness of the group. Now, turn to some of the benefits of achieving cohesiveness.

BENEFITS OF ACHIEVING COHESIVENESS

A high level of cohesiveness benefits a group in several ways. High cohesiveness often results in greater task achievement. It can be a significant source of group satisfaction. It also enhances agreement regarding goals, decisions, and norms. Let us explain.

Productivity

Productivity, of course, refers to the quality and quantity of a group's output. In every group, both cohesiveness and productivity exist in some degree. Groups may be moderately cohesive or highly cohesive. They may be minimally productive or highly productive. The point is that every group can be described by its cohesiveness and its productivity.

There is a relationship between cohesiveness and productivity. In his review of the literature, Marvin Shaw (1981, p. 225) concluded that "in spite of some equivocal evidence, it seems evident that the empirical data support the hypothesis that high-cohesive groups are more effective than low-cohesive groups in achieving their goals. The cohesive group does whatever it tries to do better than the noncohesive group." More recent research supports this conclusion (Cohen & Bailey, 1997; Wech et al., 1998). Cohesiveness is a significant factor in group productivity and is even more so when it is found in concert with strong norms (Langfred, 1998). Shaw believed that these two dimensions had a straight-line relationship—the more cohesive the group, the greater the productivity. But he provided a word of caution—groups do not always set the same goals for themselves that organizations or outside agencies set. Thus a group might achieve its own goals but be relatively unproductive in terms of the goals management sets.

Ellis and Fisher (1994, pp. 24–26) argue that this dictum—the more cohesive a group, the more productive it is likely to be—is true only up to a point. "The relationship breaks down toward the upper end of the two continuums. Extremely cohesive groups are more likely to have moderate to low productivity." The curvilinear relationship Ellis and Fisher suggest is illustrated in Figure 9.1. In this figure the vertical dimension is labeled "Productivity." The arrow suggests ever-increasing levels of productivity. The horizontal dimension is labeled "Cohesiveness." Again, the arrow shows increasing levels of cohesiveness.

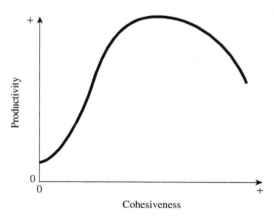

FIGURE 9.1
Relationship between Cohesiveness and Productivity

Ellis and Fisher suggest that the relationship between cohesiveness and productivity is curvilinear. The curved line in the figure suggests that in a group experiencing low levels of cohesiveness, productivity may be expected to be low. Increasing levels of cohesiveness will yield increasing levels of productivity in task groups—up to a point, a relationship confirmed by two research reports (Evans & Dion, 1991; Kelly & Duran, 1985).

At some point it is possible for a task group to be too cohesive. If cohesiveness is too intense, productivity suffers, so that the greater the cohesiveness beyond that point, the less the productivity. To illustrate this idea, take a group of friends, all of whom belong to the same church. They have agreed to plan a festival for the church. Their task is clear. They agree to meet at one of the members' houses. One of the members brings refreshments, and they snack as they work.

Soon their mood lightens. They begin to enjoy one another's company so much that they focus on their relationships rather than on their task. Soon the task group becomes a social group. Productivity falls because they are having a "party."

Productivity can fall off for another reason when a group becomes too cohesive. Members can value cohesiveness and their relationships with one another so much that they are unwilling to challenge one another's ideas. So they let ideas about which they have reservations pass unchallenged. The end product may be an inferior decision.

What are the implications of such a curvilinear relationship between cohesiveness and productivity? Members of a task group, and especially those members who wish to influence the success of the group, will do well to monitor the cohesiveness of the group. They try to increase group cohesiveness up to the point at which the group is maximally productive. After that, members who want to help the group succeed will work hard at maintaining the optimum levels of cohesiveness and keeping the group on the task.

The important point is that these dimensions affect each other. That is, productivity has an impact on cohesiveness, and cohesiveness has an impact on productivity. It is clear that both of these phenomena are the output of the group's work. What, then, can be done by individual group members to affect these important functions? Part of the answer may be found in the evolution of cohesiveness.

Satisfaction

People are usually more satisfied with their group when the group is cohesive than when it is not. Regardless of the setting—be it civic, educational, athletic, or industrial—members of highly compatible, cohesive groups report more enjoyment and satisfaction than those in noncohesive groups (Hackman, 1992). For example, in a field study, carpenters and masons who were working on a housing development were first assigned to work groups on a random basis and then arranged in work teams that were cohesive in that members were only those who liked each other. The masons and carpenters were much more satisfied than when they were randomly assigned to a work group. One worker explained that it "seems as though everything flows a lot smoother. . . . The work is more interesting when you've got a buddy working with you. Your certainly like it a lot better anyway" (Van Zelst, 1952). People experience less anxiety and

---

Looking Back: A Quick Review

POSITIVE OUTCOMES OF COHESIVENESS

Increased productivity	Enhanced agreement
Increased satisfaction	

---

tension in a cohesive group because members respond to each other more positively than in noncohesive groups (Myers, 1962; Shaw & Shaw, 1962). This suggests that working in a setting where your group is cohesive provides a healthy workplace on the psychological level. This finding has been demonstrated in both industrial groups (Seashore, 1954) and therapeutic groups (Yalom, 1995). And, of course, satisfaction is related to how members communicate with each other—a topic addressed shortly (Anderson & Martin, 1999).

Enhanced Agreement

Donelson R. Forsyth (1999, p. 161) reports that "people in cohesive groups more readily accept the group's goals, decisions, and norms. Furthermore, pressures to conform are greater in cohesive groups, and individuals' resistance to these pressures is weaker." He cites several studies to support his contention (Back, 1951; Courtright, 1978; Schachter, 1951). It appears that members want to avoid confrontation in groups where there is high cohesion so there is more agreement about goals, decisions, and norms.

PROMOTING COHESIVENESS

Leader and member behaviors make a difference in whether a group develops strong cohesiveness or does not. Leader style and member behavior need to be cohesiveness enhancing. In addition, the strength of group commitment to its goals and member identification are also important cohesiveness enhancers.

Leadership Style

Effective leadership is essential to building cohesiveness. Everyone in a group can contribute leadership, and each member's willingness and determination to do so is a part of team building. The ability to select appropriate task and social leadership behaviors, and knowing when it is appropriate to do so, is one of the most important skills.

The selection of leadership behaviors and their appropriate and skillful use is a complex issue. Task leadership and leadership styles were the topics of Chapter 7. There, alternative leadership styles, behaviors, and skills were presented. The matter of social leadership was developed fully in Chapter 8. How to be supportive, how to meet the interpersonal needs of members, and how to give appropriate feedback to improve both cohesiveness and productivity received careful treatment.

Effective Participation

Obviously, effective participation is essential to the success of a group. That statement makes fundamentally good sense at first glance. At a deeper level, we know that the ethical commitment of a group participant bears on both cohesiveness and productivity. People assume that when they join a group, they can expect the other members to behave in certain ways. If expectations are fulfilled, members will be far more likely to experience cohesiveness. John Cragan and David Wright (1999) argue that any group member must make five commitments to group members.

Commitment to do your best   You have individual skills and abilities. You have special knowledge and insight. You know some things no one else knows. If you make a commitment to do your best, then you will try to share what you know and you will try to participate in the tasks of the group. Without your commitment to do your best, the group will be shortchanged. If your group begins to believe that you are shortchanging it, conflict may ensue. You have a responsibility to try to do your best.

Commitment to the good of the group   This commitment is not the same as the last one. From time to time you have been involved in groups in which one of the members was looking out for him- or herself. This seems to happen in many different contexts.

To illustrate, consider this marketing team of a thriving business just outside Boulder, Colorado. One member of the group was an older man who had, five years earlier, personally developed the marketing program for the product being discussed. In addition, this man had a terrible anger. And so he decided that this committee assignment was his chance to gain recompense for all the shortcomings of his career. His private goals came before the good of the group. When a member suggested a new marketing approach, this man objected. If another wanted to change any particular item in the original scheme, this man obstructed the progress.

Serving with that man was maddening, but it taught a very valuable lesson. Each member of a group can undermine the group's cohesiveness and productivity by grinding his or her own private ax or by engaging in self-serving behavior. Individuals and groups have a right to expect every member will make a commitment to the group good.

Commitment to straight thinking   Sometimes individuals evolve convictions and beliefs that are important to them. Sometimes those private truths do not completely square with the facts. When this happens to members, the results can be trying, both for the group and for the individual. A commitment to straight thinking means that an individual will keep an open mind while the group works toward conclusions. Given the enormous subjectivity of perception and thinking, it often happens that a group will arrive at conclusions different from those of an individual. An individual must be willing to test private truth against the arguments and evidence presented by other members.

Commitment to fair play   When a group member makes this commitment, he or she is making a commitment to cooperative behavior. Fair play means setting self-aggrandizement aside. It means resisting the temptation to play games. It means avoiding one-upmanship. It means being straight. And it means resisting the tendency, especially in larger groups, to struggle for status when what is most important is achieving a common goal.

To illustrate the tendency to compete in our culture, quickly think of the names of five games you play. List these in your head before you read further. Have you thought of a game that is played in such a way that in order for one player to win, the other player has to win? Very rarely does anyone think of such a game. Frisbee is the only such game that comes to mind. Does this make a point about our society's commitment to competition in a compelling way?

What is common if you check with classmates is that everyone will have considered games that are played in such a way that one player can win only if the other player loses. It is significant to note that even the games we play for fun reinforce the culture's insistence that the world is competitive. Such an orientation can be especially harmful to the cohesiveness and productivity of a group.

Consider the results of this win–lose attitude at a recent meeting of the tenants' association of a condominium complex in Pensacola, Florida:

CARLOS: I think we ought to spend the money in our repair fund on a new shell for the swimming pool.

SHALOUNDA: I disagree. That's foolish. I insist that we fix the tennis courts. More people use them.

CARLOS: Since there isn't enough money for both projects, we should wait until there is enough.

SHALOUNDA: If you can't support us on this issue, Carlos, don't expect our support for your candidacy for city council this fall. I don't want someone with your kind of attitude representing me!

A commitment to fair play overcomes the damaging tendency to compete.

Commitment to careful listening   Have you participated in a conversation in which someone else responds in a way that appears he or she was not listening? A group of students engaged in a task one afternoon asked to be observed because group members had been complaining that they were unhappy with each other. Here is part of the discussion in that group:

SUNG: I think we ought to look at our evaluative criteria again. Seems to me that what you're saying doesn't meet. . . .

MARC (INTERRUPTING SUNG): You're always bringing up those criteria. What's wrong with just laying out a plan—the whole plan—then seein' if there's anything wrong with it?

SUNG: Nothing. But the criteria are really relevant on this one point. You want to give a lot of our money to the SGA [Student Government Association], and all I'm saying is that we ought to be sure that's the best way to do it. I mean, are they going to use the three thousand bucks the way we want them to?

MARC: They'll use it right. I'll see to that.

HELEN: You guys are always fighting, and I can't see why. Why don't we just give the three thousand bucks to the SGA and get on with it?

This group was spending more time talking—or planning what they would say next—than listening. Helen's comment makes clear that she was not listening. When Marc interrupted Sung, he made clear that he, too, was not willing to hear Sung out. He was not listening. When Sung responded to Marc's question with "Nothing," and then went on to point out that something was wrong with Marc's plan, he said to Marc that he, too, was not listening. Small wonder that the other members of the group complained about having to work with these three!

Making a commitment to good listening means making a commitment to more than just hearing others. It involves trying to empathize, to understand not only what is said but also what is not said. To do so is to contribute to both the cohesiveness and productivity of a working group. Not to do so is to squander the energies of the group and to undermine the sense of team.

So far, the matter of encouraging cohesiveness has been approached by looking at leadership style, group size, and effective participation by members. Perhaps the most important single variable involving cohesiveness, however, is making group progress. Recall that group members must think they are making progress toward goals in order to be satisfied with their membership. That all-important *perception* of progress is most likely if the group actually does make progress! Now a closer look at group goals is appropriate.

Commitment to Group Goals

Group goals simply cannot exist outside individual members. Individuals must subordinate, to some degree, their own goals in order to help the group reach its goals. Let us consider this idea further.

Individuals join groups because they think they will be able to accomplish some of their own private ends. Moreover, in the case of most ad hoc groups, individuals join or are appointed because they (or someone with whom they work) believe that they share some common problem that can be resolved by working together. The point is that individuals, and not groups, provide the motivation to accomplish group goals. Together they agree that some of their individual goals should become the concern of the group, and they agree to set aside other individual goals in order to accomplish those they share with other members.

Barbara joined the Public Relations Council because she thought she could receive certain benefits from that group. What she did, in this context, can be put a different way. Barbara joined the council because she believed joining was a means to achieve some individual goals. Later she saw that in order to get what she wanted from that council, she would have to set aside some of her aims. Individuals who join groups have to subordinate some of their goals in order to accomplish others. This situation creates the potential for conflict between individual goals and group goals.

Group members almost always differ when they are asked to identify their group's goals. You can imagine that perceptions of the group's goal might differ in a social sorority. For example, Jill might say that the purpose of the sorority is to provide social activities. Lerita might say the purpose is to provide support to a group of sisters as they go through their college years. Marta might say the sorority's purpose is to allow its members the opportunity to sponsor and participate in campus activities. Who is correct?

Moreover, different individuals almost never make the same level of commitment to group goals. Sometimes, too, individuals join the same group in order to achieve different ends.

To illustrate, imagine how Kosetta might feel if she realized that her intense commitment to achieving a certain group goal differs markedly from that of another member. Suppose she does a lot of planning and thinking, always comes prepared to provide leadership, and is quick to volunteer her energy and expertise. Now suppose Kosetta discovers that Martha really is not very committed to the goal toward which she has been driving so hard. Let us say that Martha joined the group because Josh was a member and she was (and still is) interested in an affiliation with Josh. At a group meeting Kosetta asks Martha if she has brought materials she said she would bring. Martha, somewhat chagrined, perhaps, says, "Oh my gosh! I'm sorry, but I just plain forgot them." Kosetta believes that Martha has reneged on her commitment. So she says, "Martha, darn it. You seem to be more interested in 'something else,' but not in our group. We are counting on your information. Now you've delayed the group. Why don't you ever follow through?" Clearly, Kosetta feels frustration and perhaps anger.

"Now just a minute, Kosetta," says Martha. "I don't like your tone of voice! And besides, you have no right to talk to me that way. After all, you're the one who makes all the moves. In fact, I *never* accepted or agreed to this."

"You didn't disagree with it either, Martha. You never said you *wouldn't* do it. And now, after a week and after we have been counting on you, you've let us down."

"Not so. I resent that you think I'd do that. And I resent your tone. You'll have to find someone else to push around. I'm leaving! Josh, are you coming?"

The point of all this is that group cohesiveness is at risk when subordination of an individual's private goals creates the potential for conflict between individual and group goals or between individual members. It is very easy for individual members of a group to reject the group's goals altogether when this kind of conflict is not managed skillfully.

Group goals tend to be long-range goals. This tendency of groups to develop and evolve long-range goals makes sense, of course. But carrying out long-range goals is a critical problem for group members because the goals are not usually stated in concrete, attainable units. But it is possible to break up long-range goals into smaller, more readily attainable units. It is also possible and desirable to talk about those goals in terms of behavior, and to reward every achievement along the way to a group's goals.

Let us examine each of these practical suggestions in turn and then look at some examples. The first was *break long-range goals into a series of intermediate goals*. Consider Figure 9.2. Suppose that the long-range goal of the group is somewhere out there on the right-hand side of the continuum. It seems obvious, but worth repeating, that breaking up the task into short ranges creates a series of readily achievable intermediate objectives. These goals should be moderately difficult. This means that they should be difficult enough to provide some challenge but also should be attainable. Each successful achievement is reinforcing in itself, because the group can observe its own progress and because the members of the group can experience the benefits of their own success.

Second, *state intermediate goals in terms of behaviors*. In setting up its goals, a group ought to try to specify *what* ought to be involved and (if the group chooses) *how* the tasks should be accomplished. Part of each meeting's agenda could be devoted to focusing upon what has been accomplished and what ought to be accomplished next.

As an illustration of how this approach might work, consider how one group of parents solved a problem through this kind of goal setting. A group of parents decided to organize a Boy Scout troop for their sons. Their long-range goal was to organize a

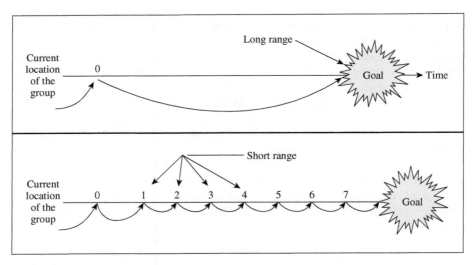

FIGURE 9.2
Illustration of Long-Range and Short-Range Goal Setting

troop that would help their boys mature and learn the valuable skills that such a program teaches. But focusing on this long-range goal did not help them be productive. They set these five intermediate goals that led them to the overall goal:

1. Conduct a survey to discover who might be interested in sponsoring a troop.

2. Locate a scoutmaster.

3. Publicize the new troop so that all interested boys would be aware of it.

4. Meet with local scout officials to charter the troop.

5. Plan and organize an orientation meeting for interested boys and their parents.

The next step was to specify what ought to be involved in carrying out each intermediate goal. Here are the short-term objectives for "Locate a scoutmaster":

a. Collect names from the scout office by Friday. (Juan)

b. Ask the sponsoring agency who from their group might be interested in being a scoutmaster by Friday. (Millie)

c. Call potential scoutmasters, and discover their level of interest by Tuesday. (David)

d. Interview the potential scoutmasters by Thursday. (All)

e. Make a selection by Monday. (All)

You can see how this kind of goal setting might work. Regardless of the task, it can lead to increased cohesiveness and productivity.

The point of all this illustration is that any production process includes not only a long-range goal but also a complex set of intermediate goals. Those intermediate goals ought to be identified in terms of some time sequence and in terms of the human behaviors required. Note who ought to be assigned to each intermediate goal.

Thus the questions we learn to ask in our sixth grade English lessons—who, what, when, where, why, and how—provide a method for setting intermediate goals and a rationale for identifying the goals that need to be set (Durham, Knight, & Locke, 1997). Brainstorming and note taking on sticky pads (or index cards)—each of which includes at least a noun and a verb—provide very useful means by which a group can accomplish the task of setting intermediate goals.

Goal Setting Theory

Edwin Locke and Gary Latham (1984) studied the issue of effective goal setting. They provide seven specific suggestions as to how to accomplish this. Here are the points they made:

1. *Goals need to be specific* so that the group will know when they are accomplished. In addition, specific goals provide clear direction to the group.

2. *Goals need to be somewhat difficult, but realistic.* The point is that goals that are simple to accomplish do not have the necessary motivating force we would hope them to have. Accomplishing simple goals is not particularly satisfying to the group since not much effort was required. On the other hand, if the goal is too difficult members may be discouraged and not put out the necessary effort to achieve it.

3. *Goals need to be accepted by the group members.* The need for this seems self-evident. Members "buy into" goals they help set. They helped set them, so presumably they agree with them and would like to see the group accomplish them. Of course, they will certainly understand that they need to do their part for this achievement to happen.

4. *Goals are a means for the group to evaluate their performance.* It is clear to all of us that if we do not know what we are trying to accomplish we will not know if we did it. Beyond this, if the goal is stated in specific terms, we will be able to make a judgment about its quality.

5. *Goals provide a basis for feedback and rewards.* Consider that a course instructor sets objectives (goals to be accomplished) and standards (statements about how these goals will be evaluated) and instruments that will be used in this evaluation (exams, papers, oral presentations and the like) and provide students with various indicators (outcomes of exams, papers, oral presentations) that provide feedback (grades and comments) on how each student is meeting those goals. And, in the end, there is a reward for the effort in accomplishing goals (the course grade). Goals in groups operate in a similar fashion—to provide feedback and a basis for reward.

6. *Goals should be set by members of the group.* There is a better chance that members will earnestly work toward meeting goals they set than goals that are imposed on them. It seems obvious that members will see the goals they set as worthwhile and, therefore, something to be achieved.

7. *Goals can promote member and group growth.* Appropriately set goals almost always lead to better success than goals that are not set well. When groups set their goals and achieve them, the process creates a more interdependent, cooperative, and cohesiveness environment in which to work. (Johnson & Johnson, 1984). These are all growth issues that are not seen in a very high level in groups as they begin a task. They are achieved through successfully working together and achieving goals. The likelihood that a group will achieve these goals is in part attributable to effective goal setting. One of the most important characteristics that differentiae between high-performing, cohesive teams form the low-performers is having a compelling, clear goal (LaFasto & Larson, 2001).

Studies have also found that self-set goals are more effective than assigned goals. This is especially true when the task is complex and strategies for reaching the goals are developed (Chesney & Locke, 1991; Durham, Knight, & Locke, 1997). One of the most important characteristics that differentiates between high-performing, cohesive teams from the low-performers is having a compelling, clear goal (LaFasto & Larson, 2001).

Thus far we have said that leadership style, group size, effective participation, and commitment to group goals enhance cohesiveness and group satisfaction. We have said also that cohesiveness and satisfaction have as an outcome valuing the group and its members. Now we turn to the concept of group identification.

Group Identification and Symbolic Convergence

Group identification is a term used to describe a state where members see themselves more as part of a group than as individual people working in a group. Members begin to see the group as something other than a collection of individuals, as having a "personality" of its own. Group identification (and identity) are fully achieved when members act as a group, believe each member belongs, and develop liking for members and the task (Henry, Arrow, & Carini, 1999). Group identification brings out some unique communication behaviors. Collective pronouns become more prominent. Members use pronouns such as *we, us,* and *ours,* rather than *I, me, mine, you,* and *yours.*

The group also adopts rituals, tells stories about its heroes and villains, and joins in group fantasies. Rituals can be as simple as always beginning the meeting with coffee and doughnuts or having special greetings for arriving members. Some groups develop a ritual of meeting after work for social time. Groups may adopt heroes, too. Perhaps a former member exemplifies the qualities for which the current group members strive. If a group has struggled against some individual or group, it may take on that person or persons as the enemy. A villain who has posed a threat to the group can push members more closely together.

Finally, members of a group that has strong identification will tell stories that exemplify their experience. Ernest Bormann called these **fantasy themes.** When scholars speak of **fantasy** in relation to a group's communication they mean the creative and imaginative shared interpretation of events that fulfill a group's psychological or rhetorical need to make sense of their experience and to anticipate the future (Bormann et al., 2001). Groups move through periods of interaction in which they move to telling stories, relating past experiences, and relating anecdotes that relate to the group and its process. Members do not usually set out to create a fantasy, but instead a group member recalls something that brings it to mind and articulates it. If other members pick up on it, their elaboration becomes a **fantasy chain.** These fantasy chains can be brief or extended and are characterized by a sense of excitement. These are not fantasies in that they are fiction. The stories usually have their basis in real-life situations that involve heroes and villains. They make a point that illustrates the group's experience. At certain times during the group's work they will divert from the task to engage in relating anecdotes or telling stories about past events.

One group we know created a story about what happens to its proposals to management that take so long to get a response. One member began with a story of trying to track down a document. He said that it had fallen into a "deep, dark hole" into which proposals mysteriously vanished. As the story unfolded, members worked together to develop it and add to its richness. Later, all that was needed to remind the group of the story was to mention the deep, dark hole.

Looking Back: A Quick Review

HOW TO DEVELOP COHESIVENESS

Effective leadership	Effective task, social, and maintenance leadership. Style appropriate to the situation. Leadership shared when needed.
Effective participation	Members using their skills and abilities toward task accomplishment. Members committed to the good of the group. Members thinking critically, weighing evidence and arguments. Members treating each other fairly and with consideration. Members listening carefully to each other. Members committed to the group's goals.
Group identification/symbolic convergence	Members see themselves more as part of the group than as individuals. Members speak in "we" terms, rather than in "I" terms. Members celebrate group success. Members are liberal in positively reinforcing each other and the group for excellent work.

Sometimes a fantasy theme will turn into a fantasy chain. A *fantasy chain* is a series of statements by members through which they jointly create a story. A particular theme catches the imagination or interest of the group, causing most or all members to participate in creating the story. These chains can last for a few minutes to a half hour, during which time members show their excitement through increased speed of interaction and volume. This storytelling is an important part of developing and sustaining a group's culture (Peterson, 1987).

Storytelling, creating logos, telling inside jokes, and taking on rhetorical visions can lead to shared perceptions and values among members. Bormann (1986) has referred to this process as **symbolic convergence.** Convergence suggests that the private symbol using of two or more people comes together or overlaps. This adoption of a shared set of symbols allows the development of a common pool of meanings. So the storytelling, fantasy themes, and symbolic convergence lead to greater group identification. Increased group identification leads to greater emotional commitment and increased cohesiveness, which, of course, can lead back to more fantasy-theme activity.

A Question of Ethics and Responsibility

A NEIGHBORHOOD GROUP

A group of neighbors met to discuss ideas for neighborhood improvements. One member described the first several meetings this way:

The group of people from the neighborhood got together today for the first time. I immediately noticed that members seemed kind of distant, physically, so I suggested we move in closer. We did. I thought that we might introduce ourselves and tell a little bit about who we are. This seemed to break the icy silence. Someone asked if we should elect a leader. I said that I didn't think we needed one in such a small group. The tone of this first meeting was quiet. People seemed a bit reserved.

Two members didn't show up for our second meeting. Someone joked that we should have elected one of the missing members to lead the group. Another member suggested we begin picking projects for neighborhood improvements. There was a long silence before I finally suggested we might improve our neighborhood park. Another person suggested improved street lighting. Not many suggestions were made. I wonder why this group isn't more enthusiastic about this opportunity. We finally adjourned after what I would describe as a brief and frustrating attempt to identify projects. No decisions were made.

Our third meeting began with three members absent. One of these people walked in thirty minutes late and made her excuses for not arriving on time. The apparent lack of interest in the task of these members did not seem to bother others. So I kept quiet, even though I thought this could become a significant problem. Nobody seemed to have any other suggestions or even to care much about what we recommended. We finally settled on improvements for our neighborhood park. One member suggested that I ought to head a group of neighbors in gathering suggestions and plans for the project. I thought that the group which had volunteered to work on this initially ought to follow through. I wonder what would have happened if they did continue to meet.

Focus on notions about cohesiveness that are presented in this chapter. What does considering this variable tell you about this group? How would you support your conclusions? Suppose that you were the leader of this group. What would you do to help this group build cohesiveness?

GROUPTHINK: A NEGATIVE EFFECT OF COHESIVENESS

Up to this point, this chapter has centered on the beneficial effects that accrue to a group with cohesiveness. The point is that for most groups the greater the cohesiveness, the better. But that idea must be tempered with a strong note of caution.

Early in the 1970s Irving L. Janis hypothesized that sometimes a decision-making group can get dangerously cohesive. The title of his famous book, which first came out in 1972 (Janis, 1972) and in an expanded and revised edition in 1982 (Janis, 1982), was both controversial and provocative.[2] The title is still a somber warning about too much cohesiveness: *Victims of Groupthink*. Janis studied decision-making fiascoes of several high-ranking presidential advisory groups. He researched the failure to adequately secure Pearl Harbor (1941), the decision to assist a group in invading the Bay of Pigs in Cuba (1962), the decision to escalate the Korean War (1950) and the Vietnam War (1964–1967), and the Nixon Watergate cover-up (1972). More recently, some have speculated that the *Challenger* space shuttle tragedy may have resulted from groupthink (Jensen & Chilberg, 1991). Shortly, we will examine an account of the *Challenger* disaster to see if you agree.

Groupthink is a phenomenon that occurs in highly cohesive groups where members ignore evidence and opinions contrary to their views, and disregard alternative choices, in order to preserve their feeling of unity. Groupthink can happen to any group (Janis & Mann, 1977). Indeed the phenomenon is common to groups.

In essence, the theory of groupthink is that situations occur in which groups take leave of reason, in part because they are too cohesive. They fail to examine evidence carefully and make incorrect assumptions about what others are thinking. When that happens, the group and its constituents are victims of groupthink. They make bad decisions that have no apparent basis in reality.

The tendency for a group to engage in groupthink is enhanced when certain conditions are present. We turn now to examine those conditions.

Conditions That Promote Groupthink

Janis's analysis yielded four conditions that lead to groupthink. The first condition is *cohesiveness*. The group has moderately high to very high cohesiveness.

A second condition is *insulation*. The group's insulation from contradictory sources inhibits members from getting information and expert opinion. Especially, insulation keeps the group from hearing criticisms and skeptical evaluations.

A third condition is *lack of a tradition of impartial leadership*. These group leaders have no traditional constraints to maintain impartiality. Janis explains: "The leader of a policy-making group will find it all too easy to use his or her power and prestige to influence the members of the group to approve the policy alternative he or she prefers instead of encouraging them to engage in open inquiry and critical evaluation." Of course, members play a part in this situation. They have to be willing to endorse the leader's view, rather than question it.

Finally, groups that experience groupthink *do not have norms or rules about the methods or procedures* they will use in dealing with the decision-making task. The leader and the members proceed as they choose. Almost certainly they will choose a path that is relatively free of criticism or countervailing evidence and argument.

Table 9.1 summarizes the conditions that lead to the groupthink syndrome. Avoiding these will help to "side-step" groupthink.

Symptoms of the Groupthink Syndrome

How do you know your group is being affected by groupthink? These tell-tale signs of groupthink (symptoms) will be evident. (See Table 9.2 for a summary.)

TABLE 9.1   Conditions That Promote Groupthink

Moderately high or very high cohesiveness.
Insulation of the policy-making group.
Lack of tradition to inhibit leadership bias.
Lack of rules or norms about methods and procedures.

TABLE 9.2   Symptoms of Groupthink

Overestimation of the group
    Members overestimate the group's power and morality.
    Members take risks and actions that a reasonable person would judge unwise.
    Members believe they can do no wrong and cannot be harmed.
Closed mindedness
    Members rationalize their decisions as being correct; they are closed minded.
    Members avoid critical thinking.
Pressures toward uniformity
    Members view outgroups as the enemy.
    Members create an illusion that they have achieved true consensus.
    Members apply pressure (through mindguards) to cause other members to conform.

Overestimations of the group's power and morality   In this category of symptoms Janis included a variety of *illusions* that groups sometimes develop. When the members of a group begin to believe that *they are invulnerable* (that they cannot be harmed), they will begin to give themselves permissions they might otherwise constrain. *They take risks* that a reasonable person would judge unwise. The illusion of invulnerability creates an optimism that may not be warranted by reality. Members believe they can do no wrong. Since they begin to believe that they cannot be harmed, group members become more and more willing to take actions that people outside the group would certainly question. Moreover, a group will sometimes become so cohesive that it begins to believe that its morality, its "rightness," is beyond question.

Closed mindedness   Closed mindedness occurs in groups when the *members attempt to rationalize their decisions* in order to discount or overcome the skepticism and warnings of people who are critical of them. *Critical thinking is discouraged.* In addition, sometimes group members rationalize away the adverse implications of information that appears to be contrary to their views. This happens especially under conditions in which members refuse to reconsider the basic assumptions on which they originally made their decisions, even in the face of countervailing evidence.

    This same category, closed mindedness, may be found in situations in which group members identify themselves as "the good guys." They stereotype as "the enemy" those who oppose their views. The enemy is so evil that it does not merit the group's attention or willingness to negotiate. The enemy is too weak or too stupid to counter the decisions of the group, and the enemy would try to delay the group from implementing its decisions.

When a group identifies an outgroup as the "enemy," this can lead to increased group solidarity. Scholars Turner and Haslam (2001, p. 38) put it like this: "We can define ourselves as a distinct we-group on the basis of our shared interests in contrast to others [the outgroup]."

Pressures toward uniformity   Sometimes it may happen that members find themselves *minimizing their own doubts and counterarguments*. Members find evidence of groupthink when they see *the illusion developing that they share a common judgment*—and they do not. In this case members do not talk about their reservations (and assume that silence on the part of their colleagues is consent); alternatively, they conform to the majority view (or what they think is the majority view) because they trust that the group is invulnerable and morally right anyway. Members think they have achieved consensus.

Janis described the emergence of **self-appointed mindguards** as one of the pressures toward uniformity that characterize groupthink. These are group members who take it upon themselves to protect the group from information or opinions that might cause the group to veer from its course. Mindguards work to protect group complacency about its ethical and moral posture and about the likely success of its decisions. These members apply pressure to those who voice opinions or present evidence that does not support the group.

Consequences of the Groupthink Syndrome

To understand what goes wrong, it is useful to review the six characteristics of sound decision making:

1. The group has thoroughly understood the problems it is trying to solve or resolve.

2. The group has set up criteria against which to evaluate the bits and pieces of the evolving solutions. Members have carefully weighed the costs and risks of any negative consequences of their plan as well as the positive consequences.

3. The group has thoroughly studied a broad range of alternative courses of action that might solve or resolve the problem.

4. The group has considered and weighed all the information available, taking into account any expert opinion or evidence that does not support the evolving decisions or the preferred course of action.

5. Having evolved a potential solution in advance, the group has consistently reevaluated the solution and both the positive and the negative consequences.

6. The group determines a final choice and makes detailed provisions for executing the final plan, paying attention to contingency plans that might be required if any of the known risks should occur.

Imagine the effects of these symptoms on a decision-making task group. If most or all the symptoms are present, then members probably will work very ineffectively.

Focus on Research

GROUPTHINK: SOME FINDINGS

Groupthink continues to intrigue scholars. Veiga (1991) extends Janis's research by identifying some additional conditions when groupthink is likely to occur. This study indicates it occurs when

1. The group is apathetic about the task.
2. The group's members have low expectations about success.
3. There is at least one highly qualified and credible group member.
4. There is one highly persuasive member.
5. There is a norm of conformity, rather than express negative opinions.

Here are some findings from other scholars:

- Cline (1990) found that groups that are experiencing groupthink spend about 10 percent more of their discussion time making statements of agreement or disagreement than nongroupthink groups.

- Cline (1994) concluded that groups think they have arrived at a unanimous decision and terminate their deliberations prematurely.
- Street (1997) discovered that groupthink is more likely to occur when there is no structured method for evaluating alternative ideas in place.

R. J. W. Cline (1990). Detecting groupthink: Methods for observing the illusion of unanimity. *Communication Quarterly, 38,* 112–126.

R. J. W. Cline (1994). Groupthink and the Watergate cover-up: The illusion of unanimity. In L. R. Frey (ed.), *Group communication in context: Studies of natural groups.* Hillsdale, NJ: Erlbaum, pp. 199–223.

M. Street (1992). Groupthink: An examination of theoretical issues, implications, and future research suggestions. *Small Group Research, 28,* 72–93.

J. F. Veiga (1991). The frequency of self-limiting behavior in groups: A measure and an explanation. *Human Relations, 44,* 877–895.

They are not likely to achieve their objectives, because their process of decision making is defective. You will see these violate the characteristics of sound decision making. Janis lists the following seven consequences of faulty decision making:

1. Incomplete survey of alternatives.

2. Incomplete survey of objectives.

3. Failure to examine the risks of preferred choices.

4. Failure to reappraise initially rejected alternatives.

5. Poor information search.

6. Selective bias in processing information at hand.

7. Failure to work out contingency plans.

Earlier we said that we would present an account of the *Challenger* disaster to see if you agree that groupthink contributed to the situation. This is in Figure 9.3.

Figure 9.4, on page 277, provides a real-life incident of groupthink and a tragic outcome.

On January 28, 1986, the space shuttle *Challenger* exploded 72 seconds after takeoff. The tragedy shocked a nation that had come to expect spaceflights to be as routine as daily flights in and out of major airports everywhere. But it also caught the management at NASA off guard. No one was prepared for a failure of this magnitude. But should they have been?

Within the week, President Reagan assigned a special group, the Rogers Commission, to investigate the disaster. The U.S. House of Representatives also sought a report from its Committee on Science and Technology. The results of those investigations revealed a number of serious flaws in the decision-making process at NASA as well as at Morton Thiokol, the contractor that had built the solid rocket booster, which was ultimately identified as the physical cause of the accident.

As it turned out, information on the flaws in design of the solid rocket booster was widely known at almost every level of the space shuttle management. Long-term plans were being made to phase in a new type of joint design for the solid rocket booster, but there was no sense of urgency to do anything soon. On the evening before the launch, some engineers at Thiokol objected to a launch because of the potential effects of low temperature on the O-ring joint seals. Morton Thiokol management initially recommended against the launch as well but reversed that decision over the protests of its own engineers. Some senior-level NASA officials later claimed to be unaware of these objections. Crucial information had not been passed on to them. The various flaws in the decision-making process read like a veritable laundry list of groupthink symptoms:

1. Erosion of the joint seals on previous flights was not reported in the flight-readiness review for the January 28 flight (adverse information rationalized away).

2. Thiokol engineers raised objections only to their immediate supervisors, not wanting to override the chain of command (a form of self-censorship by the engineers and mindguarding by their superiors).

3. Thiokol management reversed its initial decision to postpone the launch at the urging of managers at the Marshall Space Flight Center. Thiokol then put pressure on its own engineers to "prove" that the solid rocket boosters would not work at the temperature projected for launch time (external pressure by Marshall; direct pressure on dissenters at Thiokol).

4. NASA's 25-year history of success and incredibly good luck led management on a course that increasingly underestimated risks and overestimated the likelihood of further success (illusion of invulnerability).

5. NASA management was so convinced of its own safety record that it considered the shuttle program to be fully operational—the testing phase was viewed as complete. NASA management actually held some discussions with various airlines about taking over the space shuttle program. Airline officials were astounded. Most experts said the system was still in a research and development phase. (Collective rationalization created a mind-set that the system was fully operational.)

6. In a speech at Edwards Air Force Base in 1982, President Reagan reinforced this mind-set in public: "The test flights are over, the groundwork has been laid, now we will move forward to capitalize on the tremendous potential offered by the ultimate frontier of space" (external pressure to maintain faulty mind-set).

7. The plan to mention the teacher-in-space program in President Reagan's State of the Union address on the evening of the scheduled launch may have contributed to the feeling that *Challenger* had to be launched on time (implied external pressure).

FIGURE 9.3
The Shuttle *Challenger* Tragedy: Was It Groupthink?

Source: A. D. Jensen and J. C. Chilberg (1991, pp. 361–362). Reprinted by permission.

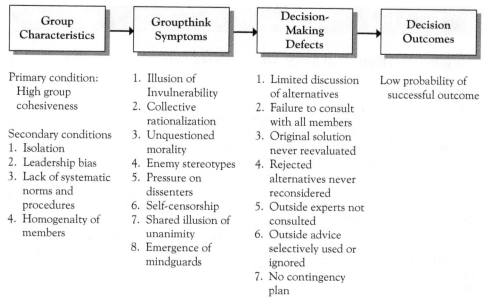

| Group Characteristics | Groupthink Symptoms | Decision-Making Defects | Decision Outcomes |

Primary condition:
  High group
  cohesiveness

Secondary conditions
1. Isolation
2. Leadership bias
3. Lack of systematic
   norms and
   procedures
4. Homogenalty of
   members

1. Illusion of
   Invulnerability
2. Collective
   rationalization
3. Unquestioned
   morality
4. Enemy stereotypes
5. Pressure on
   dissenters
6. Self-censorship
7. Shared illusion of
   unanimity
8. Emergence of
   mindguards

1. Limited discussion
   of alternatives
2. Failure to consult
   with all members
3. Original solution
   never reevaluated
4. Rejected
   alternatives never
   reconsidered
5. Outside experts not
   consulted
6. Outside advice
   selectively used or
   ignored
7. No contingency
   plan

Low probability of
  successful outcome

FIGURE 9.4
A Review of Janis's Groupthink

How to Avoid Groupthink

If the groupthink syndrome happens to your groups, how can it be avoided? Janis was concerned about this question too. His prescription makes excellent sense, and so we will present it here in abbreviated form:

1. Leaders should assign the role of critical evaluator to each member.

2. Leaders should avoid stating preferences and expectations at the outset.

3. Each member of a policy-making group should routinely discuss the group's deliberations with trusted associates and report back to the group.

4. One or more outside experts should be invited to each meeting on a staggered basis. The outside experts should be encouraged to challenge the views of the members.

5. At least one articulate and knowledgeable member should have the role of devil's advocate.

6. Leaders should make sure that a sizable block of time is set aside to survey all warning signals from rivals, and they and the group should construct alternative scenarios of the rivals' intentions.

Focus on Research

GROUPTHINK AND UNETHICAL BEHAVIOR

Ronald R. Sims has investigated the link between groupthink and unethical behavior in organizations. He suggests that groupthink can yield outcomes that are more than just purely bad decisions. It can yield decisions that commit the group to unethical behavior.

Sims (1992) argues that the same pressures that lead a group to groupthink push it to unethical behavior. Notice the similarities between the characteristics he identified (below) and those that Janis identified as conditions that set the stage for groupthink. Here are the eight factors in a group that lead to unethical decisions:

1. Group cohesiveness—a strong belief in the group's goals and values.
2. Willingness to exert considerable effort on behalf of the group.
3. Strong desire to continue as a group member.
4. Excessive and almost blind loyalty to the group.
5. Arrogance and overconfidence.
6. A "bottom-line" mentality.
7. Insulation from ethical opinion and control.
8. Leader promotion of unethical solutions (*any* winning behavior is promoted).

Sims provided examples of groups from Beech-Nut, E. F. Hutton, and Salomon Brothers that support these characteristics. Beyond these his research identified the following six decision-making defects that lead to unethical decisions:

1. Few ethical alternatives perceived.
2. No reexamination of preferred unethical alternatives.
3. No reexamination of rejected ethical alternatives.
4. Rejection of dissenting opinions.
5. Selective bias of new information.
6. Win at all costs.

Sims recommends that a group "program conflict" by appointing a devil's advocate—a person to argue the opposing side—or that the group deliberately develop a proposal and counterproposal and then appoint advocates of each position to debate their proposal. Thus Sims is suggesting that the group find a way to deliberately introduce ideational conflict. What merits and liabilities do you see in this proposal for avoiding groupthink and unethical decisions?

R. R. Sims (1992). Linking groupthink to unethical behavior in organizations. *Journal of Business Ethics, 11,* 651–662.

Research by Cline (1990) points to an additional suggestion that is based on the fact that these groups do not do a thorough analysis. She found that groups experiencing groupthink express more agreement without clarification and use fewer and simpler substantiated agreements than nongroupthink groups.

It would be difficult to pinpoint any of the reasons in Figure 9.3 as the primary causes of the *Challenger* disaster. But taken together, they constitute a groupthink situation. The groupthink syndrome can attack any group, no matter how prestigious or successful. NASA's reputation had always been that it erred on the side of caution. Delays in the launching of flights had been common. But success can breed complacency, and that may have been the most serious symptom of all.

SUMMARY

Cohesiveness is a sort of social "chemistry" that groups have that transforms a set of individuals into a working team. It is the bond that links group members to the group, the degree to which members are attracted to one another and the group, and the unity a group has toward its members.

One of the determinants of cohesiveness is attraction. People are attracted to group membership by shared similar attitudes, a clear sense of how to achieve goals, the kinds of conflict and the way a group handles conflict, and the frequency and nature of feedback provided by the group.

Beyond attraction, however, three conditions are necessary for membership satisfaction in groups, without which cohesiveness simply cannot emerge. Group members must perceive freedom to participate; they must believe that they are making progress toward their goals; and they must agree that the status position they hold in the group, relative to the status positions of the other members, is at once right for them and right for their group.

Productivity refers to the quality and quantity of a group's output. These two variables display a curvilinear relationship in that the more cohesive a group, the more productive it is likely to be, up to a point. Productivity drops off because of the effect of too much cohesiveness. Too much cohesiveness may move the group from its designated task to socializing, or may cause a group to think less critically about its task.

Commitment to doing your best, commitment to the good of the group, commitment to straight thinking, commitment to cooperation rather than to competition, and commitment to careful listening are all relevant to the whole matter of group goals.

Group goals cannot exist outside individual members, who must subordinate some of their individual goals in order to achieve others. This idea sets up the potential for conflict between individual goals and group goals—so much so that it is easy for individuals to lose sight of group goals. Of course, should that happen, group cohesiveness will be at risk.

So the intelligent setting of group goals is an issue. This can best be accomplished by breaking long-range goals into a series of intermediate goals. Those intermediate goals ought to be stated in terms of behavior—specifically who should do what, when, and under what conditions. After carefully defined intermediate goals are assigned, the achievement of those goals ought to be monitored by every member. Every time a goal is achieved, the achievement should be mentioned and reinforced.

Group identification is a factor that enhances valuing group members more as part of a group than as individuals working in a group. Members begin to see the group as having a personality of its own. Group identification brings out some unique communication behaviors. Collective pronouns become more prominent. Group members tell stories that exemplify their group experience. Ernest Bormann calls these fantasy themes—stories that make a point and illustrate the group's experience. Sometimes a fantasy theme turns into a fantasy chain. Stories are an important part of developing and sustaining the group's culture.

Storytelling, creating logos, telling inside jokes, and taking on rhetorical visions lead to shared perceptions and values among members. Bormann refers to this process as symbolic convergence. Convergence suggests that the private symbol using of two or more people comes together or overlaps. This adoption of a shared set of symbols allows the development of a common pool of meanings. The result is greater understanding, increased identification, greater cohesion, and a greater emotional commitment to the group and its product.

Groupthink happens when very cohesive groups become insulated from criticism, when they lack a tradition of impartial leadership, and when they have no rules about methods and procedures. Under these conditions groups sometimes come to believe that they are invincible and utterly moral. When that happens, they may develop closed mindedness, stereotyping anyone who does not agree with them as "the enemy" and discounting any disagreements on that basis. Typically, such symptoms keep individual members from speaking about their own reservations.

The consequences of groupthink can be summarized in these words: *defective decision making*. The victims of groupthink do not adequately survey their alternatives; they do not survey their objectives or examine the risks of what they are doing. They usually do not reappraise anything they have once rejected. They do not search for information very actively, since they believe that they know all they need to know. They slant their processing of the available information in the direction of what they want rather than what is sensible. Rarely do groups afflicted with the groupthink syndrome ever work out contingency plans. What can you do to overcome the groupthink syndrome? Janis suggested six prescriptions that will help. What they make clear is that all groups, but especially highly cohesive groups, need to set themselves up in advance to guard the quality of their thought.

KEY TERMS AND CONCEPTS

closed mindedness	goal setting theory	pressures toward uniformity
cohesiveness	group identification	productivity
fantasy	groupthink	status consensus
fantasy chain	mindguards	symbolic convergence
fantasy themes	overestimation of the group	

EXERCISES

1. Adapt the Seashore index of group cohesiveness, Chapter 11, Table 11.7, to the requirements of a classroom group. Ask members to respond to the index you have created. Using these data and the concepts from this chapter, describe and analyze your group's cohesiveness.

2. Select a group that is known for its high cohesiveness. Interview members to see how they account for the high cohesiveness. Make a list of the factors they suggest. Compare your list with the lists of classmates who are investigating other groups. How are your lists similar? How are they different?

3. Consider the most cohesive and least cohesive groups to which you have belonged. List the characteristics of these groups that account for their cohesiveness. How do these characteristics compare with those described in the text? Share your work in class. How are the lists of others similar and different? How do you account for this?

4. Form a small group to role-play this situation. Presume that you are asked to help the leader of a special small group formed recently in your organization. You recognize that cohesiveness is important to the group's productivity. What steps would you suggest to this leader to attempt to build cohesiveness in this group?

5. Class question: "Why does cohesiveness decrease?" Speculate about factors that cause decreases in cohesiveness. Make a list of causative factors and suggest ways to prevent each cause.

6. Select a group to use in the analysis of cohesiveness. What do you see as evidence of this cohesiveness? How do you see this cohesiveness as facilitating, or not facilitating, the group task? What can members do to enhance cohesiveness in this group?

7. Using the experience of members of a small group, identify groupthink encounters they have had. Describe several of these situations and then compare them with the conditions presented in this chapter. How did they differ? How were they similar? Did any group work its way out of groupthink? How did they do that?

RECOMMENDED WEBSITES

The site www.accel-team.com/work_groups/index.html contains a well-organized description of informal group dynamics and team building in the workplace. There are also additional links to related topics such as group formation, leadership, communications, cohesion, and group norms.

The site www.css.edu/users/dswenson/web/6300-OBOD/cohesion.htm provides information about group norms, cohesion, and groupthink. There are also links that take users to various sections including ways to prevent groupthink.

At www.geocities.com/Athens/Forum/1650/htmlobtoc02.html is a class site for organizational behavior at the British Columbia Institute of Technology. Even though this is an organizational behavior website, it contains a great section on groups, including groupthink and group cohesion, as well as conflict. There is also a meeting evaluation form addressing the effectiveness of the team.

The site oak.cats.ohiou.edu/~kr323396/fantasy.htm provides interesting information on fantasy themes and symbolic convergence theory.

Team Building: Informal Dynamics at Work is devoted to various elements affecting an organization, but that can be related to any type of process, and includes sections on cohesion, at www.accel-team.com/work_groups/index.html.

A site devoted to small group communication, with an excellent section on Groupthink relating to the *Challenger* space shuttle disaster, may be found at lynn_meade.tripod.com/id62.htm. There are also links to sites of verbal and nonverbal communication.

Group Cohesiveness Assessment can assess the degree of cohesiveness in a small group in order to determine and encourage an acceptable level: webhome.idirect.com/~kehamilt/obgca.html.

RECOMMENDED READINGS

A. V. Carron & L. R. Frawley (2000). Cohesion: Conceptual and empirical examination. *Small Group Research, 31,* pp. 89–116.

N. Clark (1994). *Teambuilding: A practical guide for trainers.* New York: McGraw-Hill.

I. L. Janis (1982). *Groupthink: Psychological studies of policy decisions and fiascoes,* 2d ed. Boston: Houghton Mifflin.

J. Stewart (2002). *Bridges not walls,* 8th ed. New York: McGraw-Hill.

NOTES

1. The literature has been inconsistent in its findings about the relationship between group communication behavior and problem-solving effectiveness, but the author agrees with Hirokawa's (1982c) critique of that literature.

2. For a critique of Janis's theory, see Longley and Pruitt (1980).

chapter 10

MANAGING CONFLICT
IN THE GROUP

OBJECTIVES

After reading this chapter you should be able to
- Explain the nature of a situation that produces conflict.
- Identify substantive and affective conflict in decision-making groups.
- Describe when conflict is functional and when it is dysfunctional.
- Identify the sources of conflict in group discussion.
- Specify the conflict-management strategies that are not helpful.
- Explain techniques that are viable for managing both ideational and interpersonal conflict in groups.

EVOLUTION OF CONFLICT IN A SMALL GROUP: A MEMBER'S REPORT

First Meeting

The group of people from the Maryknoll Neighborhood Association got together today for the first time. I noticed that members were "lounging around" in a loose circle. I suggested that we move in closer, and we did. Carol got us started by suggesting that we introduce ourselves and tell where we work. This broke the ice. It turned out that Yuka, Carol, and Nancy are neighbors and socialize frequently. Yuka works as a speech pathologist at the hospital, Carol works in her home, while Nancy works as a bank manager. Juan is from Mississippi, working as the manager of a fast-food store and living alone. Doug is a coordinator of recreation for city parks.

I suggested that we could always get along without a leader. People seemed satisfied with this suggestion.

Assume that you are part of this neighborhood group and that you were taking those notes. Yuka, Carol, Nancy, Juan, and Doug are also members. The members are volunteers, but you know the others from talking to them in the neighborhood. Some know one another better than others. The president of the association has asked your group to select projects to propose to the association. These ideas for neighborhood improvement are to be presented to the next meeting. Suppose that you took the following notes, too.

Second Meeting

Doug missed this meeting. Juan said we ought to elect him "leader." Some folks laughed, but I thought that Doug's absence might be a sign of a problem. Carol suggested we get started picking projects. Juan wanted us to talk about the bad lighting at the corner of Hillcrest and Maryknoll. He apparently had a recent visitor who could not see the street signs. After a long silence, I said we ought to investigate what could be done to get better neighborhood parks. Yuka wanted to know what I meant by "better."

I said that I had never heard of parks without sandboxes for the kids and baseball diamonds. She agreed with me; Carol and Nancy nodded in agreement. Juan asked if we should agree to this project without consulting Doug. We all agreed that Juan will talk to Doug before the next meeting. We are to meet on Friday at seven o'clock.

Third Meeting

Doug, Juan, and Nancy hadn't arrived by 7:45. I knew this was a bad sign! Carol was really ticked off at her neighbor, Nancy, for not showing. Nancy finally arrived a few minutes later with an apology. She had to work an extra half hour when someone didn't show up. We really didn't feel like doing anything, since two of the members weren't there. Yuka said that she thought Juan was cutting our meeting because the group didn't treat his idea for a project seriously. Carol said that maybe Juan didn't even talk to Doug—just to get even.

She said that some guys couldn't accept female leadership. After elaborating for several minutes on this idea, she concluded with, 'They are just going to have to accept it this time.' I felt very uneasy with all this. I didn't object, but didn't agree. We ended the meeting with a vow to do a good job even if Doug and Juan didn't join in.

Fourth Meeting

All the members were present. I got there a few minutes late and found Yuka, Carol, and Nancy sitting close together on one side of the living room. They had reserved an empty seat for me right next to them. It was as if Yuka, Carol, and Nancy had agreed to fight Doug and Juan. I sat down. I could sense the tension. There was small talk, with Juan making several jokes and no one laughing. It seemed as if a coalition had formed against Doug and Juan. We were making no progress. Finally, I . . .

How would you complete that sentence? What would you do in this situation? What would you have others in the group do if you were the leader? The group hasn't been able to pull together yet. It doesn't seem that the group is going to complete its work. What would you do? Much depends on your attitude about conflict.

Self-analysis is an important step to take if you want to improve your ability to manage conflict. Self-analysis helps you discover your attitude toward conflict and how you might manage it. For example, if you believe that conflict is evil, you might try to avoid it. If you have a positive attitude, you might make the best of it. Consider the various aspects of your attitude and compare them with what this chapter has to say.

We begin with a discussion of the nature of conflict, including some definitions and introductory material. Next we examine several ideas about the role of conflict in groups, which leads to a distinction between functional and dysfunctional conflict. Then we explore the major sources of conflict in groups. The chapter concludes by providing practical suggestions for managing conflict in small groups.

THE NATURE OF CONFLICT

Conflict can be defined as a struggle involving opposing ideas, values, and/or limited resources. Morton Deutsch (1973, p. 10) stated this idea more formally when he said that conflict exists when there is an "action that is incompatible with another [and it] prevents, obstructs, interferes, injures, or in some way makes the latter less likely or less effective." Conflict also has been described as a struggle over values and claims to scarce status, scarce power, and/or scarce resources (Coser, 1964). The goals of those involved in the struggle are to damage, neutralize, or actually eliminate one another. The important ideas in these definitions are (1) the incompatibility of opposing ideas or values; (2) the struggle over perceived scarce status, scarce power, and/or scarce resources; and (3) the goal of preventing, obstructing, interfering, injuring, or in some way making it less likely that the opposing goal will be achieved.

Incompatibility of ideas, values, and/or goals provides the motivation for conflict. The incompatibility may be either real or imagined, but there must be a sense that important differences exist. This feeling leads to an attempt to prevent, obstruct, interfere, injure, or in some way intervene to achieve the desired end.

The intensity of the conflict, and thus the stress involved, is related to several contextual variables. First, the more important and attractive the individual goals, the more intense the conflict is likely to be. If I am the leader of a group and know that the evolving decision is going to be difficult to implement, and if I think the decision will cause me a great deal of grief, I may fight hard to defeat it.

Second, the relative attractiveness of the options affects the intensity of the conflict. If the group perceives two ideas to be equally attractive, there is likely to be great conflict if the members also see the alternatives as being important. Conflict of this type has been called **approach–approach conflict.** On the other hand, when one alternative seems somewhat more attractive than the other, there is less conflict.

Third, a group may find that the ideas it is considering have both attractive and unattractive features. A solution to a parking problem at a local plant might provide more space for people to park, but it also might cause them to walk much farther to their workstations. Such a situation produces **approach–avoidance conflict.**

Finally, the number of ideas to consider may affect the conflict. The group that sees several possible alternatives as equally attractive *and* sees its decision as important may experience very intense conflict. Members want to make the best decision, but they are likely to have trouble sorting through the many alternatives.

THE EFFECT OF CONFLICT IN GROUPS

The term **conflict management** is used to refer to handling conflict. This term does not imply that conflict necessarily ought to be brought to a swift conclusion. Nor does it promote the idea that conflict is good or bad. To suggest that conflict must be swiftly resolved denies that it might be "good" and implies that it would be "bad." A more sensible approach is that conflict can be either functional or dysfunctional for a group.

Functional and Dysfunctional Conflict

A number of people have grown up with the idea that conflict should be avoided. Many students believe in harmony in their groups. They seek interaction with little or no conflict, as if conflict were bad (Wall, Galanes, & Love, 1987). This attitude may have its root in the fact that conflict is often painful. The argument goes something like this: "Pain is bad. Conflict is painful. Therefore conflict must be bad." This argument is an easy one for people to believe, because it is sometimes true. Painful experiences are sometimes bad, but they also can be good. Likewise, conflict can be bad for us, but it also can be good.

Whether conflict is bad or good depends in part on how skillfully it is managed. Skillfully managed conflict has a good chance of being functional for the group. Poorly managed conflict may tear the social fabric of the group and may be dysfunctional.

The objectives of those involved may affect the usefulness of the conflict. Conflict is most likely to be functional when members value both the group task and each other. This valuing produces the incentive to work through differences. When members do not value each other, they often take on self-centered goals in the end, sometimes adopting an all-or-nothing attitude. When members possess the wrong goal orientation, conflict is likely to be dysfunctional.

Finally, conflict seems to be functional for some kinds of group activities and dysfunctional for others. Leonard C. Hawes and David H. Smith (1973), after examining the results of several studies, concluded that conflict is functional when a group is searching for and evaluating information. Conflict facilitates the search-and-analysis processes. On the other hand, conflict is dysfunctional in choice activity (selecting outcomes). Successful groups avoid this kind of dysfunction by concentrating most of their conflict in the middle of their group process, where they are searching for and evaluating information. The emergence phase marks the end of most of the conflict and is a period of substantial agreement.

There is evidence that groups gain confidence when they successfully manage conflict. "Groups that manage conflict collaboratively increase group efficacy, which in turn encourages member to believe that they can also handle subsequent conflicts" (Apler, Tjosvold, & Law, 2000). Moreover, groups that master collaboration as a conflict management strategy incorporate it into their decision making more so than groups that rely on confrontation or avoidance (Kuhn & Poole, 2000).

SUBSTANTIVE AND AFFECTIVE CONFLICT

Many years ago Harold Guetzkow and John Gyr (1954) conducted a classic field study of conflict in decision-making groups. They collected data by observing more than 100 groups from business and government. Two dimensions of conflict were identified:

Looking Back: A Quick Review

WHEN IS CONFLICT FUNCTIONAL?

Functional	When conflict is managed skillfully
	When members value the task
	When members value each other
	When members are searching for and evaluating information
Dysfunctional	When conflict is poorly managed
	When members possess the wrong goal orientation—individual instead of group
	When members are involved in choice activities, selecting outcomes

substantive and affective. These dimensions coincide with the task and social dimensions of communication. This distinction is important because these different types of conflict produce different effects in groups.

Substantive conflict typically involves opposition related to ideas or issues. The focus is on the content—the ideas. Suppose the director of the mental health center calls together his staff to discuss follow-up support groups for their chemical dependence program. George thinks they should meet in support groups at least twice a week for approximately one hour. Joy thinks they should meet for a longer period, approximately two hours, once a week. These staff members are engaged in substantive conflict.

Ideational conflict is disagreement over thoughts and concepts. If it is not managed well, it has a tendency to turn into affective conflict. Dennis Devine and colleagues (1999) report that when group members get locked into a disagreement about substantive issues it soon evolves into emotionally charged discussion that then turns to affective conflict. It would seem that this could be avoided if members took their role as participant–analyst seriously and used their conflict management skills to intervene.

Affective conflict, on the other hand, is rooted in emotional and interpersonal relations. Consider again this staff meeting. Suppose, instead, that after lengthy debate about the composition of these self-help groups, Bill says, "Joy, you want to meet only once a week because it would be convenient for you to do so. You know that these folks need more contact than that. I really resent your attitude about this." You can imagine how Joy responded to a remark that seemed to challenge her professionalism. "I can't imagine that you would say anything like that, Bill. Who do you think you are to read my mind and tell me what I think? You're dead wrong!"

Bill and Joy are engaged in affective conflict. This type of conflict is often characterized by clashes over self-oriented or personal needs. Thus the focus is on the interpersonal and social rather than on the substantive and topical.

Guetzkow and Gyr (1954) found that the type of conflict affected how the group best achieved consensus. They summarized their findings as follows:

> A group in substantive conflict tends to achieve consensus by emphasizing those factors that positively promote consensus. A group in affective conflict tends to achieve consensus by reducing those forces that hinder the achievement of consensus. This reduction is largely achieved by withdrawing from a situation in which these forces are present. (p. 373)

The group that is experiencing primarily substantive conflict solves its conflict largely through availability and use of facts and through efficient problem solving. Such groups are aided by warm, friendly, and nonrestrictive interpersonal relationships (Guetzkow & Gyr, 1954). George and Joy might have solved their substantive conflict by presenting their reasons for wanting different formats for meetings. Groups experiencing affective conflict, on the other hand, seem to handle conflict best by avoidance. They often withdraw in order to avoid meeting the issue head on. Withdrawal in this case reduces the force hindering consensus (Guetzkow & Gyr, 1954). In the case of Bill and Joy, after the brief interchange Bill withdrew from the conflict. In fact, he remained silent for the rest of the meeting.

Looking Back: A Quick Review

SUBSTANTIVE AND AFFECTIVE CONFLICT

Substantive	Differences related to issues or ideas
	Differences related to the content of the discussion
Affective	Differences related to the emotions
	Differences related to interpersonal relations
	Differences related to personalities

Edward E. Sampson and Arlene C. Brandon (1964) confirmed these findings. They called group members who engaged in substantive conflict *opinion deviates*; the members who engaged in affective conflict were termed *role deviates*. Sampson and Brandon found that an opinion deviate was met with increased interaction, presumably in order to exert pressure to conform. This interaction is largely affirming, since it focuses upon the person's ideas through rational discussion. Others may ask for reasons, suggest alternatives, explain their own positions, and the like. But behavior toward the role deviate was not affirming! Role deviates were almost completely ignored as punishment.

FUNCTIONS OF CONFLICT

Conflict is functional when it serves useful purposes such as the following.

Conflict Increases Involvement

Consider the last conflict you experienced. Did you care very much about the issues? (If not, you might have been unwilling to engage in a conflict over your differences.) Most of us are willing to risk the "pain" of conflict over important issues. This caring provides the stimulus for our initial involvement. But beyond this, hearing the issues and presenting arguments for our position increase this involvement.

A group of local church members met to discuss the church's strengths and weaknesses. These were leaders of the various church groups. As you might imagine, they had a high level of commitment. They came to the meeting with a certain level of involvement. But as they clashed over their differing views, they became even more interested and involved. Conflict drew them into a deeper commitment.

Once we become involved, we are likely to risk more, to say more, and to draw others into the discussion of an issue. Lively debate is often satisfying, especially if conflict is managed satisfactorily.

Conflict Provides an Outlet for Hostility

Groups can develop deep-seated hostilities that can be damaging to the social climate and task achievement. If a group can permit conflict, it might be a healthier group. Members realize they are accepted as whole people who express both positive and negative feelings. That same group of church leaders profited from airing their views. The leaders discovered their differences, were willing to disagree, and thereby came to a new level of understanding. They came to the meeting feeling a bit apprehensive, but engaging in conflict in this supportive atmosphere allowed its release. If the atmosphere had been nonsupportive, they may have released some tension but might have added new tension.

Conflict Promotes Cohesiveness

Many factors promote cohesiveness, and several are related to successful conflict management. A group establishes a history of being successful under difficult conditions by working through conflict. In addition, successful conflict management often means increased productivity, which promotes cohesiveness. Finally, when groups manage their conflict successfully, members develop commitment to one another.

Conflict Focuses Attention

Conflict can be beneficial in that it focuses attention on a problem that needs to be solved, clarifies the need for changes, exposes our values and what is important to us, and helps us understand the other person and his or her values (Johnson & Johnson, 2000).

Conflict Increases Group Productivity

We engage in group decision making to seek high-quality decisions. We expect that a group can make a better decision than an individual can make in a particular case. If speed rather than quality were primary, we would ask one individual to make the decision.

The time spent in conflict often yields a better product and therefore greater productivity than conflict-free decision making. L. Richard Hoffman and his associates (1962) investigated how groups that were engaged in conflict used their time. Conflict about ideas causes a group to search for more alternatives. The searching is responsible for improved decision quality. Further, Thomas Beisecker (1969) discovered that as the conflict over issues increased, the group's members increased their effort to arrive at solutions. Thus it seems clear that conflict over issues promotes critical thinking and thereby increases group productivity.

Conflict Increases the Chance of Genuine Commitment

The commonsense view of conflict is that a clash might cause members to retreat and be less committed. This view appears not to be the case (Riecken, 1952). If group members feel free to express their opposition and their arguments and if consensus is achieved, that announcement of support motivates group members to support the decision. Donald Ellis and B. Aubrey Fisher (1994, p. 225) conclude: "If members are committed enough to sustain social conflict over issues, they should remain committed once consensus is achieved. Superficial or false consensus is more likely to result from suppressed conflict than from expressed conflict."

A group that avoids conflict has much to lose. Interpersonal conflict in a group increases involvement, provides an outlet for hostility, promotes cohesiveness, increases productivity, and increases the chances for genuine commitment. But perhaps all these benefits presume successful conflict management. Conversely, conflict that tears the social fabric of the group is generally dysfunctional.

SOURCES OF CONFLICT

Knowing the source of conflict can help you isolate its causes, sort through alternative strategies, and decide what to do. The major sources of conflict are ideas, status, power, and goals.

Ideational and Value Conflict

Decision making requires presentation and testing of ideas. In this process, differences become evident, and arguments may ensue, creating a conflict that is useful. Thus productive groups encourage ideational conflict as a basis for emerging consensus.

Ideational conflict may sometimes focus on the values that underlie preference for a particular idea. Observe the intensity and length of conflict. Value-related conflict is generally more intense and more prolonged than purely ideational conflict.

For example, a case study used by teachers of small group communication is titled "Nat Bronson." This case involves a 14-year-old boy who has been caught taking a car for a joy ride. The discussion question is "What should the court do with Nat Bronson?" This is certainly a question of value—and very intense discussion, even turning into debate, often results. The decision revolves around religious and moral questions that center on the participants' values.

Value conflict centers on goals and means. If your group is having trouble making a decision, ask whether members agree on basic goals. Sometimes members submit one proposal after another that is rejected. This behavior is often a sign of a goal problem.

Verbally aggressive people attack both the ideas and the self-concepts of others. Without speculating about the causes, note that such behavior in groups violates the ethic of being a good member (Infante & Wigley, 1980). Aggression in a group usually dampens the spirit of free discussion and thereby reduces the quality of the group's decision.

Sometimes the problem is basic disagreement about how the group is proceeding. For example, overall goals are clear but no agreement has been reached about procedure. Be aware that sometimes a group member chooses to create procedural conflict to mask either interpersonal conflict or disagreement regarding the solution (Putnam, 1980). Nevertheless, value questions must be met before a group can productively weigh issues.

Status and Power Conflict

Status is the position of a member in a group hierarchy—a ranking of each member on the basis of the person's perceived importance. **Status consensus** is agreement about where various members fit in this hierarchy. Dissatisfaction with one's status will generally lead to tension and conflict.

All groups, as they meet to complete a task, work out a status hierarchy. The status the group members work out among themselves is called **achieved status.** Members weigh one another's contributions, personalities, and so forth and come to some sense of their importance to the group. This, of course, is usually not a topic of discussion, but people do size up other members. One of the high-status roles, for example, is that of leader. If the group accepts a person's influence attempt, it is saying, "We give you status in this group." In addition, some groups have an **ascribed status** hierarchy. This status is based upon designations given to members by the parent organization. In a business context, for example, the ascribed status comes from the organization's management. The achieved status would come from the relative importance members give to one another. Conflict can occur as the group members work through the process of establishing status.

Power is intimately related to status. **Power** is the perceived influence one person has over another. Conflict can arise when members think a person is using power inappropriately. For example, a member might try to use coercive power to gain acceptance for a plan. Group members might resist and cause conflict. At a different level, group members will not usually follow a person who is not prepared. Conflict ensues when someone with appointed rank tries to lead without preparation. You may be able to think of other examples of power abuse.

Goal Conflict

Of course, you may not always be able to identify a single source of conflict. Indeed, when conflict occurs in a group, it is usually drawn from more than one source. At other times, conflict may derive from someone who is pursuing personal goals.

Stanley E. Jones, Dean C. Barnlund, and Franklyn S. Haiman (1980) assert that one source of conflict is the **hidden agenda.** This term refers to goals or objectives that a member or members have, and choose not to reveal, that differ from those of the group. For example, a member may try to dominate the group in order to increase his or her status. Goal conflict from a hidden agenda is likely to take one of two forms. "It may be a *status conflict* masquerading as an ideational dispute." Or "although the issue is purely a *socioemotional* one at heart, it surfaces as ideational conflict" (Jones, Barnlund, & Haiman, 1980, p. 140).

In the status dispute, a person may want to be more influential and so challenges ideas in order to seem influential. Perhaps the person wants to be taken more seriously but cannot say that directly, so he or she tries to gain status by challenging the ideas of higher-status members. A socioemotional problem happens when a person, disliked by some group members, challenges their ideas to get even.

But how do you know when a member is pursuing a hidden agenda? Look to nonverbal behavior and watch for the excessively negative. Suppose a person makes several

---

Looking Back: A Quick Review

SOURCES OF CONFLICT

Ideas and values	*Ideas*—Center on information and concepts *Values*—Center on desires and means
Status and power	*Status*—Centers on one's position in the group *Power*—Centers on influence one person has over the other
Goals	Center on anticipated outcomes of the group's effort

---

judgmental statements in a row. Perhaps the person can't seem to see anything positive about a particular person and/or that person's ideas. Expect disagreements to be couched in antagonistic terms, but notice overly cutting and negative remarks. You might observe one member not respecting another. Perhaps the person makes remarks that directly call into question the other's intellect or competence. Perhaps the person jokes about the other's personality. Disagreements can happen without negativism and personal attacks. When they do happen that way, though, they may signal a hidden agenda. Also, watch the patterns of interaction. Two high contributors vying for status will sometimes attack each other. A challenger will direct attacks at the high-status person.

A hidden socioemotional agenda is more difficult to spot. The person may avoid eye contact while engaged in ideational conflict. Such behavior, coupled with argument, may signal a hidden socioemotional agenda. If group members can agree to and become committed to a goal that every member can support, this goal is likely to become more important than their individual goals. This can enhance each member's desire to work together and provide an opportunity for the leader to reward the members collectively, a leadership activity that enhances team building (Kirkman & Shapiro, 2000).

You can tell from this discussion that there are many sources of conflict and that it may be difficult to discover an exact cause. It makes sense to try to understand as much about conflict as possible. But what method might best help you to manage conflict? The next section addresses conflict-management strategies.

MANAGING CONFLICT

The manager of a marketing department handled conflict by raising his voice to shouting level. Then he reminded the others of their respective status in the department. He made it clear that whatever they had to say was not really important. This man won the issue because he had power. He lost whatever respect these people had for him. He damaged relationships. The resentment he created also affected those who had to carry out decisions that resulted from such sessions. They were reluctant to expend effort.

This section begins by pointing out kinds of conflict management to avoid. Then we examine appropriate strategies you can learn. But first, a word of caution: You must weigh a situation carefully to make judgments about what will work for you in a particular group context. For example, in a work group under some circumstances, a strategy of using power and confrontation may be the best. Change the situation or the context, and this forcing strategy may be the worst alternative.

Dysfunctional Conflict-Management Strategies

Do not say, "Communicate more"   Some people naïvely believe that if they would just communicate more, then they would agree. More communication may occasionally be the answer, but not necessarily. You may understand something perfectly and still be in hot disagreement! When people suggest this strategy, they may mean we should communicate differently. Good advice. To communicate differently is to turn to another strategy.

Do not say, "Cooperate more"   Cooperation is certainly helpful, but it is not easy, and it may not be enough. People in conflict are usually unable to cooperate on an issue. Telling them to cooperate is not particularly useful. Can you imagine how effective this strategy might be when two angry members are abusing each other over one's hidden agenda? Harold finally says, "Okay, bub. If that's the way you want it, you'll have to do it over my dead body!" Kenneth says, "Step outside." You say, "Aw, come on, guys, cooperate!"

Do not blame the other person or the group   Even if you believe the other person is the cause of your differences, blaming behavior leads to defensiveness. Defensiveness leads to a rigid position, which leads to poor communication, which often leads to lashing out. The people you blame will not be at a loss for a response. They are likely to blame back!

Do not attack the other person or persons   Name-calling is a very common mode of attack, a mode of self-defense, and a common reaction as conflict escalates (Waln, 1982). It also involves fallacies in reasoning, as was suggested in the "Errors in Reasoning" section of Chapter 2. This refers to making judgmental statements about another person. To illustrate, you might say, "You're so lazy. You never come to the meeting prepared." This statement attacks the person by calling him or her lazy. This behavior would produce defensiveness, and so it is not a very helpful strategy for dealing with conflict.

Do not be too general   Some people figure you're better off stating your complaint in general terms. They reason that the more specific you are, the easier for an opponent to argue against it. The idea that general statements do not give the opposition ammunition with which to fight back is right in one sense. This kind of behavior confuses an opponent. But it also makes constructive action difficult. Defining the conflict in terms of specific behaviors gives members a starting point to discuss the problem.

Do not avoid conflict   Groups often create a norm that emphasizes the need for agreement. For example, the boss who tried to manage conflict by shouting also tried to head off all conflict in public meetings. Some of the strategies he employed would make amusing stories if they were not true. This boss seemed to believe in these strategies—at least, he often used them! He would:

- Tell group members that they were in danger of losing something and therefore must present a united front.

- Tell those who disagreed that they were not "team players."

- Tell group members that he knew they would do the "right thing."

- Hold the controversial agenda item until the end of the meeting when the opposition may have left or become tired.

You can see that a strategy of heading off conflict can create resentment and can decrease productivity.

Do not try to keep people talking so long that they give up   Group members who use this strategy try to manage conflict by sustaining it. They often make statements that appear to be group centered but are actually designed to keep people talking. One might say, "I'm glad we are able to take as much time as we need to resolve this problem. It's good to get it all out." This strategy may seem legitimate, but if the group has ever experienced a "keep 'em talking" strategy before, members are likely to feel considerable tension next time they meet. People often vote yes to bring an issue to a close! Considerable hostility and distrust may result from the experience.

Strategies for Managing Conflict

A small group can use a number of strategies to manage conflict. What is important is that they prove to be functional for your group. Disagreement is a frequent phenomenon in groups, so what is important is that we learn how to disagree effectively.

Here we present several strategies and show their likely outcome so that you can evaluate what might work for your group. You can probably compose a list of strategies yourself by recalling your last several experiences with conflict. Your list might look something like this (Burke, 1977):

1. *Forcing*   Using power to make the other person accept a position; each party tries to figure out how to get the upper hand, causing the other person to lose. For example, "I think we've talked long enough about this. As chair, I'll settle the issue. We will install a light at the corner of Maryknoll and Hillcrest."

2. *Withdrawal*   Retreating from the argument. For example, "Let's not talk about that today. I'd rather move on to something else."

3. *Smoothing*   Playing down the conflict (differences) and emphasizing the positive (common interests), or avoiding issues that might cause hard feelings. For example, "I know

Looking Back: A Quick Review

AVOID THESE CONFLICT-MANAGEMENT STRATEGIES

Saying, "Communicate more."	Stating a complaint in general terms.
Saying, "Cooperate more."	Avoiding the conflict altogether.
Blaming a person or the group.	Keeping the people talking until they give up.
Attacking a person or the group.	

that we have our differences, but I hope we can put these aside, be professionals, and get on to making a decision."

4. *Compromise*   Looking for a position in which each gives and gets a little, splitting the difference; nobody wins all, each loses something. For example, "It looks like Joe would like to give the Athletic Boosters $1,000. Cindy would like to give the Intramural Programs the $1,000. Let's give each $500."

5. *Confrontation–problem solving*   Directing energies toward defeating the problem and not the other person; open exchange of information is encouraged; parties try to reach a solution that is optimal to all; the situation is defined as one in which everyone wins. For example, "I can see that we have a difference of opinion as to where to spend $1,000 for athletics. What are some of the options for handling this?"

In his book *Interpersonal Conflict Resolution,* Alan Filley (1988) has given us some insights about these methods. He classified them according to their likely outcomes: win–lose, lose–lose, and win–win. A win–lose outcome occurs when one party in the conflict achieves his or her goal and the other loses. Lose–lose outcomes occur if, as a result of a conflict-management episode, both parties lose or fail to achieve all or part of their goals. A win–win strategy results in conflict management that is to be applauded. If two parties in a conflict manage their differences so that both parties achieve their goals, they have employed a win–win strategy. Since most of the time we are better off when both parties achieve their goals, we aim for a win–win strategy.

Win–lose methods   **Forcing** is primarily a win–lose situation because it calls for one person's view or goals to be accepted and the other's to be rejected. Small groups employ a number of forcing strategies. For example, the very powerful leader of a work group may let it be known that those who do not go along will suffer. A not-so-obvious method of forcing in groups where a vote is appropriate is the majority vote. The neighborhood PTA may tire of discussion and may take a vote to force a decision.

Voting forces one group to accept the other's views or goals or solutions. If the minority complains too much, the "good loser" ethic is often evoked—this states that it is not appropriate to complain after the majority has voted. Although voting can be an acceptable method of conflict management, a win–win method might be attempted initially.

Withdrawal is employed as a method of obstructing a decision. Often the withdrawing person only obstructs the effort temporarily, and those who remain in the group win the issue. This is a win–lose method because withdrawal of support is rarely effective. Instead, there is now no opposition, and the person's absence in effect gives tacit permission to do what it wants. On the occasions when this is effective, it is usually so because the group needs the person's support. Once in a while the "loser" actually becomes the winner.

Members who have a high concern for the social dimension often pursue this style. They are likely to withdraw their concern and accommodate that of others when conflict seem likely, even if it means a less effective outcome. This outcome is frequently viewed as undesirable, but might be viewed as good when it is a cooperative effort to get beyond a long period of intense, unproductive argument.

Lose–lose methods   Alan Filley (1988) suggests that **compromise** is generally a lose–lose situation. We refer to it as lose–lose because neither party is fully satisfied. Sometimes it may be necessary to seek a compromise, but if this is the initial effort at managing conflict it can create a problem. The problem is that each gives something *and* may resent having to do so. Compromise implies some reluctance, unless people have been genuinely unsuccessful at achieving consensus. If they have worked hard at consensus and failed, then they may be less resentful at having to compromise. Compromise is usually a second-best outcome. It generally provides a workable solution, but not the best solution. Scholars Pruitt and Rubin (1986) believe it is a result of lazy problem solving or simply yielding by both sides of the issue.

Smoothing is also a lose–lose strategy. Playing down, or perhaps "burying," the differences rarely dissolves the underlying tension in the group. Instead it allows the problematic situation to simmer and fester. This is apt to undermine the group's potential. The conflict may even emerge later at an escalated level. Since the conflict may only be set aside for the time being, both parties are potential losers.

Win–win methods   Donald Ellis and Aubrey Fisher (1994, p. 244) suggest that "the best decisions and conflicts are integrative and collaborative, which means the members integrate resources to work toward the common goal." These two notions are operative in confrontation–problem solving. **Confrontation–problem solving** is a win–win strategy because it allows the group to collaborate in an attempt to gain consensus. When the members of the group are not particularly far apart, they may be able to make a decision merely by focusing on goals and discussing information that relates to the problem.

Consensus means there is agreement among all the group's members. Sometimes it may be relatively easy to achieve. However, when parties are polarized in opinions or

Looking Back: A Quick Review

CONFLICT STRATEGIES AND OUTCOMES

Strategy	Definition	Likely Outcome
Forcing	Using power to gain acceptance Voting	Win–lose
Withdrawal	Retreating from the conflict	Win–lose
Smoothing	Playing down the conflict Avoiding the issue and pretending it is not important	Lose–lose
Compromise	Each side gives a little of what they want Nobody wins all; each loses something	Lose–lose
Confrontation–problem solving	Directs energies to defeat the problem Attempts to reach an optimal solution A collaborative effort	Win–win

when various possible solutions seem equally acceptable, a more systematic approach is needed. The key is to shift attention from solutions to goals. We will examine this in the next section, which addresses conflict management directly.

In general, you will be seen more negatively and as having lower competence if you manage conflict with a win–lose strategy. On the other hand, if you use an integrative win–win strategy, focusing on the issue or content of the conflict, you are likely to be perceived more positively, especially by others who use the distributive strategy also (McKinney, Kelly, & Duran, 1997). The competent communicator usually uses the confrontation–problem solving management style, while the less competent communicator chooses the forcing strategy most often (Canary & Spitzberg, 1987; Gottman & Silver, 1994, 1999).

MANAGING INTERPERSONAL CONFLICT

Most of us find it easier to confront ideas than to confront people. This difficulty is easy to understand. Consider the difference between saying, "I disagree with you," and saying, "I believe that you are obstructing the group by your continual objections." Most of us would find the first statement easier to make than the second.

Interpersonal problems may be group problems because they hinder goal achievement. But they are also personal problems. Thus they necessitate a decision about whether they are best handled in the group or individually. It may well be that one person can find an effective channel through some other group member to the second party in an interpersonal conflict. Individuals can be unnecessarily embarrassed when approached about their behavior in an open meeting. A member who possesses good interpersonal skills, is respected by the disruptive person, and is willing to approach that person may be successful in managing the conflict with a private conversation. If a private conversation doesn't work, the group can make the problem an agenda item. Rensis Likert (1961, p. 176) provides a clear statement of this process and its likely results. He indicates:

> At such times, it may be necessary for the group to stop its intellectual activity and in one way or another to look at and deal with the disruptive emotional stress. After this has been done, the group can then go forward with greater unity.

Open confrontation, then, involves making the interpersonal problem an agenda item. When the group has managed the conflict, positive results generally accrue.

Preliminary Considerations

Here are six guidelines you may find useful if you decide to confront a member.

1. *Talk with other group members to confirm your perceptions and conclusions.* Your attempt to confront may not be successful if others in your group disagree, so ask them what they are thinking about the problem or let them know that something is bothering you (Jarboe & Witteman, 1996).

2. *Make a list of the specific behaviors you have observed as being disruptive.* Presenting general statements about the disruptive behavior is likely to produce arguments from the person involved. Description of days, times, and actual behaviors may minimize both defensiveness and argument.

3. *Have some tentative suggestions in mind to present if needed.* The person may say, "You've said what you don't like. Now tell me what you want." Beyond this possibility, it is important that you have some tentative, positive suggestions.

4. *Be prepared to listen carefully to the other person's view.* Listening is very important in confrontation. Most people believe that they have good reasons for their behavior. They want you to hear those reasons. When you have listened carefully and the other person knows that you have, the person feels understood and may be more open to change.

5. *Be prepared to use supportive communication behaviors.* Review the discussion of supportive and defensive communication in Chapter 8. Supportiveness in interpersonal conflict is essential to its skillful management.

6. *Attempt to integrate the views of others when possible.* A certain type of argument seems to facilitate consensus. Daniel J. Canary, Brent G. Brossmann, and David R. Seibold (1987) found that the only argument structure that proved to be statistically different between consensus and dissensus groups was the convergent argument. This argument integrates the views of others while the issue is being contested.

Looking Back: A Quick Review

INITIAL CONSIDERATIONS IN INTERPERSONAL CONFLICT MANAGEMENT

1. Confirm your perceptions about the situation with at least one other person.
2. Objectively list specific disruptive behaviors you have observed.
3. Consider tentative solutions.

4. Understand how to and be prepared to listen effectively.
5. Understand how to and be prepared to use supportive communication.
6. Attempt to integrate the views of others if possible.

A final suggestion for managing interpersonal conflict involves the group's discussing how it is doing. Some ongoing groups are able to spend some time during each meeting—usually at the beginning or end—to discuss how they are getting along. The leader of a weekly meeting of religious leaders said, "Let's take a few minutes to review our progress and see how you think our last meeting went." If the leader can promote this kind of activity, then the group can gain a sense of progress as well as handle interpersonal issues. Concerns will not come out unless the group is convinced that it is all right to talk about feelings and the problems. A session in which the group successfully manages conflict provides an advantageous time to initiate this sort of procedure.

But the skills of direct confrontation have not yet been described. Is there a better way to confront someone? Is there a skillful way to be clear about another person's disruptive or boorish behaviors in a group? Fortunately, there is.

EFFECTIVE CONFRONTATION IN GROUPS

Suppose you have decided to confront an individual in your group. Experience and a good deal of research suggest the following advice.

Be Sure You Want to Confront

Often people get themselves into trouble in groups because they act too hastily. Something occurs that creates a conflict and then, without thinking things through, one member confronts another. Every confrontation is important enough that you ought to make sure you want to confront. But what should you consider in deciding whether to confront?

First, put some time between the conflict moment and your decision. This pause allows you to examine your motives for the choice to confront. Here are some questions to ask yourself: What do you want to accomplish? What is motivating you? Is there some perceived injustice that another is imposing upon you or the group? Are you grinding a private ax? Do you have a private hidden agenda? What are you feeling that triggers the inclination to confront? If what is motivating you is the good of the group, you might go ahead. If you are trying to get even, you may want to reconsider.

Second, examine the situation from all relevant points of view. You may not be fully aware of your own point of view. Of course, that is the reason for the first comment above. But you may not be aware of the other's point of view either. Perhaps there are reasons for his or her behavior. You might examine the situation from the other person's perspective. Ask yourself whether you have discovered, so far as you are able, what the individual is thinking. What motives could there be for the behavior? For example, does Herb know something you do not know? Is his point of view correct? Even from his point of view, what does he want from the group? What is he feeling? Suppose that his child has been hospitalized. Would that be important?

Third, determine whether or not confrontation is appropriate from a commonsense perspective. Ask yourself these questions: Is the payoff worth the price? For example, in the task dimension, are you likely to get what you want by confrontation? In the relationships of the group, will confrontation create greater problems than it solves? Perhaps Herb will become disruptive if confronted. Is there a power relationship that creates an ineffective payoff–price ratio? (For instance, perhaps Herb is the chair of this committee. Is it wise to confront him on this issue?) And in the final analysis, are you likely to achieve enough of your goal by confrontation to justify going ahead? How much of what you want would you be likely to get without the confrontation?

Set Your Goals

Do not confront someone until you are clear about what you want to accomplish. What do you want that you are not getting? Do you want Herb to come fully prepared even if his son is hospitalized? Do you really mind if he needs to be a little late? Sometimes people do things you do not want. So the question is, What are you getting that you do not want? Ask these questions about the tasks of the group and about your task goals. Then ask them about your relationship with the other person. Do you want to feel differently? Do you want Herb to change any of his attitudes? Maybe Herb is short-tempered and not tolerant of other members.

The other person can choose to behave differently if you are able to ask in particular terms about the behavior you want changed. So after you have identified your goals in the most primitive way, put them into positive statements about the other person's behavior. For example, you might write, "I want Herb to be more tolerant, tentative, and considerate of others' ideas when he talks." That would be much more helpful to Herb than telling him (and writing down), "I want Herb to stop bullying the group." To you, both statements may mean the same thing. To Herb they will mean quite different things indeed.

When you have identified the goals you want to accomplish, determine whether the other person can give you what you want. If the other cannot do so, there does not seem to be any reason to confront. Perhaps the fact that Herb's son is hospitalized leaves him no alternatives. If the other person can give you what you want, then continue.

Select the Right Channel

Given the goal you have identified and your determination that a confrontation is appropriate, are you the right person to do it? If not, who is? Either way, should the confrontation be oral? Written? Both? Should it be face to face? By telephone? There may be very good reasons to confront a person face to face, but there may be other, equally good reasons not to do that. Similarly, it might be wise for you to confront the individual personally, and it might be wise for someone other than you to do the confronting. For instance, suppose that you have been a very verbal group member. You have taken a position opposing Herb before. There might be a risk that now, if the confrontation comes from you, Herb and the group members will perceive it as a continuation of earlier disagreements. Thus you might get someone else to do the confronting.

Set the Time for the Confrontation Carefully

Confrontation almost always follows a conflict situation. If the appropriate time is not selected, you run the risk that neither party will be open to communication. Moreover, emotions may still run high immediately following a conflict or potential conflict. Thus the latitude of acceptance of both parties is down. This can be a critical issue in selecting the time for a confrontation.

Do not confront someone when there is not enough time to do so. A 30-minute conversation cannot occur in 10 minutes. If you cannot anticipate the time required, err on the side of too much time. For example, you may suppose that you can handle the situation in about half an hour. Do not select a time when you have only 30 minutes available. You cannot know how things will go during the confrontation.

Do not confront someone while the flood of feelings is still running high. Rather, put enough time between the conflict moment and the confrontation to allow both parties to get their emotions under control and to get some perspective. Perhaps, if you decide to confront Herb, you should do so at the end of the meeting. Assume that the other individual is working on the conflict situation just as you are. Allow time for that to happen.

Allow enough time for advance planning to occur. If you are going to confront an individual, asking for a goal that will take time to implement, it makes no sense to ask for that goal if there is no time for the implementation.

A sign on the wall of an executive office at International Paper Company reads: "We can manage difficult problems in a couple of days. The impossible ones require a little more time." If you ask another group member for something you want, allow that person enough time to give it!

Choose the Setting Carefully

Where you elect to confront Herb may make the difference in success or failure. Should the location be neutral? Should it lend support to you, at the risk of being perceived as threatening by Herb? Should the location give the advantage to Herb? For instance, a person's office or home is his territory. He probably feels comfortable there. He probably has arranged the space so that he can control the flow and ebb of power and interaction. He may have a barrier he can choose to use. Should the confrontation occur in a private or a more-or-less public setting? If you take Herb to lunch, will that setting allow for the full range of expression that must occur if you are to be successful? With that thought in mind, would it be best to put the confrontation into a setting that will impose itself upon the confrontation? If Herb is prone to making scenes, will the setting invite that?

Stay in the Present Tense

You have now determined to confront; you have a clear set of goals in mind, stated in terms of the other's behaviors. You have determined to meet the individual through a particular select channel, and you have carefully set the time and setting for the confrontation. You are ready to talk. Resist talking about the past.

Herb cannot do anything to retrieve past behaviors. If you are confronting, you are beyond the conflict moment. But that does not mean that you must dwell on that moment. Neither you nor the other can restructure the past—and you do not have to. Your relationship with the other individual, including what you remember of any conflict situation, is a present-tense phenomenon. So stay in the present. Perhaps you can tell Herb how much the group needs his help. You might ask him if there is anything you can do to help in the future.

Negotiate for future behavior changes. Herb cannot take back something he said or did yesterday, but he can agree not to say or do it again. He cannot undo what he did yesterday, but he can agree to behave differently tomorrow. And it is clearly the case that, if he cannot take back or undo the past, neither can you. If you try to hold Herb to his transgressions and omissions, you create an impossible situation for both of you. Stay in the present and talk about the future.

Personalize Your Talk

The term **personalize** means that you should talk about yourself. Personalized talk makes clear that the person doing the talking is owning up to his or her own responsibilities, feelings, weaknesses, and strengths. Steven Winer and Randall Majors (1981) found this kind of talk is perceived as more supportive than other types of pronoun construction. It is characterized by references to your own feelings and wants and judgments, rather than references to the other person's feelings, wants, and judgments. Thus if you say to Herb, "You behaved foolishly," you are putting your judgment on him. It would be far better to refer to your own feelings: "It *seems to me* that your behavior was foolish." Don't use foolish here either. Describe his behavior.

Table 10.1 provides both personalized and other-directed versions of the same sentences. Some of these are exaggerated in order to make the point. You will see instantly that the underlying principle is that effective communication is honest and self-aware. Learning to talk honestly may take some practice, and it is absolutely essential if you are going to confront someone like Herb.

TABLE 10.1 Some Personalized and Other-Directed Sentences

Other-Directed Sentences	Personalized Sentences
You make me angry.	I get angry when I see that behavior.
You're always acting silly and horsing around.	Your behavior seems silly to me. I don't like it.
That idea doesn't make sense.	I can't make sense out of that idea.
I can see the point you're trying to make, but you're wrong. The real issue is . . .	I can see the point you're trying to make, but I don't agree. From my point of view . . .
There isn't enough evidence to make that claim.	I don't think the evidence is sufficient to support that claim.
You're late again. Looks like you don't care very much about this group.	You're late again. I'm guessing that you don't care very much about this group.
It's important that we meet before next Wednesday.	I'm not satisfied, and I think we need another meeting before next Wednesday.
It's just not fair for you to shirk on your share of the group effort.	I'm feeling resentful. Based on what I can tell, you have chosen not to follow through on your commitment to do these things.
You ought to say what you mean.	My guess is that you are not saying what you mean, and I have a rule in my head that I would like to impose upon you.
You simply must learn to prepare for these weekly meetings.	I don't believe you have been preparing for these meetings, and I am feeling frustrated.
I can't do that.	I choose not to do that.

Be Supportive

We have come full circle. If you are going to confront Herb successfully, you must learn to be supportive. The kinds of behaviors that minimize defensiveness and tend to maximize supportiveness have already been described. Review Table 8.1 (p. 236) very carefully. A large part of learning to be supportive is learning to talk to another person in ways that are descriptive, problem oriented, spontaneous, and empathic. So be descriptive and problem oriented in describing Herb's behavior. You cannot be supportive if you are also suggesting superiority. Equality and tentativeness thus characterize supportive discourse as well.

Constructive confrontations include exploring and clarifying the issues, the needs of the group members, and their feelings (Johnson & Johnson, 2000). They involve planning, tact, and truth telling (Lerner, 1989). Constructive conflict is cooperative; it has its basis in joint problem solving, and in attempting to maintain a working relationship (Johnson, Johnson, & Tjosvold, 2000; Wilmont & Hocker, 1998).

These ideas have been drawn together into a checklist to help you manage confrontations better.

Looking Back: A Quick Review

CONFRONTATION CHECKLIST FOR MANAGING CONFLICT

1. Am I sure I want to confront?
   - Have I examined my own motives?
   - Have I examined the situation from the other's view?
   - Is confrontation appropriate in this case?
     a. Is the payoff worth the price?
     b. Have I examined the power relationship?
     c. If the confrontation is successful, what percentage of the goal will I likely achieve?
2. Have I selected the appropriate channel?
   - Have I stated my wants and expectations in terms of the other person's behavior?
   - Have I stated my wants in terms of both task and relationship?
   - Can the other person give me what I want?
3. Have I selected the appropriate channel?
   - Face to face?
   - In writing?
   - By telephone?
   - Should someone else do the confronting?
4. Have I selected the best time for the confrontation?
   - Latitude of acceptance?
   - Closure?
   - Emotions under control?
   - Enough time to implement what I am asking?
5. Have I selected the best location or setting?
   - Private or public?
   - My space, the other's space, neutral space?
6. Have I committed myself to the present tense?
7. Have I rehearsed the situation, taking care to personalize the talk?
8. Have I practiced being supportive?

MANAGING IDEATIONAL CONFLICT

Figure 10.1 shows a sequence of choices with respect to managing ideational conflict.

Confrontation–problem solving

↓

Compromise

↓

Majority vote

↓

Arbitration

FIGURE 10.1
Sequence of Choices for Managing Ideational Conflict

Focus on Research

INSTILLING TRUST DURING CONFLICT

Sometimes group members find themselves engaged in disagreement, confrontation, and escalating conflict. If they are locked in this pattern very long, they may find that mutual trust has been severely damaged. What suggestions do researchers offer to break this cycle?

Lindskold (1978, pp. 772–773) offers this bit of wisdom: "If the other party could only be trusted to be cooperative in search of the mutually beneficial solution, then the cycle could be reversed, and both parties could gain rather than lose." Others agree that one solution is to try to show a spirit of cooperation. Deutsch (1973) and Lindskold (1978) suggest that communication, consistency, and cooperative initiatives are crucial.

According to the researchers, to restore trust and cooperation, you should do the following (Lindskold, Han, & Betz, 1986):

1. Communicate your intent in specific terms and make clear reference to trust, cooperation, and fairness where appropriate.

2. If your actions are to be viewed as credible, make sure your behavior matches your stated intention. If you promise something, you must do it.

3. Respond cooperatively to those who are being competitive, even if you know the others intend to compete.

4. Respond with behavior that matches that of those who failed to respond to your invitation to cooperate.

M. Deutsch (1973). *The resolution of conflict.* New Haven, CT: Yale University Press.

S. Lindskold (1978). Trust development, the GRIT proposal, and the effects of conciliatory acts on conflict and cooperation. *Psychological Bulletin, 85,* 772–793.

S. Lindskold, G. Han, and B. Betz (1986). Essential elements of communication in the GRIT strategy. *Personality and Social Psychology Bulletin, 12,* 179–186.

Confrontation–Problem Solving

Ideational conflict needs to be confronted and kept at the ideational level if possible. This kind of conflict can easily escalate to the interpersonal level if people become ego-involved. Stanley Jones, Dean C. Barnlund, and Franklyn S. Haiman (1980) have suggested a method of managing ideational conflict that attempts to avoid this problem. They call this process the "cone of consensus seeking."

Jones argues that issues have their *beginning in assertions* of group members. For example, if we were sitting in on the deliberations of a personnel committee, such an assertion might be "We should fire Smith." This might be countered by "No, we should give her another chance." Then the discussion of Smith's job performance might go on in this manner for a minute or two. If the differences are merely semantic, the members might be able to resolve them at this level. However, when groups do not achieve consensus, members may find their discussion moving from assertions about the issue to assertions about one another. One such comment might be "You know, Pete, you really do not understand this issue. If you did, you couldn't possibly believe as you do." Note that the conflict has moved to the interpersonal level. Interpersonal conflict is generally more difficult to deal with than ideational conflict. Shifting the conflict to the interpersonal level might be avoided by moving the argument to *the next level of ideational conflict—reasoning*.

Reasoning involves more rationality than assertion does. The group leadership should ask those in the conflict to provide the reasons behind their assertions. This strategy forces members to expose the logic behind their ideas, providing a new area for discussion and potential agreement. In the case of firing Smith, the group might agree to wait one more year when it discovers that a member believes this is reasonable because Smith has not been adequately informed of the expected standards.

Members may believe that no particularly valid argument has been presented at this level, and before long they may move toward a premature vote. Conflict should be moved to the *third level* rather than *voting*. *Evidence needs to be provided*. The group may need to go out and conduct more research. In Smith's case, perhaps she needs to be interviewed and observed, and her work needs to be studied carefully. Armed with this evidence, the group may be more ready to continue its discussion. A stalemate at this point suggests that the group needs to move to a final level—values.

People who hear the same evidence and arrive at different conclusions may be in conflict over values. An individual's willingness to accept a particular idea may hinge upon what he or she thinks is good or proper or desirable. This is the most difficult of the levels of ideational conflict, but values can and should be questioned. Values ought to be subject to critical examination just as ideas are.

The easiest way of testing a value is through direct observation. To illustrate, suppose the president of a tennis club believes that strong, autocratic control is not a desirable method for leading a group whose membership is voluntary. But Don Johnson, who is chairperson of the membership committee, is fond of this style of leadership. The president of the club could attend one of Don's meetings and observe his style. Objective observations allow him to test the value of the method in the specific context. He might even formulate questions that would allow him to examine the underlying basis for this value. He might ask: Why is the autocratic leadership method undesirable to me? What is my basis for believing this? Is this basis valid? Why? So you see that the suggestions offered by Stanley Jones, Dean Barnlund, and Franklyn Haiman can be used to guide your group through a logical sequence as you address ideational conflict. Some groups do this without prompting. Other groups need leadership. Of course, you ought to provide this leadership when it is needed.

There is other evidence that Jones's suggestions really work. Researchers Harold Guetzkow and John Gyr (1954) produced the following conclusions from their extensive study of groups in conflict:

A degree of conflict is necessary and helpful when related to the task.

Facts and expert judgment help resolve substantive conflict.

An orderly treatment of topics is helpful.

Members should discuss one issue at a time rather than discuss several issues.

Members must understand what is being said.

Leaders of groups with substantive conflict should do much more direct seeking for information of an objective factual nature, largely by questioning, and should offer tentative solutions.

One apparently helpful technique for increasing the chance of achieving consensus is to *backtrack and review areas of agreement*. Research by VanLear and Mabry (1999) discovered that groups that were able to keep refocusing the group's attention on areas of agreement, especially following episodes of disagreement, were more likely to reach consensus than groups that continued to focus on the negative.

At this point, if the conflict still persists, a group may have exhausted its ability to reach consensus. The question becomes, Is there some middle ground in which those involved are willing to give what it takes to move together? Notice that the assumptions here are that further talk will not yield consensus and that no particular position that has already been stated should emerge as the decision.

Compromise

Compromise can result in pseudoconsensus. Once a group has compromised its original position and has agreed upon a decision, members may still have reservations about the decision. When people give up something, they lose, and they may not be at all satisfied with the outcome. If you were to question group members privately, they might say, "We couldn't reach an agreement, so I gave in for the sake of the group. I don't really like the outcome, and I don't agree with the decision."

Compromise may be necessary when confrontation–problem solving does not work. When a group has met and struggled with a problem *and* talked back and forth about the issue and cannot achieve consensus, then compromise is appropriate.

The problem you face beyond actually finding some acceptable middle ground is achieving as much commitment to the decision as possible. It is a good idea to reestablish commitment to the group's goals. People have been willing to participate in a struggle to attain consensus. They apparently value the group's goals. You might say something like "We've been struggling hard to come up with a decision and haven't been able to do it. Is that how other people see it?" (Stop here and see whether you have agreement.) "It seems like we could abandon the project or try to work out a compromise. What do you think?" (Pause and let group members affirm the group's goal or say that they want to abandon it. If they show commitment, confirm their commitment.) You might say, "I'm glad you think the project is important enough that we continue. One of the problems that I've experienced with compromise is that everyone gives and takes. The taking is usually easy; the giving is hard, and it creates disappointments. Are you folks committed enough to seeing us complete our work that you are willing to give and take?" (If the answer is yes, you are ready to discuss a compromise.)

Keep in mind that the language suggested here is only a sample. Students often ask for some model—a concrete sense of how to verbalize the text's suggestions. If you decide to try it, you should carry out this idea using your own words.

A Question of Ethics and Responsibility

PROBLEMS AT THE DEPARTMENT OF MOTOR VEHICLES

Charles Peterson is the manager of the State Department of Motor Vehicles office in Midville, a city of 162,000. He supervises six driver inspectors, an administrative assistant, seven clerk-typists, and an assistant branch manager.

Charlie seemed to be liked by all, until recently. Now there seems to be a good bit of ill will toward him from some of his employees. Dave Stone, a driver inspector, reflects this attitude. He said, "Charlie seemed to care about me, and I thought I could talk to him. But I have changed my mind. Now I don't trust him at all. That 'nice guy' facade he wears is phony."

Marisa Pina, a clerk-typist, reports, "I went to him about a problem I was having with one of the clerks in the headquarters at the capital. He smiled and said, 'Marisa, I'll look into this right away. Is there anything else wrong?' But I never heard anything about it. I went to him again, and it was the same old story—big smile and no response."

Lynn Holstein, the assistant branch manager, complains, "He told me that he was going to rec-

ommend me for a branch manager's position that was open in Hamilton. I went to see him about the opening one day. He told me how he thought I was ready for such a career move and would support my application by personally calling the state personnel director that afternoon. I submitted my letter of application and my résumé. About three weeks later, I called personnel to find out the status of my application. They said they were holding it because they needed a letter or some other kind of input from my immediate supervisor."

The situation is getting worse as morale continues this downward trend. Lynn talked at lunch one day with Dave, Marisa, and two others who had complaints. They all agreed that Charlie was probably not aware of the problem. Further, they thought if they approached him informally he would be receptive to making some changes in the way he approached them and their work.

What advice would you have for this group regarding how to manage interpersonal conflict and talk to Charlie?

Majority Vote

Stanley Jones, Dean Barnlund, and Franklyn Haiman (1980, p. 151) provide three very good questions that will help you decide whether a majority vote is called for to resolve conflict:

> First, are the motives of the members really so much in conflict that, given more time for exploration, they might not be able to come to an agreement?

You might size up how close member positions are. Are there some points of agreement? Do members seem to be moving closer? Are their statements becoming more general? Often as groups are moving to agreement they drop the presentation of evidence and make less absolute statements. For example, "The best way of handling the increase in violence in our neighborhood is a crime watch patrol. And here is why . . ." may become "One way to handle the violence is a crime watch patrol." You might also ask the group if it wishes to continue talking or if it is ready to vote.

> Second, is time really at a premium?

Is there a deadline for a decision? If not, try to discover whether members have time to meet again. Ask whether they think it would be valuable to continue by either extending this meeting or calling another. If they think further discussion is a good idea, proceed with it.

> Third, will a majority vote truly produce the greatest good for the greatest number when the members of that majority have not had an opportunity to come to a full appreciation of the minority's feelings?

Often a vote is taken without adequate opportunity for the minority to be heard. Decide whether the minority position has been fully explained. You might do so by trying to summarize the minority position, including its arguments, in your own words. Ask whether other members believe you have accurately reflected the minority's ideas.

If you can answer yes to all three of these questions, your group can appropriately take a vote. But keep in mind these problems:

> If the vote seriously disadvantages the minority, then resentment sets in.

> If the minority is needed to carry out the plan, minority members may resist.

> If membership in your group is voluntary, minority members may quit.

If you answer no to some of these, your group may need to employ third-party intervention.

Arbitration

Arbitration involves the presentation of the group's arguments to a neutral third party, with the group agreeing in advance to accept the decision the person makes. The assumption on which arbitration rests is that the group cannot work out its problem and that voting would not work either. It is also assumed that the neutrality of the third party will produce a fair decision without causing either side the embarrassment of having to personally give in (Rubin, 1980).

Obviously, this method of managing conflict is open to the same criticism as compromise. Members will have given and taken and thus may be less than satisfied with the outcome. Sometimes it is possible to use a member of the group in this role. The group may recognize an uncommitted member who it trusts to make a fair decision. The role of arbitrator requires a very exceptional member, and it also places the person under extreme pressure. It is better to find an impartial outsider if possible. Perhaps the group

---

Looking Back: A Quick Review

CHOICES FOR MANAGING IDEATIONAL CONFLICT

Confrontation–problem solving	A collaborative settlement in which people talk directly about differences and relationship issues in order to achieve consensus.
Compromise	A negotiated settlement in which each party gives up part of what is wanted in order to get the other part.
Majority vote	A decision technique used to resolve conflict by polling members to determine which is the most favored view. This view is adopted.
Arbitration	A decision process in which the factions present their views of the situation and their favored outcomes to a third party (usually not a group member) who decides.

---

might even adopt an advisory role and allow the person who called the group together to make the final decision.

TRUST IN A CONFLICT SITUATION

Research by Lewicki & Wiethoff (2000) suggests three ways to restore trust in a conflict management situation. The first is to be consistent and reliable, meeting deadlines consistently over time. This might involve conciliatory actions, and giving one another time to see that these are made in good faith. The second is to establish common goals, values, purposes, or identities. Focus on the reasons for your meeting and discuss the importance of achieving the group's task. The third is to agree to a strategy for managing any situations that may appear to be trust violations. Perhaps members will agree to explain, apologize, and express regret for any harm done.

CONFLICT STYLES AND CULTURES

Your culture has norms that influence how you engage in conflict in groups (Mayer, 2000). Your culture may endorse a rational, direct approach, while another may endorse an intuitive, indirect approach. Your culture may favor the expression of strong feelings, but another may not. Your culture may teach you the message is in *what is said,* while another culture will teach members the message is in *how it is said* and even *what is not said.*

Studies of conflict style focus on examining the conflict styles of individuals within the cultures and then comparing their findings to the style identified from other cultures. Their generalizations are usually based on whether the culture is individualistic or collective in its orientation. **Individualistic cultures** are those that encourage individuals to pursue independence, self-interests, and autonomy. **Collectivistic cultures** encourage individuals to conform to group norms and show concern for the group. Researchers report that people from individualistic cultures are more direct and competitive when they engage in conflict. People from collectivistic cultures are more likely to avoid conflict out of concern for other members and are more likely to try to find a solution that takes into account both their needs and those of the others. This finding was evident in a study by Carnevale & Leung (2000) that compared Brazilians and Mexicans with citizens of the United States. The Brazilians and Mexicans were found to have more styles of conflict that showed high concern for others—accommodation and collaboration—than did people from the United States. Keep in mind, though, that although a culture may favor a particular style, there is likely to be a wide variation among individual members of that culture (Mayer, 2000).

CONFLICT AND CULTURAL DIFFERENCES

Different cultures represent a potential for conflict because they represent diverse values, beliefs, and attitudes. Of course, there are many shared beliefs if the members of the group share a common language. There are cultural diversities among the various groups represented by the U.S. population. We are male, female, Republicans, Democrats, Independents, African Americans, Caucasian Americans (of many varieties), Asian Americans, and Hispanic Americans, just to name a few differences.

The possibilities for differences in values, beliefs, and attitudes are enhanced when there are also members in our group from various international communities. Consider that various cultures view confrontation and argument differently. A major difference is a collectivist versus individualist view of the goals of communication. A member of an Asian culture may have the attitude that what is good for the group is good for me. A member of the U.S. culture may have the attitude that what is good for me is good for the group. The difference is obvious. You can easily see how this situation can become complicated and difficult to manage.

Awareness is the key to successful management of these kinds of differences. We will probably do nothing if we are not aware of the differences. The obvious question is, "What should we be looking for so that we will be able to anticipate any problems and manage them?"

1. Begin with understanding how you deal with the issue of participation in your group. Do you make a special effort to be sure all people in your group know that their ideas are welcome? It may be difficult for a member of another cul-

ture to be as assertive as members of the U.S. culture in expressing his or her ideas. You may need to encourage without being "pushy."

2. Understand there may also be a translation problem. The person may be translating back and forth from their language to English. This translating takes time and you will need to learn to be patient and not interrupt them.

3. Know that vigorous debate may be stimulating to you and intimidating or seen as in bad taste by a person from a collectivist culture, like Japan. Be careful that you do not automatically view this person as uninterested in the debate or "strange" if he or she holds back.

4. Check out your perceptions as best as you can. You may think you are correct in reading the situation or the other person's motivations or the other person's attitudes, but you are probably wrong.

A PARTING PLEA

Conflict is generally uncomfortable and tension producing, which is why people avoid it if possible. Problems that produce this high level of tension are not likely to go away on their own. Confronting the differences usually produces beneficial results. Screw up the courage to confront the differences that affect your group.

SUMMARY

Your personal definition of conflict can influence the way in which you approach it. If you think of conflict as evil, then you are likely to try to avoid it. If you think of it as good, then you may approach it directly and attempt to manage it skillfully. Conflict has potential for being beneficial to groups if you understand it and are able to manage it well.

Conflict can be defined as a struggle involving opposing ideas, values, and/or scarce resources. This definition implies (1) the incompatibility of opposing ideas or values; (2) the struggle over perceived scarce status, scarce power, and/or scarce resources; and (3) the goal of preventing, obstructing, interfering, injuring, or in some way making it less likely that the opposing goal will be achieved.

Conflict can be functional or dysfunctional, depending on how skillfully it is managed and its outcome. Conflict is more likely to be functional if group members value each other and the group's goals. Conflict also tends to be functional when the group is searching for and evaluating information. It tends to be dysfunctional when a group is in the process of generating information and selecting outcomes.

Conflict can serve many useful functions for a group. When managed skillfully it (1) increases member involvement, (2) provides an outlet for hostility, (3) promotes cohesiveness, (4) increases group productivity, and (5) increases the chance for genuine commitment to the decision.

There are four sources of conflict: ideas, personality, status, and power. Understanding the source of conflict is the first step in managing it. These four fall into two basic categories: ideational and interpersonal conflict.

Sometimes those who suggest how to manage conflict give bad advice. It is not helpful to suggest communicating more, cooperating more, blaming the other person, attacking the other person, keeping the talk general, or trying to keep others talking long enough that they give up. Other strategies that are often not productive include withdrawal, smoothing, compromise, and forcing. The strategy that is most promising is confrontation–problem solving.

Interpersonal conflict is usually best handled by confrontation. There are several things you ought to do if you decide to engage in confrontation: (1) talk with other members of the group to confirm your perception and conclusions, (2) make a list of the specific behaviors you have observed as disruptive, (3) have some tentative suggestions in mind to present, (4) be prepared to listen carefully, and (5) be prepared to utilize supportive communication behaviors. In addition, you need to decide whether to confront the person in your group meeting or privately. A private confrontation may be successful if the person doing the confronting is a respected and skillful communicator. A confrontation checklist can help you manage interpersonal confrontation.

As an alternative, you might consider bringing up the behavior in the group. One creative technique is to role-play the disruptive behavior of the other person. The person may realize that he or she is creating a problem and may be able to correct the situation.

There is a sequence of strategies that you might follow when your group experiences ideational conflict. First, try confrontation–problem solving. You can use the "cone of consensus seeking" as a model for confrontation–problem solving. Move from the assertion level to the reasons behind the assertions to the evidence and finally to the underlying values. Then move to compromise if your group cannot achieve consensus. If compromise doesn't work, your group may need to take a vote and go with the majority opinion. If a vote seems unwise, you might submit the data to a neutral third party for arbitration.

Compromise can result in pseudoconsensus. It is therefore a second-best method. It is appropriate if members cannot achieve consensus and are willing to give and take. Majority vote forces the minority to accept the dominant view. You might resort to this if the good of the group is likely to be achieved and the minority has had sufficient opportunity to present its view. Arbitration might be the answer when members believe they are sufficiently biased that they may not make a decision that is for the good of the group. Arbitration also may be wise when members know that strong feelings may keep the minority from supporting the decision of the group. Both the minority and majority may be able to agree to support the decision of a neutral third party.

Finally, confrontation can be facilitated by creating a norm and a time for the group to discuss the group's progress and problems. This provides a forum for interpersonal conflict. If you decide that the conflict is ideational, you will want to move the group through the cone of consensus seeking. This involves the relative attractiveness of the options in relation to each other and the mixture of positive and negative outcomes related to the options.

KEY TERMS AND CONCEPTS

achieved status
affective conflict
approach–approach conflict
approach–avoidance conflict
arbitration
ascribed status
collectivistic culture
compromise
conflict
conflict management
conflict resolution

confrontation–problem
   solving
consensus
constructive confrontation
cultural differences
forcing
hidden agenda
ideational conflict
individualistic culture
lose–lose methods

majority vote
personalize
power
smoothing
status
status consensus
substantive conflict
win–lose methods
win–win methods
withdrawal

EXERCISES

1. Describe your personal style of conflict management. Describe what usually happens when you employ this management strategy. How do you feel? How do other group members feel? Would you describe your strategy as win–win, lose–lose, or win–lose? Is the relationship between you and the group usually strengthened as a result of the conflict? Is it weakened? Based on the information presented in this chapter, describe what you believe to be the best conflict management strategy for you personally.

2. Select a controversial issue for members of your class. Identify class members who would describe themselves on different sides of the issue. Pick the five or six class members, balancing for viewpoint, who feel the most strongly about the issue. Have this group discuss the issue and attempt to come to a consensus. The remainder of the class should observe and record any incidents of conflict and how they were managed. When the discussion is concluded, discuss as a class the group's management of conflict.

3. In small groups, create a skit in which a member of a problem-solving group disagrees with another member. First, model ineffective management of the situation. Next, model effective management of the situation. Present the two versions of managing the disagreement to your class.

4. Write a short paper that analyzes your personal style of conflict management. Describe your style. Describe what usually happens when you employ this management strategy. How do you feel? How does the other person feel? Would you describe it as a win–win, lose–lose, or win–lose strategy? Is the relationship between you and the other person usually strengthened as a result of the conflict? Is it weakened? Based on the information presented in this chapter, describe what you believe to be the best conflict management strategy for you personally.

5. A group is discussing the problem of plagiarism. One member says, "I think there is nothing wrong with cheating. Everyone does it. That is the way people survive." Another member says, "I am shocked that you would admit that you believe such things. Don't you understand that there is more to morality than just doing what others are doing? I can't believe you said that!" You know that both participants are likely to believe strongly in their positions. You know that they will need help in working through this conflict. Describe the steps you might take to help this conflict.

6. Role-play the following incidents in a small group to which you are assigned. Be sure to apply the confrontation checklist presented in this chapter. After each role-playing situation, the conflict-management behavior should be critiqued. (Note: This exercise is also used in Chapter 8.)

    a. A member is continually late for group meetings.

    b. A member displays superiority when talking to other members.

    c. A member's need for inclusion is not being met by the group.

    d. A member's need for affection is not being met by the group.

    e. A person believes that the group moves off the topic too much; the person wants more control.

    f. A person resents the parentlike relationship that another member adopts when talking to her.

    g. A person resents the fact that another member wants to play rather than work.

7. Consider a group conflict that did not turn out as well as you would have liked. Can you account for why it turned out the way it did? Using the material in this chapter, tell how you would handle this situation differently if you could start over on it.

RECOMMENDED WEBSITES

The site adrr.com/adr0/index-9.htm contains many links to small group and individual dispute resolution websites.

The site www.work911.com/conflict/index.htm has quite a few sections concerning conflict in the workplace, whether it involves co-workers, group members, or customers. This site has a variety of resources, including a free newsletter, which can help in such areas as conflict resolution and management.

The Institute for International Mediation and Conflict Resolution, at www.iimcr.org/, includes an online library and other links to conflict resolution.

A site with a training module of different types of conflict, including basic backgrounds of conflict of various types, may be found at p2001.health.org/CTW06/Ctw06ttl.htm. The site also contains several suggestions for small group exercises.

Ernest Bormann's Symbolic Convergence Theory and Fantasy Theme analysis is the topic at oak.cats. ohiou.edu/~mw389897/fantasy.htm. At the bottom of the site is a compilation of others' contributions to the site, including links on various pages to other sites.

Managing Conflict in the Leadership Development in Groups is devoted to providing techniques and creative methods for managing conflicts and includes useful tips as well: www.ext.nodak.edu/extpubs/yf/leaddev/he500w.htm.

RECOMMENDED READINGS

L. A. Erbert (1996). Conflict management styles, strategies, and tactics. In R. S. Cathcart, L. A. Samovar, & L. D. Henman (eds.), *Small group communication: Theory and practice,* 7th ed. Madison, WI: Brown & Benchmark, pp. 211–222.

A. C. Filley (1988). *Interpersonal conflict resolution,* 2d ed. Glenview, IL: Scott, Foresman.

T. Kuhn & M. S. Poole (2000). Do conflict management styles affect group decision making? Evidence from a longitudinal field study. *Human Communication Research, 26,* 558–590.

K. M. O'Connor, D. H. Gruenfeld, & J. E. McGrath (1993). The experience and effects of conflict in continuing work groups. *Small Group Research, 24,* 362–382.

W. W. Wilmot & J. L. Hocker (2001). *Interpersonal conflict,* 6th ed. New York: McGraw-Hill.

ANALYZING SMALL GROUP
DECISION MAKING

chapter

11

OBSERVING AND EVALUATING GROUPS

OBJECTIVES

After reading this chapter you should be able to
- List and explain the ground rules for observing group discussion.
- Utilize an interaction diagram in observing a group and interpret the results.
- Code and tabulate categories of interaction using Bales's interaction process analysis and interpret the results.
- Identify the various roles being played in a group and interpret the results.
- Evaluate the leadership of a group and interpret the results.
- Evaluate the decision making and member participation of a group discussion and interpret the results.
- Evaluate the cohesiveness of a group and interpret the results.

Paul Smith has been a manager in a research group of a food canning company for five years. His way of working with problems assigned to his department is to hand them over to members of a research team. He frequently sits in on parts of their meetings to check. If you could listen to him talk to himself, you would hear something like this: "I don't understand how it could take so long to deal with such a simple problem. I sure wish I could help them. Well, I'm not sure how they got where they are and what I might suggest. I better keep out of it." Paul Smith is a real person who expressed a thought like this one day. What he was trying to say was, "I wish I had some way of being able to tell what is going on in this situation. And beyond that I wish I had the knowledge to know what to do to help these groups when they are having trouble."

The first 10 chapters of this book provide information to enable you and people like Paul Smith to analyze what is going on in groups (and why) and to understand what your options are for helping. This chapter focuses on the other half of Paul's dilemma. He must be able to observe and collect data to use in attempting to help with a group's problem. The chapter's aim is to give you some tools to systematically collect data about a group. The chapter begins with some basic suggestions about observing groups and collecting data about them. Then various data-collecting instruments are presented so that you can choose those that will allow you to look at the particular aspect of a group that is of most interest to you.

The content of this chapter was selected with several assumptions in mind. First, it is assumed that you are not interested in observing groups for the purpose of constructing theories. It is also assumed that you are not interested in doing formal research. Rather, I assume that you are interested, as was Paul Smith, in observing groups and collecting data in order to make sense out of what is going on in them and, further, that you are collecting data for the purpose of improving a group's performance and making the experience better for the members. Consequently, the data-collecting tools presented here are developed as simply as possible. Several of them have been used as research tools; for those of you who might have an interest in that use, I include the citations for the reports that describe the instruments and their use.

OBSERVING SMALL GROUP INTERACTION

Observing a small group in a classroom setting is usually quite different from observing a group out in the community or at work. The classroom setting allows more freedom for the observer and a variety of observer interventions. In the classroom the observer might interrupt the discussion at predesignated points and discuss with the group what he or she has observed. Sometimes an observer is assigned to a particular member and whispers suggestions based upon his or her observations to the member. This kind of observer intervention is normally inappropriate in community or work groups.

Ground Rules for Observing Groups

The roles of observer, analyst, and critic can be quite frustrating if you do not know something about observation techniques. Here are five suggestions:

1. Set a goal for your observation and criticism. You might want to observe the interaction, the roles being played, the leadership, the problem-solving process, or the overall effectiveness. But you are unlikely to be effective in an effort to examine all of these. Focusing allows you to examine more closely and make refined judgments.

2. Be careful to distinguish between judgments made on the basis of your data and judgments that go beyond your data. The data serve as evidence for what you have to say. Use them to describe the group's behavior and then to suggest your conclusion. When you move beyond the data, cue the group in to that fact. You might say, "Here is what I saw. I am wondering whether the group also. . . ."

3. Do not try to comment on everything you observe. Focus on key points. Your major reason for observation and criticism is to help groups improve. If you comment on everything, members will not know how to focus their efforts to improve.

4. Balance the positive and the negative. Being too negative can adversely affect the climate of your critique. Groups expect that they have faults and are usually ready to hear them. But they also expect that they are doing some things right. Keep a balance and be careful not to give too much negative criticism. Perhaps you can give them two or three things to work on for their next effort.

5. Avoid focusing on one particular discussant. Try to give a balanced critique that includes comments for all members. Show trends and group characteristics when possible. This approach will help you avoid singling out a particular member for criticism.

INSTRUMENTS FOR COLLECTING DATA

Groups will generally profit from periodic observation and evaluation. A typical time for reflection in groups outside the classroom is upon completion of a project. This seems like an appropriate time for the leader to ask members to fill out reaction sheets and to discuss how they experienced the group. The group can take note of any difficulties they experienced and can reinforce each other for their achievements.

Groups that meet in a classroom setting, where the focus is on learning to be better discussants and studying small group theory, can profit by more frequent observation and criticism. Sometimes the instructor will ask these groups to fill out reaction forms, discuss group progress, and set goals about once a week. At other times, the groups will be subject to a "fishbowl" discussion. Here other class members serve as observer-critics. The instruments that follow are applicable to both in-class and out-of-class groups. Some are suited to self-evaluation, and others are especially useful to an observer.

Interaction Observation Forms

Interaction observation serves a variety of purposes. One purpose is to discover how much individual members talk and to whom they talk. The most efficient form for gathering these kinds of data is the **interaction diagram.** Here the observer draws a series of circles on a paper to represent the various group members. Once the members are represented, the observer draws arrows to represent the initial interaction of a member with another. Members' comments that seem to be made to the whole group are shown by arrows pointing toward the outside of the paper. Then each subsequent interaction is coded by a slash mark across the appropriate arrow. An example of this kind of observation sheet is found in Figure 11.1.

Consider this completed interaction diagram. Can you identify the most vocal member of this group? Which group members tend to talk to each other most? Can you identify the member who is not contributing verbally to the group? What kinds of inferences can you make from these interaction patterns?

A second kind of interaction observation instrument is represented by Bales's interaction category scheme, shown in Table 11.1. The purpose of this kind of assessment is to identify what kinds of behaviors are being performed in a group. With an understanding of the behaviors that are needed for a group to perform well, the observer is able to discuss with the group how it might improve. This category system allows the observer to identify comments; it can be set up to record who made the comments and when they were made.

Notice that certain items are mostly social-emotional (categories 1 through 3 and 10 through 12), whereas others (categories 4 through 9) are mainly task.

A tabulation sheet is set up to list the 12 categories down the left side of a paper. The categories are set off by horizontal lines. Vertical lines are drawn from the top to the bottom of the page, across the paper. A member's name or code number is then placed in each column.

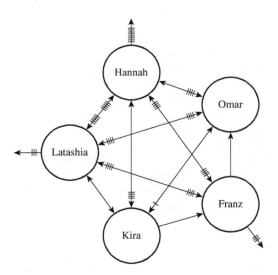

FIGURE 11.1
Completed Interaction Diagram

TABLE 11.1   Bales's Interaction Categories

1. *Seems friendly:* Raises others' status; provides assistance and rewards.
2. *Dramatizes:* Jokes; tells stories; gives indirect suggestion.
3. *Agrees:* Engages in head nodding; gives verbal suggestions of commitment about information, opinion, or suggestion.
4. *Gives suggestion:* Takes the lead; tries to assume leadership on the task.
5. *Gives opinion:* Provides evaluation, analysis, expression of feeling or wish.
6. *Gives information:* Provides orientation, repetition, clarification, confirmation.
7. *Asks for information:* Requests orientation, repetition, clarification, confirmation.
8. *Asks for opinion:* Requests evaluation, analysis, expression of feeling or wish.
9. *Asks for suggestion:* Requests direction while maintaining a submissive position; asks questions designed to call for initiative of others.
10. *Disagrees:* Gives passive rejection, mild disagreement; failure to respond.
11. *Shows tension:* Laughs; shows signs of emotional anxiety; holds back.
12. *Seems unfriendly:* Reduces others' status; defends or asserts self; conveys negative feelings.

A more elaborate analysis can be made of the categories if you use a wide paper with one column for each comment. This method allows you to keep track of the flow of discussion comment by comment throughout. That is, you can tell what kind of comment follows what kind of comment. And if you assign a number to each group member and a separate number to the group, you can tell to whom a comment is addressed and by whom it was made. For example, a 2–0 would be a comment from member 2 to the group. A 3–2 would be a comment from member 3 to member 2.

Once you have completed charting the interaction, you will be able to answer questions like these: What kind of balance do you have between social-emotional and task behaviors? Do certain members engage in certain behaviors more than others? Do the kinds of comments vary from phase to phase as suggested in Chapter 5? And, finally, do some members address other members more frequently?

Role Analysis in Discussion

Kenneth Benne and Paul Sheats are responsible for one of the oldest category systems for classifying roles. We discussed their work in Chapter 6. Recall that they divided roles into three broad classifications: task roles, group-building/maintenance roles, and self-centered roles. An observer can keep track of the kinds of roles played by each member and then can analyze the effect roles had on the interaction.

Task roles are the functions that members contribute that directly help the group with its work. They include contributions of information, opinion, elaboration, orientation, and evaluation. An observer can keep track of the kinds of task behaviors members contribute by constructing a form like the one displayed in Figure 11.2.

Group-building and maintenance roles are behaviors that contribute to the social dimension of the group. The person who seems to play these more frequently than any

Participants' names

Functional task roles								
1. Initiator								
2. Information seeker								
3. Information giver								
4. Opinion seeker								
5. Opinion giver								
6. Elaborator-clarifier								
7. Coordinator								
8. Diagnostician								
9. Orienter								
10. Energizer								
11. Procedural technician								
12. Recorder								
13. Evaluator-critic								

FIGURE 11.2
Functional Task Roles of Discussants

Source: Based on K. D. Benne and P. Sheats (1948).

other is usually identified as the social-emotional leader. The performance of these roles is important to a group because they enhance the group climate and help to build cohesiveness. Construct a form like the one in Figure 11.3 to observe and record the social-emotional roles of your group. You can discover what roles are being played and by whom. See what kind of attention is being paid to the climate of your group.

Recall that *self-centered roles* are behaviors performed to satisfy personal goals rather than group goals. Sometimes these goals produce behavior that is disruptive. For example, aggressor, blocker, and dominator are disruptive roles. Other self-centered roles merely deprive the group of the energy and input the person might have contributed if he or she had not engaged in them. Examples of these roles are the playboy/playgirl, special-interest pleader, and self-confessor.

When you are concerned about members who are playing nonfunctional roles, construct a form like that in Figure 11.4 and collect data about member roles. After

Participants' names

Social-emotional roles								
1. Supporter-encourager								
2. Harmonizer								
3. Tension releaser								
4. Compromiser								
5. Gatekeeper								
6. Feeling expressor								
7. Standard setter								
8. Follower								

FIGURE 11.3
Functional Social-Emotional Roles

Source: Based on K. D. Benne and P. Sheats (1948).

Participants' names

Self-centered roles								
1. Blocker								
2. Aggressor								
3. Deserter								
4. Dominator								
5. Recognition seeker								
6. Self-confessor								
7. Playboy/playgirl								
8. Special-interest pleader								

FIGURE 11.4
Self-Centered Roles

Source: Based on K. D. Benne and P. Sheats (1948).

Focus on Research

A SYSTEM OF MULTIPLE-LEVEL OBSERVATION OF GROUPS (SYMLOG)

Robert F. Bales and associates (Bales, 1950, 1970, 1980, 1985; Bales, Cohen, and Williamson, 1979) of the Harvard University Social Interaction Laboratory have spent years developing a system of multiple-level observation of groups. Their system, called SYMLOG, receives its name from the first letters of the words they used to describe their scheme.

These researchers describe interpersonal behavior in groups using three dimensions:

1. *Dominant versus submissive,* what is called upward (U) versus downward (D).
2. *Friendly versus unfriendly,* what is called positive (P) versus negative (N).
3. *Instrumentally controlled (task oriented) versus emotionally controlled,* what is called forward (F) versus backward (B).

The scale that has been used to rate group members on these dimensions is displayed in Table 11.2. The results of this rating allow the researcher to create directional profiles of members.

A *directional profile* is a description of how the group member is communicating according to these three dimensions. A group member named George,

for example, might be described by the dimension upward (U), which means this individual is active, is dominant, and talks a lot. Another member, Yuka, might be described as upward, positive, and forward (UPF). These dimensions would suggest this person is dominant, friendly, and instrumentally controlled. Bales would say that she is probably a purposeful, democratic, task leader.

SYMLOG has been an extremely useful way of describing group dynamics. It has been used to describe individual behaviors and values of group members. It also has been used to describe interpersonal relations among group members. You may wish to explore its use with members of your class.

R. F. Bales (1950). *Interaction process analysis: A method for the study of small groups.* Reading, MA: Addison-Wesley.

R. F. Bales (1970). *Personality and interpersonal behavior.* New York: Holt, Rinehart & Winston.

R. F. Bales (1980). *SYMLOG case study kit.* New York: Free Press.

R. F. Bales (1985). A new field theory in social psychology. *International Journal of Small Group Research, 1,* 1–18.

R. F. Bales, S. P. Cohen, & S. A. Williamson (1979). *SYMLOG: A system for the multiple level observation of groups.* New York: Free Press.

the roles and role players are identified, the group can choose to do something about them.

Leadership Rating Form

Leadership can be supplied by a number of different members. It does not matter so much whether one person provides most of the leadership or not. What is of concern, however, is whether the leadership is sufficient for the group to perform its task. The focus of the Barnlund-Haiman leadership rating scale is assessment of the adequacy of leadership activities. It divides the kinds of leadership into three categories: influence in procedure, influence in creative and critical thinking, and influence in interpersonal relations. This scale can be reproduced for use without permission of the publisher when it is to be used for nonprofit purposes, but it must be labeled as shown

TABLE 11.2   The SYMLOG Adjective Rating Form (Bales & Cohen, 1979)

Your name _____ Group _____

Name of person described _____ Circle the best choice for each item.

		(0)	(1)	(2)	(3)	(4)
U	active, dominant, talks a lot	never	rarely	sometimes	often	always
UP	extroverted, outgoing, positive	never	rarely	sometimes	often	always
UPF	a purposeful democratic task leader	never	rarely	sometimes	often	always
UF	an assertive businesslike manager	never	rarely	sometimes	often	always
UNF	authoritarian, controlling, disapproving	never	rarely	sometimes	often	always
UN	domineering, tough minded, powerful	never	rarely	sometimes	often	always
UNB	provocative, egocentric, shows off	never	rarely	sometimes	often	always
UB	jokes around, expressive, dramatic	never	rarely	sometimes	often	always
UPB	entertaining, sociable, smiling, warm	never	rarely	sometimes	often	always
P	friendly, equalitarian	never	rarely	sometimes	often	always
PF	works cooperatively with others	never	rarely	sometimes	often	always
F	analytical, task oriented, problem solving	never	rarely	sometimes	often	always
NF	legalistic, has to be right	never	rarely	sometimes	often	always
N	unfriendly, negativistic	never	rarely	sometimes	often	always
NB	irritable, cynical, won't cooperate	never	rarely	sometimes	often	always
B	shows feelings and emotions	never	rarely	sometimes	often	always
PB	affectionate, likeable, fun to be with	never	rarely	sometimes	often	always
DP	looks up to others, appreciative, trustful	never	rarely	sometimes	often	always
DPF	gentle, willing to accept responsibility	never	rarely	sometimes	often	always
DF	obedient, works submissively	never	rarely	sometimes	often	always
DNF	self-punishing, works too hard	never	rarely	sometimes	often	always
DN	depressed, sad, resentful, rejecting	never	rarely	sometimes	often	always
DNB	alienated, quits, withdraws	never	rarely	sometimes	often	always
DB	afraid to try, doubts own ability	never	rarely	sometimes	often	always
DPB	quietly happy just to be with others	never	rarely	sometimes	often	always
D	passive, introverted, says little	never	rarely	sometimes	often	always

Source: Bales & Cohen (1979).

in Table 11.3. Chapter 7 provides suggestions for promoting more effective leadership after difficulties are identified.

TABLE 11.3   Barnlund-Haiman Leadership Rating Scale

Instructions: This rating scale may be used to evaluate leadership in groups with or without official leaders. In the latter case (the leaderless group) use part A of each item only. When evaluating the actions of an official leader, use parts A and B of each item on the scale.

INFLUENCE IN PROCEDURE
Initiating Discussion

A. 3   2   1   0   1   2   3

Group needed more help in getting started	Group got right amount of help	Group needed less help in getting started

B. The quality of the introductory remarks was:

Excellent	Good	Adequate	Fair	Poor

Organizing Group Thinking

A. 3   2   1   0   1   2   3

Group needed more direction in thinking	Group got right amount of help	Group needed less direction in thinking

B. If and when attempts were made to organize group thinking, they were:

Excellent	Good	Adequate	Fair	Poor

Clarifying Communication

A. 3   2   1   0   1   2   3

Group needed more help in clarifying communication	Group got right amount of help	Group needed less help in clarifying communication

B. If and when attempts were made to clarify communication, they were:

Excellent	Good	Adequate	Fair	Poor

Summarizing and Verbalizing Agreements

A. 3   2   1   0   1   2   3

Group needed more help in summarizing and verbalizing agreements	Group got right amount of help	Group needed less help in summarizing and verbalizing agreements

B. If and when attempts were made to summarize and verbalize agreements, they were:

Excellent	Good	Adequate	Fair	Poor

TABLE 11.3 Barnlund-Haiman Leadership Rating Scale *(Continued)*

Resolving Conflict

A. 3   2   1   0   1   2   3

| Group needed more help in resolving conflict | Group got right amount of help | Group needed less help in resolving conflict |

B. If and when attempts were made to resolve conflict, they were:

Excellent   Good   Adequate   Fair   Poor

INFLUENCES IN CREATIVE AND CRITICAL THINKING
Stimulating Critical Thinking

A. 3   2   1   0   1   2   3

| Group needed more stimulation in creative thinking | Group got right amount of help | Group needed less stimulation in creative thinking |

B. If and when attempts were made to stimulate ideas, they were:

Excellent   Good   Adequate   Fair   Poor

Encouraging Criticism

A. 3   2   1   0   1   2   3

| Group needed more encouragement to be critical | Group got right amount of help | Group needed less encouragement to be critical |

B. If and when attempts were made to encourage criticism, they were:

Excellent   Good   Adequate   Fair   Poor

Balancing Abstract and Concrete Thought

A. 3   2   1   0   1   2   3

| Group needed to be more concrete | Group got right amount of help | Group needed to be more abstract |

B. If and when attempts were made to balance abstract and concrete thought, they were:

Excellent   Good   Adequate   Fair   Poor

INFLUENCE IN INTERPERSONAL RELATIONS
Climate Making

A. 3   2   1   0   1   2   3

| Group needed more help in securing a permissive atmosphere | Group got right amount of help | Group needed less help in securing a permissive atmosphere |

B. If and when attempts were made to establish a permissive atmosphere, they were:

Excellent   Good   Adequate   Fair   Poor

TABLE 11.3   Barnlund-Haiman Leadership Rating Scale *(Concluded)*

Regulating Participation

A. | 3 | 2 | 1 | 0 | 1 | 2 | 3 |

| Group needed more regulation of participation | Group got right amount of help | | Group needed less regulation of participation |

B. If and when attempts were made to regulate participation, they were:

| Excellent | Good | Adequate | Fair | Poor |

Overall Leadership

A. | 3 | 2 | 1 | 0 | 1 | 2 | 3 |

| Group needed more control | Group got right amount of control | Group needed less control |

B. If and when attempts were made to control the group, they were:

| Excellent | Good | Adequate | Fair | Poor |

Source: D. C. Barnlund and F. S. Haiman (1960), pp. 401–404.

OBSERVING AND REPORTING GROUP PROCESSES

The next two information-processing instruments take a broader focus. They are useful for examining the group's effort when the task is decision making. The first allows you to record judgments about the decision-making process and the group's interaction. The decision-making discussion rating sheet is displayed in Table 11.4.

Coding data about a group are based on a question you want answered. Of course, as an investigator, you do not code everything. Your coding scheme serves as a sort of "lens" through which you observe the group (Bakeman, 2000).

The Brilhart problem-solving process scale is especially useful if your group is following a full agenda that is based on the reflective thinking process. If you were using a decision-making agenda based on Dewey's reflective thinking pattern, this would be an appropriate rating sheet. The Brilhart problem-solving scale is in Table 11.5.

Sometimes you will want to focus on the individual members' contributions to the group process. This may be the case especially when you believe that there is a wide variation in individual participation. You may have as your goal helping members to set goals for improvement of their own effort. Table 11.6 provides an evaluation form that focuses your attention on some of the key variables in small group member participation.

TABLE 11.4   Decision-Making Discussion Rating Scale

Problem: _____   Group: _____

I. Rate the group on the following:

	Poor	Fair	Average	Very Good	Excellent
1. How well did the group understand the problem?	1	2	3	4	5
2. How adequately did the group discuss causes?	1	2	3	4	5
3. How adequately were criteria generated?	1	2	3	4	5
4. How adequately did the group explore solutions?	1	2	3	4	5
5. How systematically did the group apply criteria?	1	2	3	4	5
6. How well did the group's solutions meet causes?	1	2	3	4	5
7. How well did the group interact?	1	2	3	4	5
8. How well did the group handle conflict?	1	2	3	4	5
9. How well did the group involve its members?	1	2	3	4	5
10. How well did the group use available information?	1	2	3	4	5
11. How well were the group's conclusions summarized as it progressed?	1	2	3	4	5

II. Did the group achieve consensus on the decision? Yes _____ No _____

III. How do you know what you have said above? Present examples, evidence, and reasoning for your ratings of the group's performance.

IV. Place an X on the continuum to describe the group's overall performance.

Poor	Fair	Average	Very Good	Excellent

SELF-REPORT RATING FORMS

Self-report measures can help you discover what group members are thinking and how they are experiencing the group. But a word of caution is appropriate: Sometimes members will report what they believe the person collecting the data *wants* to hear, rather than what they *actually* think. This tendency creates a bias in the data. Sometimes you can minimize the bias by asking for anonymous reports.

This chapter includes three self-report instruments. The first is for collecting data about cohesiveness in a work group. The Seashore index of group cohesiveness, Table 11.7, asks three basic questions: How much do you feel you are a part of this

TABLE 11.5   Brilhart Problem-Solving Procedure Scale

Instructions: Based on behaviors and interaction you observed, rate the degree to which the group measured up to each criterion.

	Poor 1	Fair 2	Average 3	Good 4	Excellent 5				
1. Concerns of all members were established regarding the problem.					1	2	3	4	5
2. Components of the undesirable situation and obstacles to change were clearly described.					1	2	3	4	5
3. The goal was clearly defined and agreed upon by all members.					1	2	3	4	5
4. Possible solutions were listed and clarified before extensive evaluation of them.					1	2	3	4	5
5. Criteria for evaluation were previously understood and accepted, or discussed and agreed upon by all members.					1	2	3	4	5
6. Based on facts and reasoning, predictions were made regarding the probable effectiveness and possible negative consequences of each proposed solution.					1	2	3	4	5
7. Consensus was achieved on the most desirable/acceptable solution.					1	2	3	4	5
8. A realistic plan was developed for implementing the solution and, if appropriate, for evaluating its effectiveness.					1	2	3	4	5
9. Overall, the problem-solving process was thorough, vigilant, and systematic.					1	2	3	4	5

Source: J. K. Brilhart, G. J. Galanes, & K. Adams (2001), p. 383.

group? How willing are you to leave the group? How does your group compare with similar groups with respect to member relations? If the ratings are low, you will want to engage in some of the cohesiveness-building behaviors recommended in Chapter 9.

The open-ended nature of the postmeeting open-ended reaction sheet, Table 11.8, avoids observer bias in collecting data. It does so by allowing the individual group members to identify strengths and weaknesses as they see them. It also asks for member suggestions for improvement and change in the group. These kinds of data are valuable because group members may point out problems not known to the person collecting the data. A group might use this form to evaluate its performance. If so, the group would set aside a time at the end of a work session to evaluate and decide on alternative ways of working together.

TABLE 11.6   Discussion Participant Evaluation

Participant: _____

Poor	Fair	Adequate	Good	Excellent
1	2	3	4	5

Circle the number that describes the participation of the member indicated above.

1	2	3	4	5	1. Prepared to discuss.
1	2	3	4	5	2. Comments were relevant.
1	2	3	4	5	3. Listened to others.
1	2	3	4	5	4. Open-minded.
1	2	3	4	5	5. Argued constructively.
1	2	3	4	5	6. Frequency of participation.
1	2	3	4	5	7. Contribution to analysis.
1	2	3	4	5	8. Contribution to evaluation.
1	2	3	4	5	9. Overall rating of discussant.

How do you know what you have said above is true? Give your specific evidence and reasoning for your ratings.

Evaluator: _____

The Brilhart postmeeting reaction questionnaire, Table 11.9, provides a focused means of collecting self-report data. Asking members to respond to the same ideas has an advantage over the open-ended questionnaire. It allows you to compare answers to the question and discover whether members are perceiving the group consistently. Notice that the items correspond to various chapters of this book. Table 11.10 lists each topic with the chapter or chapters that focus on it so that you can use this book as a reference to help your group improve its performance.

Finally, there are two other forms for evaluating your group. The first measures efficacy. You will recall that efficacy is the collective belief that the group can be effective. The form for assessing this is displayed in Table 11.11. The last self-report assessment allows you to poll members regarding their sense of your group's development. This is displayed in Table 11.12.

TABLE 11.7 Seashore Index of Group Cohesiveness

Check one response for each question.

1. Do you feel that you are really a part of your work group?

_____ Really a part of my work group

_____ Included in most ways

_____ Included in some ways, but not in others

_____ Don't feel I really belong

_____ Don't work with any one group of people

_____ Not ascertained

2. If you had a chance to do the same kind of work for the same pay in another work group, how would you feel about moving?

_____ Would want very much to move

_____ Would rather move than stay where I am

_____ Would make no difference to me

_____ Would want very much to stay where I am

_____ Not ascertained

3. How does your work group compare with other similar groups on each of the following points?

	Better than most	About the same as most	Not as good as most	Not ascertained
a. The way the members get along together				
b. The way the members stick together				
c. The way the members help each other on the job				

Source: S. Seashore (1954). Used by permission.

TABLE 11.8   Postmeeting Open-Ended Reaction Form

1. I would rate today's discussion as

  _____ Excellent   _____ Very Good   _____ Good   _____ Fair   _____ Poor

2. I would rate the decision we reached as

  _____ Excellent   _____ Very Good   _____ Good   _____ Fair   _____ Poor

3. The strong points of the group's decision making were

4. The weak points of the group's decision making were

5. The group's climate could be described as

6. I would recommend the following changes for the group:

7. I would set the following goals for this group's future meetings:

Signed (Optional): _____

TABLE 11.9   Postmeeting Reaction (PMR) Form

Instructions: Check the point on each scale that best represents your honest judgment. Add any comments you wish to make that are not covered by the questionnaire. Do *not* sign your name.

1. How clear were the *goals* of the discussion to you?

very clear	somewhat vague	muddled

2. The *atmosphere* was

cooperative and cohesive	apathetic	competitive

3. How well *organized and vigilant* was the discussion?

disorderly	just right	too rigid

4. How effective was the *leadership* supplied by the chairperson?

too autocratic	democratic	weak

5. *Preparation for this meeting* was

thorough	adequate	poor

6. Did you find yourself *wanting to speak* when you didn't get a chance?

almost never	occasionally	often

7. How satisfied are you with the *results* of the discussion?

very satisfied	moderately satisfied	very dissatisfied

8. How do you feel about *working again* with this same group?

eager	I will	reluctant

Comments:

TABLE 11.10   Postmeeting Reaction Questionnaire with Corresponding Chapters

1. *Adequacy of communication:* To what extent do you feel members were understanding each other's statements and positions?
Chapter 4, "Communication Processes"
Chapter 6, "Roles and Role Emergence"

2. *Opportunity to speak:* To what extent did you feel free to speak?
Chapter 4, "Communication Processes"

3. *Climate of acceptance:* How well did members support each other, show acceptance of individuals?
Chapter 8, "Relational Communication in Groups"
Chapter 9, "Promoting Group Cohesiveness and Satisfaction"

4. *Interpersonal relations:* How pleasant were members, how concerned with interpersonal relations?
Chapter 8, "Relational Communication in Groups"

5. *Leadership:* How adequate was the leader (or leadership) of the group?
Chapter 3, "Participating in Group Meetings"
Chapter 7, "Leading Group Meetings"

6. *Satisfaction with role:* How satisfied are you with your personal participation in the discussion?
Chapter 6, "Roles and Role Emergence"

7. *Quality of product:* How satisfied are you with the discussion, solutions, or learnings that came out of this discussion?
Chapter 3, "Participating in Group Meetings"
Chapter 5, "Encouraging Group Development and Evolution"
Chapter 8, "Relational Communication in Groups"
Chapter 9, "Promoting Group Cohesiveness and Satisfaction"

8. *Overall:* How do you rate the discussion as a whole?

TABLE 11.11   Collective Efficacy Self-Report Assessment

Answer each of the questions below to assess your sense that the group believes it can be effective. Use these ratings in your assessment: 1 = to no extent; 3 = to a limited extent; 5 = to some extent; 7 = to a considerable extent; 10 = to a great extent.

1. My group has confidence in itself.	1	3	5	7	10
2. My group believes it can become unusually good at producing high-performance work.	1	3	5	7	10
3. My group expects to be known as a high-performance group.	1	3	5	7	10
4. My group believes it can solve any problem it encounters.	1	3	5	7	10
5. My group believes it can be very productive.	1	3	5	7	10
6. My group can get a lot of work done when it works hard.	1	3	5	7	10
7. No task is too difficult for my group.	1	3	5	7	10
8. My group expects to have a lot of influence in our organization.	1	3	5	7	10

Total your score: _____

Compare your score to the other group members' scores. If your group or some group members score low on several items, use these items as a guide to discuss how to increase your group's efficacy.

Source: Adapted from Gibson, Randel, & Earley (2000).

TABLE 11.12 Group Development Assessment

Circle the numbers of statements that describe your group.

1. We keep asking what we are doing and why.

2. Members do not know one another.

3. We are unclear about what we are supposed to do.

4. We are having trouble getting along.

5. We jockey for power.

6. We disagree about how to proceed.

7. We are seeing progress in our work.

8. We are open and honest in asking questions and giving feedback.

9. We are working more smoothly as we get to know each other.

10. We feel pride in our accomplishments.

11. We congratulate each other on a job well done.

12. We all believe we know what it takes to get the job done.

If you mostly circled items 1 through 3, then your group is in the orienting stage.

If you mostly circled items 4 through 6, then your group is in the conflict stage.

If you mostly circled items 7 through 9, then your group is in the emergence stage.

If you mostly circled items 10 through 12, then your group is in the reinforcement stage.

Source: Adapted from Gardenswartz and Rowe (1994).

A Question of Ethics and Responsibility

Where Does the Leader Go from Here?

A management group for a local department store met in their training room. The time chosen for the meeting was the middle of a very busy week just before a holiday. The meeting was held at 1 P.M.—just after lunch and just before a 2 P.M. change of shift when several department managers had to check employees in. The meeting included about 15 people from a variety of different departments and some of the department managers. The agenda for the meeting was to gather input about two questions: (1) What problems might result from changing store hours? and (2) If store hours were changed, what might be the best hours?

It seemed as though there might have been a hidden agenda, too. One of the high-ranking managers was opposed to the proposed change, and more than that, he appeared to be "gunning" for another manager who favored the change. This manager seemed to want to "teach" the lower-ranking manager a lesson or two—perhaps well intended, but perhaps motivated by some animosity generated over a period of time.

The meeting lasted more than an hour, and some managers left before it ended in order to check employees in. The store manager received plenty of "input." Unfortunately, it was not input that helped answer questions about store hours. The manager who was opposed to changing the hours came away from the meeting feeling more hostile than before; the meeting had brought out the soreness in a relationship that had been buried before.

Suppose that you had a videotape of this meeting. Suppose further that you could interview the members of this group. Which research tools from this chapter would be useful, and why? What do you think you would find if you did some investigation? In what ways did the high-ranking manager not behave ethically and/or responsibly?

SUMMARY

This chapter focused on observing and evaluating groups. The following ground rules were established for observing groups: The observer should decide what he or she wants to observe, be careful to distinguish between judgments made on the basis of data and those that go beyond the data, try not to comment on everything that is observed, and balance the positive and the negative.

Instruments for collecting data were presented. They included interaction-observation forms, role-analysis forms, leadership-observation forms, and a variety of decision-making and performance-rating forms.

KEY TERMS AND CONCEPTS

Barnlund-Haiman leadership
    rating scale
Brilhart problem-solving
    procedure scale
cohesiveness
collective efficacy self-report
    assessment
discussion participant
    evaluation form
efficacy
functional social-emotional
    roles of discussants

functional task roles of
    discussants
group development
    assessment
interaction analysis
interaction diagram
interaction observation form
open-ended reaction form
postmeeting reaction
    questionnaire
role analysis

Seashore Index of group
    cohesiveness
self-report rating form
self-centered roles of
    discussants
SYMLOG
SYMLOG adjective rating
    form
system for multiple-level
    observation of groups

EXERCISES

1. Examine the flow of communication in a discussion group you observe. Record the number of times a person speaks and to whom the person speaks. Consider these questions: Which members contribute the most? To whom do they speak? What conclusions can you draw from these data? Who are the low participators? Do you see any attempt to speak directly to them to draw them into the discussion? What would you recommend to this group with respect to the low participators? How often are comments made to the entire group? What does this pattern look like? What suggestions do you have for the group about its inclusiveness? Report your findings to the group you assessed.

2. As a group, pick an area to assess the small group communication. Develop an assessment form and bring it to class. Share your form with others in your group who have been developing similar forms. Now, using the input of individual members, work together to develop a form. Share your results with the class.

3. Use Bales's interaction categories to analyze a prerecorded discussion. Keep track of ten-minute intervals. What types of questions were asked in each period? How often were they asked? Were more questions asked during a particular period? What comments can you make about the discussion based on your data? Now focus on the question answering. What percentage of the questions were answered? Were members ignored when they asked questions? Write a two-page report critiquing the question asking and answering.

4. Observe a decision-making group in your community for three or four meetings. Focus on a different aspect of the communication or dynamics each time. Submit a report to your instructor that includes a description of the group, the data you collected, your conclusions, and an appendix with the completed instruments you used.

5. Record a classroom discussion. Use the forms in this chapter to analyze the functional roles played. Now consider the adequacy of the roles played for the achievement of the group's goals. Bring a written analysis to class and compare your analysis with those of other members in your group.

6. Talk with relatives and friends about groups to which they belong. Try to identify at least one group that has had formal feedback about an aspect or aspects of their group process. Ask them to explain this experience. Report back to the class.

RECOMMENDED WEBSITES

A group leadership evaluation form used in a business and professional communication class of Dr. Lisa Millhous at West Chester University can be found at communication.wcupa.edu/faculty/millhous/230/formb.htm. The page also has a rating key to evaluate the group members' leadership skills.

At dante.med.utoronto.ca/peereval/Small%20Group%20Evaluation.html is a small group evaluation scale that has a detailed analysis of members' group task and group maintenance functions.

The Student Organization Solutions at Vanderbilt University at www.vanderbilt.edu/sos/Communication.htm has several measures for assessing the quality of small group communication including links to motivating members and leadership.

Student Peer Review at www.uwp.vt.edu/html/online_resources/teaching/olr_menu_03_sub_2.htm is a detailed site devoted to procedures for assembling a peer response group, as well as questions to ask in order to determine their effectiveness.

Technidigm is devoted to self-assessments and leadership evaluations and allows participants to fill in the blanks. The site can be found at technidigm.org/formev.htm.

A University of Texas site, www.utexas.edu/academic/cte/sourcebook/evalform.pdf, has a small group evaluation form for use in assessing the effectiveness of group members.

RECOMMENDED READINGS

S. A. Beebe & J. K. Barge (2003). Evaluating group discussion. In R. Y. Hirokawa, R. S. Cathcart, L. A. Samovar, & L. D. Henman (eds.), *Small group communication: Theory and practice,* 8th ed. Los Angeles: Roxbury, pp. 275–288.

J. Keyton (2003). Observing group interaction. In R. Y. Hirokawa, R. S. Cathcart, L. A. Samovar, & L. D. Henman (eds.), *Small group communication: Theory and practice,* 8th ed. Los Angeles: Roxbury, pp. 256–266.

G. J. Galanes, K. Adams, & J. K. Brilhart (2004). Observing and evaluating group discussion. In *Effective group discussion,* 11th ed. New York: McGraw-Hill, pp. 425–454.

Appendix A

Public Small Group Presentations

Susan Holbrook works in the engineering department of a power company in the southeast. One Monday morning she arrived at work to discover a note on her desk:

Susan,
Please see me as soon as possible. Public Relations has decided we should mount a public information campaign on the use of nuclear energy as a power source. I understand you have the background we need to do this. I'd like you to plan a public meeting at which our people can present our position on this issue.

Phil

Susan was surprised at the request to organize and participate in the upcoming public information meeting. She was prepared to do so, though she admits she felt "butterflies" in her stomach at the thought of being in front of a large audience.

Organizations that are interested in how they are viewed by the public attempt to provide information about issues that involve them. These frequently take the form of a public meeting. Civic organizations and other groups that are concerned about community issues do the same. Sometimes classroom teachers ask students to present a discussion for their fellow classmates. Thus you are likely to find yourself participating in or perhaps organizing a public group meeting.

This appendix focuses on public group meetings. We begin by discussing formats for public group meetings. We describe typical formats and tell when they are useful. Then we move to provide information on public group oral presentations. Here we show you how to prepare, practice, and present.

FORMATS FOR PUBLIC GROUP MEETINGS

Public discussions usually differ in purpose from private discussions. The principal difference is that public discussion is conducted for the benefit of the audience. Even if a group is engaged in decision making, the fact that an audience is expected means that special

343

attention is being paid to audience needs. For example, in a political group—say a city council meeting—one would sense that members are talking to the audience part of the time, rather than to each other. Thus it seems reasonable to conclude that these discussions are to some extent performances. This section considers several types of public discussion formats and their uses. These include the forum, panel discussion, symposium, and colloquium.

Forum

A **forum** is a public discussion that involves full audience participation. Its most familiar form is the New England town meeting. The citizens of the town gather to propose issues, discuss them, and make decisions. Impromptu speeches are made from the floor, members debate each other, questions are asked and responded to, and comments are made. The purpose of these meetings is to share information and ideas and to take care of the affairs of the town.

Most of us will not experience the forum in its pure form. Instead, we will experience a forum coupled with some other kind of communication activity. Generally a speech, film, panel discussion, symposium, or interview is presented as a stimulus for the audience discussion. Leading this form of discussion is the responsibility of a chairperson or moderator. This difficult role requires skillful control by the chair. The goals of this leader include the following items:

1. Stimulating the group further by posing provocative ideas and questions.

2. Providing an opportunity for as many people as possible (or practical) to talk. This means urging speakers to keep their comments brief.

3. Recognizing the various viewpoints and trying to give an opportunity for all of them to be heard.

One way to help your audience meet these goals is to suggest some guidelines for managing participation in this discussion. Here are several basic guidelines:

1. Tell them that there will be a forum after the presentation. Suggest that they write down questions and comments as they are listening so that they are ready to participate fully in the discussion.

2. Ask them to wait to be recognized before they begin to speak.

3. Ask them to hold their comments if they have already spoken, thereby allowing others who have not spoken to have a turn.

4. Suggest a time limit on individual speeches. Suggest some signal you will give when the limit is reached.

5. Let them know how much time is allotted for the forum interaction.

6. Have floor microphones available for use.

7. Call for a different point of view if several persons have presented a similar view.

Panel Discussion

A **panel discussion** is an interaction involving specialists or reasonably well-informed people who share their points of view about a common topic or question. The discussion is carried out for the benefit of, but not with, the audience. Panel members generally react to stimulus questions posed by a moderator. A moderator plans such a session by developing five or six primary questions, with several follow-up questions for each. The primary questions are usually given to the participants prior to the discussion so that they can prepare.

A city police department used this format to discuss personal security issues with a group of high school students. The director of community services for the department gathered a group of experts to discuss the question "What should young people know about self-defense?" Subquestions were "What are some common characteristics of attackers?" "What situations should be avoided if possible? Why?" "How should you defend yourself against an armed attacker?" The panel members discussed each possible subquestion for about ten minutes in front of the audience.

This kind of public discussion demands special attention to the physical arrangement. The panel members and leader should be seated facing the audience, but in such a way that they can see each other also. A V-shaped arrangement is often preferred. Name cards are provided for the participants. The name cards are especially important if the discussion is to be followed by a forum.

The moderator's job includes the following steps:

1. Preparing the discussion question outline and distributing it to the participants. This step includes distribution of the ground rules and stressing the need for fair play and limiting each comment to about a minute.

2. Introducing the topic and the main discussion question or questions.

3. Introducing the panel of participants.

4. Posing questions, maintaining order, and summarizing agreements and differences.

5. Closing the discussion by summarizing, thanking the speakers, and asking the audience for questions.

Symposium

By itself, a **symposium** is not a discussion; it is instead a series of brief speeches all related to a central topic, each usually taking a different position on the issue. Its chief purpose in a discussion situation is to provide a stimulus for discussion. It is generally followed either by a discussion among the members of the symposium (a panel discussion) or by audience participation in a discussion (a forum). The ideas suggested for forum and panel discussions apply when they are used in connection with a symposium.

Colloquium

A **colloquium** is a format for public discussion that involves a panel of experts who are asked questions by an audience. The audience knows the general topic of discussion and frequently prepares questions in advance. Often each questioner has an opportunity to ask a question and then to ask a follow-up question. The experts generally answer questions but do not ask them. This format seems best suited to enlightenment of the audience, as it does not provide for meaningful two-way communication.

A news conference at which scientists are gathered to announce a medical break-through would be an example of a colloquium. Such a colloquium followed the implantation of the first artificial heart. Another example of the colloquium format would be a variation on the police department's panel discussion about personal security described earlier. If the students and faculty had come prepared to ask questions, instead of the members' addressing advance questions, this would have been a colloquium. Also, instead of interacting with one another, the group members would need to interact with the audience.

Larry L. Barker and his colleagues suggest a version of the colloquium that provides two-way communication. In this case the panel of experts actually engages in problem solving. Here is how the authors suggest this process operates:

> When either the chairperson or the panel members determine that some matter is deterring the pursuit of a satisfactory solution to the problem or subproblem, the audience is invited to participate by asking questions or making remarks. For example, as a chairperson you might observe that two panel members disagree on a matter; that a salient issue, subproblem, or solution is being omitted or ignored in the discussion; or that a questionable point is not being challenged. At this point, you would shift from the panel discussion to the forum discussion until the matter is settled. Then you would shift back to the panel discussion until the next opportunity for the audience's participation occurs. This process continues until the discussion is concluded, either by the time limit or by arrival at an agreed-upon solution to the problem and interrelated subproblems. (Barker, Wahlers, & Kibler, 1991, pp. 201–204)

Selecting a Public Discussion Format

Recall the goal of public discussions is to inform the public, including segments of the public, such as members of clubs and organizations. Regardless of the group, some questions will help you to decide which format you want to use.

Start by asking how informed your audience will be. Then determine the basic purpose of the meeting. Table A.1 summarizes some of the problems posed by these questions, with the formats that seem most useful for each. Thus if members of a professional group of speech pathologists in your community want to know about computer applications to speech pathology, they may invite a panel to their meeting. If they know about some applications but want to be exposed to others, they may choose a symposium-forum. Or if members are well informed, they may choose to share among themselves in a pure forum format. But if they wish instead to inform the public about the services that speech pathologists perform for the community, they may arrange for a colloquium to be video-taped and played on cable TV. The type of public discussion format you select is related to how informed your membership is and the specific purpose you have in mind for the event. Consider how informed your membership is and your purpose with respect to format selection.

TABLE A.1   Selecting a Public Discussion Format

Situation and/or Problem	Solution
1. First exposure of the group to the topic.	1. Group may not be able to generate much dialogue. Invite experts for panel discussion or colloquium.
2. Audience is reasonably well informed but would like to be exposed to different perspectives.	2. A likely format is a symposium-forum.
3. The group is well informed, and there are diverse views in the group.	3. A pure forum type of format will permit an exchange of views.
4. The group wishes to help inform the public about an issue on which its membership is well informed.	4. The format that may best serve this need is a colloquium. Invite a group of experts to quiz your group. Videotape this session for replay over a local cable station.

ORAL PRESENTATIONS TO AN AUDIENCE

You will be faced with the task of preparing an oral presentation when you select a forum or symposium. The aim of this section is to help you with this activity. We begin with a plan you can use to prepare the presentation. Then we present helpful information for preparing to deliver your speech. Finally, we give advice to help you polish your delivery.

Preparing for an Individual Oral Presentation

1. *Identify Your Purpose*
The purpose of your presentation is often dictated by the situation. Most likely, you will need to inform or persuade. You may have the task of presenting your group's decision to an audience. This is often largely an informative task if the decision is not controversial. The task becomes persuasive if the decision is controversial. Your group may find the situation requires presenting opposing sides in a debate-style format. This too would be a persuasive task.

You may occasionally find your group has an assignment that requires entertainment. You may be heading a committee to plan a "roast" of a colleague at the year-end banquet. Typically, you would meet to make decisions regarding how to organize the "event" and then prepare entertaining speeches. Your goal is to make the audience laugh and enjoy themselves. Having a clear sense of what the situation requires is the first step in preparing to speak to an audience.

2. *Identify and Analyze Your Audience*
You will want to find out as much as you can—given your time constraints—about your audience. This task will help you select and narrow your subject and select what points you want to make. Your analysis centers on answering several

questions. Who are the audience members in terms of their attendance at the presentation? What do they know about the topic? What attitudes do they have about the topic? Why will they be there to listen to you? What expectations do they have? Are these people present voluntarily or are they required to attend?

Your analysis of the answers to these questions will allow you to know how to go beyond what your audience knows. It will allow you to plan carefully to present ideas that may be controversial. It will allow you to be sensitive to the needs of those who are required to attend and be especially careful to make the information interesting and relevant. This kind of analysis is a key to a successful presentation.

3. Select and Narrow Your Subject

You may find you are assigned a topic or that the situation requires you present on a specific topic. For example, you would be expected to present your plans if your group has been meeting as a long-range planning committee. On the other hand, you may find you have a general assignment with the specific topic left to your selection. We recommend self-examination as the place to start in this second case. The best topics are often ones where you have expertise and experience. In fact, you were probably selected for the assignment because of these. Sit with a sheet of paper and list all of the logical possibilities you can. Then, narrow the list to a few. Pick the one about which you know the most or ask the person who asked you to speak to identify the most appealing topic.

You will probably find you have more to say than the time allotted to your presentation. Sometimes you will not be told how long to speak, but merely told to "fill us in" or "be brief." Unless you know what these mean from understanding the traditions of the audience, see if you can get a better idea of what is expected. You will want to time your presentation when you practice. Our experience suggests that, unless you time your speech, it will be difficult to judge how long it will take you to present your ideas.

4. Identify and Organize Your Major Ideas

Your next step is to decide what you want to say. You might start this process by listing the things that you might present, then narrow the list to the two or three things that are most important for you to say. On the other hand, you already may know what you need to say from working with the topic in your group.

Presumably, the ideas relate to each other in some way. So your next step is to organize these ideas. Clear organization helps your audience understand better what you have to say. Here are some frequently used patterns of arrangement you can consider:

Chronological arrangement is the discussion of ideas based on a time sequence. This arrangement applies if you are covering a series of steps or presenting historical information.

Topical arrangement is used to organize a topic into its natural divisions. You may find that "background," "plan," and "implementation" are logical divisions if your group was assigned a problem-solving task and you want to give a full description of your deliberations.

Spatial arrangement organizes ideas in terms of location or position. A plan for laying out a new building or department area might be organized in this fashion. Each main point might indicate a floor of the building. The component areas of each floor also might be presented spatially. Visual aids might help the listener orient to what you are saying.

Cause to effect or **effect to cause** is an organization you might use if you are presenting a problem. This pattern does exactly what the terms say. You state why the problem exists—the causes—and then show their impact—the effect. The effect-to-cause pattern reverses this sequence. This type of organization can be used to present your group's deliberations regarding any type of problem they have been assigned.

Problem–solution arrangement is a pattern where you first talk about a problem and then present a solution to it. Discussion of the problem often includes presentation of the harm in the situation, the significance of the problem, and its causes. Discussion of the solution generally presents a proposal to solve the problem and evidence that shows the plan can reasonably be expected to work. This is usually a persuasive presentation in this form. It would be an informative speech if the presentation traces the course of an already solved problem.

We recommend that you organize your ideas, rather than just let your speech flow by presenting ideas related to the topic as they occur to you. The "letting the speech flow" method can be confusing to your audience and does not allow you to preview your points in your introduction to the speech—an idea suggested shortly in our discussion of the introduction.

Looking Back: A Quick Review

HOW TO ORGANIZE YOUR IDEAS

Chronological	Use a time sequence.
Topical	Use the natural divisions of the topic.
Spatial	Use the location or position to lay out your points.
Cause to effect	State why the problem exists; state the impact of the problem.
Effect to cause	State the impact of the problem; tell why it exists.
Problem–solution	Present the problem; provide a plan for dealing with it.

5. *Support Your Major Ideas*

The goals of any oral presentation are for the audience to remember and believe the main points. These goals are achieved through careful support of each idea with examples and evidence of various types.

Examples are instances that serve as an illustration. An example might include a lot of detail (a victim or victims of the problem your group is studying, with names, dates, etc.) or very little detail (just the names of victims of your problem). An example might be factual in that it describes real events, people, and so forth, or it might be hypothetical in that it describes a plausible event, typical event, person, and so forth. The number of examples you offer may vary too. You will want a few vivid examples if you are merely illustrating a situation so your audience "will get the picture." You will want many examples, and may summarize these with statistics, if you are using the examples to persuade the audience there is a problem.

Statistics and testimony are two other kinds of evidence that you will probably want to use. *Statistics* are numbers used to quantify or explain a situation. Statistics can help members of your audience understand how serious your problem is and even how it might relate to them. For example, if your group researched a parking problem at your institution, you might be able to say that there are parking spaces for only 70 percent of the students—based on the notion that not all students attend class at the same time. And, further, three students will be five or more minutes late every day for each class offered.

Testimony is a personal statement about your topic that is quoted directly or paraphrased. Such statements may be from a recognized authority or merely from a person who has experienced your problem firsthand. Be sure to tell your audience the credentials of the person making the statement. This can be accomplished by a simple introductory clause to the statement. For example, "Bill Gates, CEO of Microsoft, was quoted in *Newsweek* as saying, . . ." or "Hannah Fahndrich, a victim of this telephone scam, reports. . . ."

Visual support for your ideas can take many forms and help hold the audience's interest. Visuals help your audience remember and often make the point more vivid. The options for visual materials are many. Sometimes it is practical to bring in an **object** that is central to your presentation. The object may be too big, so you may select the option of either a **model** or a **picture** of it. A **map,** be it a topographical map or a diagram of the floor plan for a building, is certainly useful for visualizing the territory. A **chart** is useful if you need to display data so your audience can easily digest it. This may take the form of a pie chart or bar graph. You may prepare paper **handouts** for a variety of purposes. A handout could be an outline with space for people to write, with the aim of helping them stay involved. It might be copies of slides you will use. It might be related materials you want them to read later. Be sure to time the distribution of your handouts to meet the purpose you have in mind for them. **Transparencies** or a **multimedia presentation** of slides or video clips can be especially effective for presentation of your support if the equipment is available. You will find helpful information on how to construct professional-quality graphics in Appendix B.

Looking Back: A Quick Review

KINDS OF SUPPORT FOR A POINT

Examples	Provide an illustration.
	Provide specific instances.
	Provide real or hypothetical examples.
Statistics	Provide numerical quantification.
	Provide percentages to show breakdowns.
Testimony	Provide a statement from an expert as backing.
	Provide the credentials of your expert.
Visual support	Provide a model or picture.
	Provide an actual object.
	Provide printed handouts.
	Provide visual images via a projection unit.

Of course, you will want to make sure the evidence you use meets acceptable standards. Refer to Chapter 2 where we discussed standards for evidence, whether you get your information from the library or from the Internet.

6. Develop an Introduction and a Conclusion

A final and very important step in planning your oral presentation is to construct an introduction and a conclusion. We strongly recommend that you give careful attention to developing an effective introduction and an effective conclusion.

The introduction.   The introduction to an oral presentation has three audience-oriented goals. It gains their attention, shows them how the topic is related to them, and reveals the thesis of the talk.

Gain attention.   There are five opening techniques you can use to gain attention. Use of *humor* can be effective if you are good at providing it. You will know whether what you say when you are attempting to be humorous is actually funny to others. If so, humor may work for you. Here are a couple of pointers. First, be sure the humor actually relates to the topic. Second, humor that belittles is often inappropriate.

Offer a **striking statement** or a **striking quotation.** Your statement must be something out of the ordinary if it is to catch the audience's attention. Of course, the statement has to be true but something the audience does not already know.

Often people are not aware of the seriousness or significance of a problem. You might use the most potent data that describe the problem as an opener if you are presenting a problem.

You might ask an **intriguing question** that you want your audience to answer or that you will later answer. You could call your audience's attention to the seriousness of a parking problem by asking a series of questions: "How many of you have been late to class because of not finding a parking space? Did you know how many others have been experiencing the same problem? Your experience is like mine and so I'd like to talk to you about this problem." Your intriguing question might be a **rhetorical question** that you expect to answer later. One speaker started this way, "I was late to class this morning. Maybe you were too. Is there any way to solve this problem? I think there is. Today I will offer you a practical solution to this nagging problem."

Telling a story is an excellent way to gain your audience's attention. The story can be true or fictional. Be sure the story is plausible and consistent with the material you will present if it is fictional. Of course, the story should make a point that is related to your topic in a significant way. If you are presenting a problem, telling a brief story about a victim of your problem can be especially effective.

Demonstrate the need.   People want to know how your topic relates to them personally. You will want to do some careful thinking here since this must relate to the specific topic. Ask yourself, "Why is this important to you?" "How are you connected to the topic?" The answers to these questions often point to needs to know in others since you may share a lot in common with the audience—presumably you are there because you share something. For example, in the parking problem we mentioned above, you probably share frustration with other audience members. You might say, "Undoubtedly, you share my frustration in not being able to find a parking space when you are late for class. I will show you how you can help me solve this problem."

Provide a thesis statement. Here is where you provide your audience the key idea around which all else you say revolves. Here is where you ensure that your audience will know where you are headed. The thesis is a single sentence that reveals your point. "We have a serious student parking problem that we can solve" provides a thesis statement for the parking presentation. Here you also might preview the points you will make. After the one-sentence statement, say, "First, I will describe the parking problem, then I will share a plan to solve that problem, and finally I will show you why this plan will work."

The conclusion. A conclusion should do two things: summarize ideas and tie the speech together. Your conclusion should summarize your points if your purpose was to inform. This is your opportunity to reinforce what you hope your audience will remember from your speech. You should summarize your arguments if your speech was persuasive. Tie the speech together with a final statement. This statement might refer to the attention-getting device with which you began or might be a challenge if the speech is persuasive.

Looking Back: A Quick Review

PURPOSES OF INTRODUCTIONS AND CONCLUSIONS

Introduction	Gain attention Demonstrate need Provide a thesis
Conclusion	Provide a summary of the points or arguments Tie the speech together with a final statement

STEPS IN PREPARING A FORMAL PRESENTATION

1. Identify your purpose.
2. Identify and analyze your audience.
3. Select and narrow your topic.
4. Identify and organize your main points.
5. Plan how to support your points.
6. Develop an introduction and conclusion.

Presenting Your Ideas to the Audience

Presenting your ideas to the audience will require preparation of notes, practice of the actual speech, and some specific behaviors during the speech.

PREPARING TO DELIVER YOUR SPEECH   We recommend you deliver your speech extemporaneously. An **extemporaneous speech** is a prepared speech that is delivered using note cards you made during your preparation. You should not generally expect to use extensive notes as they can get in the way of your ability to maintain adequate eye contact with audience members. We recommend a "key word" outline that includes everything you need to say, but not written out in sentences. Specific quotations may appear on a single card and be read. You may not need note cards at all if you have prepared a visual program that uses slides. Many speakers find that these slides substitute well for note cards.

Practice your speech, including use of visual aids. Keep your practice sessions brief and flexible. It is better to have several sessions rather than one long session. We suggest going over the speech two or three times. You also might practice in different settings. You may wish to practice in the actual room you will use if the presentation is an especially important one. Pay attention to the kind of eye contact you maintain and the gestures you use as you practice. Eye contact and gestures don't just happen naturally for most people, so practice can be a benefit. Also, be aware of where you focus your attention when using a visual aid. Many speakers have a tendency to talk to the visual aid rather than to the audience. Finally, pay attention to your voice. You will want to speak loudly enough and with enough vocal energy to hold your audience's attention.

If you have access to videotaping equipment, you can benefit greatly from the review of a videotaped practice session. If you do not have the equipment, you might have a colleague view your presentation and offer a critique.

DURING YOUR PRESENTATION   What should you do during the presentation? Obviously, you are a unique person. Try to be yourself when you speak. Let your personality show. It is usually a mistake to pretend to be someone you are not or to hide what you are feeling. We do not mean to say that you should not try to control your nervousness, but know that you as a person are something you want to reveal. Beyond this, we offer these suggestions: (1) Speak up and slow down; (2) stand or sit still; move only for a reason; (3) gesture naturally; and (4) maintain eye contact with your audience.

SPEAK UP AND SLOW DOWN   Unless a public address system is available, the listeners will depend upon you to make yourself heard. The larger the audience, the greater the floor noise it generates. There are two ways to overcome the noise. You can speak up and you can slow down. This will allow your audience to hear and understand you.

STAND OR SIT STILL; OR MOVE FOR A REASON   You may get so involved in what you are saying and how you are feeling that you move aimlessly. An audience always notices aimless and purposeless movement and, usually, it signals that the speaker is uncomfortable. Standing or sitting still may feel awkward to you, but it will look natural to your audience. Let your movement be intentional and work for you. For example, if you want to emphasize a point and are standing, actually move a step or two.

GESTURE NATURALLY   Understand that gestures do reinforce points you are making just as they do in conversation. You will probably be animated in your presentation if you allow yourself to gesture in your practice session. Most people cannot plan to gesture and have it appear as being a natural movement. So allow yourself to move naturally as you practice your presentation.

MAINTAIN EFFECTIVE EYE CONTACT   It seems safe to say that all of us expect a speaker to give some visual attention. We all notice when this does not happen. Eye contact allows your audience to know your message is for them. So how much eye contact is enough? The answer is simple: You should give your audience most of your attention if you want to be effective. So give your audience as much eye contact as you can give.

Looking Back: A Quick Review

CHECKLIST FOR DELIVERING YOUR PRESENTATION

1. Speak loudly enough to be heard.
2. Avoid random movement.

3. Gesture to reinforce important ideas.
4. Maintain effective eye contact.

SUMMARY

Public discussions are those small group interactions carried on for the benefit of an audience. Forums involve full participation of the audience, either through question-and-answer sessions involving a group of experts or well-informed people or through actual discussion within the audience. A panel discussion is interaction involving specialists or reasonably well-informed people who share their points of view about a common topic or question. A symposium is a series of brief speeches with an audience present. It is often coupled with a forum or a panel discussion. A colloquium is an interaction that involves a group of experts being questioned by the audience. The selection of a format is related to how informed the members of the audience are and the purpose of the meeting.

There are six steps to follow in preparing for an individual oral presentation: (1) identify your purpose, (2) identify and analyze your audience, (3) select and narrow your subject, (4) identify and organize your major ideas, (5) support your major ideas, and (6) develop an introduction and conclusion. Ideas may be organized chronologically, topically, spatially, as cause to effect, and as problem–solution. Examples, statistics, and testimony may support ideas. Visual support may include an actual object, a model, a picture, a map, handouts, or slides—either transparencies or multimedia slides and clips. The introduction should gain the attention of the audience, show how the topic is related to audience members, and provide a thesis with a preview of your points. Methods of gaining attention are using humor, making striking statements or quotations, asking intriguing questions, and telling stories. Conclusions should summarize the ideas and tie the presentation together.

We recommend extemporaneous delivery for a speech. This means speaking with notes. Practice your speech several times using any visual aids intended for the presentation. Pay attention to developing effective eye contact, gestures, and movement. You may wish to practice using video equipment.

During a presentation let your personality show and try to be natural in your behavior. Beyond this, we suggest speaking up, slowing down the speaking rate, standing or sitting still, moving only for a reason, gesturing naturally, and maintaining significant eye contact with the audience.

KEY TERMS AND CONCEPTS

chart
chronological arrangement
colloquium
effect to cause
example
extemporaneous speech
forum
handout
intriguing question

map
model
multimedia presentation
object
panel discussion
picture
problem–solution
rhetorical question
spatial arrangement

statistics
striking statement
striking quotation
symposium
testimony
topical arrangement
transparencies
visual support

Appendix B

DESIGNING PRESENTATION GRAPHICS

Groups are often asked to present their work to other interested parties. The audience might be the larger group of which they are a part, a group of interested citizens, or management decision makers. These presentations can have significantly greater impact if you support them with presentation graphics. **Presentation graphics** are visual materials, designed with the aid of a computer, that support an oral presentation. They take the form of verbal outlines, graphs, pictures, and videoclips, with the outcome of a series of transparencies for an overhead projector or a series of computer-generated graphics for video output or some display system.

Even the person who is not a graphic artist can design presentation graphics with the aid of powerful software. Several popular presentation graphics programs are Adobe Persuasion, Corel Presentations, Gold Disk Astound, Lotus Freelance Graphics, and Microsoft® PowerPoint. These programs allow the designer to use attractive, audience-specific backgrounds, sophisticated graphs, text animation, and even videoclips.

The goal of this discussion is to help you develop credible presentation packages to present your group's deliberations. You will learn basic concepts and practices as well as what to embrace and what to avoid in designing your materials. However, this text is not a software manual. You will need to refer to your software manual to know how to achieve a particular effect with the program you use.

WHAT PRESENTATION GRAPHICS CAN DO FOR YOU

Presentation graphics serve three purposes: They can make it easier for the audience to follow your organization and ideas, they can make complex and abstract ideas clearer, and they can provide the speaker with an aid for organizing and pacing the presentation.

Help the Listener Organize Ideas and Remember Them

Organizing ideas is not a difficult task if your presentation has only two or three rather simple points. Suppose, however, that your presentation has two points and you want to break down each of these into two or three subpoints. Perhaps your group has been solving a problem, so you have two points: a problem and solution. Regarding the problem itself, you want to show the harm and the causes; you also want to discuss the solution by presenting a plan and its benefits. Suddenly, your presentation becomes complex.

One way to organize your material is to develop a series of slides. A **slide** is a single unit of a visual presentation. It might be one part of a series of transparencies to be projected with an overhead projector or one element of a series of computer-generated graphics to be projected on a screen or a video display unit.

These slides will be useful in presenting the main points in the body of the presentation and also will help your audience remember the points you made earlier when you wrap up and review in the conclusion part of your presentation.

Make Complex and Abstract Ideas Clear

Sometimes you will need to present complex materials that listeners may have trouble following. Often this material is in the form of statistics, cost projections, or complex procedures or policies. Charts, graphs, tables, models, and flowcharts will make complex information much easier for listeners to understand.

Help the Speaker Stay Organized

Your graphics program can take the place of the notes you might use during your presentation. The beauty of using graphics is that it allows you to give more direct attention to your audience and frees you from being tied to a podium and your notes. As you practice your presentation, you will discover the slides can become a substitute for your notes.

AVOIDING DESIGN TRAPS

The graphics package is not a substitute for the actual presentation. The focus of your listeners needs to be on you and what you are saying. So put in the necessary time to fully develop your speech before you turn to developing the graphics to support it. Keeping this perspective in mind as you develop presentation graphics will actually help you develop a better set of slides.

This section presents several important guidelines for avoiding situations that actually detract from your presentation. Design traps can distract your listener and actually make it harder for the person to focus on the point you are making. Here are several suggestions for avoiding these traps:

1. Be Judicious in Your Use of Words
If you include too much text, audience members can spend so much time reading the slide that they miss what you are saying. Edit each slide so that you use only as much language as needed to make the point.

2. Be Judicious in Your Use of Special Effects

Many graphic design packages allow you to incorporate sound effects, videoclips, and other multimedia elements. Careful use of special effects can enhance the presentation. However, including animation on every slide, constantly playing background music, and the like can seriously detract from the message.

3. Be Judicious in What You Place on Each Slide

Of course, you can use "hot and wild" colors. You can use clip art on every slide. You can bend the font. You can use a multitude of other special text manipulations. You can decorate the slide with seasonal references. Just because you can, though, doesn't mean you should.

The default colors and fonts of most templates have been chosen by the computer program designer to engage the audience and to promote clarity. They provide a visual unity that is important to your presentation. For example, if triangles are used to indicate main points on one slide, they will be used on the next. You should not add to or change these features unless you have a good reason to do so.

4. Be Judicious in the Number of Large Graphic Elements Placed on a Slide

Do not try to use more than one large graphic element, such as a picture or graph, on a single slide. The one exception is a slide that is designed to show a side-by-side comparison.

5. Be Judicious in Selecting a Design That Is Appropriate to Your Audience and Topic

All sorts of design treatments are available, so consider your audience. You might use more graphic experimentation with a younger audience than with older folks. You might use a template with balloons and confetti for a light topic—presenting a proposal for campus entertainment for the academic year—and a much more subdued template for a more serious topic—a plan for curbing campus violence.

CONSTRUCTING YOUR PRESENTATION GRAPHICS

Most presentation graphics software is designed to be used by people with varying levels of expertise. All feature a point-and-click design of the templates that allows a novice to be up and running very quickly. So you will be able to select from the already designed slides—the templates—and point at the feature with which you want to work. A click of the left button on the mouse activates the feature. The packages also include more advanced drawing and templating features to support the expert user.

The slide is the basic element of design, and a wide variety of slide templates are available. Typical slides are for titles, bullets, graphics, and other combinations of text and graphic material.

Plan Your Presentation

You will need to plan your presentation before you begin the process of producing slides. First, decide on the important points. What do you want the audience to remember?

What can you simplify with a graph or illustration? What do you need to help you keep on track?

After you have answered these questions, develop a rough plan for the graphic program to go with your presentation, which should include a thumbnail sketch of each slide. Remember that each slide is only a piece of your presentation, so resist the urge to put too much information on one slide.

Select a Template

Next, select one of the predefined templates that is appropriate for your audience and topic. This template will help you place bullets, arrange text on the page, and choose colors. If you have a great deal of experience and artistic ability, you may wish to modify the design of the template. You can do so by invoking the template master command in your software. When you make this change in the template master, you will make it for every slide in your presentation.

Make sure the template you select does not have a background design feature that will interfere with the text or images you may impose over it. For example, think about how a color design might look if you will present it in black and white. A color background that does not interfere with reading the slide may make reading difficult if it is produced in black and white.

Work with the Slide Window

All your design work takes place in the slide window of your presentation software. This window is surrounded with icons that allow you to use various tools for inserting text, for drawing, and for a number of other functions. Don't be intimidated. You don't need to use everything all at once. In fact, you probably shouldn't try. Get acquainted with the basic functions first. The button bars across the top, bottom, and sides provide tools to customize text, navigate the screen or the entire slide show, insert new slides, and play back what you have done so far.

Features vary from program to program, so you will need to follow your software manual for the details. For example, PowerPoint and other programs tell you where to click and where to insert the content.

USING FONTS   You will want to pay attention to the font size you use. A 16-point font is adequate for a slide that is being projected onto a screen but will look much smaller if displayed on a 27-inch monitor. Generally, a 16-point font is a good starting point on any display, but some items, such as titles, will have to be much larger, perhaps as large as 54 points. The defaults in your display package will get you started, but remember the display environment dictates the appropriate font size.

USING THE BUILD FEATURE   The build feature allows you to reveal the ideas on a particular slide progressively. You can hide text on the slide until you are ready to use it and thus focus your audience's attention on what you are saying. If you select this feature, you will want to use it with each slide to maintain a sense of consistency. (This principle is true for all design elements: bullets, colors, fonts, and so forth.)

Pay attention, too, to the level of detail of the build on each slide. Each level is generally cued by indenting the text. You will probably not want to use more than two levels. And more than three levels of text present a cluttered screen that overly complicates the visual task of your audience.

USING GRAPHS   Most presentation graphics software has a slide formatted specifically for graphs. The pop-up table that appears when you double-click on the graph icon allows you to supply the values for the graph output. After you create this slide, check the graph's colors. Will your display equipment be able to differentiate the color bars or lines displaying the data? If not, check in your user manual under the term *series* or *data series* to find out how to manipulate the output.

You should probably resist the urge to use three-dimensional graphics. You can check the results if you wish, but this kind of display can be confusing to the audience. A two-dimensional graphic often provides the clearest display of data.

USING IMAGES   Most presentation graphics packages allow you to import a variety of images from other programs or files. Many packages even include clip art, such as simple line drawings, symbols, and backgrounds. More sophisticated clip art is available from a number of vendors.

You may wish to scan an image if you have access to a scanner. You should get permission from the owner of copyrighted material for its use, especially if you are presenting in a commercial setting rather than a classroom.

A most important consideration in the use of an image is its relevance to the idea you are presenting. If you can't come up with a better reason than "it looks nice," don't use it. Also, remember that images take up a great deal of space on your computer's hard drive. You can make these files smaller if you use fewer colors, but there is a cost to the image quality. Follow two rules in making decisions about the use of colors: (1) don't reduce the colors to the point that the image doesn't make your point and (2) don't use more colors than your display device can produce. If your display can produce only 256 colors, it makes no sense to use images with 16.7 million colors.

Using Handouts

Presentation graphics software makes it easy to produce handouts with the content from your slides. Because the slides focus on the larger concepts in the presentation, the corresponding handouts can help members of the audience take notes.

However, you do have to decide when to distribute the handouts. Note-taking assistance is the advantage of handing them out before the presentation. The disadvantage is that the audience may read the package of handouts, rather than pay attention to you. Distribution after the presentation allows for greater focus on the speaker at the expense of the note-taking advantage.

Practicing Your Presentation

You will want to invest some time in practicing the presentation because coordinating the verbal presentation with the slides can be tricky. Also, the practice session will allow you to check the presentation equipment for problems. You may find a unique piece of equipment. You may find the placement of the presentation equipment doesn't serve your needs. You may discover that the projection screen is too small. The only way to check these details is to hold a practice session in the actual room and with the equipment you will use.

SUMMARY

Many powerful graphics programs enable you to create attractive, audience-specific backgrounds; sophisticated graphs; text animation; and videoclips. Graphics serve three purposes: they make it easier for the audience to follow your organization and ideas, they make complex and abstract ideas clearer, and they provide an aid for organizing and pacing the presentation.

You can increase the effectiveness of your presentation graphics by being judicious with words, special effects, and the placement of large graphics and by making sure the design is appropriate for the audience.

Several considerations are important in the construction of presentation graphics slides. Generally, predefined templates will help you avoid major design errors. Beyond this help given by the program, font size should be at least 16 points, and titles should be 45 to 54 points. The build feature enables you to hide some text until it is needed. You also can use handouts easily generated from the slide package. And, finally, be sure to practice the presentation with the equipment to be used in the actual presentation.

KEY TERMS AND CONCEPTS

build feature	presentation graphics	template
defaults	slide	transparency
fonts	slide window	
graphics	special effects	

glossary

abdicrat A person who gives up all power and responsibility.

abstraction Process of deriving a general concept from specific details; partial representation of something whole.

accommodation Situation in which individuals who are experiencing interpersonal conflict refrain from overt expression of the conflict.

active listening Process of paraphrasing the other's ideas or statements, including the provision of feedback about nonverbal messages.

activity track A category that designates dimensions of group interaction—task, relational, and topic.

adaptable social A person who looks to the group situation to determine what is an appropriate level of interaction and involvement.

affection, need for The desire to like and be liked by others.

affective conflict Conflict among people that is generated from differences in emotions or from relational frictions.

affiliation Attachment or unity on basis or terms of fellowship.

agenda Agreed-on arrangement of topics for discussion. Sometimes this term is applied to the private issues or problems that individuals bring to a group meeting.

agenda, hidden Secret plan that a group member has to achieve goals or objectives that are his or her own, rather than those of the group.

aggressor A self-centered role in which the member attempts to enhance his or her status or agenda by behavior, often abusive, that lowers the status of others and demands acceptance of his or her agenda or position.

anchoring Point of decision in the process of reach-testing. The cycle that includes an anchoring point follows the sequence: suggestion of an idea; agreement to the idea by others; presentation of examples to clarify the idea; and finally, affirmation, or confirmation, of the idea.

antecedent condition Any condition that precedes, and thus influences, an event or decision.

approach–approach conflict Conflict over mutually exclusive but equally attractive outcomes.

approach–avoidance conflict Conflict resulting when outcomes from an act or decision are perceived as both desirable and undesirable. The actor is attracted by one of the outcomes but put off by another.

arbitration Process of hearing and determining the outcome of a dispute between factions or persons; hearing given to disputants by an arbitrator, the aim of which is reaching a settlement.

assembly effect Ability of a group to be more productive, working together, than the sum total of productivity that individual members can achieve working on their own.

authoritarian leadership Sometimes called *autocratic leadership*; leadership style in which the leader directs the behavior of others by resort to power and rules.

autocrat   A person who exerts strong control over others.

autocratic leadership   See *authoritarian leadership*.

avoidance–avoidance conflict   Conflict that results when avoiding an undesirable outcome will yield a different undesirable outcome.

barrier (or) breakdown   Interruption in the flow of communication assigned or attributed to some structural defect in the communication process. This idea is controversial among communication scholars, who perceive it as inconsistent with a "process model" of communication.

blind area   A quadrant of the Johari window that describes a situation in which information about a person is not known to the person, but is known to others.

blocker   A self-centered role in which the member attempts to prevent progress on the group's task or agenda, often by raising objections, rejecting others' ideas, or taking a negative stand on the issue.

brainstorming   Group procedure for generating a large and diverse idea base quickly. Members of a group select a "recorder" and then generate as many ideas as may occur. Ground rules prohibit any editorial or judgmental remarks about member contributions. Brainstorming sessions are usually timed, and often a member creates a "group memory" by placing key words or phrases on a chalkboard or flip chart as they are offered by the group.

breakpoint   Transition in the developmental process of a group that is represented by a change in the group activity, topic, or task.

breakpoint, normal   Most common breakpoint by which a group moves from one topic to the next, or from one activity to the next, or moves to plan a task.

Burelle's Broadcast Database   A large and comprehensive print and broadcast media directory.

buzz groups   To maximize the input of members in a large group meeting, the large group is divided into subgroups of six persons. Each group discusses a designated question for a specific length of time and reports its conclusions back to the large group's leader. The leader collects the results and then displays them for the membership.

causal fallacies   The error is a mistaken causal relationship. A causal relationship between two events is present when one circumstance provides the basis or impetus for some other happening.

causal relationship   A relationship between two events that suggests the first event is responsible for the second event happening.

cause to effect   Reasoning that links two things together based on the idea that the first happens before the other. The first event is why the second event, the result, happens.

centrality   Term used to refer to the location of an individual in a communication network. Centrality is measured by the number of "linkages" required for a position to communicate, through channels, to every other position in the network.

certainty   In logic, the position that what is being observed could not have occurred by chance; 100 percent level of confidence. *Certainty* also refers to an attitude that is closed-minded, thus not considerate of alternative positions or points of view. The opposite of certainty, from this perspective, is *provisionalism*.

channel Means of transmission; the vehicle through which messages are sent.

channel capacity Measure of the maximal amount of information that a communication channel can handle at any given moment.

chronological arrangement Ordering ideas in a listing based on when they happened, usually beginning with the first happening.

closed mindedness A mental set in which the person assumes he or she is thinking correctly and therefore rejects opposing views without careful thought about these views.

coalition Alliance or agreement between two (or more) individuals. Coalitions are usually temporary and usually have to do with a controversial position.

code System of signs and symbols used to transmit messages between people; sometimes used to suggest a system of symbols used to translate messages from one form to another.

cognition Act, power, or faculty of apprehending, knowing, or perceiving.

cognitive complexity is a mental operating ability that allows a person to process complex information effectively.

cohesiveness Group's sense of unity, or "togetherness"; characterized by mutual attractiveness and willingness to work together; a measure of an individual's commitment to the group.

collection A gathering of individuals.

collectivistic culture A culture that encourages individuals to conform to group norms and show concern for the group.

collective efficacy The belief among members that their work on a particular task will lead to success.

collective evaluation A belief shared by members of a group about how members ought or ought not to act.

collective expectation A standard applied to behavior to discover whether it classifies as a norm.

colloquium Public group meeting format designed to inform an audience through the use of planned questions that produce unprepared responses from a panel of experts.

communication apprehension An individual's level of fear or anxiety associated with either real or anticipated communication with another person.

complex cyclic model A path of group development that is characterized by repeated cycles of focus on problems followed by focus on solutions.

compromise Negotiated conflict settlement in which each party gives up part of what is wanted in order to get the other part. From a game theory perspective, compromise is a lose–lose solution.

compromiser A maintenance role in which the member seeks a middle ground between two or more positions through mutual concessions.

computer-mediated culture A situation within a group where technology and group process are brought together so each affects and alters the other.

computer-supported cooperative work A group decision support situation in which a group uses computer support to help them in idea generation or decision making or both.

confederate   An accomplice and active participant who works with a researcher in an experimental study.

confessor   A self-centered role in which the member presents to a group his or her personal matters that are unrelated to the group's task.

conflict   A struggle between/among members of a group or groups involving incompatibility of opposing ideas, values, and/or limited resources.

conflict management   The functional handling of conflict.

conflict phase   A time in a group's task effort that is characterized by free presentation of ideas and counter ideas supported by evidence and reasoning in an attempt to arrive at some decision or decisions regarding the group's task. This is often preceded by an orientation phase and followed by an emergence phase.

conflict resolution   An attitude or mindset about conflict that includes a goal of settling the issue. The goal of bringing to an end or settling a conflict.

conformity   Behaviors produced by an individual that are uniform, consistent with the expectations of a social system, and least likely to produce negative consequences or influences from the other members of the social system.

confrontation   Conflict management technique in which participants talk directly about the conflict and relationship issues; sometimes called *confrontation–problem-solving method*.

confrontation-problem solving   A win-win conflict strategy that allows a group to collaborate in an attempt to gain consensus on an issue or situation.

connotation   Affective value or meaning of a word; emotional associations an individual user brings to a word.

consensus   Measure of the extent of agreement or commitment that members feel toward the decisions of a group. Generally, consensus means that all members agree with a decision.

content and relationship dimensions   Notion that language refers both to the world external to a speaker—the objects, phenomena, and events outside of the individual (content dimension)—and to the relationship existing between the speaker and the other individual (relationship dimension).

context of communication   Physical, social, psychological, and temporal environment in which a communication event occurs.

contingency model   Both Fiedler's and Poole's model of group leadership that predicts leader and group effectiveness.

contingency perspective   A leadership perspective that suggests selection of a particular leadership style (or perspective) is dependent on one or more factors.

coordinator   A task role in which the member draws together information, opinions, and ideas or checks relationships among information, opinions, and ideas.

control   The exercise of power and authority over self and others.

cooperation   Process of working together toward a common goal; sharing effort, expertise, and resources to achieve some mutually desirable outcome.

credibility   Degree to which a receiver believes a source; believability of an individual.

credibility gap   Tendency of people to disbelieve one another; difference between the image of integrity an individual attempts to project and the perception of integrity that another holds of that individual.

criteria   Standards of judgment based upon what is valued.

critical advisor   A person who suggests disadvantages to proposals, questions assumptions, sees errors in reasoning, and offers constructive criticism.

cross-functional   Team members understand each other's responsibilities and are ready to step in to perform these when a member is absent.

cross training   One way teams plan to pick up the slack when members are absent.

cultural diversity   The differences people possess because of their specific background and heritage.

culture (group)   History, traditions, and rules concerning appropriate and inappropriate behaviors of a group.

decision   Choice among available or imagined alternatives. A group decision is a decision reached by the process of consensus or by some other decision-making procedure validated by the group.

decision making   Process of choosing among alternatives; process of arriving at a decision.

decision-making meeting   A meeting at which group members interact for the purpose of considering action related to some concern.

decode   Process of taking message value from language or actions.

defective decision making   Victims of groupthink do not adequately survey their alternatives; they do not survey their objectives or examine the risks of what they are doing. They usually do not reappraise anything they have once rejected.

defensive behavior   Acts designed to ward off what is perceived to be an attack by another.

defensiveness   Behavior that has as its purpose preventing or minimizing a verbal attack from another person.

delay   A breakpoint that happens when a group moves back to repeat an analysis or activity.

delegating approach   An approach to leadership in which the leader turns over responsibility for decisions and their implementation to a group.

Delphi method   A group decision-making technique in which individuals respond to questionnaires until a final composite list is obtained that represents the opinions of the group. This is *not* a group discussion technique, since the group members do not typically or necessarily meet to talk about their responses to the questionnaires.

democrat   A person who can either take charge or allow others to take charge, depending on the situation and the needs of the group.

democratic leader   A group leader who stimulates the involvement of group members and encourages them to arrive at decisions through the process of consensus.

denotation   Associations usually called up by a word among members of a speech community; the "dictionary definition" of a word; the features of meaning of a word that are usually accepted by native speakers of a language.

description   An objective report of an observation and inferences.

deserter   A self-centered role in which the member withdraws from the group's deliberation in some way.

designated leader   Any individual who is appointed to a position of leadership, as opposed to an individual who emerges as the result of his or her perceived leadership potential.

deviance   Behavior of a group member that does not conform to the norms or expectations of the group.

deviant role   is one that detracts from the group's productivity because it focuses on the individual's goals and away from achieving the group's goals.

diagnostician   A task role in which the member analyzes and identifies task-related problems and brings them to the attention of the group.

disruption   A breakpoint that is represented by either a major disagreement or a conflict.

dominator   A self-centered role in which the member frequently talks more than what is his or her share of the available time.

Dow Jones News/Retrieval   This database provides business-related information. This includes company and industry news, economic and financial news, and stock trading information.

dyadic communication   Communication between two people. A dyad is not a group, since the minimum number that can be called a group is three.

dysfunctional conflict   Conflict that does not contribute to the group's progress toward its goals, or that is not productive. Not all conflict is dysfunctional, since conflict is inherent in change and in relationship management.

effect to cause   This is an argument or statement that represents a relationship of an end result (the effect) that has as its beginning in another event (the cause).

either-this-or-that reasoning   An argument that suggests to a listener that there are only two alternatives from which to make a decision. This is often a fallacy as there are generally more that two alternatives available.

elaborator-clarifier   A task role in which the member inquires about comments in order to gain greater understanding of the meaning.

electronic database   An information source that may be accessed via the Internet by visiting a particular site.

electronic journal   A scholarly reference work that is published on and accessed via the Internet.

electronic meeting systems   A group meeting where members are linked together and communicate via computers.

emergence   Gradual process in which groups develop the roles individual members will play, the norms that govern group behavior, and the decisions the group will validate by consensus.

emergence phase   Period in a decision-making discussion in which dissent dissipates as a group comes to agreement on a decision.

emergent leader   An individual who rises to a position of leadership as a result of the group's perception of his or her leadership potential.

empathic listening   A process of receiving information in which the receiver attempts to understand what is being said by a source from that person's perspective.

empathy   Experiencing what another person experiences; feeling what another person feels.

encode   To translate thoughts into words and behavior.

encoder Component of the communication process in which information is translated from one form into another. In speech, to encode is to translate ideas into spoken words. A telephone mouthpiece serves as an encoder as it translates spoken sounds into electrical impulses.

encyclopedia on disc A source of general information that may be accessed via a computer and a compact disk.

energizer A task role in which the member raises the group's level of enthusiasm for its work.

equality The attitude, reflected in communication choices, that each individual is inherently of worth. Equality encourages supportiveness. The behavioral opposite is *superiority*.

ERIC The Educational Resources Information Center (ERIC) is a national system that provides access to an extensive body of education literature.

ethics are the rules or standards for right conduct or practice.

ethics The branch of philosophy that studies moral value, rightness or wrongness.

ethnic diversity Group membership made up of two or more cultures or subcultures.

ethos Perception of an individual's character, as, for example, an audience's perception that a speaker is honest, knowledgeable, and of goodwill and intention.

evaluation Process of making a value judgment about some person, object, or event.

evaluative listening A process of receiving information in which the receiver attempts to understand what is being said by considering it through his or her experience and knowledge base.

evaluator-critic A task role in which the member analyzes or causes the group to analyze its work in terms of appropriate standards of productivity and quality.

evolution History of an object, idea, or event; enduring changes.

examples Support for an idea or argument by citing an instance to illustrate it.

exigency A need, demand, or requirement that is a result of some particular circumstance that motivates the desire to communicate.

expert power The influence a person has based on what the person knows and/or the person's abilities.

extemporaneous speaking Talking to an audience with preparation and notes regarding the message to be delivered.

fact Statement about an observation that can be demonstrated to be true.

fallacy An error in the reasoning process that makes an argument unsound.

fantasy The creative and imaginative shared interpretation of events that fulfill a group's psychological or rhetorical need to make sense of their experience and to anticipate the future.

fantasy chain A series of statements by members in which they jointly create a story.

fantasy theme The creative and imaginative shared interpretation of events that fulfills a group's psychological or rhetorical need to make sense of their experience and to anticipate the future.

faulty comparison An error in the reasoning process where two or more things are thought to be like each other, but are not.

feedback   Messages sent from a receiver to a source that have the effect of correcting or controlling error. Feedback can take the form of talk, applause, yawning, puzzled looks, questions, letters, increases or decreases in subscription rates, and so on. In groups, feedback sometimes is used by members to teach an individual his or her role, or to extinguish the behavior of a deviant member.

feeling expresser   A maintenance role in which the member monitors the mood and relationships within the group and articulates his or her mood and that of the group as appropriate.

field of experience   The image of the world that an individual holds as a result of interacting and communicating with it. The field of experience is dependent on language (how you talk about the world—the things you say to yourself and others) and on such things as memory and forgetting. Thus an individual field of experience is unique.

FIRO   *Fundamental interpersonal relationship orientation;* an analytical system developed by William Schutz for examining and understanding human relationships based upon need for inclusion, control, and affection.

focus group   Group with relatively unstructured interaction whose members meet to share their ideas about and experiences with a particular idea, product, or problem.

forcing   Method of managing conflict in which the person attempts to gain compliance by applying some sort of pressure.

forgetting curve   A model that traces the amount of material retained or forgotten over time.

forum   A large group meeting designed to encourage audience participation on issues surrounding a topic. Typically, a moderator introduces a speaker and a topic. The speaker presents a brief statement and then interacts with the audience. The moderator encourages audience participation and involvement.

function   Appropriate activity or action of a person or thing; purpose for which something is designed or exists; role.

functional perspective   In group communication theory, the study of the group processes in terms of the functions of a group or its individual members. When applied to leadership of groups, an examination of what the individual does—as opposed, for example, to a *trait perspective,* which would study individual features of the leader's character.

game   Simulation, with rules governing the behaviors of the participants. In game theory, games may be played in three forms: win–win, win–lose, and lose–lose.

gatekeeper   A maintenance role in which the member regulates the communication of members by keeping communication channels open, attempting to discourage monopolizing the talk and encouraging the low contributors.

gatekeeping   The act or process of filtering messages sent. Some messages are allowed to pass intact, others are distorted, and still others may be eliminated altogether.

gender   Learned characteristics and psychological attributes of masculinity and femininity.

goal conflict   Conflict among group members about what they want to accomplish.

goals   Anticipated outcomes of a group's interaction.

group   Three or more people who perceive themselves as a unit, who are mutually interdependent, and who interact about some common goal.

group decision support systems (GDSS)   A computer program used to assist a group in idea generation or decision making.

group failure   A disruption-type breakpoint that is a result of a group's realizing that its effort is not going to be sufficient to meet the task goals.

group identification   A state in which members see themselves more as part of a group than as individual people working in a group.

group mind   The idea that a group's way of thinking and feeling can exist apart from its individual members. The notion is out of date.

groupthink   A phenomenon that occurs in highly cohesive groups when the members ignore evidence and opinion contrary to their own views and disregard alternative choices in order to preserve their feeling of unity. Groupthink often leads to a faulty decision.

groupware   Software designed to integrate the use of a computer in group decisions making.

harmonizer   A maintenance role in which the member helps other members reconcile disagreements, mediate differences, and reduce conflict.

hidden area   A quadrant of the Johari window that describes a situation in which information about a person is known to the person, but not to others.

high-context culture   A society whose meaning in a communication relies heavily on nonverbal behaviors, the context of the message, the history of the relationships among the people, and the social rules governing the interaction.

hitchhiking   Use by a member of an idea of another member to stimulate his or her imagination, thereby creating an idea that is a variation of the original.

homepage   The primary page of an Internet website.

hypothesis, motivational-hierarchy   A thesis that Fred Fiedler presented to explain some of his findings about leadership style. It suggests that people are motivated to attain more than one goal at a particular time and these goals are ranked.

ideal solution sequence   A plan in which a group is asked to take into account the various ideal solutions the involved parties (groups) might favor.

ideational conflict   Disagreements among group members about conceptualizations.

inclusion, need for   The desire to be accepted, to feel wanted, and to be a part of a group.

individualistic culture   A culture that encourages individuals to pursue independence, self-interests, and autonomy.

inference   A guess; a judgment, based upon observational data, about the meaning of those data.

informal role   A set of behaviors taken on by an individual and regulated very subtly between the group and person. This contrasts with a formal role.

information   In information theory, available data. The more the available data, the more the information, and the greater the uncertainty. More commonly used to mean anything that reduces uncertainty.

information giver   A task role in which the member provides data from his or her personal knowledge and/or research.

information overload   Condition in which the amount of information is too great to be processed; typically, in groups, occurs when the number and complexity of messages are too great to be dealt with.

information processing   Using perceptions to transform data into information, usually followed by action on those perceptions. Can be either an individual or a group process.

information-processing system   A group of component parts ordered in such a way as to access data and assess it, conduct a sequence of events that allows it understand the data, and use this understanding to draw conclusions.

information seeker   A task role in which the member asks questions that prompt revealing of additional data.

information-sharing meeting   A meeting at which a group interacts for the purpose of enlightenment of members.

initiator-contributor   A task role in which the member instigates discussion of ideas and issues.

input   In group communication, the contributions of individual members; what the members bring to a group decision-making situation.

input variable   An element of the communication environment or attribute of a group that impacts the group's productivity.

interaction   Two acts by group members that occur in sequence and are related to each other.

interaction diagram   A diagram used to record the flow and number of messages sent in a group.

interaction process analysis (IPA)   A method of content analysis developed by Robert F. Bales that classifies messages into four categories: social-emotional positive, social-emotional negative, questions, and attempted answers.

Internet search engine   These sites provide key word searches of the Internet for sites that include information about the key words presented for the search.

interpersonal communication   Communication between or among people, characterized by give-and-take; distinguished from public communication by its more personal nature (as opposed to the impersonal nature of public communication).

interpersonal conflict   Competitive situation in which one person's behaviors are designed to interfere with or harm another individual (expressed); disagreement or opposition of ideas or opinions (unexpressed).

interpersonal needs   Motives that produce affiliation; reasons for establishing a relationship; in William Schutz's system, inclusion, control, and affection.

interrole conflict   The attempt to play two or more contradictory roles in two different groups.

intrapersonal communication   Communication within oneself.

intrapersonal conflict   Condition or status of emotional tension. See also *approach–approach, approach–avoidance,* and *avoidance–avoidance conflict.*

intrarole conflict   The strife that comes from an attempt to play a role in a group when members have different ideas about how the role should be played.

intriguing question   A technique for beginning a public speech that involves asking a puzzling question.

intrinsic interest   A level of concern and involvement generated by a particular issue or idea.

IPA   See *interaction process analysis*.

irresponsible member   A member who knows his or her obligations to a group, but often fails to meet them.

issue   A question that is central, or critical, to an argument. Issues may be of fact (something is), value (something is good), or policy (something should be).

jargon   Technical language evolved by specialists so that they can communicate more accurately and efficiently about their interests or concerns.

Johari window   A model of self-disclosure that uses an area divided into quadrants—open, blind, hidden, unknown—to illustrate different kinds of knowing in two-person relationships.

laissez-faire leadership   A behavioral style employed by some designated leaders in which the leader withdraws from the group process, leaving the group members to their own devices.

leader   One who directs and influences a group to move toward group goal achievement. A leader may be designated or may emerge.

leader as medium   A leader as the mechanism through which an organizing scheme of rules and procedures for problem solving is created.

leader, designated   A person appointed by someone in authority to direct the activities of a group.

leader, emergent   A group member, not appointed to lead by someone in authority, who directs the activities of a group because the majority of group members accept this person's willingness to do so.

leadership   In a group, the functional behaviors of a person, usually of high status, that contribute to the group's movements toward its goals.

leadership-structuring style   In a group, the functional behaviors of a person who directs the activities of a group by helping the group plan and organize its activities and set goals, while encouraging relative equality among its members.

legitimate power   The influence a person has over others because of being elected, appointed, or selected to lead.

leveling   Communication phenomenon in which messages are distorted by reduction of details, intensity, or complexity when they are repeated in a series.

LEXIS   LEXIS/NEXIS is an interdisciplinary, full-text database that includes newspapers, journals, wire services, newsletters, company reports, case law, government documents, transcripts of broadcasts, and selected reference materials.

linear model   A model of the communication process that describes or implies a straight-line direction of message flow.

listening   Active process of receiving and processing stimuli.

lose-lose method   Any method of conflict management where the outcome is such that each party loses some of what they had hoped to gain.

low-context culture   A society whose meaning in a communication relies heavily on verbal behaviors, the spoken words.

maintenance   Behaviors by group members that contribute to the cohesiveness of the group.

maintenance function   Behavior that is performed in a group that serves to support a group and its members.

maintenance roles   Sets of behavior that have as their aim the harmony and well-being of the group.

majority vote   A decision technique sometimes used by a group to resolve conflict; not recommended except when an attempt at consensus has failed.

meaning   The idea represented by a word or series of words.

meaningfulness   The significance of a word or series of words.

mediation   A conflict management technique in which disputing parties agree to negotiate with the help of an arbitrator; usually understood to be binding.

mental set   A psychological orientation produced by prior events or perceptions that contributes to bias in perception or comprehension.

message   Any sign or symbol, or any combination of signs or symbols, that functions as stimulus for a receiver.

method of residues   A process in which members are gradually eliminated as potential leaders until one person emerges to lead.

mindguards   Members of a group who take it upon themselves to protect the group from any information or opinion that might cause the group to deviate from its current position.

model   A physical representation of an object or a process. Models may be visual or verbal, and may be two- or three-dimensional.

modification, nonverbal   A cue or message sent, nonverbally, to modify the meaning of the verbal message.

motivational-hierarchy hypothesis   See *hypothesis, motivation-hierarchy.*

multimedia presentation   A public speech that uses computer-generated slides, video clips, and the like to support the ideas.

multiple sequence model   A model of group development that portrays a group as moving along three activity tracks.

mutual influence   The effect that two persons or things have on each other.

need for inclusion   An interpersonal dimension that represents the level of a person's desire to be part of the interaction in a group.

network, communication   In a group, the structure of channel linkages between and among members; a description of who communicates with whom, how often, and through what channels.

neutrality   An impersonal communication response pattern that suggest the responder does not care about the person or his or her ideas. It often creates defensiveness; opposite of *empathy*.

NEXIS   LEXIS/NEXIS is an interdisciplinary, full-text database that includes newspapers, journals, wire services, newsletters, company reports, case law, government documents, transcripts of broadcasts, and selected reference materials.

NGT (or) NGP   See *nominal group technique*; sometimes called *nominal group process*.

noise   Any source of interference or distortion in message exchange. Noise exists in the process to the extent that message fidelity is damaged. Three broad categories are (1) physical, or channel noise; (2) semantic, or psychological noise; and (3) systemic, or system-centered noise.

nominal group technique (NGT)   A group procedure for increasing productivity by asking members to follow a five-step sequence: (1) silent listing of ideas, (2) creation of a master list of ideas, (3) clarification of ideas, (4) straw vote or rank ordering for testing acceptance of ideas, and (5) follow-through.

nonparticipant   A group member who engages in very little to no interaction in the group to which he or she belongs.

norm   An unspoken rule that evolves out of a group's interactions to control and govern the behavior of group members.

normal breakpoint   A transition in the group development process where a group moves from one topic to the next or one activity to the next.

online catalog   A database of a library's holdings, accessed by a computer.

open area   A quadrant of the Johari window that describes a situation in which information about a person is known to the person and also to others.

openness   In language, the phenomenon that allows native speakers to talk about matters that they have not discussed before and to understand talk they have never heard before. In relationships, the willingness of an individual to receive and consider ideas from another.

operational definition   Definition by example.

opinion   An inference or conclusion; a personal or professional judgment.

opinion giver   A task role in which the member offers his or her evaluation of an issue and/or ideas related to it.

opinion leader   Person whose opinion molds public opinion; in a group, an individual whose ideas influence the direction or decision of a group.

opinion seeker   A task role in which the member encourages other members to offer their evaluation of an issue and/or ideas related to it.

organization   A human system designed to achieve some set of specific goals; characterized by a recurring sequence of events, such as a calendar year.

orientation phase   The initial period in a decision-making process; characterized by the members' establishing goals and getting to know other members.

orienter-summarizer   A task role in which the member attempts to keep the group or members on the task of the group. Reviewing the group's progress and then asking the group to move on to the next step in the decision-making process may accomplish this role.

output   In group communication, the productivity of a group or its individual members; the yield that is derived from communication in the task dimension.

overestimation of the group   Faith in a group's ability to accomplish a task that is beyond what most reasonable people would think prudent.

overgeneralization   A conclusion that results when data for some reason are not strong enough to support it.

overpersonal   Behavior of a person who goes to great lengths to be liked by others.

oversocial   Behavior of a person who goes to great lengths to join and be a part of groups.

panel discussion   Interaction of a group of experts on a predetermined topic or issue.

participant-analyst   A person in a group who observes and evaluates what is going on and takes action to provide whatever the group needs at that moment.

participant-analyst role   The behavior of a member of a group that is characterized by monitoring its progress and providing guidance based on the observations.

participating approach   A leadership style in which the leader shares ideas and facilitates group decision making.

perception   The process of becoming aware of stimuli that impinge on the five senses.

personal   The balancing of a situation in order to be liked when affection is desired but also maintaining distance when affection is not needed.

personal prejudice   A error in reasoning about an issue that has its basis in biases the individual employs in the process.

personalize   To indicate ownership of an idea or judgment by casting it in terms of first person pronouns, e.g., "I believe. . . ."

persuasion   The process of influence; the process of changing attitudes, beliefs, and behaviors.

persuasive power   The use of one's persuasive ability to gain acceptance of an idea or move people to action.

physical noise   See *noise.*

physiological noise   Disruption in the receiving and/or processing of information due to physical functioning of the body.

playboy/playgirl-clown   A self-centered role in which the member uses humor or "horseplay," or cynicism inappropriately so that it distracts from the group's productivity.

population familiarity   A feature of a group task having to do with the extent to which the group has had experience with the task.

positive feedback   Feedback that reinforces behaviors for the purpose of increasing the likelihood that the behaviors will recur; for example, nods of agreement, or laughter in response to an anecdote.

positive reinforcement   Increasing the likelihood of a particular response by rewarding it.

power   The perceived influence one person has over another.

primary tension   An experience of tension that individual group members feel during the early stages of group evolution or at the beginning of a meeting.

problem orientation   A focus upon the components of a problem and its possible solutions, as opposed, for example, to imposing one's own idea on another or the group; encourages supportiveness; the opposite is *control*.

problem-solution   Any communication or deliberation that seeks to lay out a difficulty and propose a plan for dealing with it.

procedural assistant   A task role in which the member helps a leader by making sure a group has what it needs so that its meeting moves along in an effective, efficient, and timely manner.

procedural leadership   Behavior that contributes to group productivity by focusing upon and providing guidance concerning group tasks.

procedural leadership functions   Those things that a leader does to ensure that the group is moving along in an effective, efficient, and timely manner.

process   Ongoing activity; continuous changing in the pursuit of a goal.

process variable   Behaviors of members that help a group move through its task.

productivity   Quantity and/or quality of a group's work in the task dimension.

programmed decision situation   A routine meeting that has as its aim coordination and information exchange. Very little, if any, decision making takes place in a programmed decision situation.

provisionalism   Behavior suggesting an attitude of open-mindedness, tentativeness with respect to a conclusion; opposite is *certainty*.

psychological noise   Disruption in the receiving and/or processing of information because of thinking that pulls thoughts away from the message.

punctuated equilibrium model   A group development scheme that is characterized by sequences of stable behavior, followed by disruptive behavior, with the return of stable behavior.

punctuation   In group communication, the arbitrary process of creating the meaning of a sequence of messages by selecting the beginning and ending points of the sequence.

punishment power   Exerting influence by withholding benefits or subjecting a person to unpleasant situations.

question of cause   A problem for group discussion that requires the group to examine data and evidence to determine the cause of the particular situation or issue.

question of definition   A problem for group discussion that requires the group to examine data and evidence to discover the meaning or significance of the issue.

question of fact   A discussion issue that does not involve value decisions or policies and that can be resolved by collecting information that addresses the issue.

question of policy   A problem for group discussion that requires the group to examine data and evidence to recommend a course of action to resolve or handle a particular situation or issue.

question of value   A problem for group discussion that requires the group to examine data and evidence to determine the desirability or preference of the group regarding a particular situation or issue.

reach-test cycle   A pattern of testing an idea that involves the suggestion of the idea, agreement with the idea, presentation of examples to clarify the idea, and affirmation or rejection of the idea.

reach testing   Introduction of a new idea based upon some anchored position in the spiral model. Group members accept, revise, or reject the idea through group discussion.

readiness level   The group's ability, motivation, and education or experience.

receiver   A person or thing that takes in messages.

reciprocity   An assumption that people will respond to behaviors with similar behaviors.

recognition seeker   A self-centered role in which the member seeks to call attention to himself or herself in some exaggerated manner.

redundancy   In information theory, a measure of the predictability of a message. The greater the redundancy, the greater the predictability and the less the uncertainty.

referent   An object or event to which a symbol refers.

referent power   The influence a person has because others identify with or are attracted to the person.

reflective thinking   A pattern, or sequence, of logical thought that provides the following convenient agenda for the tasks of a discussion group: (1) identify the problem, (2) define and delimit the problem, (3) develop evaluative criteria against which to test alternative proposals, (4) seek alternative solutions to propose and test, and (5) develop a final solution to advocate.

reflexiveness   A feature of all languages that allows the language to refer to itself. Language for talking about language is said to be self-reflexive.

regulation   In groups, substitution of nonverbal messages for words in order to control the behavior of group members.

reinforcement   Increasing or strengthening the likelihood of a response.

reinforcement phase   The final period in decision making, in which members congratulate themselves on completing their task effectively.

relational activities   Categories of interaction that focus on the social process.

relationship   Who a person is with respect to others. (*See* content and relationship dimensions)

relationship dimension   Behavior and ideas related to how group members connect socially.

reliability   Measure of the extent to which independent observers agree; measure of the extent to which a measuring instrument will measure the same phenomenon in different cases.

reward power   The influence that comes from a person's ability to provide or withhold benefits another person values.

rhetorical question   A method of beginning a public presentation in which the speaker poses an idea in the interrogative form, but does not immediately answer the question. Generally the answer will become evident as the speaker continues.

risky shift   The tendency of a group to be less conservative in decision making than an individual; the tendency of a group to take a greater risk than an individual. A group is more likely to gamble—to "go for" the greater payoff—than is an individual.

role   The part an individual plays in a group; behaviors evidenced by a group member that have been sanctioned by group approval; expectations that a group has of an individual's behavior.

role conflict   The result of a person's attempting to play two or more roles that are contradictory in function.

role, self-centered   A role that serves the purpose of personal enhancement of the role player at the expense of progress toward achievement of group goals.

role stability   The point at which a group member performs a particular role function in a group and the group reinforces the practice of the function, resulting in general agreement that the member should continue to perform that function.

role strain   Tension that results from a person's trying to perform a role, but being unable to do so.

scapegoating   Blaming others for one's own mistakes.

Scenario I   A pattern of leadership emergence, identified by the Minnesota Studies, in which a leadership candidate picks up support of another member and emerges to lead because no other member picked up support.

Scenario II   A pattern of leadership emergence, identified by the Minnesota Studies, in which a leadership candidate picks up support of another member and another leadership candidate picks up support of a different member. A leader may emerge from this leadership struggle.

Scenario III   A pattern of leadership emergence, identified by the Minnesota Studies, in which the group was confronted by a crisis and the member who managed the crisis emerged to lead.

Scenario IV   A pattern of leadership emergence, identified by the Minnesota Studies, in which a leadership candidate picks up support of another member and another leadership candidate picks up support of a different member. A leader does not emerge from this leadership struggle. The group may solve this problem by electing a leader or by having a series of leaders who serve for a short time.

secondary tension   Discomfort that a group experiences, or that is experienced by individual group members, it may be beyond the *tolerance threshold* for tension; that is, tension experienced by the group or its members that is so great that the group may no longer ignore it. Produced from sources other than orienting activities.

secretary-recorder   A task role in which the member makes a written record of the group's deliberations.

selective perception   The unconscious process of sorting through available stimuli, and selecting those to be perceived.

self-centered roles   Sets of behavior that have as their aim promoting the individual and his or her agenda.

self-concept   An image of oneself that has evolved out of interaction with significant others over time.

self-directed work teams   Mature groups that are given the authority to manage and accomplish a particular task.

self-disclosure   Revealing oneself—thoughts, feelings, beliefs, and the like—to another.

self-fulfilling prophecy   Process of making a prediction come true; for example, predicting that a group experience will be exciting and then fulfilling the prediction by experiencing the group as exciting.

self-reflexiveness   Ability of something to refer back to itself. Language is self-reflexive. People can be self-reflexive.

self-report rating form   Form used to report self-appraisals of performance in a group context.

selling approach   A leadership style that involves the group by asking for inputs and then selling these as important goals in a supportive climate.

semantic noise   Error introduced into a communication event because of peculiarities in the use of language; sometimes called psychological noise.

sensing   The act of receiving stimuli through the five senses.

sidetracker   A self-centered role in which a member moves a group away from its agenda or task.

single question sequence   A decision-making sequence formulated to help groups identify issues that flow from a problem.

situation/context   Terms used interchangeably to refer to the immediate surroundings of an event; the environment in which an event takes place; the presence of variables that may influence a communication event.

situational perspective   A perspective that relies on examination of a situation in order to guide decisions about appropriate leadership.

small group   Three or more individuals, up to about 11 individuals, who perceive themselves as joined to achieve some common goal.

smoothing   A conflict-management strategy in which a member attempts to play down or ignore differences in order to keep a disagreement from being addressed by the group.

social dimension   The relationship dimension of group communication, having to do with such relational matters as cohesiveness.

socialization   A two-way process of influence and change whereby group members use verbal and nonverbal messages to integrate a new person into their group.

social facilitation   The positive effect that comes to the group's effort from members working in the presence of each other.

socialization   A two-way process of influence and change whereby group members use verbal and nonverbal messages to integrate a new member into their group.

social leadership   Behaviors of individual group members that serve to maintain the group's relationships and cohesiveness.

social leadership functions   Functions members perform that facilitate the relational dimension of a group.

social loafer   A group member who makes minimal or no contributions to the group's effort. He or she does not feel the need to participate because the effort of other group members is accomplishing the task.

social loafer   is a person who does not contribute much to the group effort to achieve its goals because he or she is willing to let others carry the load.

social responsibility   The ethical obligation a group and its members have to act in the best interest of their society.

social tension   Uneasiness that group members feel when they are uncertain about members' relationships.

socioemotional   The dimension of a group that refers to its social and emotional make-up.

solution multiplicity   The number of reasonable alternatives to solve a problem.

solution-oriented model   A decision-making pattern that focuses almost exclusively on finding an acceptable plan for dealing with a problem.

source   Location of an idea; originator of a message.

source/encoder   A person who translates an idea or message into language and nonverbal behavior.

spatial arrangement   A pattern of ideas that makes use of their place in a space, e.g., the description of the rooms based on their location in a building.

special-event meeting   An unusual, not regular, one-of-a-kind meeting, or an occasional and traditional event meeting, such as the annual sales meeting of a company's marketing division.

special interest pleader   A self-centered role in which the member speaks on behalf of his or her private interests or those of an outside group, rather than those of the group of which he or she is a part.

spiral model   Model of decision development that encompasses backtracking and reach testing until group consensus is achieved.

spontaneity   A characteristic of interaction in which individuals speak freely and straightforwardly without editing or developing strategies of control; encourages supportiveness; opposite is *strategy*.

stability in perception   A phenomenon of the perceptual process that renders perceptions of people and things relatively constant or consistent with previous conceptualizations of those people and things.

standard setter   A maintenance role in which the member suggests rules, criteria, or other aids to engaging in appropriate task behavior.

statistics   Numerical representation of a situation; data.

status   One's place in a hierarchy; in a group, one's social position, either appointed or achieved as the result of interactions.

status, achieved   The position or ranking that a group member gains in a group's hierarchy because of other members' perceptions of the person's contribution and personality.

status, ascribed   The position or ranking that a group member has in a group's hierarchy because of the function that person is assigned to play by the organization of which the group is a part.

status conflict   Conflict over relative, or comparative, status among group members.

status consensus   Agreement among group members that the members' place in the status hierarchy is agreeable and appropriate.

stereotype   Application of a fixed set of characteristics about a group or subgroup to an individual member of that group or subgroup in such a way that the uniqueness of the individual is ignored.

stimulus   Data to be perceived; anything in the experiential field that arouses an individual or impinges upon the perceptual mechanisms of that individual.

strategy   Application of a plan to control another; the opposite is *spontaneity*. In interpersonal communication, strategy often fosters defensiveness.

striking quotation   A method of beginning a formal presentation in which the speaker repeats a statement from a book, speech, or the like.

striking statement   A method of beginning a formal presentation in which the speaker provides a memorable or surprising idea.

structure   The arrangement of components of a system at any given moment in time.

style   The general approach that an individual takes in providing leadership to a group.

substantive conflict   Conflict over ideas and issues. In group communication theory, conflict in the task dimension rather than in the social, or relationship, dimension of communication.

substitution   Using nonverbal messages instead of words to regulate another individual during a communication event.

superiority   An attitude or opinion communicated to another that the individual is beneath oneself. The opposite is *equality*.

supporter-encourager   A maintenance role in which the member offers warmth, solidarity, and recognition to the group's members.

supportiveness   A category of behavior identified and described by Jack Gibb that implies or suggests an interpersonal attitude characterized by candor, freedom from fear, and a sense of equality. Behaviors that yield a sense of supportiveness are description, problem orientation, spontaneity, empathy, and equality.

survey interview   A method of collecting data in which a representative group of respondents is asked to answer standardized questions, and the data are tallied and analyzed to make statements about the group, its attitudes, and its opinions.

symbol   Anything that arbitrarily "stands for" something else. Symbols do not usually bear any natural relationship to the things for which they stand. For example, a flag bears no natural relationship to the country for which it stands. A word bears no natural relationship to the thing it represents.

symbolic convergence   A process by which members of a group come closer together in their perceptions and values. The members achieve a common understanding of a set of symbols and a common pool of meanings.

symmetry   In communication, any response that mirrors the antecedent stimulus.

symposium   A form of group meeting used to present a variety of views in the form of short speeches or reports for the benefit of an audience. A moderator introduces a panel, provides a history of the issues, presents each speaker, monitors time, and ends the meeting with a brief charge to the audience or a summary of the ideas and issues presented.

synergy   is the energy or power that comes from people working together.

system   The sum total of all the components of a thing, plus all the relationships among those components, joined to form a single entity, and interdependent in such a way that any change in some part of the system affects the entire system.

systemic noise   A disruption that affects a group and has as its source something that is external to the group's immediate environment.

task The focus of a group's effort that leads to the achievement of the group's goal.

task difficulty Amount of effort required to complete a task. As a general rule, complex tasks (those that have multiple causes and multiple solutions) are more difficult than simple tasks (those that have few causes and few solutions).

task dimension Part of a communication event having to do with objects or ideas, as opposed to relationships.

task experience The extent to which a group is familiar with a task.

task leadership functions Efforts to facilitate group processing and thinking about the task, such as generating ideas and information, processing that information, thinking critically about decisions, and clarifying ideas.

task-process activities Categories of interaction that focus on the group's work.

task roles Behaviors that are performed in a group that relate to accomplishment of its goals.

team A mature group of three or more individuals who interact on a regular basis about some common problem or interdependent goal (task), provide their own leadership for development and performance, and exert mutual influence over one another.

teleconference A meeting where members are in different physical locations and are connected through the technology of audio and video.

telling a story A method of beginning a formal presentation in which the speaker repeats a story in order to introduce the topic.

telling approach A leadership style in which the leader provides specific instructions and close supervision.

tension releaser A maintenance role in which the member engages in various behavior in an attempt to relax group members.

territoriality The notion of ownership or attitude of possessiveness that individuals develop toward a particular space or particular objects.

testimony A method of support for an idea or topic that uses a quote from an expert or someone who has personal knowledge of the idea or topic.

theory The foundation of an explanation or description of any complex phenomenon; sometimes described as a complete set of "if-then" statements that serve to allow explanation or prediction.

thinking for yourself Independent consideration of an issue based on a person's own understanding of the issue, data, and reasoning process.

tolerance threshold The level of tension experienced by an individual or group such that any tension beyond that threshold must be addressed; the maximal tension that will not debilitate an individual or a group.

topic activities Categories of interaction that depict areas of content.

topical arrangement An ordering of ideas such that it makes use of a typical division of the topic into distinct parts.

trait perspective Attempt to understand leadership by examining the features of personality and behavior that are evidenced by leaders.

transaction Pattern of interaction between people.

transformational leadership   A leadership style that elevates, motivates, inspires, and develops a group or team. It is characterized by providing a vision and sense of mission, communication of high expectations, intelligent and rational problem solving, and personal attention to the individual members that is represented by a coaching and advising relationship.

transparencies   Clear plastic film on which words are superimposed and then placed on a device that allows projection on a screen.

triangle of meaning   A theoretical model that shows the relationship among an object, phenomenon, or event; thinking about that object, phenomenon, or event; and the symbolic representations people generate about their observations.

trust   Confidence in another person; belief that we can predict the behavior of another person.

20 percent rule   The rule that, when 20 percent or more of a group's membership is of a particular minority, acts of discrimination against that minority decrease.

underpersonal   The behavior of a person who has a low need for affection.

undersocial   The behavior of a person who isolates him or herself from group involvement.

unitary sequence model   A model of group development posed by B. Aubrey Fisher that suggests a group moves through stages of orientation, conflict, emergence, and reinforcement.

value   The worth of something; the characteristic or quality of a thing that renders it desirable.

variable   Something that can increase or decrease in some dimension, as in the variable worth of the American dollar overseas; something that can have different values.

vigilant interaction theory   A functional theory that suggests a group's productivity and effectiveness are enhanced through careful examination of the problem, clarifying objectives, developing all available alternatives, and examining potential consequences of accepting various alternatives.

visual support   Any method of supporting ideas that uses sight as a primary method of conveyance.

win-lose method   A conflict management strategy that leads to one person gaining his or her goal and the other person forfeiting his or her goal.

win-win method   A conflict management strategy that leads both parties in the conflict to achieving their goal.

withdrawal strategy   A conflict-management strategy in which a disputant leaves the conflict, either physically or psychologically.

references

Abrams, D., Wetherell, M., Cochrane, S., Hogg, M. A., & Turner, J. C. (1990). Knowing what to think by knowing who you are: Self-categorization and the nature of norm formation, conformity, and group polarization. *British Journal of Social Psychology, 29,* 97–119.

Adams, T., & Clark, N. (2001). *The Internet: Effective online communication.* Fort Worth, TX: Harcourt.

Adelman, M. A., & Frey, L. R. (1994). The pilgrim must embark: Creating and sustaining community in a residential facility for people with AIDS. In L. R. Frey (Ed.), *Group community in context: Studies of natural groups* (pp. 3–22). Hillsdale, NJ: Erlbaum.

Adler, N. (1986). *International dimensions of organizational behavior.* Boston: Kent.

Alderton, S. M., & Frey, L. R. (1986). Argumentation in small group decision making. In R. Y. Hirokawa & M. S. Poole (Eds.), *Communication and group decision making* (pp. 157–173). Beverly Hills, CA: Sage.

Alexander, E. R., III (1977). Communication and conflict resolution. In R. C. Huseman, C. M. Logue, & D. L. Freshley (Eds.), *Readings in interpersonal and organizational communication* (3d ed., pp. 287–304). Boston: Holbrook Press.

Alper, S., Tjosvold, D., & Law, K. S. (2000). Conflict management, efficacy, and performance in organizational teams. *Personnel Psychology, 53,* 625–642.

Altman, I., & Taylor, D. (1973). *Social penetration: The development of interpersonal relationships.* New York: Holt, Rinehart and Winston.

Anderson, A. B. (1975). Combined effects of interpersonal attraction and goal-path clarity on cohesiveness of task oriented groups. *Journal of Personality and Social Psychology, 31,* 68–75.

Anderson, C., John, O. P., Keltner, D., & Kring, A. M. (2001). Who attains social status? Effects of personality and physical attractiveness in social groups. *Journal of Personality and Social Psychology, 81,* 116–132.

Anderson, C. M., & Martin, M. M. (1999). The relationship of argumentativeness and verbal aggressiveness to cohesion, consensus, and satisfaction in small groups. *Communication Reports, 12,* 21–32.

Anderson, L. R., & Blanchard, P. N. (1982). Sex differences in task and social-emotional behavior. *Basic and Applied Social Psychology, 3,* 109–139.

Anderson, S. D., Riddle, B. L., & Martin, M. M. (1999). Socialization processes in groups. In L. R. Frey, D. S. Gouran, & M. S. Poole (Eds.), *The handbook of group communication theory & research* (pp. 139–163). Thousand Oaks, CA: Sage.

Andrews, P. H. (1992). Sex and gender differences in small group communication: Impact on the facilitation process. *Small Group Research, 23,* 72–74.

Argyle, M. (1975). *Bodily communication.* New York: International Universities Press.

Argyle, M. (1991). Intercultural communication. In L. A. Samovar & R. E. Porter (Eds.), *Intercultural communication: A reader* (6th ed., pp. 1–36). Belmont, CA: Wadsworth.

Argyle, M., Lalljee, J., & Cook, M. (1968). The effects of visibility on interaction in a dyad. *Human Relations, 21,* 3–17.

Aries, E. J. (1982). Verbal and nonverbal behavior in single-sex and mixed-sex groups. *Psychological Reports, 51,* 127–134.

Associated Press (1999, September 3). Demographics challenge employers and government. *The Mobile Register,* p. 15B.

Atwater, L. E., Carey, J. A., & Waldman, D. A. (2001). Gender and discipline in the workplace: Wait until your father gets home. *Journal of Management, 27,* 537–566.

Back, K. W. (1951). Influences through social communication. *Journal of Abnormal and Social Psychology, 46,* 9–23.

Baird, J. E., Jr. (1977). Some nonverbal elements of leadership emergence. *Southern Speech Communication Journal, 42,* 352–361.

Baird, J. E., Jr., & Schubert, A. (1974). Nonverbal behavior and leadership emergence in task-oriented and informal group discussion. Paper presented at the International Communication Association Convention, New Orleans.

Bakeman, R. (2000). Behavioral observation and coding. In H. T. Reis & C. M. Judd (Eds.), *Handbook of research methods in social and personality psychology* (pp. 138–159). Cambridge: Cambridge University Press.

Baker, D. C. (1990). A qualitative and quantitative analysis of verbal style and the elimination of potential leaders in small groups. *Small Group Research, 38,* 13–26.

Baker, W. H. (1980). Defensive communication: Its causes, effects, and cures. *Journal of Business Communication, 17,* 5–17.

Bales, R. F. (1958). Task roles and social roles in problem-solving groups. In E. E. Maccoby, T. M. Newcomb, & E. L. Hartley (Eds.), *Readings in social psychology* (3d ed., pp. 437–447). New York: Holt, Rinehart and Winston.

Bales, R. F. (1976). *Interaction process analysis.* Chicago: University of Chicago Press.

Bales, R. F., & Cohen, S. P. (1979). *SYMLOG: A system for the multiple level observation of groups.* New York: Free Press.

Ballard, D. I., & Seibold, D. R. (2000). Time orientation and temporary variation across work groups: Implications for group and organizational communication. *Western Journal of Communication, 64,* 218–242.

Bandura, A. (2000). Exercise of human agency through collective efficacy. *Current Directions in Psychological Science, 9,* 17–20.

Bantz, C. R. (1993). Cultural diversity and group cross-cultural team research. *Journal of Applied Communication Research, 21,* 1–20.

Barge, J. K. (1994). *Leadership: Communication skills for organizations and groups.* New York: St. Martin's.

Barge, J. K., & Hirokawa, R. Y. (1989). Toward a communication competency model of group leadership. *Small Group Research, 20,* 167–189.

Barker, J. R., & Tompkins, P. K. (1994). Identification in the self-managing organization: Characteristics of target and tenure. *Human Communication Research, 21,* 223–240.

Barker, L. L., Wahlers, K. J., Watson, K. W., & Kibler, R. J. (1991). *Groups in process: An introduction to small group communication* (4th ed.). Englewood Cliffs, NJ: Prentice Hall.

Barnard, W., Baird, C., Greenwalt, M., & Karl, R. (1992). Intragroup cohesiveness and reciprocal social influence in male and female discussion groups. *Journal of Social Psychology, 132,* 179–188.

Barnlund, D. C., & Haiman, F. S. (1960). *The dynamics of discussion.* Boston: Houghton Mifflin.

Bass, B. M. (1981). Traits of leadership: A follow-up to 1970. In R. M. Stogdill, *Handbook of leadership* (pp. 73–96). New York: Free Press.

Bass, B. M. (1990). From transactional to transformational leadership: Learning to share the vision. *Organizational Dynamics, Winter 1990,* 19–31.

Bass, B. M., & Avolio, B. J. (1993). Transformational leadership: A response to critiques. In M. M. Chemers & R. Ayman (Eds.), *Leadership theory & research: Perspectives and directions.* San Diego, CA: Academic Press.

Beachler, C., & Johnson, S. C. (1995). Leadership and listening: A study of member perceptions. *Small Group Research, 26,* 77–85.

Beisecker, T. (1969). Communication and conflict in interpersonal negotiations. Paper presented to the annual meeting of the Speech Communication Association, New York.

Belcher, C., & Johnson, S. C. (1995). Leadership and listening: A study of member perceptions. *Small Group Research, 26,* 77–85.

Bell, M. A. (1982). Phrases in group problem solving. *Small Group Behavior, 13,* 475–495.

Benne, K. D., & Sheats, P. (1948). Functional roles of group members. *Journal of Social Issues, 4,* 41–49.

Berkowitz, L. (1953). Sharing leadership in small decision-making groups. *Journal of Abnormal and Social Psychology, 48,* 231–238.

Birdwhistell, R. L. (1970). Masculinity and femininity as display. In R. L. Birdwhistell (Ed.), *Kinestics and context.* Philadelphia: University of Pennsylvania Press.

Blanchard, F. A., Weigel, R. H., & Cook, S. W. (1975). The effect of relative competence of group members upon interpersonal attraction in cooperating interracial groups. *Journal of Personality and Social Psychology, 32,* 519–530.

Blau, P. M. (1980). Cooperation and competition in a bureaucracy. *American Journal of Sociology, 59,* 530–535.

Blickensderfer, E., Cannon-Bowers, J. A., & Salas, E. (1998). Cross-training and team performance. In J. A. Cannon-Bowers & E. Salas (Eds.), *Making decisions under stress: Implications for individual and team training* (pp. 299–311). Washington, DC: American Psychological Association.

Bogardus, E. S. (1931–1932). Leadership in social situations. *Sociology and Social Research, 16,* 165.

Bonito, J. A. (2000). The effect of contributing substantively on perceptions of participation. *Small Group Research, 31,* 528–553.

Bonner, B. L. (2000). The effects of extroversion on influence in ambiguous group tasks. *Small Group Research, 31,* 225–244.

Booth-Butterfield, M. (1984). She hears: What they hear and why. *Personal Journal, 53,* 39.

Bordia, P., DiFonzo, N., & Chang, A. (1999). Rumor as group problem solving: Development patterns in informal computer-mediated groups. *Small Group Research, 30,* 8–28.

Borisoff, D., & Merrill, L. (1992). *The power to communicate: Gender differences as barriers.* Prospect Heights, IL: Waveland.

Bormann, E. G. (1986). Symbolic convergence theory and communication in group decision-making. In R. Y. Hirokawa & M. S. Poole (Eds.), *Communication and group decision-making* (pp. 221–231). Beverly Hills, CA: Sage.

Bormann, E. G. (1990). *Small group communication: Theory and practice* (3d ed.). New York: Harper & Row.

Bormann, E. G., & Borman, N. C. (1992). *Effective small group communication* (3d ed.). Edina, MN: Burgess Press.

Bormann, E. G., Cragan, J. F., & Shields, D. C. (2001). Three decades of developing, grounding, and using symbolic convergence theory. In W. B. Gudykunst (Ed.), *Communication yearbook, 25* (pp. 271–313). Thousand Oaks, CA: Sage.

Bown, V., Tumer, M., Larey, T. S., & Paulus, P. B. (1997). Modeling cognitive interactions during group brainstorming. *Small Group Research, 28,* 459–526.

Brewer, M. B. (1995). Managing diversity: The role of social identities. In S. E. Jackson & M. N. Ruderman (Eds.), *Diversity in work teams: Research paradigms for a changing workplace* (pp. 47–68). Washington, DC: American Psychological Association.

Brilhart, J. K., & Galanes, G. J. (1982). *Effective group discussion* (4th ed.). New York: McGraw-Hill.

Brilhart, J. K., Galanes, G. J., & Adams, K. (2001). *Effective group discussion* (10th ed.). New York: McGraw-Hill.

Broome, B. J., & Fulbright, L. (1995). A multi-stage influence model of barriers to group problem solving: A participant-generated agenda for small group research. *Small Group Research, 26*, 24–44.

Brown, V., Tumeo, M., Larey, T. S. & Paulus, P. B. (1997). Modeling cognitive interactions during group brainstorming. *Small Group Research, 28*, 495–526.

Buck, R., Miller, R. E., & Caul, W. F. (1971). Sex, personality, and physiological variables in the communication of affect via facial expressions. *Journal of Personality and Social Psychology, 17*, 314–318.

Bugental, D. B., & Lewis, J. C. (1999). The paradoxical misuse of power by those who see themselves as powerless: How does it happen? *Journal of Social Issues, 55*, 51–64.

Burgoon, J. K. (1996). Spatial relationships in small groups. In R. S. Carthcart & L. A. Samovar (Eds.), *Small group communication: Theory & practice* (7th ed., pp. 241–253). Madison, WI: Brown & Benchmark.

Burke, R. J. (1977). Methods of resolving superior-subordinate conflict: The constructive use of subordinate differences and disagreements. In R. C. Huseman, C. M. Logue, & D. L. Freshley (Eds.), *Readings in interpersonal and organizational communication* (3d ed., pp. 254–255). Boston: Holbrook Press.

Burn, S. M. (1996). *The social psychology of gender.* New York: McGraw-Hill.

Burn, S. M. (2004). *Groups: Theory and practice.* Belmont, CA: Wadsworth.

Buzan, T. (1991). *Use both sides of your brain* (3d ed.). New York: E. P. Dutton.

Byrne, D., Clore, G. L., Jr., & Worchel, P. (1966). Effect of economic similarity–dissimilarity on interpersonal attraction. *Journal of Personality and Social Psychology, 4*, 220–224.

Byrne, D., Griffitt, W., & Stefaniak, D. (1967). Attraction and similarity of personality characteristics. *Journal of Personality and Social Psychology, 5*, 82–90.

Cady, S. H., & Valentine, J. (1999). Team innovation and perceptions of consideration: What difference does diversity make? *Small Group Research, 30*, 730–750.

Campbell, D. (1958). Systematic error on the part of human links in communication systems. *Information and Control, 1*, 334–369.

Canary, D. J., Brossmann, B. G., & Seibold, D. R. (1987). Argument structures in decision-making groups. *Southern Speech Communication Journal, 53*, 18–37.

Caple, R. B. (1978). The sequential stages of group development. *Small Group Behavior, 9*, 470–476.

Carli, L. L. (1999). Gender, status, and influence. In E. J. Lawler, B. Markovsky, C. Ridgeway, & H. A. Walker (Eds.), *Advances in group process* (vol. 8, pp. 89–113). Greenwich, CT: JAI Press.

Carli, L. L. (2001). Gender and social influence. *Journal of Social Issues, 57*, 725–742.

Carli, L. L., & Eagly, A. H. (1999). Gender effects on social influence and emergent leadership. In G. N. Powell (Ed.), *Handbook of gender and work* (pp. 203–222). Thousand Oaks, CA: Sage.

Carnevale, P. J., & Leung K. (2001). Cultural dimensions of negotiation. In M. A. Hogg & S. Tindale (Eds.), *Blackwell handbook of social psychology: Group processes* (pp. 482–496). Oxford UK: Blackwell.

Carrocci, N. M. (1985). Perceiving and responding to interpersonal conflict. *Central States Speech Journal, 36*, 215–228.

Chemers, M. M., & Murphy, S. E. (1995). Leadership and diversity in groups and organizations. In M. M. Chemers, S. Oskamp, & M. A. Costanzo (Eds.), *Diversity in organizations: New perspectives for a changing workplace* (pp. 157–188). Thousand Oaks, CA: Sage.

Chen, Z., Lawson, R. B., Gordon, L. R., & McIntosh, B. (1996). Groupthink: Deciding with the leader and the devil. *The Psychological Record, 46*, 581–681.

Chesney, A. A., & Locke, E. A. (1991). Relationship among goal difficulty, business strategies, and performance on a complex management simulation activity. *Academy of Management Journal, 34*, 400–424.

Cline, R. J. W. (1990). Detecting groupthink: Methods for observing the illusion of unanimity. *Communication Quarterly, 38*, 112–126.

Cline, R. J. W. (1994). Groupthink and the Watergate cover-up: The illusion of unanimity. In L. R. Frey (Ed.), *Group communication in context: Studies of natural groups* (pp. 199–223). Hillsdale, NJ: Erlbaum.

Cohen, S. G., & Bailey, D. E. (1997). What makes teams work: Group effectiveness research from the shop floor to the executive suite. *Journal of Management, 23*, 239–290.

Coleman, D. (1992). Welcome to groupware '92. *Proceedings of Groupware '92* (pp. xii–xv). San Mateo, CA: Morgan Kaufmann.

Comer, D. R. (1995). A model of social loafing in real work groups. *Human Relations, 48*, 647–667.

Cooper, L. O., Seibold, D. R., & Suchner, R. (1997). Listening in organizations: An analysis of error structures in models of listening competency. *Communication Research Reports, 14*, 312–320.

Cooper, W. H., Gallupe, R. B., Pollard, S., & Cadbsy, J. (1998). Some liberating effects of anonymous and identified electronic brainstorming. *Small Group Research, 29*, 147–177.

Coser, L. (1964). *The functions of social conflict.* New York: Free Press.

Counsleman, E. F. (1991). Leadership in a long-term leaderless group. *Small Group Behavior, 22*, 240–257.

Courtright, J. A. (1978). A laboratory investigation of groupthink. *Communication Monographs, 43*, 229–246.

Cox, T., Jr. (1995). The complexity of diversity: Challenges and directions for future research. In S. E. Jackson & M. N. Ruderman (Eds.), *Diversity in work terms: Research paradigms for a changing workplace* (pp. 235–253). Washington, DC: American Psychological Association.

Cragan, J. F., & Wright D. W. (1999). *Communication in small group: Theory, process, skills* (4th ed.). St. Paul, MN: West.

Davis, J. H. (1969). *Group performance.* Reading, MA: Addison-Wesley.

Deese, J. F. (1958). *The psychology of learning* (2d ed.). New York: McGraw-Hill.

DeKlerk, V. (1991). Expletives: Men only? *Communication Monographs, 58*, 156–169.

Delbecq, A. L., Van de Ven, A. H., & Gustafson, D. H. (1986). *Group techniques and Delphi process* (2d ed., pp. 7–16). Glenview, IL: Scott, Foresman.

Den Hartog, D. N., House, R. J., Hanges, P. J., Ruiz-Quintanilla, S. A., & Dorfman, P. W. (1999). Culture specific and cross-culturally generalizable implicit leadership theories: Are attributes of charismatic/transformational leadership universally endorsed? *Leadership Quarterly, 10*, 219–257.

Den Hartog, D. N., Van Muijen, J. J., & Koopman, P. L. (1997). Transactional versus transformational leadership: An analysis of the MLQ (multi-factor leadership questionnaire). *Journal of Occupational and Organizational Psychology, 70*, 19–35.

De Souza, G., & Klein, H. J. (1995). Emergent leadership in the group goal-setting process. *Small Group Behavior, 26*, 475–496.

Deutsch, M. (1960). The effect of motivational orientation upon trust and suspicion. *Human Relations, 13*, 123–140.

Deutsch, M. (1968). Field theory in social psychology. In G. Lindzey & E. Aronson (Eds.), *The handbook of social psychology* (2d ed., pp. 412–487). Reading, MA: Addison-Wesley.

Deutsch, M. (1973). *The resolution of conflict.* New Haven, CT: Yale University Press.

Deutsch, M. (1985). Trust and suspicion. *Journal of Conflict Resolution, 2*, 65–79.

Deutsch, M. (1990). Cooperation, conflict and justice. In S. A. Wheelan, E. Pepitone, & V. Abt (Eds.), *Advances in field theory* (pp. 149–164). Newbury Park, CA: Sage.

Devine, D. J., Clayton, L. D., Philips, J. L., Dunford, B. B., & Melner, S. B. (1999). Teams in organizations: Prevalence, characteristics, and effectiveness. *Small Group Research, 30*, 678–711.

DeVito, J. A. (1994). *The interpersonal communication book* (7th ed.). New York: Harper & Row.

Dewey, J. (1910). *How we think*. Boston: D. C. Heath.

Dierks-Stewart, K. (1976). The effects of protracted invasion on an individual's action territory. Unpublished master's thesis, Bowling Green State University.

Dierks-Stewart, K. (1979). Sex differences in nonverbal communication: An alternative perspective. In C. L. Berryman & V. A. Eman (Eds.), *Communication, language and sex: Proceedings of the first conference on communication and gender* (pp. 112–121). Rowley, MA: Newbury House.

Dobbins, G. H., & Zaccaro, S. J. (1986). The effects of group cohesion and leadership behavior on subordinate satisfaction. *Group and Organizational Studies, 11*, 203–219.

Dodd, C. H. (1997). *Dynamics of intercultural communication*. Dubuque, IA: Brown.

Dominick, P. G., Reilly, R. R., & McGourty, J. W. (1997). The effects of peer feedback on team member behavior. *Group & Organization Management, 22*, 508–520.

Donnell, S. M., & Hall, J. (1980). Men and women as managers: A significant case of no significant difference. *Organizational Dynamics, 8*, 60–76.

Downs, C. W., & Pickett, T. (1977). An analysis of the effect of nine leadership group compatibility contingencies upon productivity and member satisfaction. *Communication Monographs, 44*, 220–230.

Dreksell, G. L. (1984). Interaction characteristics of emergent leadership. Unpublished doctoral dissertation, University of Utah.

Duerst-Lahti, G. (1990). But women play the game too: Communication control and influence in administrative decision making. *Administration and Society, 2*, 182–205.

Durham, C. C., Knight, D., & Locke, E. A. (1997). Effects of leader role, team-set goal difficulty, efficacy, and tactics on team effectiveness. *Organizational Behavior and Human Decision Processes, 72*, 203–231.

Eadie, W. F. (1982). Defensive communication revisited: A critical examination of Gibb's theory. *Southern Speech Communication Journal, 47*, 163–177.

Eagly, A. H., & Johnson, B. T. (1990). Gender and leadership style: A meta-analysis. *Journal of Personality and Social Psychology, 60*, 685–710.

Eagly, A. H., Karau, S. J., & Makhijani, M. G. (1995). Gender and the effectiveness of leaders: A meta-analysis. *Psychological Bulletin, 111*, 3–22.

Ebbinghaus, H. (1885). *Über das Ged ächtnis: Untersuchungen der Experimentalen Psychologie*. Leipzig: Dancher und Humbolt.

Edney, J. J. & Grundmann, M. J. (1979). Friendship, group size and boundary size: Small group spaces. *Small Group Behavior, 8*, 124–135.

Ellis, D. G. (1979). Relational control in two group systems. *Communication Quarterly, 46*, 153–166.

Ellis, D. G., & Fisher, B. A. (1994). *Small group decision making: Communication and the group process* (4th ed.). New York: McGraw-Hill.

Ellsworth, P. C., Carlsmith, J. M., & Henson, A. (1972). The stare as a stimulus to flight in human subjects: A series of field experiments. *Journal of Personality and Social Psychology, 21*, 302–311.

Ellsworth, P. C., & Ludwig, L. M. (1972). Visual behavior in social interaction. *Journal of Communication, 22*, 375–403.

Evans, C. R., & Dion, K. L. (1991). Group cohesion and performance. *Small Group Behavior, 22*, 175–186.

Exline, R. V. (1963). Explorations in the process of person perception: Visual interaction in relation to competition, sex and the need for affiliation. *Journal of Personality, 31*, 1–20.

Exline, R., Gray, D., & Shuette, D. (1965). Visual behavior in dyad as affected by interview content and sex of respondent. *Journal of Personality and Social Psychology, 1*, 201–209.

Farmer, S. M., & Roth J. (1998). Conflict-handling behavior in work groups: Effects of group structure, decision processes, and time. *Small Group Research, 29*, 669–713.

Fiedler, F. (1965). Engineer the job to fit the manager. *Harvard Business Review*, September–October, 115–122.

Fiedler, F. E. (1967). *A theory of leadership effectiveness*. New York: McGraw-Hill.

Fiedler, F. E. (1978). The contingency model and the dynamics of leadership process. In L. Berkowitz (Ed.), *Advances in experimental psychology* (vol. 12). New York: Academic Press.

Fiedler, F. E., & Chembers, M. M. (1974). *Leadership and effective management*. Glenview, IL: Scott, Foresman.

Filley, A. (1988). *Interpersonal conflict resolution* (2d ed.). Glenview, IL: Scott, Foresman.

Fisher, B. A. (1970). Decision emergence: Phases in group decision making. *Speech Monographs, 37,* 53–66.

Fisher, B. A. (1979). Content and relationship dimensions of communication in decision-making groups. *Communication Quarterly, 27,* 3–11.

Fisher, B. A. (1986). Leadership: When does the difference make a difference? In R. Y. Hirokawa & M. S. Poole (Eds.), *Communication and group decision making* (pp. 197–215). Beverly Hills, CA: Sage.

Foels, R., Driskell, J. E., Mullen, B., & Salas, E. (2000). The effects of leadership on group member satisfaction. *Small Group Research, 31,* 676–701.

Folger, J., Poole, M., & Stutman, R. (1993). *Working through conflict: A communication perspective*. Glenview, IL: Scott, Foresman.

Forsyth, D. R. (1999). *Group dynamics* (3d ed.). Belmont, CA: Brooks/Cole.

Frances, S. J. (1979). Sex differences in nonverbal behavior. *Sex Roles, 5,* 519–553.

Franz, R. S. (1998). Task interdependence and personal power in teams. *Small Group Research, 29,* 226–253.

French, J. R. P., & Raven, B. (1981). The bases of social power. In D. Cartwright & A. Zander (Eds.), *Group dynamics: Research and theory* (pp. 259–269). New York: McGraw-Hill.

Frey, L. (1994). *Group communication in context: Studies of natural groups*. Hillsdale, NJ: Lawrence Erlbaum Associates.

Gagne, M., & Zuckerman, M. (1999). Performance and learning goal orientations as moderators of social loafing and social facilitation. *Small Group Research, 30,* 524–541.

Galanes, G. L., Adams, K., & Brilhart, J. K. (2004). *Effective group discussion: Theory and practice*. New York: McGraw-Hill.

Gardenswartz, L., & Rowe, A. (1994). *Diverse teams at work: Capitalizing on the power of diversity*. Chicago: Irwin.

Geen, R. G. (1991). Social motivation. *Annual Review of Psychology, 47,* 377–399.

Gero, A. (1985). Conflict avoidance in consensual decision processes. *Small Group Behavior, 16,* 487–499.

Gersick, C. J. G. (1988). Time and transition in work teams: Toward a new model of group development. *Academy of Management Journal, 31,* 9–41.

Gersick, C. J. G. (1989). Marking time: Predictable transitions in task groups. *Academy of Management Journal, 32,* 274–309.

Gersick, C. J. G. (1990). The students. In J. R. Hackman (Ed.), *Groups that work (and those that don't): Creating conditions for effective teamwork* (pp. 146–153). San Francisco: Jossey-Bass.

Gersick, C. J. G., & Hackman, J. R. (1990). Habitual routines in task-performing groups. *Organizational Behavior and Human Decision Processes, 47,* 65–97.

Gibb, J. R. (1961). Defensive communication. *Journal of Communication, 11,* 141–148.

Goktepe, J. R., & Schneier, C. E. (1989). Role of sex and gender roles, and attraction in predicting emergent leaders. *Journal of Applied Psychology, 74,* 165–167.

Goss, B. (1982). Listening as information processing. *Communication Quarterly, 30,* 304–307.

Gouran, D. S. (1986). Inferential errors, interaction, and group decision making. In R. Y. Hirokawa & M. S. Poole (Eds.), *Communication and group decision making* (pp. 93–111). Beverly Hills, CA: Sage.

Gouran, D. S., & Baird, J. E., Jr. (1972). An analysis of distributional and sequential structure in problem-solving and informal group discussion. *Speech Monographs, 39,* 16–22.

Gouran, D. S., & Hirokawa, R. Y. (1983). The role of communication in decision-making groups: A functional perspective. In M. S. Mander (Ed.), *Communication in transition* (pp. 168–185). New York: Praeger.

Gouran, D. S., & Hirokawa, R. Y. (1996). Functional theory and communication in decision-making and problem-solving groups. In R. Y. Hirokawa & M. S. Poole (Eds.), *Communication and decision making* (pp. 55–80). Thousand Oaks, CA: Sage.

Gouran, D. S., Hirokawa, R. Y., Julian, K. M., & Leatham, G. B. (1993). The evolution and current status of the functional perspective on communication in decision-making and problem-solving groups. In S. A. Deetz (Ed.), *Communication Yearbook, 16* (pp. 573–600). Newbury Park, CA: Sage.

Graham, E. E., Papa, M. J., & McPherson, M. B. (1997). An applied test of the functional communication perspective of small group decision-making. *Southern Communication Journal, 62,* 269–279.

Grob, L. M., Meyers, R. A., & Schuh, R. (1997). Powerful/powerless language use in group interactions: Sex differences or similarities? *Communication Quarterly, 45,* 282–303.

Grob, L. M., Meyers, R., & Schuh, R. (1997). Powerful/powerless language use in group interaction: Sex differences or similarities? *Communication Quarterly, 16,* 481–495.

Gudykunst, W. B., & Ting-Toomey, S. (1988). *Culture and interpersonal communication,* Newbury Park, CA: Sage.

Guetzkow, H., & Gyr, J. (1954). An analysis of conflict in decision-making groups. *Human Relations, 7,* 367–381.

Gully, S. M., Devine, D. J., & Whitney, D. J. (1995). A meta-analysis of cohesion and performance effects on level of analysis and task interdependence. *Small Group Research, 26,* 497–520.

Guzzo, R. A., & Dickson, M. W. (1996). Teams in organization: Recent research on performance and effectiveness. *Annual Review of Psychology, 47,* 307–338.

Hackman, J. R. (1992). Group influences on individuals in organizations. In M. D. Dunnette & L. M. Hough (Eds.), *Handbook of industrial and organizational psychology* (3d ed., pp. 199–267). Palo Alto, CA: Consulting Psychologist Press.

Hall, E. T. (1959). *Beyond culture.* New York: Doubleday.

Hall, E. T. (1976). *Beyond culture.* Garden City, NY: Doubleday.

Harris, T. E. (1997). Diversity: Importance, ironies, and pathways. In C. D. Brown, C. Snedeker, & B. Sykes (Eds.), *Conflict and diversity* (pp. 17–34). Cresskill, NJ: Hampton Press.

Harris, T. E., & Sherblom, J. C. (1999). *Small group and team communication.* Boston: Allyn and Bacon.

Harrison, D. A., Price, K. H., & Bell, M. P. (1998). Beyond relational demography: Time and the effects of surface and deep-level diversity on work group cohesion. *Academy of Management Journal, 41,* 96–107.

Harrison, R. (1972). Nonverbal communication: An approach to human communication. In R. W. Budd & B. D. Ruben (Eds.), *Approaches to human communication.* New York: Spartan.

Hartung Hagen, B. J., & Burch, G. (1985). The relationship of group process and group task accomplishment to group member satisfaction. *Small Group Behavior, 16,* 211–233.

Haslett, B. B., & Ruebush, J. (2002). What differences do individual differences in groups make? In L. R. Frey (Ed.), *The handbook of group communication theory and research* (pp. 115–138). Thousand Oaks, CA: Sage.

Hawes, L. C., & Smith, D. H. (1973). A critique of assumptions underlying the study of communication and conflict. *Quarterly Journal of Speech, 59,* 423–435.

Hawkins, K. W. (1995). Effects of gender and communication content on leadership emergence in small task-oriented groups. *Small Group Research, 26,* 234–249.

Hawkins, K. W., & Fillion, B. P. (1999). Perceived communication skill needs for work groups. *Communication Research Reports, 16,* 167–174.

Hayakawa, S. I. (1991). *Language in thought and action* (5th ed.). San Diego: Harvest House.

Hearn, G. (1957). Leadership and the spatial factor in small groups. *Journal of Abnormal and Social Psychology, 54,* 269–272.

Henley, N., & Thorne, B. (1977). Womanspeak and manspeak: Sex differences and sexism in communication, verbal and nonverbal. In A. Sargent (Ed.), *Beyond sex roles.* St. Paul, MN: West.

Henry, K. B., Arrow, H., & Carini, B. (1999). A tripartite model of group identification: Theory and measurement. *Small Group Research, 30,* 558–581.

Hersey, P., Blanchard, K. H., & Johnson, D. E. (1996). *Management of organizational behavior: Utilizing human resources* (7th ed.). Upper Saddle River, NJ: Prentice Hall.

Hirokawa, R. Y. (1980). A comparative analysis of communication patterns within effective and ineffective decision-making groups. *Communication Monographs, 47,* 312–321.

Hirokawa, R. Y. (1982a). Consensus group decision making, quality of decision, and group satisfaction: An attempt to sort "fact" from "fiction." *Central States Speech Journal, 33,* 407–415.

Hirokawa, R. Y. (1982b). Improving intra-organizational communication: A lesson from Japanese management. *Communication Quarterly, 30,* 35–40.

Hirokawa, R. Y. (1982c). Group communication and problem solving: A critical review of inconsistent findings. *Communication Quarterly, 30* (Spring), 134–141.

Hirokawa, R. Y. (1983). Group communication and problem-solving effectiveness II: An exploratory investigation of procedural functions. *Western Journal of Speech Communication, 47,* 59–74.

Hirokawa, R. Y. (1985). Discussion procedures and decision-making performance. *Human Communication Research, 12,* 203–224.

Hirokawa, R. Y. (1987). Why informed groups make faulty decisions. *Small Group Behavior, 18,* 3–29.

Hirokawa, R. Y. (1988). Group communication and decision-making performance: A continued test of the functional perspective. *Human Communication Research, 14,* 487–515.

Hirokawa, R. Y. (1990). The role of communication in group decision-making efficacy: A task–contingency perspective. *Small Group Research, 21,* 190–204.

Hirokawa, R. Y. (1996). Communication and group decision-making efficacy. In R. S. Cathcart & L. A. Samovan (Eds.), *Small group communication: A reader* (7th ed., pp. 108–119). Madison, WI: Brown & Benchmark.

Hirokawa, R. Y., & Rost, K. M. (1992). Effective group decision making in organizations: Field test of vigilant interaction theory. *Management Communication, 5,* 267–288.

Hirokawa, R. Y., & Sheerhorn, D. R. (1986). Communication in faulty group decision-making. In R. Y. Hirokawa & M. S. Poole (Eds.), *Communication and group decision-making* (pp. 63–80). Beverly Hills, CA: Sage.

Hirokawa, R. Y., DeGooyer, D., & Valde, K. (2000). Using narratives to study task group effectiveness. *Small Group Research, 31,* 573–591.

Hoffman, L. R. Harburg, E., & Maier, N. R. F. (1962). Differences and disagreements as factors in creative group problem-solving. *Journal of Abnormal and Social Psychology, 64,* 206–214.

Hollingshead, A. B. (1998). Group and individual training: The impact of practice on performance. *Small Group Research, 29,* 254–280.

Hollingshead, A. B., McGrath, J. E., & O'Connor, K. M. (1993). Group task performance and communication technology: A longitudinal study of computer-mediated versus face-to-face work groups. *Small Group Research, 24,* 307–333.

Honeycutt, J. M., Knapp, M. L., & Powers, W. G. (1983). On knowing others and predicting what they say. *Western Journal of Speech Communication, 47,* 157–174.

Howell, J. M., & Avolio, B. J. (1993). Transformational leadership, transactional leadership, locus of control, and support for innovation: Key predictors of consolidated-business-unit performance. *Journal of Applied Psychology, 78,* 891–902.

Howell, L. T., & Becker, S. W. (1962). Seating arrangement and leadership emergence. *Journal of Abnormal and Social Psychology, 64,* 148–150.

Howell, W. S. (1982). *The empathic communicator.* Belmont, CA: Wadsworth.

Infante, D. A., & Gordon, W. I. (1991). How employees see the boss: Test of argumentative and affirming model of supervisors' communication behavior. *Western Journal of Speech Communication, 55,* 295–304.

Infante, D. A., Rancer, A. S., & Womack, D. F. (1997). *Building communication theory.* Prospect Heights, IL: Waveland.

Infante, D. A., & Wigley, C. J., III (1986). Verbal aggressiveness: An interpersonal model and measure. *Communication Monographs, 53,* 61–67.

Jackson, S. E., May, K. E., & Whitney, K. (1995). Understanding the dynamics of diversity in decision-making teams. In R. A. Guzzo, E. Salas, & associates (Eds.), *Team effectiveness and decision making in organizations* (pp. 204–261). San Francisco: Jossey-Bass.

Janis, I. L. (1972). *Victims of groupthink.* Boston: Houghton Mifflin.

Janis, I. L. (1982). *Groupthink.* Boston: Houghton Mifflin.

Janis, I. L., & Mann, L. (1977). *Decision making.* New York: Free Press.

Jarboe, S. (1988). A comparison of input–output, process–output, and input–process–output models of small group problem-solving effectiveness. *Communication Monographs, 55,* 121–142.

Jarboe, S. (1996). Procedures for enhancing group decision-making. In R. Y. Hirokawa & M. S. Poole (Eds.), *Communication and group decision making* (pp. 345–383). Thousand Oaks, CA: Sage.

Jarboe, S., & Witteman, H. R. (1996). Intragroup conflict management in task-oriented groups: The influence of problem sources and problem analyses. *Small Group Research, 27,* 316–338.

Jensen, A. D., & Chilberg, J. C. (1991). *Small group communication: Theory and application.* Belmont, CA: Wadsworth.

Jessup, L. M., & Valacich, J. S. (Eds.) (1993). *Group support systems: New perspectives.* New York: Macmillan.

Johansen, R., Vallee, J., & Spangler, K. (1979). *Electronic meetings: Technical alternatives and social choices.* Reading, MA: Addison-Wesley.

Johnson, D. W. (1980). Group processes: Influences of student–student interaction on school outcomes. In J. H. McMillan (Ed.), *The social psychology of school learning.* New York: Academic Press.

Johnson, D. W., & Johnson, F. P. (2000). *Joining together: Group theory and group skills* (7th ed.). Boston: Allyn Bacon.

Johnson, D. W., Johnson, R. T., & Tjosvold, D. (2000). Constructive controversy: The value of intellectual opposition. In M. Deutsch & P. T. Coleman (Eds.), *The handbook of conflict resolution* (pp. 65–85). San Francisco: Jossey-Bass.

Johnson, D. W., Maruyama, G., Johnson, R., Nelson, D., & Skon, L. (1981). Effects of cooperative, competitive and individualistic goal structures on achievement: A meta-analysis. *Psychological Bulletin, 89,* 47–62.

Johnson-Lenz, P., & Johnson-Lenz, T. (1992). Groupware in computer-mediated culture: Some keys to using it. In D. Coleman, *Proceedings of groupware '92* (pp. 130–132). San Mateo, CA: Morgan Kaufmann.

Johnson, S., & Bechler, C. (1998). Examining the relationship between listening effectiveness and leadership emergence: Perceptions, behaviors, and recall. *Small Group Research, 29,* 452–471.

Jones, S. E., Barnlund, D. C., & Haiman, F. S. (1980). *The dynamics of discussion: Communication in small groups* (2d ed.). New York: Harper & Row.

Jourard, S. M. (1971). *The transparent self* (2d ed.). New York: Van Nostrand.

Jungeward, D. (1974). *Everybody wins: Transactional analysis applied to organizations.* Reading, MA: Addison-Wesley.

Jurma, W. E. (1979). Effects of leader structuring style and task-orientation characteristics of group members. *Communication Monographs, 46,* 282–295.

Kameda, T. (1996). Procedural influence in consensus formation: Evaluating group decision making from a social choice perspective. In E. H. Witte & J. H. Davis (Eds.), *Understanding group behavior: Consensual action by small groups* (pp. 137–161). Mahwah, NJ: Erlbaum.

Kanekar, S., & Rosenbaum, M. E. (1972). Group performance on a multiple-solution task as a function of time available. *Psychonomic Science, 27,* 331–332.

Karakowsky, L., & Siegel, J. P. (1999). The effects of proportional representation on intergroup behavior in mixed-race decision-making groups. *Small Group Research, 30,* 259–279.

Karau, S. J., & Williams, K. D. (1993). Social loafing: A meta-analytic review and theoretical integration. *Journal of Personality and Social Psychology, 65,* 681–706.

Katzenbach, J. R., & Smith, D. K. (1993). *The wisdom of teams: Creating the high-performance organization.* Boston: Harvard Business School Press.

Kelly, C. (1984). Empathic listening. In R. S. Cathcart & L. A. Samovar (Eds.), *Small group communication: A reader* (4th ed., pp. 296–303). Dubuque, IA: Wm. C. Brown.

Kelly, J. R., & Karau, S. J. (1993). Entrainment of creativity in small groups. *Small Group Research, 24,* 179–198.

Kelly, L., & Duran, R. L. (1985). Interaction and performance in small groups: A descriptive report. *International Journal of Small Group Research, 1,* 182–192.

Kendall, R. A. (1995). Death of the encyclopedia salesman. *Computer Life, June,* 119–124.

Kenny, D. A., & Zaccaro, S. J. (1984). An estimate of variance due to traits in leadership. *Journal of Applied Psychology, 68,* 678–685.

Keyton, J. (1994). Going forward in group communication research may mean going back: Studying the groups of children. *Communication Studies, 45,* 40–51.

Keyton, J. (2000). *Communicating in groups.* New York: McGraw-Hill.

Keyton, J. (1999). Relational communication in groups. In L. Frey, D. S. Gouran, & M. S. Poole, (Eds.), *The handbook of group communication and research* (p. 192). Thousand Oaks, CA: Sage.

Kinlaw, D. C. (1991). *Developing supervised work teams: Building quality and the competitive edge.* Lexington, MA: Lexington Books.

Kirkmann, B. L., & Shapiro, D. L. (2000). Understanding why team members won't share: An examination of factors related to employee receptivity to team-based rewards. *Small Group Research, 31,* 175–209.

Kleinke, C., Bustos, A. A., Meeker, F. F., & Staneski, R. (1973). Effects of self-attributed and other attributed gaze on interpersonal evaluations between males and females. *Journal of Experimental Social Psychology, 9,* 154–163.

Kline, S. L., Hennen-Floyd, C. L., & Farrell, K. M. (1990). Cognitive complexity and verbal response mode use in discussion. *Communication Quarterly, 38,* 350–360.

Knouse, S. B., & Dansby, M. R. (1999). Percentage of work-group diversity and work-group effectiveness. *Journal of Psychology: Interdisciplinary and Applied, 133,* 486–495.

Kolb, J. A. (1997). Are we still stereotyping leadership? A look at gender and other predictors of leader emergence. *Small Group Research, 28,* 370–393.

Kolb, J. A. (1999). The effect of gender role, attitude toward leadership, and self-confidence on leader emergence: Implications for leadership development. *Human Resource Development Quarterly, 10,* 305–320.

Konrad, A. M., Winter, S., & Gutek, B. A. (1992). Diversity in work group sex composition: Implications for majority and minority members. In I. P. Tolbert & S. B. Bacharach (Eds.), *Research in the sociology of organizations* (vol. 10, pp. 115–140). Greenwich, CT: JAI Press.

Koomen, W. (1988). The relationship between participation rate and liking ratings in groups. *British Journal of Social Psychology, 27,* 127–132.

Kotlyar, I., & Karakowsky, L. (2006). Leading conflict? Linkages between leader behaviors and group conflict. *Small Group Research*, 37, 397.

Kramer, M. W., Kuo, C. L., & Dailey, J. C. (1997). The impact of brainstorming techniques on subsequent group processes: Beyond generating ideas. *Small Group Research*, 28, 218–242.

Krichevskii, R. L. (1983). The phenomenon of the differentiation of the leadership role in small groups. In H. H. Blumberg, A. P. Hare, V. Kent, & M. Daves (Eds.), *Small groups and social interaction* (vol. 1). Chichester, UK: Wiley.

Kuhn, T., & Poole, M. S. (2000). Do conflict management styles affect group decision making? Evidence from a longitudinal field study. *Human Communication Research*, 26, 558–590.

LaFasto, F. & Larson. C. (2001). *When teams work best*. Thousand Oaks, CA: Sage.

Langfred, C. W. (1998). Is group cohesiveness a double-edged sword? An investigation of the effects of cohesiveness on performance. *Small Group Research*, 29, 124–143.

Larkey, L. K. (1996). The development and validation of the workforce diversity questionnaire: An instrument to assess interactions in a diverse workplace. *Management Communication Quarterly*, 9, 296–337.

Larkin, T. J. (1986). Humanistic principles for organizational management. *Central States Speech Journal*, 37, 37.

Larson, C. E. (1969). Forms of analysis and small group problem-solving: *Speech Monographs*, 36, 453.

Larson, J. R., Jr. (1997). Modeling the entry of shared and unshared information into group discussion: A review of the BASIC language computer program. *Small Group Research*, 28, 454–479.

Lau, S. (1982). The effect of smiling on person perception. *Journal of Social Psychology*, 117, 63–67.

Laughlin, P. R., Van der Steop, S. W., & Hollingshead, A. B. (1994). Collective versus individual induction: Recognition of truth, rejection of error, and collective information processing. *Journal of Personality and Social Psychology*, 61, 50–67.

Leathers, D. G. (1969). Process disruption and measurement in small group communication. *Quarterly Journal of Speech*, 55, 288–298.

Leathers, D. G. (1976). *Nonverbal communication systems*. Boston: Allyn and Bacon.

Leathers, D. G. (1979). The informational potential of the nonverbal and verbal components of feedback responses. *Southern Speech Communication Journal*, 44, 331–354.

Lewicki, R. J., & Wiethoff, C. (2000). Trust, trust development, and trust repair. In M. Deutsch & P. T. Coleman (Eds.), *The handbook of conflict resolution* (pp. 21–40). San Francisco: Jossey-Bass.

Likert, R. (1961). *New patterns of management*. New York: McGraw-Hill.

Little, B. L., & Madigan, R. M. (1997). The relationship between collective efficacy and performance in manufacturing work teams. *Small Group Research*, 28, 517–535.

Littlejohn, S. (1992). *Theories of human communication* (5th ed.). Belmont, CA: Wadsworth.

Locke, E. A., & Latham, G. P. (1984). *Goal setting: A motivational technique that works!* Englewood Cliffs, NJ: Prentice-Hall.

Locke, E. A., Shaw, K. N., Saari, L. M., & Latham, G. P. (1981). Goal setting and task performance: 1969–1980. *Psychological Bulletin*, 90, 125–152.

Longley, J., & Pruitt, D. G. (1980). Groupthink: A critique of Janis's theory. In L. Wheeler (Ed.), *Review of personality and social psychology* (vol. 1). Beverly Hills, CA: Sage.

Ludwig, T., & Geller, E. S. (1997). Assigned versus participatory goal setting and response generalization: Managing injury control among professional pizza deliveries. *Journal of Applied Psychology*, 82, 253–261.

Luft, J. (1990). *Group processes: An introduction to group dynamics* (3d ed.). Mountain View, CA: Mayfield.

Manz, C. D., & Gioia, D. A. (1983). The interrelations of power and control. *Human Relations*, 36, 461.

Martin, J. N., & Nakayama, T. K. (2001). *Experiencing intercultural communication: An introduction*. Mountain View, CA: Mayfield.

Martin, M. M., & Anderson, C. M. (1997). Aggressive communication traits: How similar are young adults and their parents in argumentativeness, assertiveness, and verbal aggressiveness? *Western Journal of Communication, 61,* 299–314.

Maslow, A. H. (1970). *Motivation and personality* (2d ed.). New York: Harper & Row.

Maslow, A. H., & Mintz, N. L. (1965). Effects of esthetic surroundings: Initial effects of three esthetic conditions upon perceiving "energy" and "wellbeing" in faces. *Journal of Psychology, 41,* 247–254.

Mayer, B. (2000). *The dynamics of conflict resolution: A practitioner's guide.* San Francisco: Jossey-Bass.

McCauley, C. (1989). The nature of social influences in groupthink: Compliance and internalization. *Journal of Personality and Social Psychology, 57,* 250–260.

McCroskey, J., Larson, C., & Knapp, M. (1971). *An introduction to interpersonal communication.* Englewood Cliffs, NJ: Prentice Hall.

McCrosky, J. C., & Richmond, V. P. (1992). Communication apprehension and small group communication. In R. S. Cathcart & L. A. Samovar, eds. Small group communication: A reader, 6th ed. Dubuque, IA: Wm. C. Brown.

McGrath, J. E. (1984). *Groups: Interaction and performance.* Englewood Cliffs, NJ: Prentice Hall.

McIntyre, R. M., & Salas, E. (1995). Measuring and managing for team performance: Emerging principles from complex environments. In R. A. Guzzo & E. Salas (Eds.), *Team effectiveness and decision making in organizations* (pp. 9–45). San Francisco: Jossey-Bass.

McKinney, B. C., Kelly, L., & Duran, R. L. (1997). The relationship between conflict message styles and dimensions of communication competence. *Communication Reports, 10,* 185–196.

McShane, S. L., & Von Glinow, M. A. (2000). *Organizational behavior.* Boston: Irwin McGraw-Hill.

Mehrabian, A. (1972). *Nonverbal communication.* Chicago: Aldine-Atherton.

Mehrabian, A., & Diamond, S. G. (1971). Seating arrangement and conversation. *Sociometry, 34,* 281–289.

Mehta, S. N. (2000, July 10). What minority employees really want. *Fortune,* pp. 181–186.

Millard, R. J., & Smith, K. H. (1985). Moderating effects of leader sex on the relation between leader style and perceived behavior patterns. *Genetic, Social, and General Psychology Monographs, 111,* 305–316.

Miller, G. A. (1965). The magic number seven plus or minus two: Some limits on our capacity for processing information. *Psychological Review, 63:* 81–97.

Miller, G. R. (1978). The current status of theory and research in interpersonal communication. *Human Communication Research, 4,* 164–178.

Miranda, S. M. (1994). Avoidance of groupthink: Meeting management using group support systems. *Small Group Research, 25,* 105–137.

Mudrack, P. E., & Farrell, G. M. (1995). An examination of functional role behavior and its consequences for individuals in group settings. *Small Group Research, 26,* 542–571.

Muirhead, R. D., & Goldman, M. (1979). Mutual eye contact as affected by seating position, sex, and age. *Journal of Social Psychology, 109,* 201–206.

Mulac, A., Studley, L. B., Wiemann, J. M., Widenmann, S. J., & Gibson, T. W. (1988). Male/female differences and effects in same-sex and mixed-sex dyads: The gender-linked language effect. *Communication Monographs, 55,* 315–335.

Mullen, B., Anthony, T., Salas, E. & Driskell, J. E. (1994). Group cohesiveness and quality decision making. *Small Group Research, 25,* 189–204.

Mulvey, P. W., & Klein, H. J. (1998). The impact of perceived loafing and collective efficacy on group goal performance and group performance. *Organizational Behavior and Human decision Processes, 74,* 62–87.

Munduate, L., Ganaza, J., Peiro, J. M. & Euwema, M. (1999). Patterns of styles in conflict management and effectiveness. *The International Journal of Conflict Management, 10,* 5–24.

Murphy, A. J. (1941). A study of the leadership process. *American Sociological Review, 6,* 674–687.

Myers, A. E. (1962). Team competition, success, and adjustment of group members. *Journal of Abnormal and Social Psychology, 65,* 325–332.

Neck, C. P., & Moorhead, G. (1995). Groupthink remodeled: The importance of leadership, time pressure, and methodical decision-making procedures. *Human Relations, 48,* 537–557.

Newcomb, T. M. (1961). *The acquaintance process.* New York: Holt.

Nichols, R. (1957). Listening is a 10-part skill. *Nation's Business, 45,* 56–60.

Nichols, R., & Stevens, L. A. (1957). *Are you listening?* New York: McGraw-Hill.

Nierenberg, G. I., & Calero, H. H. (1973). *How to read people like a book.* New York: Pocket Books.

Northcraft, G. B., Polzer, J. T., Neale, M. A., & Kramer, R. M. (1995). Diversity, social identity, and performance: Emergent social dynamics in cross-functional teams. In S. E. Jackson & M. N. Ruderman (Eds.), *Diversity in work teams: Research paradigms for a changing workplace* (pp. 69–96). Washington, DC: American Psychological Association.

Oetzel, J. G. (1995). Intercultural small groups: An effective decision-making theory. In R. L. Wiseman (Ed.), *Intercultural communication theories* (pp. 247–270). Newbury Park, CA: Sage.

Oetzel, J. G. (1998). Explaining individual communication processes in homogeneous and heterogeneous groups through individual-collectivism and self-construal. *Human Communication Research, 25,* 202–224.

Oetzel, J. G., & Bolton-Oetzel, K. (1997). Exploring the relationship between self-construal and dimensions of group effectiveness. *Management Communication Quarterly, 10,* 289–315.

Offner, A. K., Kramer, T. J., & Winter, J. P. (1996). The effects of facilitation, recording, and pauses on group brainstorming. *Small Group Research, 27,* 283–298.

Ogden, C. K., & Richards, I. A. (1923). *The meaning of meaning.* New York: Harcourt, Brace.

Olaniran, B. A. (1994). Group performance in computer-mediated and face-to-face communication media. *Management Communication Quarterly, 7,* 256–281.

Osborn, A. F. (1959). *Applied imagination: Principles and procedures of creative thinking.* New York: Scribners.

Osborn, A. F. (1993). *Applied imagination: Principles and procedures of creative thinking* (3d ed.). New York: Scribners.

OSS [Office of Strategic Services] Staff Report (1969). *The assessment of men.* New York: Rinehart.

Ostendorf, V. A. (1989). Audio conference with ease. In K. J. Hansell (Ed.), *The teleconferencing manager's guide* (pp. 37–56). White Plains, NY: Knowledge Industry Publications.

Palme, J. (1995). *Electronic mail.* Norwood, MA: Artech House.

Palmer, G. J., Jr. (1981). Task ability and effective leadership. Technical Report No. 4, Contract No. 1575(05), No. 6, Contract No. 1575(05), Louisiana State University, 1962. In M. E. Shaw, *Group dynamics* (p. 190). New York: McGraw-Hill.

Park, H. S., & Levine, T. R. (1999). The theory of reasoned action and self-construal: Evidence from three cultures. *Communication Monographs, 66,* 199–219.

Parlee, M. B. (1979). Women smile less for success. *Psychology Today, 12,* 16.

Pavit, C. (1993). What (little) we know about formal group discussion procedures: A review of relevant research. *Small Group Research, 24,* 217–235.

Pavitt, C., & Johnson, K. K. (2002). Scheidel and Crowell revisited: A descriptive study of group proposals sequencing. *Communication Monographs, 69,* 19–32.

Pavitt, C., & Sackaroff, P. (1990). Implicit theories of leadership and judgments of leadership among group members. *Small Group Research, 21,* 374–392.

Pearson, J. C., Turner, L. H., & Todd-Mancillas, W. (1991). *Gender and communication* (2d ed.). Dubuque, IA: Wm. C. Brown.

Pescosolido, A. T. (2001). Informal leaders and development of group efficacy. *Small Group Research, 32,* 74–94.

Peterson, E. E. (1987). The stories of pregnancy: On interpretation of small-group cultures. *Communication Quarterly, 35,* 39–47.

Peterson, P. (1975). An investigation of sex differences in regard to nonverbal body gestures. *Proceedings of the Speech Communication Association summer conference.* Austin, TX.

Pettigrew, T., & Martin, J. (1987). Shaping the organizational context for black American inclusion. *Journal of Social Issues, 43,* 41–78.

Phillips, J. D. (1948). Report on discussion 66. *Adult Education Journal, 7,* 181–182.

Podsakoff, P. M., Ahearne, M., & MacKenzie, S. B. (1997). Organizational citizenship behavior and the quantity and quality of work group performance. *Journal of Applied Psychology, 82,* 262–270.

Poole, M. S. (1981). Decision development in small groups, I: A comparison of two models. *Communication Monographs, 50,* 20.

Poole, M. S. (1983). Decision development in small groups, III: A multiple sequence model of group decision development. *Communication Monographs, 50,* 321–341.

Poole, M. S. (1991). Procedures for managing meetings: Social and technological innovation. In R. A. Swanson & B. O. Knapp (Eds.), *Innovative meeting management* (pp. 53–220). Austin, TX: 3M Meeting Management.

Poole, M. S., & Doelger, J. A. (1986). Development processes in group decision making. In R. Y. Hirokawa & M. S. Poole (Eds.), *Communication and group decision making* (pp. 35–61). Beverly Hills, CA: Sage.

Poole, M. S., & Holmes, M. E. (1995). Decision development in computer-assisted group decision making. *Human Communication Research, 22,* 90–127.

Poole, M. S., Holmes, M. E., Watson, R., & DeSanctis, G. (1993). Group decision support systems and communication: Comparison of decision making in computer-supported and nonsupported groups. *Communication Research, 20,* 176–213.

Poole, M., & Roth, J. (1989a). Decision development in small groups IV: A typology of group decision paths. *Human Communication Research, 15,* 323–356.

Poole, M., & Roth, J. (1989b). Decision development in small groups V: Test of a contingency model. *Human Communication Research, 15,* 549–589.

Porter, L. W., & Lawler, E. E. (1986). *Managerial attitudes and performance.* Homewood, IL: Dorsey.

Powers, R. B., & Boyle, W. (1983). Common dilemma choices in small vs. large groups. Paper presented at the American Psychological Association Annual Meeting. Anaheim, CA.

Prapavessis, H., & Carron, A. V. (1997). Cohesion and work output. *Small Group Research, 28,* 294–301.

Pratt, J. M. (1997). A case study of male-female leadership emergence in small groups. Unpublished doctoral dissertation, University of Minnesota.

Proff, K. M. (1995). An experimental examination of biological sex as a status cure in decision-making groups and its influence on information use. Small Group Research, 26, 451–474.

Propp, K. M. (1995). An experimental examination of biological sex as a status cue in decision-making groups and its influence on information use. *Small Group Research, 26,* 451–474.

Pruitt, D., & Rubin, J. (1986). *Social conflict: Escalation, stalemate, and settlement.* New York: Random House.

Prussia, G. E., & Kiniki, A. J. (1996). A motivational investigation of group effectiveness using social-cognitive theory. *Journal of Applied Psychology, 81,* 187–198.

Putnam, L. L. (1986). Conflict in group decision making. In R. Y. Hirokawa & M. S. Poole (Eds.), *Communication and group decision making* (pp. 175, 196). Beverly Hills, CA: Sage.

Richmond, V. P., & McCroskey, J. C. (1995). *Communication: Apprehension, avoidance, and effectiveness,* 4th ed. Scottsdale, AZ: Gorsuch, Scarisbrick.

Riecken, H. W. (1952). Some problems of consensus development. *Rural Sociology, 17,* 245–252.

Riordan, C., & Shore, L. (1997). Demographic diversity and employee attitudes: Examination of relational demography within work units. *Journal of Applied Psychology, 82,* 342–358.

Rodriquez, R. (1998). Challenging demographic reductionism: A pilot study investigating diversity in group composition. *Small Group Research, 28,* 744–759.

Rogelberg, S., & Rumery, S. (1996). Gender, diversity, team decision quality, time on task, and interpersonal cohesion. *Small Group Research, 27,* 79–90.

Rogers, C. (1942). Releasing expression. *Counseling and psychotherapy.* Boston: Houghton Mifflin.

Rogers, C. R. (1962). The interpersonal relationship: The core of guidance. *Harvard Educational Review, 32,* 416–429.

Rogers, C. R., & Roethlisberger, F. J. (1952). Barriers and gateways to communication. *Harvard Business Review, July–August,* 28–34.

Rommetviet, R. (1974). *On message structure: A framework for the study of language and communication.* New York: Wiley.

Rosenfeld, L. B., & Pax, T. B. (1975). Personality determinants of autocratic and democratic leadership. *Speech Monographs, 42,* 203–208.

Rosenthal, S. B., & Buchholz, R. A. (1995). Leadership: Toward new philosophical foundations. *Business & Professional Ethics Journal, 14,* 25–41.

Rosin, H. (2010, July/August). The end of men. *The Atlantic,* 56–72.

Roy, M. C., Gauvin, S., & Limayem, M. (1996). Electronic group brainstorming: The role of feedback on productivity. *Small Group Research, 27,* 215–247.

Rubin, J. Z. (1980). Experimental research on third-party intervention in conflict. *Psychological Bulletin, 87,* 380.

Rubin, R. B., Rubin, A. M., & Jordan, F. F. (1997). Effects of instruction on communication apprehension and communication competence. *Communication Education, 46,* 104–114.

Rubin, Z. (1970). Measurement of romantic love. *Journal of Personality and Social Psychology, 16,* 265–273.

Russo, N. F. (1967). Connotations of seating arrangements. *Cornell Journal of Social Relations, 2,* 37–44.

Salas, E., Rozell, D., Dirskell, J. E., & Mullen, B. (1999). The effect of team building on performance. An integration. *Small Group Research, 30,* 309–329.

Salazar, A. J. (1996). An analysis of the development and evolution of roles in the small group. *Small Group Research, 27,* 475–503.

Samovar, L. A., & Porter, R. E. (1995). *Communication between cultures* (2d ed.). Belmont, CA: Wadsworth.

Sampson, E. E., & Brandon, A. C. (1964). The effects of role and opinion deviation on small group behavior. *Sociometry, 27,* 261–281.

Sargent, J. F., & Miller, G. R. (1971). Some differences in certain behaviors of autocratic and democratic leadership. *Journal of Communication, 21,* 233–252.

Sagrestando, L. M. (1992). Power strategies in interpersonal relationships: The effects of expertise and gender. *Psychology of Women Quarterly, 16,* 481–495.

Schachter, S. (1951). Deviation, rejection, and communication. *Journal of Abnormal and Social Psychology, 46,* 190–197.

Schaible, T. D., & Jacobs, A. (1975). Feedback III: Sequence effects. Enhancement of feedback acceptance and group attractiveness by manipulation. *Small Group Behavior, 6,* 151–173.

Scheidel, T. M., & Crowell, L. (1964). Idea development in small group discussion. *Quarterly Journal of Speech, 50,* 140–145.

Scheidel, T. M., & Crowell, L. (1966). Feedback in small group communication. *Quarterly Journal of Speech, 52,* 273–278.

Schiffenbauer, A., & Babineau, A. (1976). Sex role stereotypes and the spontaneous attribution of emotion. *Journal of Research in Personality, 10,* 137–145.

Schittekatte, M., & Van Hiel, A. (1996). Effects of partially shared information and awareness of unshared information on information sampling. *Small Group Research, 27,* 431–449.

Schmitt, D. R. (1981). Performance under cooperation or competition. *American Behavioral Scientist, 24*, 649–679.

Schriesheim, C. A. (1982). The great high consideration-high initiating structure leadership myth: Evidence on its generalizability. *Journal of Social Psychology, 116*, 221–228.

Schultz, B. (1986). Communicative correlates of perceived leaders in the small group. *Small Group Behavior, 17*, 61–65.

Schultz, B., Ketrow, S. M., & Urban, D. M. (1995). Improving decision quality in the small group: The role of the reminder. *Small Group Research, 26*, 521–541.

Schutz, W. C. (1958). *FIRO: A three-dimensional theory of interpersonal behavior.* New York: Holt, Rinehart and Winston.

Seashore, S. E. (1954). *Group cohesiveness in the industrial work group.* Ann Arbor, MI: Institute for Social Research.

Seibold, D. R. (1979). Making meetings more successful: Plans, formats, and procedures for group problem solving. *Journal of Business Communication, 16*, 3–20.

Senge, P. M. (1990). *The fifth discipline: The art and practice of the learning organization.* New York: Currency Doubleday.

Shaw, M. E. (1973a). Change in sociometric choices following forced integration of an elementary school. *Journal of Social Issues, 29*, 143–158.

Shaw, M. E. (1973b). Scaling group tasks: A method for dimensional analysis. *JSAS Catalog of Selected Documents in Psychology, 8*, 294.

Shaw, M. E. (1981). *Group dynamics: The psychology of small group behavior* (3d ed.). New York: McGraw-Hill.

Shaw, M. E., & Blum, J. M. (1965). Effects of leadership styles upon group performance as a function of task structure. *Journal of Personality and Social Psychology, 49*, 238–242.

Shaw, M. E., & Gilchrist, J. C. (1955). Repetitive task failure and sociometric choice. *Journal of Abnormal and Social Psychology, 50*, 29–32.

Shaw, M. E., & Rothschild, G. H. (1956). Some effects of prolonged experiences in communication nets. *Journal of Applied Psychology, 40*, 281–286.

Shaw, M. E., & Shaw, L. M. (1962). Some effects of sociometric grouping upon learning in a second grade classroom. *Journal of Social Psychology, 57*, 453–485.

Sherif, M., & Sherif, C. W. (1973). *Groups in harmony and tension.* New York: Harper & Row.

Short, J. A., Williams, E., & Christie, B. (1976). *The social psychology of telecommunications.* London: Wiley.

Shuter, R. (1979). A study of nonverbal communication among Jews and Protestants. *Journal of Social Psychology, 109*, 31–41.

Siegel, J., Dubrovsky, V., Kiesler, S., & McGuire, T. W. (1986). Group processes in computer-mediated communication. *Organizational Behavior and Human Decision Processes, 33*, 157–187.

Sillince, J. A. A. (2000). Rhetorical power, accountability and conflict in committees: An argumentation approach. *Journal of Management Studies, 37*, 1125–1156.

Silver, W. S., & Bufanio, K. M. (1996). The impact of group efficacy and group goals on group task performance. *Small Group Research, 27*, 347–359.

Smeltzer, L. R., & Watson, K. W. (1985). An analysis of communication skills in productivity improvement groups. Paper presented at the annual meeting of the International Communication Association, Honolulu.

Smith, C. M., & Powell, L. (1988). The use of disparaging humor by group leaders. *Southern Speech Communication Journal, 53*, 279–292.

Smith, P. B. (1963). Differentiation between sociometric rankings: A test of four theories. *Human Relations, 16*, 335–350.

Smith, P. B., & Bond, M. H. (1999). *Social psychology across cultures* (2d ed). Boston: Allyn & Bacon.

Sorenson, R. L., & Savage, G. T. (1989). Signaling participation through relational communication: A test of the leader interpersonal influence model. *Group & Organizational Studies, 14,* 325–345.

Sorenson, S. (1981). Grouphate. Paper presented at the annual meeting of the International Communication Association, Minneapolis, MN.

Sosik, J. J., Avolio, B. J., & Kahai, S. S. (1998). Inspiring group creativity: Comparing anonymous and identified electronic brainstorming. *Small Group Research, 29,* 3–31.

Spencer, T. (1995). There is no place like a home page! *Spectra,* July, 10–11.

Spich, R. S., & Keleman, K. (1985). Explicit norm-structuring process: A strategy for increasing task group effectiveness. *Group and Organizational Studies, 10,* 55.

Spillman, B., Spillman, R., & Reinking, K. (1981). Leadership emergence: Dynamic analysis of the effects of sex and androgyny. *Small Group Behavior, 12,* 139–157.

Stafford, L., Dainton, M., & Haas, S. (2000). Measuring routine and strategic relational maintenance: Scale revision, sex versus gender roles, and prediction of relational characteristics. *Communication Monographs, 67,* 306–323.

Stasson, M. F., & Bradshaw, S. D. (1995). Explanations of individual-group performance differences: What sort of "bonus" can be gained through group interaction? *Small Group Research, 26,* 296–308.

Stein, R. T., & Heller, T. (1979). An empirical analysis of the correlations between leadership status and participation rates reported in the literature. *Journal of Personality and Social Psychology, 37,* 1993–2002.

Steinzor, B. (1950). The spatial factor in face-to-face discussion groups. *Journal of Abnormal and Social Psychology, 45,* 552–555.

Stewart, D. D. (1998). Stereotypes, negativity bias, and the discussion of unshared information in decision-making groups. *Small Group Research, 29,* 643–668.

Stewart, J. (2002). *Bridges not walls* (8th ed.). New York: McGraw-Hill.

Stewart, L. P., & Stewart, A. D. (1985). *Communication between the sexes: Sex differences and sex role stereotypes.* Scottsdale, AZ: Gorsuch Scarisbrick.

Stewart, L. P., Stewart, A. D., Friedley, S. A., & Cooper, P. J. (1990). *Communication between the sexes: Sex differences and sex role stereotypes* (2d ed., pp. 43–114). Scottdale, AZ: Gorsuch Scarisbrick.

Stogdill, R. M. (1981). *Handbook of leadership: A survey of theory and research.* New York: Free Press.

Stogdill, R. M., Shartle, C. L., Scott, E. L., Coons, A. E., & Jaynes, W. E. (1956). *A predictive study of administrative work patterns.* Columbus: Ohio State University, Bureau of Research.

Straus, S. G. (1996). Getting a clue: The effects of communication media and information distribution on participation and performance in computer-mediated and face-to-face groups. *Small Group Research, 27,* 115–142.

Straus, S. G. (1997). Technology, group process, and group outcomes: Testing the connections in computer-mediated and face-to-face groups. *Human-Computer Interaction, 12,* 227–266.

Straus, S. G. (1999). Testing typology of tasks: An empirical validation of McGrath's (1984) group task circumplex. *Small Group Research, 30,* 166–187.

Street, M. C. (1997). Groupthink: An examination of theoretical issues, implications, and future research suggestions. *Small Group Research, 28,* 72–93.

Strodtbeck, F. L., & Hook, L. H. (1961). The social dimensions of a twelve-man jury table. *Sociometry, 24,* 397–415.

Tandy, C. H. (1992). Assessing the functions of supportive messages. *Communication Research, 19,* 175–192.

Tannen, D. (1990). *You just don't understand: Women and men in conversation.* New York: Ballantine Books.

Terborg, J. R., Castore, C., & DeNinno, J. A. (1976). A longitudinal field investigation of the impact of group composition on group performance and cohesion. *Journal of Personality and Social Psychology, 34,* 782–790.

Thayer, L. (1968). *Communication and communication systems.* Homewood, IL: Richard D. Irwin.

Thayer, S., & Schiff, W. (1975). Eye-contact, facial expression, and the experience of time. *Journal of Social Psychology, 95,* 117–124.

Thomas, R. R., Jr. (1995). A diversity framework. In M. M. Chambers, S. Oskamp, & M. A. Costanzo (Eds.), *Diversity in organizations: New perspectives for a changing workplace.* Thousand Oaks, CA: Sage.

Tjosvold, D. (1995). Cooperation theory, constructive controversy, and effectiveness: Learning from crisis. In R. A. Guzzo & E. Salas (Eds.), *Team effectiveness and decision making in organizations* (pp. 79–112). San Francisco: Jossey-Bass.

Triandis, H. C. (1995). A theoretical framework for the study of diversity. In M. M. Chambers, S. Oskamp, & M. A. Costanzo (Eds.), *Diversity in organizations: New perspectives for a changing workplace* (pp. 11–36). Thousand Oaks, CA: Sage.

Tsui, A. S., Egan, T. D., & O'Reilly, C. A., III (1992). Being different: Relational demography and organizational attachment. *Administrative Science Quarterly, 37,* 549–579.

Tubbs, S. L. (1995). *A system approach to small group interaction* (5th ed.). New York: McGraw-Hill.

Tuckman, B. W. (1965). Developmental sequences in small groups. *Psychological Bulletin, 63,* 384–389.

Turner, J. C., & Haslam, S. A. (2001). Social identity, organizations, and leadership. In M. E. Turner (Ed.), *Groups at work: Theory and research* (pp. 25–65). Mahwah, NJ: Erlbaum.

Tyler, T. R., & Blader, S. L. (2000). *Cooperation in groups: Procedural justice, social identity, and behavior engagement.* Philadelphia: Psychology Press.

VanLear, C. A., & Mabry, E. A. (1999). Testing contrasting interaction models for discriminating between consensual and dissentient decision-making groups. *Small Group Research, 30,* 29–58.

Van Zelst, R. H. (1952). Sociometrically selected work teams increase production. *Personnel Psychology, 5,* 175–185.

Veiga, J. F. (1991). The frequency of self-limiting behavior in groups: A measure and an explanation. *Human Relations, 44,* 877–895.

Volpe, C. E., Cannon-Bowers, J. A., Salas, E., & Spector, P. E. (1996). The impact of cross training on team functioning: An empirical investigation. *Human Factors, 38,* 87–100.

Vroom, V. H., & Jago, A. G. (1988). *The new leadership: Managing participation in organizations.* Englewood Cliffs, NJ: Prentice Hall.

Wall, V. D., Jr., Galanes, G. J., & Love, S. B. (1987). Small, task-oriented groups: Conflict, conflict management, satisfaction, and decision quality. *Small Group Behavior, 18,* 31–55.

Warnemunde, D. E. (1986). The status of the introductory small group communication course. *Communication Education, 35,* 392.

Watson, K. W. (1996). Listener preferences: The paradox of small-group interactions. In R. S. Cathcart, L. A. Samovar, & L. D. Henman (Eds), *Small group communication: Theory & practice* (7th ed., pp. 268–282). Madison: Brown & Benchmark.

Wech, B. A., Mossholder, K. W., Steel, R. P. & Bennett, N. (1998). Does work group cohesiveness affect individuals' performance and organizational commitment? A cross-level examination. *Small Group Research, 29,* 472–494.

Weick, K. (1978). The spines of leaders. In M. McCall & M. Lombardo (Eds.), *Leadership: Where else can we go?* (pp. 37–61). Durham, NC: Duke University Press.

Weisband, S. P. (1992). Group discussion and first advocacy effects in computer-mediated and face-to-face decision making groups. *Organizational Behavior and Human Decision Processes, 53,* 352–380.

Wheaton, H. B. (1974). Interpersonal conflict and cohesiveness in dyadic relationships. *Sociometry*, *37*, 328–348.

White, R. K., & Lippitt, R. (1960). Leader behavior and member reaction in three "social climates." In D. Cartwright & A. Zander (Eds.), *Group dynamics: Research and Theory* (2d ed., pp. 527–553). New York: Harper & Row.

Wilmont, W. W., & Hocker, J. (1998). *Interpersonal conflict* (5th ed.). New York: McGraw-Hill.

Wilson, G. L., & Goodall, Jr., H. L. (1991). *Interviewing in context*. New York: McGraw-Hill.

Winer, S., & Majors, R. E. (1981). Research done on supportive and defensive communication: An empirical study of three verbal interpersonal variables. *Communication Quarterly*, *29*, 166–172.

"Women in U.S. Management. (2011, March). Catalyst. [Online]. Available: http://www.catayst.org/publications/206/women-in-us-management.

Wong, C. L., Tjosvold, D., & Lee, F. (1992). Managing conflict in a diverse workforce: A Chinese perspective in North America. *Small Group Research*, *23*, 302–321.

Wood, J. T. (1977). Leading in purposive discussions: A study of adaptive behaviors. *Communication Monographs*, *44*, 152–165.

Wood, J. T. (1981). Sex differences in group communication: Directions for research in speech communication. *Journal of Group Psychotherapy, Psychodrama, and Sociometry*, *34*, 31–34.

Wood, J. T. (1984). Consensus and its alternatives: A comparative analysis of voting, negotiation and consensus as methods of group decision-making. In G. M. Phillips & J. T. Wood (Eds.), *Emergent issues in human decision-making*. Carbondale, IL: Southern Illinois University Press.

Woodall, W. G., Burgoon, J. K., & Markel, N. (1980). The effects of facial–head cue combinations on interpersonal evaluations. *Communication Quarterly*, *28*, 47–55.

Woodward, M. S., Rosenfeld, L. B., & May, S. K. (1996). Sex differences in social support in sororities and fraternities. *Journal of Applied Communication Research*, *24*, 260.

Worchel, S. (1994). You can go home again: Returning group research to the group context with an eye on developmental issues. *Small Group Research*, *23*, 205–223.

Yalom, I. D. (1995). *The theory and practice of group psychotherapy* (4th ed.). New York: Basic Books.

Yarmey, D. A. (1979). Through the looking glass: Sex differences in memory for self-facial poses. *Journal of Research in Personality*, *13*, 450–459.

Zajonc, R. (1965). Social facilitation. *Science*, *149*, 269–274.

Zimmerman, D. H., & West, C. (1975). Sex roles, interruptions and silences in conversation. In B. Thorne and H. Henley, *Language and sex: Differences in dominance* (pp. 105–129). Rowley, MA: Newbury House.

name index

Abrams, D., 20
Adams, K., 24, 79, 332, 336
Adams, T., 88
Adler, N., 242
Ahearne, M., 239
Alderton, S., 236
Alexander, E. R., 234
Alper, S., 287
Altman, I., 232
Anderson, A. B., 256
Anderson, C. M., 175, 239, 261
Anderson, L. R., 204
Anderson, S. D., 20
Andrews, P., 109
Argyle, M., 123, 124
Aries, E. J., 123
Arrow, H., 269
Atwater, L. E., 192
Avolio, B. J., 83, 206

Babineau, A., 124
Back, K. W., 261
Bailey, D. E., 259
Baird, J. E., 121, 155
Bakeman, R., 330
Baker, D. C., 195
Bales, R. F., 141, 142, 145, 152, 204,
    326, 327
Ballard, D. I., 125
Bandura, A., 28
Bantz, C. R., 12
Barge, J. K., 209
Barker, J. R., 218
Barker, L. L., 87, 346
Barnard, W., 255
Barnlund, D. C., 292, 306, 309, 326,
    328–330
Bass, B. M., 195, 206
Bechler, C., 209
Becker, S. W., 121
Bedeian, A. G., 168
Beisecker, T., 290
Belcher, C., 66
Bell, M. A., 146
Bell, M. P., 220
Bem, S., 233
Benne, K. D., 163, 168, 169, 172, 174,
    323–325

Berkowitz, L., 47
Bettinghaus, E. P., 45
Betz, B., 306
Birdwhistell, R. L., 123
Blader, S. L., 239
Blanchard, F. A., 255
Blanchard, K. H., 200, 201, 202
Blanchard, P. N., 204
Blickensderfer, E., 17
Blum, J. M., 46
Bogardus, E., 197
Bolton-Oetzel, K., 11
Bond, M. H., 142
Bonito, J. A., 256
Bonner, B. L., 193
Borders, L. D., 233
Bordina, P., 89
Borisoff, D., 63
Bormann, E. G., 45, 127, 148, 152 164,
    165, 190, 191, 269, 270
Bostrom, R. N., 45
Bowers, J. A., 17
Boyle, W., 44
Bradshaw, S. D., 13
Brandon, A. C., 289
Brehm, S. S., 233
Brewer, M. B., 15
Brilhart, J. K., 25, 79, 330, 332, 333, 336
Broome, B. J., 46, 87
Brossman, B. G., 299
Brown, V., 88
Buchholz, R. A., 206
Buck, R., 124
Bufanio, K. M., 171
Bugental, D. B., 187
Bullis, C. A., 152
Burgoon, J. K., 122, 123
Burch, G., 27
Burke, R. J., 295
Burn, S. M., 217
Buzan, T., 62, 63, 65
Byrne, D., 137

Cadsby, J., 83
Cady, S. H., 220
Calero, H. H., 121
Calhoun, J. B., 93
Campbell, D., 61

Canary, D. J., 298
Caple, R. B., 146
Carey, J. A., 192, 299
Carli, L. L., 184, 189
Carlsmith, J. M., 123, 124
Carnevale, P. J., 312
Carrocci, N. M., 204
Castore, C., 255
Caul, W. F., 124
Chang, A., 89
Chen, Z., 210
Chertkoff, J. M., 184
Chesney, A. A., 268
Chilberg, J. C., 272, 276
Clark, N., 88
Cline, R. J. W., 275, 278
Clore, G. L., Jr., 137
Cody, M. J., 45
Cohen, S. G., 259, 326, 327
Coke, J. S., 233
Coleman, D., 86
Conaty, J. C., 117
Cook, M., 124
Cook, S. W., 255
Cooper, W. H., 83
Coser, L., 285
Courtright, J. A., 261
Cragan, J., 262
Carini, B., 269
Cox, T., 242
Crowell, L., 153, 154, 155, 156

Dailey, J. C., 82, 84, 88
Dansby, M. R., 220
Davis, J. H., 47
Deese, J. F., 65
DeGooyer, D., 211
DeKlerk, V., 109
Delbecq, A., 84, 85
Den Hartog, D. N., 206, 207
DeNinno, J. A., 255
Derlega, V. A., 233
De Souza, G., 190
Deutsch, M., 73, 233, 258, 285, 306
Devine, D. J., 16, 288
DeVito, J., 128
Dewey, J., 74, 75
Diamond, S. G., 119

subject index